THE SOVIET WORLD

THE SOVIET WORLD

Luca Pietromarchi

Former Italian Ambassador in Moscow

TRANSLATED BY LOVETT F. EDWARDS

NEW YORK: A. S. BARNES AND CO., INC.

CONTENTS

CONTENTS

CONTENTS

INTRODUCTION

IN 1958 I asked the government to send me to Moscow as ambassador. I wanted to study communism on the spot, to assess, as an eyewitness, the practical value of the ideas upon which it is based, to decide how far and with what results the fundamental tenets of Marxism had been applied and to make a comparison between communism and capitalism.

In this assessment I have tried to be as objective as possible. From the very beginning of my mission I felt the most lively sympathy for Russia, for the Russian people and its leaders. Despite difficulties and misunderstandings, I set out to improve relations between our two countries by settling various questions left in abeyance and encouraging collaboration between our two peoples, above all in economic relations and cultural exchanges. I am convinced that collaboration with the Soviet Union is not only in our vital interest but that it is also indispensable for peace, at least as long as it is possible to preserve the hope of being able to live in peace.

An indispensable requirement for collaboration with the Soviet Union is a firm defence of the principles upon which our own civilization is based. The necessity of distinguishing between questions of principle and interest is not always clearly understood. Yet relations between the Soviet and the Western world can only develop on the basis of this fundamental distinction. What is the use of maintaining diplomatic relations with countries which have an ideology contrary to our own if such relations are not to serve our concrete interests?

It may be objected that by collaborating with the Soviet Union we aid its economic progress to our own hurt. Only the ignorant can believe this. Both commercial and cultural relations are of greater advantage to the West than to the communist states. In any case, with or without the collaboration of the Western countries, the Soviet Union is bound to become the leading economic power in the world. But must one conclude from that, as Khrushchev claimed, that this will prove the superiority of communism over capitalism? No. The forces that will assure the economic rise of the Soviet Union are not ideological. The communist ideology does not assist, indeed it retards, productive effort. Marxism is a weak driving force compared with the stimulating energy of private initiative.

Naturally, when the Soviet Union has become the leading world economic power, it will also be the leading political and military power. Does this mean that communism will spread throughout the world and that we shall not be able to keep pace with it? No. The Western world has resources at least double those of the communist world and has no reason, therefore, to fear it. But it must be united or at least have a degree of cohesion as great as that of the Eastern bloc.

Is it to be foreseen that communism will make further conquests and include new countries in its orbit? This is not impossible, but a consolidation of the present balance is more probable, if Soviet propaganda, Soviet flattery and Soviet aid be matched by the Western world with the same firmness and consciousness of its own values with which it has resisted, for centuries, the ideological waves that have threatened to submerge it.

Unity and vitality are the requirements of defence as well as of counter-attack; since whoever remains simply on the defensive is lost. There is nothing for it save to accept the Soviet challenge and to counter it vigorously. Communism has its weak points and limits beyond which it cannot go and these are not always clearly seen by Western public opinion, since in most cases news of what is happening in Russia comes from Russian propaganda through its countless centres of diffusion which exist in almost every country.

It must also be borne in mind that the communist experiment, even though forty-seven years have now passed since the October revolution, has not yet begun. The mass of the public believes that the Bolshevik revolution installed a communist régime in Russia. Yet it has not yet been possible to carry out an experiment of this kind and everything leads one to believe it will never be possible. We are, therefore, on the threshold. Up to the present all attempts to put a communist régime into operation have ended in disastrous failure. In particular, the wartime communism set up by Lenin, immediately after his seizure of power, led to such a destruction of wealth that it reduced the people to famine and drove them to revolt. China has tried again with the People's Communes, despite the famine and the intolerable suffering that it inflicted on the population. The Soviet Union was forced to abandon the experiment and adopt the New Economic Policy, the NEP, which was a return to free enterprise, and then to proceed, under Stalin, to what is known as 'the preliminary phase', or socialist phase, which is still going on, despite every effort to cross to the farther bank whose outlines can scarcely be discerned.

Even if the experiment has not yet been begun, there is no lack of interest in the results it is proposed to attain, because of the weighty reasons behind it and the importance of the problems to which a solution is being sought. These problems do not leave the Western world indifferent. It was the consideration of these problems, as they appeared in the most industrialized and progressive countries, which was leading English, French and German economists and thinkers to consider programmes of radical change in their traditional economic and social structures, until Marx and Engels made their detailed accusations against capitalism and traced the outlines of a new social organization in the Communist Manifesto of 1848.

From that manifesto, and from the publications of Marx and Engels which explained it, arose the social-democratic movements. In the West, however, Marxist principles were subjected to searching criticism by the leaders of the social-democratic parties themselves, who tried to make their significance clear and variously interpreted their application. Others opposed them and accused them of creating utopias.

This diversity of interpretation and application, due also to the frequently imprecise and even contradictory nature of some of the Marxist declarations, was accentuated by the Bolshevik revolution and the course decided upon by Lenin and Stalin for the organization of a socialist state based on the dictatorship of the Party.

The fact remains that the Western democracies have found in Marxism the impulse to create in the mass of the people the consciousness of their rights and the need for trade unions and political organizations to enforce them. But the practical problems raised by Marxism were not solved basically by the revolutionary formula proposed by it, but in a reformist manner within the framework of the traditional principles of liberty, democracy and respect for individual initiative, which have triumphed in the West at the cost of so many sacrifices and struggles throughout its millenary existence. The Western world refused to renounce these values, so painfully won, to which it owes its present progress and prosperity and without which it cannot conceive how a human being can express himself and live in a fitting manner.

The need to preserve these traditional values was not, however, felt, or at least not with the same intensity, among the Russians, who lived on the outskirts of Western civilization and were the last of the Aryan peoples to form part of the concert of Europe. Cut off from every tie with the past, Russia tried to put into effect a social and economic order based on principles diametrically opposed to those of the West and justified by her organizers and her present leaders in the name of equality, justice and progress.

The paths followed by the Western and Eastern worlds for the solution of similar problems therefore diverged and only the actual results, not those which are claimed by propaganda, will in the passage of time reveal the merits of one or the other system. It is clear that the truth is not all on one side nor all on the other, and a balance sheet of assets and liabilities cannot be drawn up until the transition to communism has been attempted and one can judge of its fulfilment, within what limits and with what advantages.

For the moment one can only come to the conclusion that the economic and social problems of our times are being confronted not only by the group of Marxist countries but also with equal attention by those countries which the Soviets define as 'capitalist' but which should more suitably be called 'democratic'. It is not only divergence of principles which has set these two worlds against one another but also divergence of methods. The communists stick rigidly not only to the spirit but even to the letter of the Marxist texts, now more than a century old and which are relevant to a world economy based on a management structure and a technology very different from those now in force. The democratic countries work on a dynamic formula of the relations between society and the individual and carry out reforms and innovations pragmatically, so that only proven efficiency is the measure of their value. These reforms are, in the nature of things, less global; but they do not clash, as do the communist ones founded on a rigid application of principles, with deep-rooted psychological inclinations or founder on the skerries of economic trends which, in the Soviet Union, have resisted almost half a century of effort.

Interest in what is happening in Russia is mainly centred on the antithetical position she has adopted towards the West in the study and formulation of similar problems. It is a different viewpoint which requires an effort by the observer to adapt himself but which in the end accustoms him to seeing things from an aspect quite different from that to which he is accustomed.

Undoubtedly the audacity of the Russian attempt, the vast scale of the geographical framework in which it is being carried out, the fertility of initiative, the zeal with which exceptional brains strain to construct new suspension bridges of vast span towards the distant shore of the promised land, cannot but excite the imagination of the masses. By comparison, the policy of the Western governments often appears imprisoned in the past, afraid of what is new, deprived of pungency and imagination. Many Western countries recall former Austria, always a year, a day, an hour behind the times.

There has thus arisen a divergency of climate which, growing greater and greater as Soviet power increases, has assumed the form of a life and death struggle between two truths, between two worlds. It is not the first time that Western civilization has been endangered by movements which have shaken it to its foundations; but undoubtedly the time in which we are living is decisive, not only because of the strength of the adversary but also because of the irresoluteness and disunion of the West, paralysed and thrown off balance by the unprincipled nature of the enemy offensive which makes use of all the advantages that the freedom and the democratic institutions of the Western countries place at its disposal. The communist world thus wounds us with our own weapons, without our being able to strike back. The struggle, therefore, is not on equal terms. Furthermore the principle of publicity reigns in the West, whereas in the communist world the principle is one of closest secrecy. Thus a halo of wonder and admiration has been created among the Western peoples for everything Russian, with no precise evaluation of the reality. Such reality must be known as a point of departure to measure the strength of the adversary, even as it is absolutely necessary to appreciate the strategy of an enemy in order to combat it. Ex *inimico salus*. And since one of the components of this strategy is propaganda, we propose in this book to try objectively to confront this propaganda with reality, to indicate the present trends in the Soviet World and to draw attention to certain perspectives that are being sketched out in the relations between the Eastern and Western worlds.

PART I

COMMUNISM AND CAPITALISM

CHAPTER I

The Economic Rivalry Between
East and West

1

KHRUSHCHEV invited the world to trial by ordeal.

Let us give, he said, a practical demonstration of the advantages that communism and capitalism bring the people. It will be up to them to choose. This has been the theme of most of his speeches during his visits to America, France and Austria.

On September 16th, 1959, at the Washington Press Club, he thus defined the terms of the contest:

'I am personally convinced that the winner will be communism, a social system which offers better possibilities for the development of the productive forces of a country and which opens the way to every man to develop fully his abilities and assures his full personal freedom within such a society. Many of you will not agree, but that only means that I cannot agree with you.

'What must be done then? Let us leave it that each one of us lives in the system he prefers, you in capitalism while we go on building communism.

'Everything that does not progress is one day destined to perish. Therefore, if capitalist society is the best form of society and offers better opportunities to develop the productive forces of a nation, then it will surely be the winner; but we think that the brief history of our state does not speak in your favour.'

Here Khrushchev went on to describe at length the great advances made by Russia after the revolution and because of it.

What is the value of this challenge? Looked at carefully, it betrays its propaganda motive. Comparison is only possible between homogeneous entities. Such a basis for comparison does not exist between the United States and the Soviet Union, which has a territory two and a half times greater than America, with enormously superior natural resources (minerals, forests, water-power) and, furthermore,

23

almost untouched, since they have been for the most part discovered and exploited only in recent decades, whereas America has made wide use of its resources and for some of them at least the cost of exploitation is rising according to the well-known phenomenon of Ricardian yield.

In such conditions it is to be foreseen that the Soviet Union will attain a volume of production greater than that of America, both in total and *pro capite*. The Soviet effort to reach the finishing post is therefore comprehensible. What is less comprehensible is the deduction that Khrushchev wished to draw from the achievement of economic superiority over America, namely that it is a proof of the superiority of his régime. He himself confessed his propaganda aim in a speech to representatives of the Soviet-French Association during his visit to de Gaulle. 'In the eyes of the world,' he said, 'America is the richest and most industrially developed country in the world. For that reason the supporters of capitalism, when they argue with us communists, always refer to the example of America. Here, they say, are the United States, a capitalist country, but see what a high level of development its economy has reached, considerably higher than that of the communist countries. Yes, for the time being that is so. But the Soviet Union is a socialist country which is in the process of building communism and has taken upon itself the task of overtaking the United States, the capitalist country with the highest degree of development, in such a way as to show all the advantages of the communist system. You may be sure that we will do it and that we shall not only reach but even surpass the United States. We are now working on a twenty-year economic development plan. We believe that in twenty years we shall surpass the present *pro capite* production of the United States by a hundred per cent.'

This is the argument which the Soviet Union makes use of to convince the world, especially the countries recently freed from colonial rule and uncertain which régime to adopt, that communism is the quickest way to reach a high level of production. The contest is a clamorous publicity stunt to recommend the qualities of the régime.

On the other hand, if the working masses freely informed of the working of the rival régime which it is intended to surpass are to be the judges, then the confrontation proposed by Khrushchev should provide useful elements of assessment. It is, however, certain that knowledge of the capitalist world is neither widespread nor organized, indeed scarcely tolerated, in the Soviet Union. Khrushchev affirmed that 'ideas travel without visas and there is no man yet born who can command human thought to die and can ensure that it really does die. It was thus that communist ideas found their way into our country.'

In actual fact, the precedent that it was the Red Army which imposed communism on the countries occupied by it makes rather dubious the statement of Khrushchev that ideas impose themselves by their own force and not by force of arms.

The rigorous supervision exercised in Russia by the Party and by the police over every form of Western propaganda seems to give the lie to the convictions that Khrushchev was making every effort to diffuse. He returned to this argument in great detail in his speech to the members of the Soviet-French Association which we have already quoted. 'It is worthy of interest,' he said, 'that the Russian tsars, who feared these ideas and those of the French Revolution like the plague, themselves read in secret the forbidden books in order to find some antidote, but they kept them hidden from their people under seven seals.' This is a typical example of the unscrupulousness of Soviet propaganda which, while stigmatizing the police methods of tsarism, does not seem to be aware that what the tsars did is exactly what the present rulers are doing, that is to keep jealously hidden from their own public Western books, newspapers and reviews, naturally with the exception of papers like *L'Unità*, *Avanti* and *Il Paese*. Similarily, Western radio transmissions are systematically jammed by costly installations along the whole frontier, like a *cordon sanitaire*.

When a challenge has been launched in which the final word is to be left to those affected there must at the same time be full freedom of information. The contest is now developing between a deaf and dumb people on the one hand and the free world on the other. The free world, by showing its adhesion to democratic forms by a crushing majority, has on every occasion given its answer to Khrushchev.

2

Productivity was proposed by Lenin as an objective criterion by which to assess the superiority of one régime over another. This is a parameter of undoubted value, especially for those who, like the communists, base their propaganda on the promise to assure the people a living standard higher than that enjoyed by the working classes in the capitalist world. This is equivalent to saying that the communist régime believes itself able to produce and put at the disposal of the workers a larger quantity of consumer goods and services. The communist régime boasts that it will attain this by greater labour yield, due either to its differing social structure which abolishes the so-called parasitical classes and permits an integral use of working energies, or to technical advances due to the wide diffusion of schooling and higher education, or above all to the greater energy of the working classes, stimulated by the new spirit which animates the people's state. Lenin saw clearly that productivity was the key to economic progress and therefore made the Council of People's Commissars on June 24, 1919 pass a decree 'on the increase of labour productivity'. Two days after its signature he commented on it in an article entitled A *great beginning*. In it Lenin warned that 'in the final analysis the most important thing is labour productivity; it is the principal factor in the victory of the new social system. Communism means greater labour productivity in comparison with that of the capitalist régime. It is the product of willing workers who are united by class-consciousness and who apply advanced techniques.'

However in the Soviet Union, and even more noticeably in the other communist states, this superior productivity has not been achieved; in fact it is now markedly inferior to that of the capitalist countries. This confession comes from Khrushchev himself who, at the XXII Communist Party Congress in January 1959, declared that Soviet productivity was 40% of that of America in industry and 30% in agriculture.[1] But most Western economic experts assess the level of Soviet productivity at an even lower percentage. A person of undisputed competence told me that, on the basis of on-the-spot investigations by experts, the productivity of the Soviet worker scarcely amounts to ten per cent of the American, a percentage which can, however, be considered as too low. It may be assumed that it averages about thirty per cent.

There are many reasons for this low productivity. One of the most important is the antiquated nature of the greater number of plants. The impression reported by foreign technicians after visiting Soviet factories is that the labour systems in force there are, for the most part, very out of date. These deficiencies of productive organization

---

[1] 'American industry,' he said, 'works at a level about two or two and a half times higher than ours; American agriculture is about three times higher.' Mr Allan Wallis, Special Assistant to President Eisenhower, in a press report on June 8, 1960 on the rhythm of economic progress in America and in Russia, said that 50% of the Soviet labour force is employed in agriculture, whereas in America it is only 1.8%. A. Paskov in *Kommunist* (No. 4, 1962) published an article entitled *Economic laws in the building of communism* in which he wrote: 'At present, labour productivity in Soviet industry is approximately a half and in Soviet agriculture about a third of that of the United states.'

See Chapter IX for Khrushchev's fears about the poor increase in labour productivity.

have been noted by the Soviet leaders, especially in the post-Stalin period. In giving directives for the carrying out of the sixth five-year plan, the XX Congress of the Soviet communist party acknowledged that 'in a number of production sectors there has been a certain delay in introducing and applying the most recent discoveries in science and technology; the framework of mechanization and auto-mation of industry, agriculture, transport and construction is still inadequate'. It was a first, mild criticism of the productive organiza-tion. It is a fact, as D'Angelo and Paladini have observed, that pro-ductivity has stagnated for many years or has even definitely diminished.[2]

Little by little the criticisms have become harsher. At the next Party Congress, in January 1959, one of the most influential speakers, A. P. Kirichenko, blamed defective organization, unpro-ductive expenditure, wastage of materials, waste of manpower, delay in solving technical problems, and so on.

A reorganization of the apparatus of production was discussed by the Party Central Committee in its session from June 24th to June 29th of the same year (1959). It revealed errors, prejudices, defici-encies, negligence and slackness, and lack of discipline both among the technical directors and the workers. The debate was opened by the vice-premier of the Council of Ministers, Kosygin, president of the Gosplan. He insisted above all on the necessity of modernizing the whole textile industry. It was revealed by the statements of certain technicians that most of the plants in the Moscow province were more than a hundred years old. Aristov, a member of the Presidium, did not hesitate to declare: 'There are many things in our economy that are backward; sometimes one feels ashamed and blushes to see the old-fashioned technical processes used in our in-dustries, the heavy labour still being done by hand, the low yield and so on. Those responsible for this are the directors of the various sectors of the machine industry.'

As always, the most drastic accusations were made by Khrush-chev, who seasoned them with sharp and sarcastic gibes.

'I have visited,' he said, 'an exhibition of the machines which we are producing. Merely to look at them is enough to make one burst a blood-vessel. To think that such antediluvian machines are still being produced in our factories is enough to make one weep. There are machines there as old as our grandfathers, worthy of our an-cestors.' He quoted the switch-gear factory at Saratov which pro-duced antiquated and inefficient machines although, as he said, 'since

[2] Sergio D'Angelo and Leo Paladini in *Khrushchev's Challenge* (*La sfida di Krusciov*); *Economic and Political Problems of the Soviet Union after Stalin*, p. 26; Feltrinelli, 1960.

1955 there have been new automatic models of such machines produced which are 50% more productive than those now being made. Why is this? The reason is that the production of old lathes goes ahead without trouble but if it is necessary to produce new lathes then one must re-tool the plant. But why do this at a time when the Saratov economic council has paid the workers at the plant several hundreds of thousands of rubles for having exceeded the production plans and twenty-one thousand rubles to the director? . . . No one has called on him to account for the production of antiquated lathes and they have even paid him a bonus for his work.'

It is impossible to outline a more accurate picture of the defects of the system; on the one hand the lack of the incentive of personal interest, on the other the proof of a timorous bureaucratic parasitism that inevitably benumbs the common weal.

'Thus,' Khrushchev concluded, 'not only is material wasted but out-of-date machinery is produced, slowing up communist development. And that is not the only case of this sort.' But not all the blame should be placed on the directors. In the haste to accelerate the industrialization of the country, more attention is being paid to the construction of new factories than to the modernization of old ones; the funds set aside for amortization are, as a rule, inadequate since, as Khrushchev has pointed out, tooling is effective only for five years and no more. After that it becomes antiquated. However, during the Stalin period, no one paid any heed to modernizing old plants. Naturally there are very many extremely modern industrial sectors with mechanized assembly lines or based entirely on automation. But, for the moment at least, they are very much in the minority.

No less inadequate are the qualifications of the great majority of the workers. Those in the factories are mostly women, to whom heavy and difficult work is entrusted, such as drop forging. I have seen women handling power-drills on the streets in a temperature thirty degrees below freezing. This prevalence of feminine labour is easily comprehensible if one bears in mind that the census of January 15, 1959 revealed that there were twenty million more women than men in Russia. Another reason is that men have to do their military service, are enrolled in the vast militia, swarm into the administration and compose the greater part of the executive and Party cadres. The women, however, are in no way behind the men in physical strength and force of character. The transfer of heavy labour from the stronger to the weaker sex is so universal that it has become one of the butts of popular satire in comedies, the humorous papers and the daily press.

Talking to the Central Committee at its June 1959 session,

Khrushchev insisted on the need to improve the cultural and technical level of the employees, since the development of automation and mechanization demands a specialized labour force and above all a constantly increasing number of draftsmen, designers, scientists and engineers. The reform of the secondary school system, with the introduction of directed labour after the first eight classes, is basically aimed at the specialization of the workers. It may therefore be foreseen that the technical level of the employees will be gradually improved.

Then too labour discipline in the factories leaves much to be desired. There is no comparison possible with the order, the discipline, the correctness of relations between staff and executive that exists in the factories of Western countries. Here too Khrushchev has not failed to put his finger on the sore spot by blaming the slackness of discipline and demanding the severest control. 'Working hours,' he said in the speech quoted above, 'must be wholly devoted to productive work. There must be no toleration of unconscientious workers. If a worker is lazy, it is the duty of his companions to tell him frankly that he is a parasite . . . Watch committees should be organized,' Khrushchev explained, 'for the scrupulous observance of orders from the centre, for the good working of the factories, for the fulfilment of the programme, for the regularity and exactness of deliveries and for the quality of the product. They must make certain that all the employees of the enterprises keep the strictest discipline and fight against every harmful divergence from the directives.'

The most frequent comment made by Western technicians who visit Soviet factories is that an excessive number of workers are used for operations which in the West are carried out by a half or a third of that number. The Zil motor-car factory in Moscow employs forty thousand workers for an annual production of a hundred and fifty thousand vehicles, for the most part four-ton or four-and-a-half-ton lorries.

A large part of the personnel of the enterprises is made up of administrative employees, especially clerks. In a régime in which everything belongs to the state and in which an account of everything must be rendered to the state, bureaucracy becomes a thousand-tentacled octopus. Khrushchev has not spared this his sharpest rebukes. 'There are amongst us bureaucrats who are accustomed to riding old hacks and do not want to change them for thoroughbreds because they are afraid of being thrown; therefore they hang on to the manes and tails of their nags by hands and teeth.' This, however, is the defect of all bureaucracies. The ageing of a society is above all shown by its progressive bureaucratization, even as the ageing of a human organism by the hardening of its arteries.

But above and beyond all these causes, the low productivity is the result of the lowness of wages. It is an incontestable fact that everyone yields according to how he is paid. The badly paid, badly lodged, worker, unable to assert his rights and his interests, lacks the bite of the Western worker, considerably better paid, who works in an atmosphere of freedom, knows his rights and his duties and is eager to improve his status. The inferiority of Soviet wages compared with those of the West is the more striking in that communism was born out of reaction to the capitalist system, guilty, according to Marx, of reducing the workers' wages by their 'surplus-value'. On the whole, state capitalism as practised in the Soviet Union cheats the worker of a far higher quota of 'surplus-value' than private capitalism.

In the session of the Supreme Soviet which opened on May 5, 1960, Khrushchev reaffirmed Lenin's view that capitalism will finally be defeated by socialism which creates a new and much higher labour productivity. It is therefore very clear that productivity is the yardstick by which to measure the superiority of one régime over another. The communists anticipate that victory will come from increased productivity. It is now clear, by their own admission, that this superiority is still very far off. If the main cause of low productivity is low wages, one is justified in thinking that the situation of the working masses would be very different if they could exert on the economic and political organs of the state a pressure similar to that which the working classes in the West are constantly exerting for the improvement of their living standards.

It must be remembered that labour productivity in the Soviet Union has not followed a continuously ascending curve. Between 1938 and the entry of the Soviet Union into the war there was a marked fall in productivity. The same happened during the war. Among the causes of this diminution must not be forgotten the fall in real wages due to increasing prices and the scarcity of consumer goods.

As soon as the war was over the rise in labour productivity was resumed, not because of an increased yield from the workers but thanks to the technical and administrative progress made by Soviet industry. This progress not only continues but has been accentuated, so that the index of productivity increase which is, according to Soviet statistics, 7% in the Soviet Union has exceeded the increase in the productivity index of the United States which, according to American statistics, has been about 2% between 1950 and 1960. There is good reason to believe that the increase in the Soviet productivity index has been exaggerated; however, there seems no doubt that the difference between the two productivities tends to diminish. Robert W. Campbell observes: 'The Soviet industrial worker has much less mechanical power at his disposal than does his American opposite number . . . The Soviet worker is provided with less than half as much electric energy as the American industrial worker is . . . Nevertheless throughout the entire post-war period the Russians have been increasing the consumption of electrical power per industrial worker at a more rapid rate . . . but there is no reason to doubt that the gap in productivity will be gradually narrowed as the Russians accumulate the capital required for equipping the industrial labour force with more mechanical power.'[3]

It is a question of an increase of 'plant-productivity' rather than labour yields. This is evident in agriculture where productivity remains very low, notwithstanding the enormous employment of mechanized methods. For the moment, however, the difference between Soviet and American productivity is about one to three, as has been shown.

All the efforts of the government, the Party, the unions and the Soviet economic departments aim at raising the level of productivity. This is the basis of the programme which expects to win, within twenty years, the economic contest with America and so put into effect the transition from socialism to communism. It will, however, be shown that the growth indices of the programmes do not seem to be attainable. Furthermore, in many Western countries and in Japan the labour productivity index, both industrial and agricultural, is growing even more rapidly than in the Soviet Union. Though the difference in productivity between the Soviet Union and the United States is decreasing, that between the Soviet Union and the Common Market countries is increasing.

3

The Soviet government does its utmost to encourage moral incentives in order to increase its labour productivity. Many are the expedients adopted in order to intensify the efforts of the employees. The first of these in order of time was Stakhanovism. The tendency which prevails today is to make one gang compete with another and to cite the victors in the order of the day. These gangs form the communist labour groups and shock-workers, whose leaders met in May 1960 at Moscow in a Pan-Union Conference, which officially

[3] Robert W. Campbell, *Soviet Economic Power*, pp. 81 & 82, Chapter 4, Houghton-Mifflin Co., Boston, 1960.

approved and brought to the attention of the whole country these contests between factories and enterprises of similar nature whose object is to exceed the planned production levels. The aim of these competitions is to attain even higher levels which it may be possible to achieve in various sectors. Reliance is placed not only on the physical effort of well-trained and selected groups but also on their methods of working, their experience and the skill that they acquire and impart.

The centre of this mania for competition is the Ukraine. The movement arose out of the 'pledges' which the various enterprises made with growing frequency to exceed the quotas foreseen in the seven-year plan or to shorten the period for the fulfilment of the tasks allotted to them. Before the XXI Party Congress only ten thousand such labour groups had joined the movement; a year later there were sixty-four thousand groups with a membership of more than a million factory and kolkhoz workers. The winners were awarded the title of 'advanced worker of communist labour'. The task of these chosen groups is to encourage the laggards by example and instruction to get into step. These groups are the leaven to make the dough rise. What was wanted, in short, was to create a means of accelerating production based on moral, patriotic and, above all, ideological motives.

But, as always happens, as the movement spread it lost its initial zeal. The newspaper *Pravda* remarked that many of its promoters had resumed their former primitive rhythm of labour. Nor is it difficult to see why; any intense effort, too prolonged, exhausts the worker. Was not this one of the most severe criticisms made by Marx of private capitalism?

These are, therefore, flames which die down quickly. A method based on enthusiasm relies on the precarious, the transitory, the exceptional. Enthusiasm is born of a sudden upsurge of emotion and can even be contagious but, like all emotional states of mind, it is of short duration. It is only material interest, that is to say egoism, that releases the maximum of energy. The secret is to keep kindled the hope of still greater gains, because only on the basis of his own benefit will the individual plan his activities over a long term and aim at even higher goals. When the individual is rigidly classified, like the worker-bee in the hive, the only perspective is a flat, grey, monotonous life in which one day is exactly like the next.

4

Not being able to demonstrate the superiority of the communist

Top left: St. Basil's Church, a Moscow landmark.

Top right: Soviet citizens stroll inside the walls of the Kremlin.

Bottom left: Russian children play inside the "Freedom Bell."

Bottom right: Thousands line up in Red Square to see Lenin's tomb.

régime on the basis of the only valid yardstick recognized by Lenin and Khrushchev, that is to say labour productivity, the Soviet propaganda machine stresses the superiority of the index of production growth which is a different matter altogether. It must at once be realized that the index of growth to which the Soviets normally refer is not that of production generally but only of industrial production, since the rhythm of agricultural production is markedly less.

In a set speech at the XXI Party Congress on the character and aims of the seven-year plan Khrushchev asserted that the victory of communism was assured by the rhythm of the progress of the Soviet economy, far more rapid than that of the Western economy. According to his data, the average annual increase in industrial production was, over the fire-year period 1954-1958, 11% for the whole communist bloc, whereas the capitalist world had not reached 3%. He explained that this superiority was due to the application of two principles: the co-ordination of productive effort among the communist countries and the division of labour amongst them based on their specialization.

It will for the moment suffice to restrict this comparison to the indices of production increase in the Soviet Union and the United States, not only in order to remain within the frame of Khrushchev's challenge but also because it is impossible in practice to compare data relative to two such heterogeneous entities as the communist world and the capitalist world, in which last the Soviets include all the countries which do not form part of the communist bloc, that is to say the African countries, the Latin-American countries and a good number of the Asian countries. These are countries which have been very little industrialized and whose economic data can scarcely be taken into account with Western Europe and North America.

According to Soviet data, the rhythm of increased industrial production in the Soviet Union has been maintained from the time of the first *pyatiletka* (five-year plan) at 10%, whereas the American index was, on an average over the last four years, about 3.2%. When the seven-year plan came into operation, that is to say in 1959, the index of production increase was 10% but fell to 9.5% in 1962 to 8.5% in 1963 and 7.8% in 1964.

It is difficult to ascertain the exactness of this percentage, since it has been pointed out[4] that in the total of industrial production the

The academician S. G. Strumilin, the dean of Soviet economists, in his publication *Essay on the Social Economy of the Soviet Union*, shows that in calculating the official index of industrial production Soviet statisticians add the same item several times. Strumilin gives as an example automobile production. The official index is not limited to the value of machines built, but includes the value of individual parts and of the raw materials used in the

Russian statistics usually include the same values several times; as raw materials, as semi-manufactured goods and as finished products. It has also been pointed out that the increase in total production does not correspond to the increase of the individual items that compose it. Thus, on the basis of the increases of Soviet industrial production declared year by year, it must already have surpassed American production. This has compelled the Soviet statisticians to modify every so often the relation between the production of the two countries.

Sergio D'Angelo and Leo Paladini, who have drawn attention to these factors in their very accurate study of this matter, consider that the average annual increase of aggregate production in the Soviet Union from 1928 to 1955 is around 8%.[5]

However this may be, the Soviets stress that the volume of their production in 1960 was half that of the United States. On the basis of an annual rhythm of increase of 10% they may expect to reach in ten years, that is to say in 1970, the volume reached by American production in 1960. In another ten years they expect to double this volume and thus exceed the Americans since they, at their present rhythm of increase, cannot in twenty years double the volume of their production.

The above argument is based on the one hand on an effective increase of 10% in Soviet production and on the possibility of maintaining it for twenty years and on the other on an index of growth in American production of not more than 3.2%.

Khrushchev, speaking on January 28, 1961 to the Plenum of the Central Committee of the Ukrainian communist party, even shortened the term in which victory will be won. 'They ask us: "Comrade Khrushchev, when do you expect to overtake the Ameri-

construction of the machines. In this way the same values are added several times.

Beginning with the first plan, Strumilin shows that in 1928 the net industrial production was 10,000 million rubles (at the prices current for 1926-27) and not 21,500 million as stated in the official statistics. The figures were thus increased twofold.

Between 1928 and 1956 industrial production increased fifteen times and not twenty-three times as claimed by the official statistics.

Between 1945 and 1956 industrial production was trebled and not quadrupled.

In 1945 industrial production was about a third less than in 1940 whereas it was officially stated to be about 8% less.

In 1956 net production, calculated on the 1926-27 prices, was 147,700 million rubles, that is less than a third of the official figure of 492,400 million rubles.

Thus the increase from 1955 to 1956 was not 11% but only 8%.

[5] Sergio D'Angelo and Leo Paladini, op. cit., p. 22.

cans?" I reply: "Take this down in your notebooks; in 1970 we shall overtake them in the *pro capite* volume of production and we shall go on still farther." '

5

An essential factor to bear in mind is that the struggle between communism and capitalism is taking place on the economic plane. The fact that all efforts are being concentrated on this formidable challenge, and that on its outcome communism expects recognition of its superiority, makes the danger of war less probable.

At the opening session of the XXI Party Congress on January 27, 1959, when launching the seven-year plan, Khrushchev referred to this plan as a factor for peace. 'Its importance,' he said, 'lies primarily in the fact that it is imbued with the spirit of peace. A state that undertakes this gigantic programme of building new factories, plants, power stations, mining establishments and such things, which sets aside about four hundred thousand million rubles (about $40,000 million) for housing and public buildings and sets itself the task of substantially raising the living standards of its people, wants peace, not war.'

That is incontestable; but with the proviso that victory in this struggle, even if attained only in the economic field, must give Russia similar results to a military victory, that is to put the seal on the definite supremacy of the communist world. On this point Khrushchev, in his speech to the XXI Party Congress, was sufficiently explicit. He said that the overwhelming power of the Soviet Union will enable it to impose peace. 'It will produce more than half of the industrial articles manufactured in the world and therefore the world situation will radically change ... There will then be a real possibility of outlawing war as a means of solving international questions. As long as capitalism exists there will always be persons willing to launch out on some desperate adventure. But in such a case they will only hasten the final collapse of the capitalist system.'

He could not indicate more clearly the aim of this economic contest. The communist world wishes to attain such a reserve of means as to be able to impose peace, its peace, and therefore to impose its will. This confirms that, even if it is being fought out on the economic plane, it is a struggle for supremacy between two worlds.

6

Let us now hear the American bell toll. President Kennedy, re-

plying to the Soviet statements on June 30, 1961, said that Khrushchev has compared America to an old champion living in the past
and has said that the Soviet Union will overtake the United States
in overall production before 1970. The President then recalled that in
1913 Russian overall production was 46% of American, whereas in
1959 it reached 47%. This despite the fact that while the Soviet
Union advanced so did the tired old runner, so that in 1959 the
pro capite production of the Soviet people was scarcely 30% of the
American.

Kennedy also referred to the 6% annual development index of
Soviet production and the 3.5% of American production. He added,
however, that he was convinced that the United States could increase its rhythm of production to 4.5%, which he considered 'a
reasonable limit which takes account of our potential'.

Similar conclusions were reached by the economist Warren Nutter
of Virginia University after eight years research into, and verifica-
tion of, Soviet economic data, carried out by the National Bureau
of Economic Research. According to Warren Nutter, Russian overall
production was, in 1913, roughly equal to 13.9% of that of the
United States in the same year, in 1955 to 23.4% and in 1961 to
less than 30% of United States production in the same year.

On the other hand Khrushchev in his report to the XXII Party
Congress in October 1961, declared: 'The industrial production of
the Soviet Union is now more than 60% of the American.' In proof
of his statement he compared the production volume of the principal raw materials, consumer goods, etc.[6] 'I remember,' he said,

[6] Here are the figures referred to by Khrushchev:

	Soviet Union	United States	Percentage of Soviet production in relation to American
Iron (millions of tons)	51.1	62	82
Steel (millions of tons)	71	91	78
Coal, oil, gas and other fuels, calculated in con- ventional fuel units (millions of tons)	724	1,430	51
Electrical power (in 1,000 million kwh.)	306	872	35
Cement (millions of tons)	51	54	94
Unbleached cotton fabrics 1,000 million sq. metres	5.3	8.5	82
Woollen fabrics (millions of metres)	353	270	131
Leather footwear (millions of pairs)	443	610	73
Sugar (millions of tons)	6.5	3.7	175

'that about ten or eleven years ago the Soviet Union produced less than 30% of United States industrial production. Today the Soviet Union has already overtaken the USA in the volume of extraction of iron ore and coal, in coke production, in reinforced concrete, Diesel and electric locomotives, sawn softwoods, woollen textiles, sugar, butter, fish and other products. Our country now produces almost a fifth of world consumption, more than England, France, Italy, Canada, Japan, Belgium and Holland combined. Yet these are highly developed countries with a total population of 280 millions. The fact that our country with a population of 220 millions should have overtaken them in total industrial production shows with what speed and certainty the Soviet Union is advancing.'

The conclusion to be drawn from these comparisons is that the rhythm of Soviet production is more rapid than that of American. Yet it must be noted that the labour productivity index in the Soviet Union is less, indeed considerably less, than that of labour productivity in the United States. But this inferiority is in great measure compensated by the Soviet superiority in natural resources (land) and in investments (capital).

This last point above all needs to be clarified.

In the democratic countries, in homage to the principle of freedom, once the state has levied a part of the national income in the form of taxes and duties, what remains is at the free disposal of private individuals who devote a portion of it to consumer goods and a portion to savings which, in practice, is channelled into productive enterprises. Every citizen decides, on his unchallenged judgment, to what extent he intends to limit his consumption. Progress flourishes because of this freedom to enjoy the good things of life. Art, culture, refinement of manners, are born from this variety of tastes and individual needs.

In the communist world this is not so. The limit of every citizen's consumption is fixed by the state which, in dividing up the whole national income, of which it is the sole administrator, stabilizes on the one hand the part destined for the consumers, including therein both the returns expendable in cash and the advances for the social services, and on the other the portion allocated for administrative expenses, military expenses and productive investment. It is clear that the greater the military expenses and investments the less will be the quota allotted to the consumers. It is not easy to estimate what proportion of the national income is earmarked for armaments. Given that Soviet and American military expenditure are more or less equivalent and calculating that Soviet income is a half, or perhaps less than a half, of the American, it follows that the percentage of income set aside for armaments is more than double that destined for them by the United States.

No less high is the percentage of income allotted to productive investments. It is estimated that whereas the Soviet Union set aside for this purpose about 30% of their production, the United States allotted a percentage which varies between 17% and 20%.

What must also be borne in mind is that the Soviet state reserves the right to accelerate or retard the rhythm of production by increasing or reducing the quota devoted to investment. It then becomes obvious, bearing in mind the drastic reduction caused by military expenditure, why Soviet wages are lower than Western wages.

The Americans estimate that the Soviet citizen must content himself with scarcely a third of the consumer goods and services enjoyed by the American.

The secret of the advance in Soviet production is therefore to be found in the restrictions on consumer spending. Khrushchev continues to speak of overtaking United States production and sets a date for this, but he takes good care not to say when the *pro capite* consumption of the Soviet people will exceed that of the Americans since if consumption becomes widespread investments will begin to taper off. Only a state with a dictatorial régime can dispose at will of the product of labour and fix the scale of wages. It is therefore the working people who are paying for the communist experiment which rewards them with reduced wages, denial of the right to strike, shortage of housing, scarcity of consumer goods, in short by a lowering of its living standards.

Marx scathingly criticized accumulation of capital by curtailment of wages. Whether the accumulated capital belongs to the state or to private individuals is irrelevant to the workers, whose wages are drastically reduced in either case. It is useless to retort that state capital is accumulated in the interests of production for Marx himself has acknowledged that accumulation of private capital also has as its aim the increasing of enterprises, that is to say of capital.

7

It is clear that, by keeping the investment index higher and bearing in mind that in a new country, such as the greater part of Soviet territory is, costs are considerably lower than in a country which has long been industrialized, the difference between the volume of American and Soviet production is bound to become less until their positions are finally reversed.

The wheel of history is continually turning and bit by bit as progress, especially cultural and technical progress, extends to other lands, new powers appear to contest the leading role on the world's stage. For several centuries the leading power in the world was France. In the nineteenth century as a result of the industrial revolution the lead passed to England, which was overtaken by Germany which in its turn had to cede primacy to the United States. These are all capitalist countries, not one of which dreamed of attributing its hegemony to the wonder-working efficiency of some particular ideology or some particular régime, but rather to the interplay of economic and financial power.

It is in the natural order of things that an immense country like Russia, with almost inexhaustible resources, should, thanks to the progress of its technology and the vast scale of its investments, reach a volume of production superior to all others. Perhaps the time needed to achieve this is a good deal farther away than Khrushchev anticipates, not only because the quotas foreseen by the seven-year plan for agricultural production have not been attained but also because the difference between American industrial production and Soviet industrial production are considerable, as may be seen from the figures relative to certain key sectors given below.

In the first six months of 1959, considering Soviet production as 100, the American production indices were:

Electricity	363
Petrol	339
Steel	236
Cement	166

8

But why limit the contest to these two countries, the Soviet Union and the United States, which, even though they be the prototypes of the two rival ways of life and also the two major world powers, differ so greatly in territorial extent and by the amount of their natural resources, which are the bases of economic progress?

The picture changes if one compares the index of productive development of the Soviet Union with that of the countries of the European Economic Community. It will then be seen that the rhythm of growth is swifter in the second than in the first, since the percentage of the European Community in world production rose in 1960 from 20.8 to 21.3, whereas the quota of the Soviet Union fell from 19.9 to 19.1.

Among so many figures, let us take the most significant, that of steel production which is the foundation of industrial development. In 1960 the Soviet Union produced 65 million tons whereas the European Economic Community produced 72.8 million tons. The Soviet Union increased its steel production by 9%. Far more impressive was the leap forward by the Italian steel industry which produced 8,229,000 tons in 1960, an increase of 21.7%, a world record.

It is, therefore, a good thing to take another viewpoint on Soviet economic progress. Several capitalist countries, beginning with Western Germany, have exceeded the percentage increase of industrial production in the Soviet. Let us therefore compare two authentic prototypes of capitalism and communism: Western and Eastern Germany. On the one side there is unprecedented progress: industries with record-breaking production, a gold reserve which is second in the world, cities rebuilt and even larger than ever before, a spectacular resurrection in scarcely ten years from the ruin of the war, a prosperity never known before. On the other side a country being drained of its best, its youngest and most intellectual manpower which the government restrains by terror, transforming the whole territory into a walled camp. The drain is simply due to the difference in living standards between the two Germanys, like that which takes place between two vessels on two levels. In the Democratic Republic there is a shortage of consumer goods and rationing has been re-introduced. East Berlin is sad and lifeless in comparison with the Western sector, throbbing with life and overflowing with wealth. Yet the Soviet Union has done its best to develop the economy of Eastern Germany to the full, providing it with huge quantities of raw materials and giving it huge orders.

Comparison between the two régimes is even more striking if it is extended to a larger number of communist and capitalist countries of approximately equal size, as between Czechoslovakia and Switzerland, Austria and Hungary, Poland and Italy.

The wonder is not that mighty Russia has reached an index of 8.5%, or even 10%, of industrial production increase, but that Italy, so much smaller, poor and over-populated, should have exceeded it. The demonstration of the superiority of the régime is in the Italian miracle, because it proves that freedom stimulates creative energy sufficiently to compensate for the lack of natural resources.

9

If capitalism maintains, on the admission of the highest Soviet leaders, a productivity index at least twice or three times more than that of the communist countries, thus showing in the only manner considered valid by Lenin and Khrushchev its clear superiority over communism, how can one explain the repeated assertion of Soviet propaganda that the collapse of capitalism is imminent? What are the concrete proofs of the validity of the thesis that Marxism has repeated unchanged for more than a hundred years, despite the quite evident signs of the vitality of capitalism which is modernizing its structure, its technology, its system of financing, its productive methods and, even more, its spirit?

Khrushchev, in his closing speech at the XXI Party Congress, prophesied the imminent triumph of communism. 'Comrades,' he said, 'we are living in extraordinary times. This is a time when, by the will and the creative labour of the Soviet people guided by the communist party, the boldest dreams of men are being translated into living reality. Countless generations have dreamed of a more splendid future, of a society which should no longer be divided into rich and poor and in which the workers should not be oppressed. That dream was communism.'

Observe the technique of this propaganda. It does not dwell on immediate realities, which provoke so lively a disappointment among the workers and peasants as is shown by the very low labour productivity index, but on the promise of a morrow which recedes ever farther away in time. What matters is to maintain the expectation of the fulfilment of 'the boldest dreams of men'.

This does not mean that Khrushchev did not believe in these distant mirages. He explained his convictions to a Western statesman in these terms: 'Communism imposes itself upon the conscience. It is an ideology, it is a political doctrine. It suits us. There is no question of imposition, but of penetration into the consciences of men. We are convinced of it. Think how it used to be in Russia; we were poor and illiterate. Now we are the second power in the world. We shall become the first. In some sectors we already are. Is this because we are more intelligent? We are not racists. Every nation has an equal chance. The merit is in the system. We will wait until they understand us.'

It was not difficult for his listener to counter Soviet reality with Western reality, to confront the virtues of communism which has not yet stood the test of time with the virtues of Christian civilization confirmed by thousands of years of experience. As to the power of diffusion innate in the very nature of the Marxist idea, the Western statesman stressed the enormous resources with which the Soviet Union supported its propaganda in the democratic countries. It was no longer a struggle of ideas, but of influences and interests.

Khrushchev retorted: 'When an idea is born it becomes accessible to all peoples. The sooner it takes root in their consciences the better; the more it is delayed the more the people are punished for this delay. The Soviet Union has been punished for having stopped at the stage of feudalism. The Western countries went beyond feudalism and found themselves in the lead. In the Soviet Union instead of moribund capitalism we have a system which allows us to stride onward and to leave you behind. The positions are reversed. Stay where you are if you like.'

Statements of this kind reveal the spirit of the man. We are on the frontier between politics and Messianism. Everyone can judge for himself the validity of such an interpretation of history. What makes the discussion difficult is that the expectation of the events which must lead to the triumph of communism is not far off but immediate. 'The triumph of communism is imminent,' Khrushchev declared to the Conference of Pan-German workers at Leipzig in March 1959. 'As soon as the Soviet Union matches America in *pro capite* production, has reduced the working day and carried out its programme of communist reforms, all peoples will see the superiority of the new régime and will overthrow the disintegrating and anachronistic capitalist organization . . .The symptoms of capitalist collapse, shown by economic crises, strikes and unemployment, are evident. All we can do is wait.'

During a reception to which the whole diplomatic corps was invited Khrushchev referred to the representatives of the Western powers in more or less these words: 'Poor fellows, they are prisoners of an archaic system, forced to say not what they think but what their governments want them to say, though they are aware of the crisis which will mark the end of their system.' On that same occasion he expressed the hope of living long enough to attend the burial of capitalism. Someone wittily wished him so long a life, adding that even the years of Methuselah would not be enough.

The irony of the situation is in the fact that, while insisting on the crises and contradictions of the capitalist system, Khrushchev has been forced to realize that deviationism and dogmatism have created fissures in the communist system which is only a few decades old. And it is well known that children's illnesses are a good deal more dangerous than those of adults.

From what has been said certain conclusions may be drawn:

1. It is unrealistic to speak of a comparison between capitalism and communism, since in no country till now has the communist formula been applied. The impossibility of comparison between a fulfilled capitalist society and a communist society still in the making weakens Marxist propaganda, because it forces it to stress

a negative activity, that is a destructive criticism of capitalism, rather than a positive activity, that is a concrete proof of the superiority of the formula intended to replace it. How can it persuade men to burn their boats before reaching the unknown land, when it is by no means certain if it even exists?

2. Comparison may be made between the two realities now existent, that is between private capitalism and state capitalism. The latter, though it may not be communism, is based on Marxist tenets inimical to capitalism, that is on state possession of the sources of production and their administration by means of planning. These are two premises which will exist in a communist order and of which one can at present estimate the efficiency.

3. Such an estimate is based essentially on the level of labour productivity. This criterion has been laid down by Lenin and accepted by Khrushchev. Now the superior labour productivity in the capitalist régime is incontestable, as Khrushchev himself has acknowledged. The differential is about three to one. The reasons for this wide variance have been stated. The main reason lies in the fact that capitalist economy with its high wages stimulates to the maximum the yield of all productive effort.

4. The low level of labour productivity in the Marxist lands is a fact of primary importance for two reasons. In the first place, as can be seen from the programme of the Soviet communist party at its XXII Congress, and as Khrushchev has stressed to the utmost in his speeches about the programme, the transition from socialism to communism will be made possible by an increase in labour productivity at least three times more than at present during the next twenty years.

5. In the second place there is a reasonable doubt whether in a régime of free enterprise Russian labour productivity would not have reached levels similar to those in the Western countries. This doubt is justified, among other things, by what has been taking place in agricultural production throughout all those communist countries which have put into practice the collectivization of land. For example, in the last decades of the tsarist government, Russia achieved spectacular advances in agricultural production after the reforms of Stolypin, who had facilitated the transfer of land to private ownership. If the rhythm of progress at that time had been maintained over the past forty-five years (and there is nothing to forbid the thought that this would have taken place in a régime respectful of private property) the recession in agricultural production, to say nothing of the present agricultural crisis, would have been avoided, nor would there now be a shortage of foodstuffs.

6. If the labour productivity index in the Soviet Union is less

43

than that in the United States, the index of Soviet industrial production is higher than that of the United States and some other capitalist countries. Khrushchev attributed this high rhythm of industrial production (the annual rate of increase today is about 7.8%) to the superiority of the Marxist régime, hinting at the greater possibilities offered by a system of centralization of productive forces, of state control, of rationalized, methodical and ordered planning, of the technical formation of cadres, of a new social conscience, the high quality of the directing cadres and so on.

It would be contrary to reality to deny that the régime has in many ways made good use of the potential energies of the country, but it would also be contrary to truth to conceal that these same principles have limited the expansion of creative energy and that in many sectors one has the fixed impression that the difficulties and limitations which the régime has encountered would have been more easily overcome by the multiform, flexible and inventive forces of private activity. Undoubtedly one of the great qualities of the régime has been to form a ruling class of very high cultural and moral level, of remarkable energy and incomparable organizing ability from a people which, before the revolution, was for the most part illiterate. But in a democratic régime which allows all forms of talent to rise to positions of command, would not these men have risen just the same to the positions that they now occupy?

A dictatorial structure gives a state special advantages for centralization of power, and speed and secrecy in decision; but here the comparison is not so much between Marxism and capitalism as between dictatorship and democracy.

7. In so complex a framework as that of the Soviet Union there are both lights and shadows. How much of the one or of the other is attributable to the ideology? The reply can only be given after a detailed analysis of the Soviet organization, sector by sector, and of the problems which it has confronted and which still confront it, because only on the basis of such an analysis is it possible to decide what are the elements of strength and what the elements of weakness.

A synthetic judgment can only be given by a historian after a certain passage of time, which will enable him to take a broader viewpoint and interpret longer cycles of evolution.

Therefore this study proposes to examine:

—the strength of the Soviet Union and its chances of success;

—the obstacles and weaknesses that retard its progress.

PART II

THE ELEMENTS OF
STRENGTH

CHAPTER II

Natural Resources

1

THE first element of strength of the Soviet Union is its immense size. It extends from the Baltic to the Pacific and covers a sixth of the land surface of the world. It has an area of 22,273,700 square kilometres, two and a half times larger than the United States. It is roughly three and a half million square kilometres larger than the total area of the two next largest countries in the world, the United States with 9,363,488 square kilometres and the Chinese People's Republic with 9,560,000 square kilometres.

The Soviet Union has an almost complete range of primary raw materials. Though prospecting on its territory is still far from complete, the wealth already revealed assures it an immense superiority of economic potential over all other countries in the world. The inventory of its natural resources grows longer every year, even every month, as the work of prospecting goes on.

A member of the Presidium, Aristov, speaking at the XXI Communist Party Congress on January 31, 1959, said quite rightly about the wealth of the Soviet Union: 'We are richer than any other country in the world. I speak not only of mineral wealth, but of the limitless expansion of our fertile soil. As we study the subterranean deposits of our country we keep finding new and fabulous sources of wealth, above all in Siberia and in the Far East. We can say without fear of contradiction that these regions will remain for many centuries our basic treasure house of mineral wealth, the major source of development of raw materials for the benefit of society.

'It is often said,' he went on, 'that the United States is in a more favourable situation than the other capitalist countries because of its natural resources. But even its resources cannot in any way be compared with the natural wealth of our country. If we consider the known world reserves of the sixteen most important minerals, the Soviet Union is first in the world for thirteen of them.'

This is a statement to be borne in mind when making a comparison between the productive capacities of Russia and America.

47

Estimates already several years old, and which should in all probability be increased, attribute to the Soviet Union the following percentages of world reserves:

21% of coal (which should probably be increased to 50%);
20% of ferrous metals (which should probably be 40%);
33% of forests.

But notwithstanding the lower potential of the United States, it was in 1958 the leading power in the world for the production of twenty-nine out of the sixty-three minerals to which the mining statistics of one hundred and ten countries refer. The Soviet Union was in the lead for eight of these and Canada for three.

It would undoubtedly be a mistake to over-estimate the importance of natural resources. Adam Smith in his classic work *The Wealth of Nations* has already given a warning that the possession of natural resources is not wealth because it is to everyone's benefit to buy goods where they cost least, and that therefore the real factor of wealth is labour because of its decisive importance in the cost of transformation of the raw materials into the finished product. It is, however, clear that in an immense country like the Soviet Union, where transport costs notably affect production costs, it is indisputably an advantage to have raw materials available on the spot rather than to have to import them, and to be able to proceed with their transformation, so to speak, at the pit head. An even more striking advantage is that the greater part of these raw materials, because of the favourable conditions of exploitation, can be obtained at exceptionally low cost. Such, for example, is the case for the production of electrical energy, because of the exploitation of the immense water power of the Siberian rivers, and of the iron ore in the Ural territory and to the east of it. This wealth of mineral resources permits a development of industrial activity far in advance of agricultural activity which in certain zones becomes impossible and in others is hampered by climatic conditions. It is, moreover, surprising that, thirty-five years after the first five-year plan which gave a formidable impulse to industrialization, the peasants are nearly as numerous as the workers employed in industry, the contrary of what is taking place in America, even though in America the volume of agricultural production is far greater than in the Soviet Union. This anti-economic distribution of the labour force reveals the existence of frictions in the Soviet production system which prevent this natural flow of workers from the land to the factories, as has happened naturally in all the Western countries solely through the stimulus of personal advantage.

This in no way belies the fact that the land is, and will always remain, one of the main sources of the wealth of the Soviet Union. However, only a relatively small area of its immense territory is suitable for profitable cultivation. The well-known Russian economist Sergei N. Prokopovich[1] begins his description of the natural resources of his country with the words: 'The Russian climate is, for agriculture, one of the worst in the world. In the north the growth cycle is very short indeed, the eternal frost hinders cultivation in Eastern Siberia, drought threatens the harvests in the southern lands, in Central Asia and in Kazakstan.'

This seems too negative a judgment. From the 22,300,000 square kilometres of Soviet territory must be subtracted the part covered by the tundra, that is to say the northern part of the country, plunged in the polar night during the winter, frozen and under a cover of snow for eight or nine months of the year, devoid of humus almost everywhere and denied to cultivation because of the shortness of the summer, which is at the same time the period without night. The tundra covers 12.2% of Soviet territory.

A great part of Eastern Siberia, that is to say the country east of the river Yenisei, must also be subtracted, because it is subject to the *merzlotà*, that is to say the presence of eternal ice just below the soil. The thickness of this ice is, in the northernmost areas, about four hundred metres and becomes progressively less as one moves southward until it finally disappears. The *merzlotà* extends over 47% of Soviet territory, that is to say over ten million square kilometres. The territories in the Far East seized from China and Japan are free from it, that is to say the regions along the Amur, the Ussuri and the island of Sakhalin.

The lands subject to the *merzlotà* are not, however, sterile because, other than forest and pasture land, many forms of cultivation are possible during the short period of the cycle of growth. Indeed, were it not for the *merzlotà*, every form of vegetable life would be impossible and Eastern Siberia would be a desert, since the annual rainfall over all the zone is between a minimum of 150 mm. and a maximum of 350 mm. But in the summer heat the upper layer of the subterranean ice melts and waters the surface of the soil, giving nourishment not only to herbaceous vegetation but even to trees like larch and pine whose roots, not being able to grow downward, spread out horizontally. In the southern zone of the *merzlotà* cereals are also cultivated, such as barley and spring wheat, rye and oats.

[1] Sergei N. Prokopovich, *Economic History of the Soviet Union*; ed. Laterza, Bari, 1957, p. 11.

At Yakutsk, near the Cold Pole, there are experimental plantations, with fields and even gardens. Much has been done to extend cultivation in these areas by the selection of suitable varieties crossed with resistant strains. The Soviet Union has inaugurated studies and experiments in many research centres. The famous biologist Michurin has created varieties of fruit trees, amongst which is the northern pear—obtained by crossing an ordinary pear with a rowan —as well as various types of grapes. But to ensure that these products get beyond the palings of the experimental stations and become diffused throughout the country, it is necessary to have a class of smallholders and large landowners interested in taking up these experiments and exploiting them for their own profit. It is, moreover, evident that the range of priorities in the Soviet Union will not allow for large-scale investments in the extension of cultivation in Eastern Siberia.

The agricultural future of Russia is in the cultivation of the great southern plains or steppes, which stretch from the Rumanian frontier into the heart of Western Siberia. They are rolling downland, sometimes fringed by folds of land to which the villages cling; they are mainly treeless, monotonous, crossed and re-crossed by the wind which drives the low clouds over them for infinite distances, even as they were crossed and re-crossed by the nomad people swarming from the inexhaustible womb of Central Asia.

The most fertile part of the steppe is the belt of *chernozem*, or black earth, which stretches for more than four thousand kilometres. The humus here reaches a depth of a metre and is covered by vegetable detritus which gives it its characteristic black colour. It is the area of the highest yields in all Russia. If private initiative were given its head all this zone would become a garden because the black earth is more suitable than any other for intensive cultivation similar to that in the western European countries. Also, for wealth of agricultural yield, the Ukraine need fear no comparisons for no land exceeds or even equals its proverbial fertility. On the other hand, as will be seen when speaking of the agricultural crisis, its production has slowed down in recent years. Its cereal yield varies between ten and twelve quintals per hectare.

It is, however, true that drought makes its harvests very variable from year to year, especially in the more eastern districts. When the *sukhovei* comes, the wind from the deserts between the Caspian and the Urals, all the vegetation is shrivelled up.

There are good conditions for agricultural exploitation over a great area of Western Siberia. Cultivation prospers in a central strip where the soil has ideal conditions of humidity and temperature. Farther north the soil is waterlogged by the thaws, and the watercourses are not enough to drain off the immense stagnant meres, not only because of the very slight slope of the plains but also because when the thaw is already far advanced upstream ice is still blocking the river estuaries, causing the mass of the waters to overflow in the interior. The resulting floods extend over an area of about four million square kilometres, that is to say 18% of the territory.

But the central part, of which the most important city is Novosibirsk, is an immense granary. The local people speak enthusiastically about its soil. The commandant of the airport told me: 'This is a very fertile land which produces all kinds of cereals, forage crops and fruit. The grape too flourishes. It can feed an immense number of animals. We have resistant strains here, derived from crossing American stud animals with local varieties. Who comes for only a day stays for ever.'

Deserts and semi-deserts complete the picture of the Russian lands. These cover about four million square kilometres, that is to say 18% of the superficial area. The centre of this desolate zone is the Aral-Caspian depression, a lunar landscape, all crevasses and sharp ridges, dotted with huge white stains of saline efflorescence. This zone stretches as far as the Aral Sea, a vast expanse of metallic blue because of the density of the mineral salts. To the south of this sea is the Kizilkum desert between the tributaries of the Aral, the Amu Darya and the Sir Darya. But wherever the landscape is furrowed by these two rivers or their affluents life rapidly recovers and bursts out with tropical exuberance in gardens, orchards and great plantations of cotton.

The sterility of these deserts is due in part to lack of rainfall, which is less than 250/200mm., in part to the temperature which in summer reaches 45° C., and in part to the high saline content in the soil. But the semi-desert provides summer pastures. Many of these arid zones become very fertile if irrigated, as has been shown by the results obtained on a wide scale by the work undertaken during the last decades.

To conclude: the areas in which it is possible to extend cultivation are: in Europe the steppe and the forest up to a maximum northern limit about the 6oth parallel; Transcaucasia, the middle zone of Western Siberia, the Amur plain in the Far East and, finally, if irrigated, the sub-tropical zones.

At one time it was estimated that the cultivable part of Soviet territory did not exceed 10 to 11% of the total area, that is to say from 220 to 245 million hectares. Today, as a result of advances in agricultural techniques, of the development of irrigation and of recent experience, Soviet specialists are inclined to believe that the areas capable of agricultural exploitation can be extended to about a fifth of the territory, that is to say about 450 million hectares, double the area given in earlier estimates. Of these 450 million hectares, 250 million would be in European Russia or Caucasia, 150 million in Western Siberia and in Central Asia and the remaining 50 million in the Chita district and in the Far East.

Perhaps both these estimates err, the first by under-estimation, the second by over-estimation. But there seems no doubt that the cultivable area is greater, indeed much greater, than a tenth of the territory. Only experience can show the maximum limits of cultivable area.

Naturally not all these lands are of equal fertility. In a régime of private ownership even poorer lands would find someone to exploit them, since the lesser fruits of a poor soil find their recompense in the lower purchase cost. But in the Soviet Union, where state ownership reigns, it is logical that the most remunerative lands be put under cultivation, unless various non-economic questions come under consideration, such as the opportunity of colonizing areas, even if sub-standard, where it is wished to increase the density of population or to introduce nuclei of the ruling race. In such a case the communist state, which cannot on principle admit any difference in economic treatment between cultivators of a richer and those of a poorer area, since all work equally for the state, must take upon itself the burden of the lesser yield. In other words it must assure the risks and losses inherent in the expansion of cultivation in less productive areas.

The problem was raised in an acute form after Stalin's death, when there was a discussion about the most suitable methods for expanding agricultural production and, even more important, the choice of areas in which to concentrate the greatest productive effort. The debate ranged the anti-Party group headed by Malenkov and Molotov against the minority led by Khrushchev and Mikoyan. The former held that, in order to lessen the risk and expense of the expansion of cultivation, it was best to raise production levels in the most fertile zones of European Russia, that is to say in the *chernozem* of the Ukraine, transforming the system of cultivation from extensive to intensive and at the same time improving the equipment and the infrastructure; this could be done at relatively low cost, since the area in question was already economically developed. But Khrushchev, made sceptical by the failure of the agricultural programme included in the sixth five-year plan which had forecast an increase in the yield per hectare in the Ukraine from twelve to eighteen quintals of cereals, supported the view that the virgin lands must be placed under cultivation and fresh areas of cereal cultivation and stockbreeding created in Kazakstan and Eastern Siberia. He won; even though he could not make public the real reason for his preference.

There are two reasons above all of Khrushchev's choice. The transition from extensive to intensive cultivation requires time and mean while the need for larger harvests had become urgent. Nor should it be forgotten that intensification of cultivation in a régime of private ownership is easy to manage whereas in a régime of state ownership it is almost impossible. The agricultural crisis of 1960-61 gave a recent proof by the poor yield of the harvests in just that region of the Ukraine upon whose increase in production the anti-Party group relied.

But there was a second reason, no less important, which explained Khrushchev's preference, a political reason. The colonization of Kazakstan, as of all Central Asia, is a part of the Russianization of those areas, inhabited for the most part by Moslem populations which have never shown heartfelt sympathy for Russian rule.

The results of the exploitation of the virgin lands, pursued by Khrushchev with such indomitable tenacity, with a vast mobilization of men and means, seemed at the beginning to justify his calculations, but weather conditions in 1956, 1960 and 1961 were very irregular and jeopardized an ever greater part of the harvests.

Recently the chances of extending the areas of cultivation even farther southward have been considered, above all in the regions of Central Asia sheltered by the great mountain barrier which separates them from Afghanistan and Chinese Turkestan. Great reliance is being placed on the wealth of water in these zones which enjoy longer summers and therefore permit less speculative cultivation cycles.

Even taking into account the virgin lands under cultivation the cultivated area of Soviet territory is still far from being the 450 million hectares over which, according to the estimates given above, cultivation can be extended.

The efforts made to increase the cultivated area each year may, however, be clearly seen from the table below:

	millions of hectares
1913	105.0
1922	77.7
1932	135.3
1940	151.1
1945	104.3
1953	157.0
1959	196.3
1960	202.9
1962	216.0

As a basis for comparison one may take the relative figures of cultivated area in the United States, the People's Republic of China and the European Economic Community.

In the United States, which has a territory of more than 936 million hectares, the cultivated area in 1958 was over 188 million hectares, that is to say only 8 million hectares less than that of the Soviet Union. In Communist China, in an area of 960 million hectares, the cultivated area was 112 million hectares, equivalent to about 12% of the territory.

Lastly, in the European Community out of 116.5 million hectares about 48 million are cultivated, equivalent to 41% of the total area of its countries.

It is clear from the figures cited that both the United States and the countries of the European Economic Community have extended to the utmost, by comparison with Russia, the area of their cultivation.

Even more indicative is a comparison between the volume of agricultural production in Russia and that of agricultural production in the United States. It shows how great is the leeway which the Soviet Union has to make up to raise its *pro capite* production to the American level. In 1959 the Soviet Union produced about 126 million tons of cereals, while the United States produced almost half as much again, that is to say 185 million. As regards cotton the United States in 1959 produced 4,353,000 tons of seed and the Soviet Union 2,816,000 tons. As to stock-breeding the Soviet Union owned 74 million cattle in 1958 compared with 93.35 million in the United States in the same year.

The United States Secretary for Agriculture, Mr Ezra T. Benson, stated on July 2, 1960 that the productivity of American farmers was four or five times greater than that of Soviet farmers. It must not be forgotten that whereas in the Soviet Union a peasant population of more than a hundred million persons lives on 200 million hectares of cultivated land, on the slightly smaller cultivated area in the United States there is a population of 20,827,000 persons, equal to 12% of the inhabitants.[2] It is, moreover, to be noted that the Soviet Union, still having large areas at its disposal suitable for cultivation and especially of good irrigable land, can raise the volume of its agricultural production to very high levels. The development verified from 1953 to 1959 gives good reason to believe this; during this period the cultivable area was increased by 39 million hectares, while production increased 50%. The greatest advance was in the cereal harvest which had an increase of a good 60 million

[2] *The Statesman's Year Book* 1960, p. 164; ed. S. H. Steinberg, Ph.D., London, Macmillan and Co.

tons over that of 1953, equivalent to a 71% increase.

If, as has been said, the Soviet Union inaugurates an intensive programme of irrigation the yields per hectare will greatly exceed those now obtained in the Kazakstan steppe. Khrushchev admitted that the choice of the virgin lands, in which such enormous investments of capital and labour have been concentrated in recent years, was made when conditions were not very well-known in the even more favourable low-lying valleys of Central Asia and Siberia, closed to the south by the mountain ranges of the Pamirs, the Tien-Shan and the Altai, the sources of the huge water masses of the Amu Darya, the Sir Darya and the Ob with its affluents the Irtysh and the Yenisei. The melting of the snows in these mountains coincides with the growth period throughout this zone and therefore the mountain chains and their glaciers temper the summer heats and provide the wealth of water needed to combat the aridity of the lowlands. When this immense reserve of water has been exploited to irrigate the arid lands, agriculture will have harvests three or four times better than those obtained by the present system of 'dry farming'. All Central Asia and especially Uzbekistan will take on a new life. Already today the irrigated area of Uzbekistan is more than two million hectares, and it is expected that this will shortly be doubled. It will again become a second Mesopotamia, furrowed by a dense network of canals as it was before the hordes of Genghis Khan extinguished its life by stopping up the canals and thus depriving it of the life-giving fluid. The areas capable of irrigation cover some tens of millions of hectares. Stalin had earlier thought of transferring the centre of large-scale cultivation to southern Russia and Central Asia by irrigating 28 million hectares and planting 6 million hectares of forests as windbreaks. The scheme was abandoned because of the excessive cost; but his successors have again become interested. Hundreds of new kolkhozes are to be organized, making use of tens of millions of hectares of unused land in Western Siberia as pastures. The First Secretary of the Central Committee of the Kazakstan communist party told the Soviet Central Committee at its meeting in January 1961: 'In the last six years we have brought water to 34 million hectares of forage land. We have another 80 million hectares which lack canals, pipelines and artesian wells.'

As well as surface water, the arid zones are often rich in subterranean water. In Kazakstan there are vast underground catchments under the burnt-out steppe. Some seventy of them have already been located, rich in very fresh water, with a total volume equal to one and a half times the water volume of the Aral Sea. Soviet technicians say that when these waters have been raised to the surface the present deserts of the region will blossom as the rose. Already they have begun to lose the desolate aspect which has made them legendary. Thus the irrigation of the famous 'Hungry Steppe' has made gardens and plantations flourish. There remain more than a million hectares to irrigate; but already more than a million tons of cotton have been obtained. Another half million hectares are to be cultivated in the fertile valleys of Fergana and Zervashgan. The cultivation of the Karsh steppe will make possible the production of 1,700,000 tons of cotton. Similar projects are being carried out in Transcaucasia and in the Crimea. The advances in science, technology and electrification make it possible to solve problems at one time thought insoluble by bringing whole catchment areas to the surface. One project, drawn up by the Institute of Hydraulic Design under the direction of the engineer Gurgen Sarukhanov, forecasts the reversal of the courses of two rivers, the Pechora and the Vychegda, which now flow into the Arctic and which will then flow into the Caspian. Other cyclopaean projects that reflect honour on Soviet technology are now being studied. The aim is to form immense areas for the cultivation of rice and cotton, and for stock-breeding.

A new phase in the development of Soviet agriculture has begun, characterized by irrigation of the steppes, the deserts and the semi-deserts, which opens boundless possibilities.

To conclude: in the immensity of its territory the Soviet Union has an agricultural potential which is still far from being fully exploited. While the United States is forced to limit its cultivable area in order to avoid crises of over-production, the Soviet Union has still an exceedingly large margin for development, which could lead it to extend cultivation over an area far greater than its American competitor.

3

The Soviet industrial potential is even greater. It will be enough to pass briefly in review its sources of power: coal, oil, gas and hydro-electrical potential, to say nothing of its reserves of ferrous and non-ferrous metals and, finally, its immense timber reserves.

The Soviet Union has astronomical coal reserves. At the moment they are estimated at 8,600 milliard tons, that is to say more than all the rest of the world. The reserves of Siberia alone are estimated at 7,500 milliard tons. Then there is the Donbass basin in the Ukraine, estimated at 240 milliard tons. Third are the reserves of Kazakstan, and in particular of Karaganda, estimated at fourteen milliard tons, but which, according to a later estimate, would amount to fifty milliard tons with seams, as at Ekibastuz, almost open-cast, to a depth of roughly a hundred metres. The Kuzbass basin in Western Siberia, to the east of Novosibirsk, is also of great importance. Most of these coalfields are of very high quality, like the coking coal of the Ukraine and the bituminous coal of Vorkuta, north of the polar circle. Thanks to the scale of its resources the Soviet Union has increased its production from 29,200,000 tons in 1913 (reduced to 7,200,000 tons in 1920) to 506.5 millions in 1959 and 530 millions in 1963, making the Soviet Union first among the coal producers of the world. Of the total coal produced in the world, which in 1958 amounted to 2,436 milliard tons, 20.4% was produced by the Soviet Union and 16.1% by the United States.

The Soviet Union has decided to slow down coal-mining in order to give priority to oil production, which costs two-thirds less, and to natural gas, which is even cheaper. Notwithstanding this slowing up, the seven-year plan aimed at increasing coal production to 612 million tons before 1965 but, in the two-year plan 1964-65, production was reduced to only 553 million tons. So, while in a great part of the world the coal crisis aims at reducing the quantity mined, the Soviet Union continues to increase its output, though at a slower rate.

4

Up to World War II the main oil-bearing area of the Soviet Union was Baku in Azerbaidzhan, together with the Grozny fields in the northern Caucasus and, to a lesser extent, Maikop in the Kuban. But in 1935 the vast depression known as 'the second Baku' was discovered between the Urals and the Volga. Its reserves are about 2.5 milliard tons, roughly the same capacity as the Caucasus oil-fields. Though the quantities extracted from Baku have been increased since the war, the deposits of the Volga-Ural zone are now the basis of the Soviet oil industry. Extraction is about 100 million tons, three times that of Baku.

Very rich deposits have also been found throughout Central Asia. Soviet technicians are convinced that the Caspian depression is destined to become one of the most important oil basins, since its geological characteristics are similar to those of the Middle East oil-fields.

No less rich is the Western Siberian depression, in the zones of Tyumen, Omsk and Tomsk. Other deposits have been located in Eastern Siberia, in addition to those on the island of Sakhalin.

The potential oil-bearing area is estimated at about 11 million square kilometres, compared with that of the United States which is about 4,600,000 square kilometres. Four shelves, or oil-bearing regions, have been located in the Soviet Union: the Russian or Scythian, the Western Siberian, the Eastern Siberian and the Central Asian.

Geological prospecting is being carried out systematically and the list of prospective oil-fields grows longer. In 1962 alone more than 540 new oil-fields had been located, the richest of which were in Western and Eastern Siberia. In the former, four vast sectors with a high quality oil were located in the depression of the mid-course of the Ob and in the Irtysh basin. In the latter, shafts were sunk, which give up to a thousand tons of oil a day, on the banks of the Lena in the district of Irkutsk; it is an area which seems destined to become one of the most important oil-fields in the Soviet Union.

In both parts of Siberia commercial exploitation of the oil and gas will be begun as soon as possible, but not before 1966, for there are serious difficulties to be overcome, since many of these deposits are in the heart of the *taiga* or among the bogs and marshes.

Again in 1962 several other promising zones were located, in the Yenisei basin, in the Soviet Far East and on the island of Sakhalin.

Meanwhile the work of prospecting goes on incessantly. Well-drilling at an annual average of from 13 to 15 million metres is laid down in the plan, with a tendency to drive the drills to a preliminary depth of more than 4,000 metres and successively, above all in Azerbaidzhan and the Caspian depression, to 7,000 metres and finally, little by little, to depths of ten, twelve and fifteen thousand metres.

The richer of the new deposits are exploited immediately. Scarcely had the first Siberian oil been located in the Konda valley than production began from the first well. Out of 186 million tons of oil produced in 1962 about 12 million came from wells drilled in the course of that year.

As a result of these explorations, about 80% of the oil reserves is concentrated in about 10% of the oil-fields which the government proposes to exploit with priority over the others. Among the fields given priority those of Turkmenia and Kazakstan are the most important. In the former, drilling carried out in 1961 led to the discovery of the Lenin oil-bearing area in the western Karakum, whose production equals that of the richest fields in the Volga-Ural region. It has several layers of excellent quality oil, as well as natural gas. Drilling carried out in the first half of 1961 showed that the commercial value of its reserves is in no way inferior to half those of all Central Asia. In Kazakstan the richest oil-fields have been found in the western part and it is believed that their potential amounts to several tens of millions of tons annually.

Soviet production, which was 70.8 million tons in 1955, has more than doubled in four years and is expected to reach 240 million tons in 1965. The production increase which was 12% annually in the period 1951-1955 rose in the following five-year period to 13.4% and continues to rise. In 1962 Soviet production was 185 million tons which was more than Venezuelan which in that year was 166 million tons. The Soviet Union has thus become the second largest world producer after America, which in the same year produced 400 million tons. Soviet participation in world production has risen from 7.7% in 1950 to 14% in 1960. The development of Soviet oil production and exports in recent years, as well as estimates up to 1980, are shown in the following table:

Year	Production Tons	Exports Tons	Percentage of production exported
1955	70,800,000	—	—
1957	98,346,000	13,680,700	13.9
1958	113,216,000	18,138,000	16.0
1959	129,557,000	25,372,000	19.5
1960	147,859,000	33,217,700	22.4
1961	166,068,000	41,218,100	24.8
1962	186,000,000	50,000,000	27.0
1963	205,500,000	—	—
1965 (estimated)	240,000,000	103,000,000	—
1970 „	390,000,000	—	—
1980 „	690/710,000,000	—	—

If one bears in mind that the oil production of the capitalist world in 1959 was 885 million tons it is evident how rapid has been the advance in Soviet production which aims at exceeding Western production and contesting the export markets with the Western countries.[3]

5

The majesty of the Russian rivers, both European and Asian, has already been mentioned. The whole country is a sort of sponge

[3] To facilitate oil exports the Soviet Union is building a network of oil pipelines intended to carry the crude oil into the heart of Europe and is forming a great tanker fleet. In particular the 'Friendship' pipeline, of which the stretch to Poland was inaugurated in 1963, will bring oil also to Eastern Germany (with a more southerly branch to Hungary and Czechoslovakia). The gigantic Trans-Siberian pipeline goes eastward and links the Tatar and Bashkir oil-fields with the Siberian refineries. In 1963 it had reached Irkutsk and will extend to Chita, Khabarovsk and thence the Pacific, in order to supply the Far East and South-East Asia.

soaked with water which flows into lakes as big as seas linked by a network of affluents, tributaries, effluents and artificial canals which in winter are carriage-ways and in summer navigable routes. The energy that these immense reservoirs can provide cannot be compared with the potential of any one of the greatest rivers of other continents. As an example let us quote the potential, according to the estimates of Soviet scientists, of some of the principal rivers east of the Urals:

	Million kw.
Angarà	10
Yenisei	18
Lena	18
Amur	6.5
Ob	5.5

Soviet technology dominates these forces of nature with a genius and an audacity which need fear no comparison with anything in this field anywhere in the world. In only eight years, from 1945 to 1953, the Soviet Union has tripled its capacity and its production of energy. The electrification programmes are exceptionally ambitious. They aim at a production of 2,500 milliard kwh. by the end of a twenty-year period. For the moment the production of electrical energy in Russia is considerably less than half that of the United States. In 1959 American production was 794,000,509,000 kwh. whereas Russia, in 1960, had only reached 300 milliard kwh. But Soviet progress is rapid. In 1963 production was 411.6 milliards and in 1965 it is expected to reach 508 milliard kwh. Thenceforward its advances are expected to allow it to quintuple its production in three five-year periods.

6

Last among the sources of energy to be discovered and exploited, but by no means the least important because of the great size of the deposits now being located in various areas, is natural gas. Only in recent years and only occasionally, when sounding for oil, was this new wealth discovered, but the discoveries were on such a scale that the seven-year plan made provision for the intensification of gas prospecting by allowing for drillings to a total depth of 15 million metres.

The first deposits of gas, which are among the richest in the world, were discovered in the 'Hungry Steppe' not far from Bukhara in 1956. Some of them furnish from one and a half to three and a half million cubic metres of gas a day. In the Gazli sector alone (the city was created as a result of the discovery of the fields) the available reserves are estimated at more than 500 milliard cubic metres. In 1959 the fields of Bashkirya were located with reserves, according to a preliminary estimate, of 300 milliard cubic metres; others have been found in the Ukraine near Kharkov, the Volga area near Saratov, in Western Siberia and in Eastern Siberia. Some of these deposits (like those of Karadag, Stepnovski, Shebelinka, etc.) contain, as well as gas, condensates (hydrocarbons), suitable for transformation into liquid gases (butane and propane), benzine, naphtha, etc.

Thanks to such discoveries the gas industry has developed enormously in a few years. In August 1958, the Party Central Committee adopted a series of resolutions to raise, within five years, the production of gas to 270/320 milliard cubic metres. The discoveries in 1959 alone doubled the total of ascertained reserves.

Prospecting is now centred on Siberia, Central Asia and in the Caspian depression. Deposits of high yield are being sought to reduce to a minimum the number of wells. New techniques are being practised, including pressure boring; and the systems of extraction improved in order to increase the yield.

Industrial exploitation of gas will be centred in Uzbekistan, in the Ukraine, in Azerbaidzhan and in the northern Caucasus, applying automation on a vast scale.

In 1958 the gas extracted was 28.5 milliard cubic metres. In 1963 production was 91.6 milliard cubic metres. In 1965 it is expected to reach 132 to 150 milliards. In the United States, where this industry has had many more years of existence, production has developed as follows:

	Milliards of cubic metres
1940	75.6
1945	111.5
1950	176.8
1955	266.2
1958	310.0

The difference is a great one and America still has a good lead. However, it may be expected that this will be reduced, especially if the discoveries in the Soviet Union continue with the same rhythm as in recent years. According to the seven-year plan gas is expected, about 1965, to make up 21% of the fuel consumed in the Soviet Union. The network of gas pipelines is being extended with feverish activity. By January 1, 1960 it was 17,000 kilometres long; in six years it is expected to increase by another 26,000 kilometres. By comparison the United States in 1956 had 716,000 kilometres of gas pipeline.

The Soviet Union intends to devote almost all of its natural gas to industrial uses. The main consumers, taking about a third, are the thermal power stations, followed by the chemical industry (for the production of acetylene, nitrogenous fertilizers, ammonia, synthetic ethylalcohol, artificial rubber, polymers for plastics, etc.), the cement industry and the machinery industry. The use of gas for heating has been avoided because the Institute for Health has confirmed that it affects the purity of the air. The properties of natural gas and especially its high temperatures and the chemical inertia of its flame, as well as its purity and the homogeneity of its composition, make it invaluable for the iron and steel industry which is expected, from 1965 onward, to consume more than a fifth of the gas intended for industrial use.

7

The picture is no less impressive when one passes from sources of energy to mineral reserves. The Soviet Union is the richest country in the world in reserves of ferrous ores. Its reserves have been verified at 40% of all world reserves. Most of the discoveries have been made on the initiative of the Soviet régime.

The 'magnetic anomaly' of Kursk has been famous since tsarist times. But it was Lenin who had it investigated. Before World War II the Ukraine provided more than half of the Soviet Union's iron ore from one of the largest iron deposits in the world, that of Krivoi-Rog, which is seven hundred kilometres long and more than a hundred and fifty wide. The total reserves of this area exceed 30 milliard tons of iron ore, of a content between 45 and 60%. Its exploitation is made easier by its proximity to the Donbass coalfields. The mines are for the most part open-cast and have an annual production of forty million tons. Even richer deposits have been found in Kazakstan, both in quantity and quality. They are considered the most important in the Soviet Union. Near Karaganda a great iron and steel centre is now being built equal in importance to that of Magnitka in the Urals. In 1960 deposits of iron ore of exceptional importance, estimated at seven milliard tons, were discovered in the Turgai (northern part of Kazakstan). The Sokolovsko-Sarbaiski complex has been created to exploit them. The principal mine of this region already produces seventeen million tons a year, though it has only partially been exploited; but its production is expected to increase until it will be possible to extract thirty-six million tons a year. The ore extraction is on the open-pit method and its cost the lowest in the Soviet Union. The zone of the Urals, on the eastern slopes of the chain, is also very rich in iron. The annual production is thirty million tons of ore with 50% content. One of the richest centres is the Magnitskaya mountain at Magnitogorsk.

There are also mines at Kerch in the Crimea, rich in ore with a content of from 30 to 40% but with considerable impurities.

An enormous field of oolitic iron ore, estimated at tens of milliards of tons, has been discovered on the Upper Ob in Western Siberia.

There are many fields in Eastern Siberia, mostly in the region of the Angarà, between Krasnodar and Irkutsk, where development after World War II was exceptionally rapid. Other mines are in the Chita district, in southern Yakutya and in the Soviet Far East. The production of pig-iron, steel and sheet-metal has developed as follows: [4]

Year	Pig-Iron	Steel	Sheet Metal
		Millions of tons	
1913	4.2	4.2	3.5
1928	4.0	4.8	3.9
1932	6.2	5.9	4.4
1940	14.9	18.3	13.1
1946	10.0	13.4	9.6
1948	13.9	18.7	14.1
1949	16.5	22.3	17.9
1950	19.2	27.3	20.9
1951	22.0	31.2	23.8
1953	27.4	38.1	29.4
1955	33.3	45.3	35.3
1958	39.6	54.9	42.9
1959	43.0	59.0	47.0
1963	58.7	80.0	62.0

By comparison American production figures are:

Year	Pig-Iron	Steel
	Millions of tons	
1939	35.6	52.7
1944	62.8	89.6
1950	68.4	96.8
1955	79.2	117.0
1957	80.7	112.7
1958	58.8	85.2

It should be noted that the Soviet Union has an absolute primacy in world iron ore production, which reached 135 million tons in 1963, and that it is becoming the principal provider of iron ore to the iron and steel industries of the new countries.

[4] *The Statesman's Year-Book*, op. cit.

8

The Soviet Union is also first in the production of manganese ore, of which it claims to possess the largest reserves in the world. The main deposits are in European Russia (the Shatura ranges, at Nikopol in the Dneiper basin and those recently discovered at Tokmak). No less rich is the famous deposit of Chiatura in Georgia. Western Siberia also has huge reserves, but the quality of the ore is inferior to the Ukrainian ore and even more so to the Georgian. The Soviet Union also abounds in non-ferrous metals, including copper. The eastern flanks of the Urals south of Magnitogorsk are rich in them, especially the district of Mednogorsk, which means Copper Mountain. Kazakstan, Uzbekistan, the region of Lake Balkash, Georgia, Armenia and the Kola Peninsula are also rich in non-ferrous metals.

It would be tedious to list the mineral wealth with which this huge territory is provided: nickel, bauxite, chrome, magnesium, lead, zinc, phosphates and mineral salts.

After the Union of South Africa, the Soviet Union is the world's largest gold producer. Its mines are scattered throughout Siberia from the Urals to the Altai, from the Chita district to Yakuya, which is one of the most important gold-mining centres,[5] Yakutya is especially famous for the diamond deposits found there in 1954. The diamonds are found in the rocks as well as in 'placers', and it may be foreseen that the Soviet Union will very soon take its place as one of the leading diamond producers. Nor is there any lack of platinum, mainly from the Ural region.

Some districts of the Soviet Union are veritable safe-deposit boxes, so fabulous is the mineral wealth that they have in them. Such are the Ukraine which leads the federal republics in coal production, iron and manganese, the vast zone of the Urals because of its im-

[5] Details of gold production in the Soviet Union are jealously kept secret. According to the estimates of Western experts, whose reliability it is not possible to check, it seems that production should be valued at from three hundred to four hundred million dollars a year. It is certain that production costs are very high because the mines are in districts difficult of access, far from industrial centres and therefore without the infrastructure necessary for intensive exploitation. Larger investments to increase gold production would not, therefore, be remunerative.

On an average the gold exported annually to cover the deficit in the balance of payments is valued at about two hundred million dollars. Rather larger shipments were necessary in 1963 and 1964 to pay for grain imports (see chapter on the agricultural crisis).

According to Western experts Soviet gold reserves in 1963 were estimated at about eight milliard dollars.

mense resources in oil, coal, iron, copper, gold, platinum, manganese and other non-ferrous metals, and Kazakstan which is perhaps destined to become the most important mining centre of the Soviet Union so rich is it in rare metals such as cobalt, titanium, tungsten, molybdenum, tantalium, niobium (columbium), as well as vast reserves of coal, iron, copper, zinc, lead, aluminium, nickel, chromite, manganese, oil and gas. Also the territory of Krasnoyarsk which occupies the central part of Siberia, rich in its northern zone in polymetallic ores, amongst which several are very rare, such as palladium, ruthenium, osmium, iridium, as well as copper, nickel, cobalt, platinum and silver, so that in the heart of the tundra the great centre of Norilsk has been created with its huge metallurgical plants for non-ferrous metals.

9

Last but not least is the fabulous timber wealth of the forests which cover more than a half of Soviet territory. They abound in conifers and broad-leaved species, as well as a vast range of other timbers. Some varieties of Russian timber are considered the best in the world. It is estimated that the vast Siberian forests contain 47 milliards of cubic metres of timber. The annual natural increase exceeds by one and a half times the volume of felling carried out annually throughout the whole country.

It must be borne in mind that the greater part of these immeasurable riches has been discovered in recent years, that is after the advent of the Soviet régime. We are therefore only at the beginning of the inventory. This shows that the greater part of this wealth comes from territory inhabited for the most part by non-Russian peoples: the diamonds of Yakutya, the gold of Chita, the oil of Baku, the gas of Bukhara, the electrical power of the Angarà and the Yenisei. These are the elements of Soviet wealth and power, which the Soviet Union extracts from its immense empire.

CHAPTER III

The Human Element

1

HOWEVER impressive the natural resources of this immense territory, the physical, intellectual and moral qualities of the people, who now possess them and exploit them as the basis of Soviet wealth and power, are far more important.

The Great Russian is of exceptional physical vigour. In type he is similar to the Nordic peoples; he is tall, with a thick neck on a bull-like torso, with broad shoulders, deep chest and athletic limbs. In the young people, as De Custine has rightly pointed out, this solid construction gives a sense of force. But they do not lack elasticity and flexibility despite the power of the mass of muscle. The Great Russian race has been formed and developed in one of the most forbidding geographical areas. Forced to emigrate from the sun-drenched plains of the Ukraine before the invasion of the Asian nomads, after Kiev had already become the metropolis of a flourishing empire under the Rurik dynasty, it for the most part found refuge in the zone of forest and marsh around Moscow. How this people managed to survive in the glacial rigour of the Muscovite winters is one of the mysteries of history. Perhaps the present vigour of the Great Russian is the result of a process of selection, which confirms the Darwinian thesis of the survival of the fittest. Undoubtedly an admixture of Finnish and Scandinavian strains has helped. But how much the harshness of the climate has contributed, and is still contributing, to the health and strength of the race is shown by the emergence of a new type, the Siberian, who is even taller than the European Russian. I was able to confirm how great is the physical resistance of this race during a trip to the Soviet Far East where I went up the Amur river by boat. Though it was towards the end of August it seemed that the cataracts of heaven were pouring down on us. The boat was crowded with colonists returning from Khabarovsk where they had gone the same morning on business. At the landings there were no pontoons as they would not have been able to withstand the floods and the force of the current. The people disembarked thigh-deep in water. All, men, women and children, accepted the adventure gaily, splashing about in the water and the mud with huge burdens on their backs, which they had to carry for the whole of the journey back to their homes. So former generations had lived; so the peasants still live. Six months in the snow and two months in the mud of the thaw.

In Yakutya, close to the Cold Pole, I have admired the most beautiful people in Russia, the more striking in comparison with the slender, parchment-like, wrinkled figures of the Yakut minority of Mongoloid type. Yet the winter in that region is of a rigour that anyone else would find intolerable. There is light for a few hours a day only. The temperature goes down to 60° C., sometimes even to 65° C., below zero. At the time of the most extreme cold a black mist blankets the earth. It is total paralysis. Yet the schools go on notwithstanding, until the temperature falls to 40° C. below zero. Work, however, does not cease until it reaches −50° C. Yet Yakutya has the largest number of centenarians in all Russia.

Longevity is a characteristic of the Russian people. The 1960 census registered more than a hundred persons aged between 120 and 156. The Russian Federal Republic has eighty-one centenarians for every million inhabitants, as against thirty in the United States. In all, the census registered more than thirty thousand persons more than a hundred years old.

A proof of the strength and health of this race is the physical effort which it uncomplainingly accepts. Building work in Russia does not stop by day or night. I have seen conduits being dug in Moscow in a temperature of 35° C. below zero.

The force and agility of this race is shown in the magnificent figures of its athletes and the many gold medals that they have won at all the Olympic Games.

2

The moral resistance of the race is not less than the physical strength. The adaptability, endurance and inexhaustible patience of the Russian shows a steadiness of nerves equal to any test. The Western mentality mistakes for passive resignation the acceptance of discomforts, trials and sufferings which it could not itself endure.

Both friends and enemies have admired the courage, the steadiness, one could almost say impassivity, of the Russian soldier even in the most untenable situations. With the same imperturbability he accepts in times of peace the lack of even the most elementary comforts. The Russian is able to wait for trains for days and nights, huddled in the overcrowded railway stations or in the waiting-rooms of the airports, sleeping one alongside the other on the bare earth. The Russians squeeze into trains and put up with terrible over-crowding in the cities. This race has for centuries endured the harsh Mongol rule, the autocracy of the tsars and, finally, the tyranny of Stalin's times.

There is a whole range of misconceptions about the Russians to unmask. They come from the superficial impressions of hurried travellers and tourists, accustomed to repeat like parrots the stalest commonplaces. In Italy, De Custine especially is responsible for many of them. 'I ask myself,' he wrote, 'if it is the character of the people which has created autocracy or autocracy which has created the Russian character . . . I believe that the influence is reciprocal; the Russian government would not be able to endure anywhere save in Russia and the Russians would not have become what they are had they had a different government. One can only say of the Russians that they are intoxicated with servitude.' In proof of this thesis De Custine recalls that the best loved rulers have been the most bloodthirsty tyrants, before whom even the Caesars whose in-famies were revealed by Suetonius pale into insignificance. What De Custine has failed to remember is that all European peoples in similar circumstances have been forced to bow their necks under the most odious tyrannies. Recent history provides more than one example. Nor has he recalled that insurrections have been frequent in Russian history, far more frequent than is commonly believed. Cities and countryside alike have rebelled. The great revolts of Stenka Razin and Pugachev are the best-known of them but for centuries *jacqueries* have been endemic in the Russian lands. It is true that the sovereign power always succeeded in quelling them, but the reason for this must above all be sought in the vastness of the land, which has enabled the government to isolate the move-ment and to concentrate against it all the forces which flowed in from every part of the territory.

To understand the state of mind of a people one must mingle with the crowd, in shops, in trains, in restaurants; one must listen to the talk and take part in the conversations. Then one realizes with astonishment how caustic is the Russian sense of criticism. They criticize everything: the administrative disorganization, the poor quality of the goods on sale, the high prices. They are in-veterate grumblers, always ready to argue, to answer back, like the characters in a novel. But experience, which has now become in-sight, tells each one the insuperable limits beyond which he may not go. To speak of the gregarious spirit of the Russian people is a mere banality; it does not mean that it has not known for centuries the necessity for discretion.

3

It has been said that dissimulation has become second nature for the Russians. The impassivity of their faces is like a lowered vizor which conceals their real feelings from the outside world. Dissimulation, like camouflage, is a natural method of defence. The classical philosophers have given us the well-known maxim 'conceal in order to live' and Roman wisdom has commented on it: *Bene vixit qui bene latuit*. Terror of those in command has become so rooted, by an instinct now atavistic, that all Russians, from the officials downward, whenever they speak of the hierarchy lower their voices without being aware of it, so accustomed are they to treat so perilous a subject with the utmost precaution, secretly, in an almost imperceptible whisper.

From dissimulation to lying is but a short step. And this is one of the accusations most frequently levelled against the Russians. 'To lie in this country,' wrote De Custine, 'is to protect society; to speak the truth is to subvert the state. Russia is a nation of mutes . . . The evil of dissimulation extends here farther than one thinks.' The Russian statesmen are well-known for guile, for tortuous manoeuvres, for crafty calculations. All their propaganda is tainted by it and often also their political direction is infected with it, creating a sense of diffidence, almost always of suspicion. Their reasoning is seldom clear and straightforward; for the most part it is dialectical, casuistic, and alters facts, by the habit of forcing principles and twisting the meanings of words. The ancient sophists would have found here their most understanding pupils and their most faithful imitators. It could only occur to a Russian statesman to alter historical judgments on men and on events to suit changing circumstances, as the Soviet Encyclopaedia does in every new edition.

This example from above finds imitators in all official circles. 'Russians of all classes,' it is always De Custine who speaks, 'conspire with marvellous accord for the triumph of duplicity. They have such skill in lying, such frankness in falsehood, that their success revolts my sincerity as much as it terrifies me . . . A sincere man in this country would be regarded as a madman.'

An episode indicative of this aspect of Russian character was reported by Tatiana Tess in *Izvestia* on December 12, 1960. It was a meeting in a scientific institute. There was a debate about the activities of one of the members upon whom it was intended to confer one of the highest academic awards. The orators spoke one after the other, praising the services of their colleague, his talent and the profundity of his creative ideas. All the speeches were eloquent brilliant and persuasive. The member in question was present in the hall, listening with satisfaction to the praises showered on him. Then the members proceeded to the secret vote and the scientist in honour of whom all these laudatory speeches had been made did not receive a single favourable vote. All, unanimously, had voted against him, each believing himself to be the only one to cast a dissenting vote covered by the secrecy of the urn.

The writer commented:

'Can't we see, before our very eyes, how an actor already famous kisses his colleague and congratulates him on his success and then, immediately afterwards, behind his back, describes him as a mediocrity? . . . Does it not happen that he who has lost all sense of his own dignity merely repeats, out of respectful homage, the words that his chief has just pronounced, without himself having any personal opinions?'

We might perhaps remark that things similar to those lamented by Tatiana Tess happen in every country in the world, since the courage of one's own convictions is a rare enough thing, and perhaps what should be admired is the frankness of the Soviet writer. But it should not be forgotten that the virtues on which Soviet teachers lay the greatest stress in the education of their pupils are those of honesty and sincerity.

4

However that may be, the habit of dissimulation gives the observer the impression of being in the presence of dormant volcanoes which might erupt again at any moment, when least expected. Anyone who is familiar with Russians can read from almost imperceptible signs, even from the lack of expression on their faces, the reaction aroused in them by an event, a gesture, a word. De Custine prophesied the outbreak of revolution eighty years before it took place. This people broods for centuries over inextinguishable rancours. They still brood over them. The greater part of the population of Moscow is made up of families forced to fly from the countryside because of the collectivization of their lands; many of them had their properties confiscated, their houses burnt, their goods stolen and one or more members of their family killed or deported to distant regions. What are the real feelings of such people? I have known Italian communists who sought asylum in Russia in fascist times. Their anti-fascist past did not save them from suspicion.

Almost all of them ended in forced labour camps, like the infamous Vorkuta in the Arctic regions. Some of the survivors have told their story. But how much more often has this been repeated in Russian families?

Suddenly reaction explodes; this always happens under weak governments. They are wild, delirious, overwhelming reactions, with the blind violence of a force of nature. The story of the civil war between Whites and Reds is a chronicle spangled with countless and unspeakable atrocities. Russia was the birthplace of the great anarchists, Bakunin and Kropotkin. In *The Possessed* Dostoyevsky has drawn with a master hand the satanic figure of Nechaev.

Perhaps it is just the fear of the terrifying violence of these excesses that explains on the one hand the need for autocratic and dictatorial governments and on the other the habitual tolerance of the many. It is a fear of giving free vent to the corrosive and impassioned criticism and the anarchic individualism of the Russians.

5

All this proves that the other commonplace about the inherent goodness of the Russians must be treated with the greatest reserve. It is undeniable that the Russian has a fund of innate courtesy and an impetuosity which makes him capable of the most generous actions. His fondness for children is proverbial and his feeling for animals, his love of flowers and his almost mystical sense of communion with nature are well known. During the glacial winters, that weigh down the Russian land under a leaden hood, there is always someone to throw out millet for the birds. There is no window without a flower in it. There is in the Russian soul an inexhaustible source of affection, a fund of sadness, an insatiable yearning for ideals, a thirst for perfection, which shines out in the lovely figures of this people's history. If the Orthodox Church had not been a soulless instrument in the service of those who held the power, but had shown the way upwards to god-intoxicated souls, Russia would have made her voice, ardent with mysticism and ecstasy, heard. We can hear the first stirrings in the works of Solovev and Berdyaev. Who can forget the sublime words of the Staretz Zosimus in *The Brothers Karamazov*?

This is the most romantic people on earth, which can still be moved by the old fables made eternal in poems, music and ballet. Perhaps this is one aspect of its need to escape from everyday life. Not for nothing did the Russian people give the full measure of its literary, musical and artistic genius in the last century, since it

71

found in the romantic atmosphere of the eighteen hundreds a climate natural to it which allowed it to flower and produce fruit. It has been said that this people still lives in the eighteen hundreds. It is true; the Russians are a nineteenth century people, even as the Italians are a people of the Renaissance and the French are still the French of Louis XIV, since it is a historical climate that forms the background most suitable for the spiritual ripening of a people.

There is so much nobility in the urge of the Russian to give aid and assistance to the weak and suffering, to give service by an immediate and spontaneous impulse without any shadow of servility even before it has been asked. Everyone is ready to show you the way, to save you embarrassment. The journalist Lamberti Sorrentino told me that in the middle of the night on the Trans-Siberian an old woman, having noticed that he was shivering from cold, got up and went to find him some blankets even though she had never seen him before. However poor he may be, the Russian is always ready to share his bread with one poorer than himself. The Italian prisoners know only too well that merciful kindness of the Russian people. More than one of them has told me that he owes his life to the help of persons quite unknown to him. In his *Diary of a Writer* Dostoyevsky tells how in the trek across Siberia he and his companions were met, shortly after leaving Tobolsk, by the wives of the Decembrists exiled in that city, who were awaiting them to give them a last greeting. They blessed them and gave each of them a copy of the gospels with a ten-ruble note hidden in the cover of the book. This goodness is a reflection of the patience and tolerance natural to the Russian people. From it springs that sense of human brotherhood that, in its most representative writers, Tolstoy and Dostoyevsky, soars to the tragic commiseration of a common destiny.

Yet so much gentleness and so much humanity, by the contradictions of the human soul, do not prevent very harsh relations between Russian and Russian. There is a core of hardness, of quarrelsomeness and above all of ill-concealed envy in the soul of the masses that weighs upon everyday life and explodes at the slightest pretext. More than once have I been surprised by the frigid refusal of the tourist guide who accompanied me, almost always a cultured and well-educated girl, to reply to the questions of someone who wanted an explanation, whereas with me she was always courteous and ready with the most patient information. This brusque transition from affability to rigidity is disconcerting, even though almost always a word, a gesture, a cordial smile, is enough to change this hostility to the most attentive and courteous interest. With these sudden changes of mood the intense over-crowding is a source of frequent frictions and squabbles. The court records are full of cases, often tragi-comic, brought by persons who loathe one another and yet are forced to go on living side by side. Almost always these incidents are caused by the use of common facilities, especially in the kitchens. Every tenant uses special padlocks for her saucepans in order not to find in them rats or worn-out shoes put there maliciously by her neighbours. Everyone is spied on and the tenants' collective can demand from every family in it justification of behaviour considered contrary to the customs and morale of communism. Particularly suspect is any form of luxury or even of spending which shows that one has a little more than others. One might say that there is in the soul of this people a goad to suffer and to make others suffer, to humiliate and to be humiliated. Quite alien, indeed repugnant, to Western mentality is the practice of self-criticism which young people learn in the students' collectives and which is like a spiritual strip-tease before the indiscreet eyes of those who have no special moral title to humiliate their companions.

6

Gentleness and harshness, sympathy and cliquishness, alternate like the light and shade of a picture. Russian society has its 'toughs' and 'moderates', Russian history, like Russian literature, is rich in characters of inflexible temper who are like the ribbing in the social weave. In the Christian Science Monitor of July 19, 1960, Nate White writes: 'When the "tough ones", the Leninists and Stalinists, meet, stiff and military in bearing, there is a clash of inflexibility, roughness and cruelty, not only towards Westerners but also towards their own Soviet people.'

The frequency of these 'toughs' especially among the leaders, formed in the fanatical atmosphere of the Party which has to a great extent absorbed the logical rigidity of the old anarchism, gives the lie to another common prejudice which has been diffused by Western writers, namely that the Russian lacks will-power. This accusation comes above all from Maurice Paléologue, French ambassador at Petrograd in the last days of the tsarist régime. 'The will of the Russian is always passive and unstable,' he writes. 'He knows nothing of moral discipline and he is never happy save in a world of dreams.' Paléologue contrasts the weak character of the Russian with the American character, 'a positive and practical mentality, imbued with a sense of duty and a passion for work'. It is a picture that does not in the least correspond to the present character of the Russian people. This shows how easy it is to confuse incidental traits with typical and permanent traits. Lack of will-power is not a characteristic of the Russian, but it is rather the sort of passive resistance of one who is subject to a will with which he cannot agree. Even today, in the measure in which the Soviet régime is endured, a slowing down of productive energy is evident in certain strata of the population. But if one looks at the men holding executive posts, it must be agreed that their energy and unsparing devotion is in no way inferior to the working effort of the best men of the West.

At one time the Russians were accused of inability to carry out long-term plans and the reason was attributed to lack of trust among the masses who were inclined to a fatalism which was really a sort of resignation. Today, under the harsh discipline of communism and under the burden of new responsibilities, the old dross has disappeared and the Russian people has for the most part given countless proofs of its indomitable tenacity in war and in peace and of a spirit of sacrifice.

Some of the old habits still remain, such as the tendency to postpone decisions, the bureaucratic delays, the small margin of initiative left to the administrative cadres even among the seniors, and the persistence of alcoholism, perhaps because of the need to escape into that world which Paléologue calls the world of dreams, partly because of boredom and disgust at a petty and monotonous life.

But these are defects of small importance. For good or evil it is always the ruling class which makes the character of a people and influences its formation. The members of the Presidium, the members of the government, the heads of the great industrial enterprises, give the impression of men of remarkable energy, shrewd, broadminded and of very high technical achievement. The Russians are for the most part hard bargainers, clever but understanding, ready to seize the gist of an argument and to yield to the evidence of tangible interests. They are business men who preside in ever greater numbers over the destinies of Russia, whether they come from the ranks of the Party or from the economic enterprises, for it is up to the politicians to supervise, to encourage and to spur on economic activities. Khrushchev's challenge to the Western world pledges them, to all intents and purposes, to concentrate their interests on production. What do these men, in daily contact with reality both communist and capitalist and well able to see the advantages and defects of one and the other, think of the supposed superiority of their régime and above all of the practical possibility of translating communist ideology into practice? The observer gets the impression that all their economic plans are based on the continuance of the present system of state capitalism. The fact that it may be less productive than private capitalism loses its importance in the eyes of the executive hierarchy before the enormous advantage of being able to concentrate in their own hands all the levers of economic development. In this way economic dictatorship reinforces political dictatorship.

Notwithstanding the statements, the studies and the clamorously acclaimed preliminary reforms for the transition to total communism, very few let themselves be deceived into thinking that it is possible in practice. There is a popular anecdote which illustrates this frame of mind. A propagandist declared that man must look towards the communist horizons. One of his listeners, not really understanding what the words meant, looked up a dictionary to find the definition of 'horizon'. He found: 'An imaginary line between earth and sky which gets farther and farther away the more one tries to approach it'.

Despite these practical impossibilities and this lack of confidence, the Soviet people cannot renounce stressing the goal set by the founders of communism. The prize is the leadership of the world. Every criticism sounds like treason and depreciates that propaganda upon which communism above all relies to lure new countries to follow its lead.

The time will come when the contrast between the two worlds will be reduced to a contrast between two economic systems. But one may be sure that the realism of the Russians, even as it has led them to adapt their economic system more and more to the facts of reality, will keep them from compromising the results they have achieved and those they hope to achieve by indulging in utopian experiments.

This, as can be seen, is a conclusion based on the realism of the technicians, whose importance continues to grow, because the Soviet ruling class is more and more assuming the form of a technocracy, very similar to that in the West.

7

A similar argument might perhaps be used concerning the problem of freedom.

There is no more unfounded prejudice than that which considers the Russian people to have become insensible to the idea of freedom, having been for centuries, as it still is today, the victim of a despotic régime. Yet like all the other European peoples the Russians have indefatigably fought a hard battle for freedom. Also, though it may seem a paradox, Russia is not merely a creation of tsarism but also of free men. It has already been said that the Great Russians, rather than bow to Mongol rule, fled from the fertile lands of the south to live in freedom in the northern forests. New communities were organized, based on the very ancient democratic Slav institution of the *veché*, or assembly of fathers of families, a democratic rule common to all the branches of the Aryan race at the time of their diaspora. These Russian communities, amongst which the republic of Novgorod took pride of place, seemed a far-off echo of the western Communes. When their liberties were suppressed by the rising dynasties, of which the most powerful was that of the Princes of Moscow, there was a reflux from the north to the south. Once again men thirsting for freedom fled to the southern steppes beyond the line of fortifications which defended the Christian states and settled in the no-man's land. They lived there according to their own democratic laws and obeyed only those chiefs whom they had themselves freely elected.

These men were the Cossacks. They fought for their freedom against the Tatars, against the Turks, against the Poles and against the Tsars. Organized in *artel*, or companies, they lived for centuries as buccaneers on untilled lands. At one time the Cossacks founded the free republic of the Zaporozhie beyond the Dneiper rapids which became a rallying place for all free and adventurous spirits, the rejected, the oppressed, the fugitives from justice. The ideal was then 'to cross the steppes and live among the Cossacks'. These adventurers had leaders of indomitable energy and legendary daring, the *atamans*. Russian history has always abounded in these 'tough ones'.

Little by little as the Golden Horde disintegrated and became weak the Cossacks took advantage of this to press forward. In them Holy Russia found her mobile patrols for the advancement of her frontiers. Behind these fearless advance-guards the armies of the tsars pressed on; but it is due to the merits of the Cossacks that Tatar and Turkish rule was overthrown in the Crimea and it was they who preceded, across the Siberian *taiga*, the expansion of Russian power to the Pacific. The Stroganoffs, the Khabarovsks, were representatives of the tradition which remained alive among the people.

It is indisputable that the great majority of the Russian people was, at the time of the downfall of tsarism, in favour of a democratic system based on parliamentary institutions, as the elections for the Constituent Assembly in 1917 showed. The revolutionary violence of a minority imposed itself on the will of the majority. It was a bitter defeat.

Old and new elements alike have influenced the formation of the Russian character which, as in all young peoples, is malleable and easily takes the stamp of the great events in which it has been a protagonist. The efforts of the régime to mould the people according to the human type idealized by the founders of Marxism are intense and incessant. The schools are above all the forge of the new character. But notwithstanding the materialist and atheist propaganda which is at the base of Marxism, it cannot be said that religious feeling has been suffocated, not only because the churches are always crowded but also because there are many signs that the reaction of the anonymous masses to the anti-Christian struggle is persistent and increasing.

On the other hand it would be contrary to fact to deny the educative work that the Soviet schools have developed, with undoubted results, to inculcate in the young feelings of civic duty, patriotism, personal dignity, loyalty, courtesy, altruism, love of plants and animals, love of art and music, a passion for sport.

The morality of Soviet Russia is incomparably more healthy and austere than the morality of the Western world. No obscene publication, no immoral film, no licentious spectacle, no strip-tease, is tolerated by the authorities. There is none of that sex-frenzy which rages in the West and is an undoubted proof of degeneration. I have met in Moscow many Catholic priests, Dominicans, Jesuits, Salesians, who have come as tourists to observe the life of the Soviet Union. All of them have confessed their surprise at this moral health, at least to all external appearances.

This is not to deny that in Soviet society also there is a notable freedom in relations between the sexes. Divorces, though less frequent than at one time, are frowned on and made difficult by the authorities, but none the less they are still numerous. Overcrowding is a fertile source of adultery and licence. Abortion is permitted. The falling birth-rate, especially in the cities, has been accentuated since the advent of the new régime.

9

The principal merit of the schools is to have diffused a love of knowledge among the people, making the Russians the people with the highest level of general knowledge in the world. There is a passion for learning in the air so contagious is the enthusiasm for all forms of knowledge. The Russian gives one the impression of a neophyte, of one who discovers virgin worlds that reveal their fascination to him. Everyone studies. The libraries are crowded with readers at every hour of the day. In the Metropolitan railway stations one can always see persons reading while waiting for the trains and almost always reading technical or scientific books, not popular magazines, novels or comic strips.

In the country near Tbilisi in Georgia I noticed a youth holding a book with one hand while holding the halter of a grazing bull with the other. At Tashkent in Uzbekistan the crowd that jostles on the central square before the bookstalls is always more numerous than that around the cauldrons of rice and roast lamb or the ice-cream carts.

In his book *The Anatomy of Soviet Man*[1] Klaus Mehnert has said quite rightly:

'Every visitor to the Soviet Union is struck by the crowded book-shops and the huge editions of the classics, both Russian and foreign, that are constantly being published; by the theatrical performances that are sold out to the last seat, particularly if the play is a classic; by the unending discussions on art; by the large audiences attracted to lectures on new books; and by the many eagerly sought-after literary monthlies . . .'

From the time of Catherine, Great Russia has boasted world-famous scientists: mathematicians, physicists, biologists. In these fields she is still among the world leaders. But her contribution to philosophical studies has always been poor. The Russian intelligence turns for preference to the exact sciences, where research is bounded by precise and impassable limits of calculation and experiment.

10

The Russian, far more than the Mediterranean man, lives, like the German, in a world of his own. He has his own convictions, his own vision of the world, his own ideas of morality and law. All the characters in the Russian novel are introspective, rooted in their more or less theoretical opinions, according to which they judge themselves and others. There is always a fund of self-criticism in every Russian. This explains the logical strictness of the thinkers, the propagandists, the fanaticism of Lenin and his successors, the violence of the doctrinaire crises that break out among their followers.

But refinement of civilization sharpens the spirit of criticism and

[1] Klaus Mehnert, *The Anatomy of Soviet Man*, Chapter 10, page 138, Weidenfeld and Nicholson, 1961.

sharpens, perhaps makes more caustic, the Russian sense of humour. Anecdotes circulate and the satirical reviews carry barbed caricatures of situations and persons, often stereotyped, of the present society. Even as in Papal Rome the public was amused by the witticisms between Pasquino and Marforio, so the Soviet public is amused by the sarcasms of an imaginary 'Radio Erivan' which replies to questions from a no less imaginary enquirer who, for example, asks:

'What nationality were Adam and Eve?'

Radio Erivan replies: 'Soviet citizens.'

'Why?'

'Because they went about naked, shared an apple between them and thought they were in Paradise.'

One could fill volumes with such anecdotes.

11

But perhaps the most important result of the spread of education is to have brought the Soviet people into closer touch with the West, because that culture, that science and technology which make up the greatness and strength of the Soviet Union comes from the West. With the suppression of the political influence of the Orthodox clergy, which had for centuries been the great champion of anti-Westernism, communism removed the only obstacle which had always hindered the spread of Western culture, to which it opposed a vague orientalist tendency. The civilization which the Soviet Union is spreading throughout its vast Asian territories is that of the West. The cities that it has founded, the factories, the schools, the centres of culture, are Western. Under our eyes Western civilization is spreading over an immense area, even as in the centuries of the great European expansion in the two Americas. Whether acknowledged or not, this creates a link between Russia and the West because, as Dostoyevsky made Ivan Karamazov say, the Russians are none the less Europeans. Perhaps they have never been so profoundly so as they are today.

This expansion of Western civilization by a state on the borders of Europe may seem to be a paradox, but it is not the first time that such a thing has happened. The Macedonia of Alexander the Great brought Hellenism to the frontiers of India, though Macedonia had fought bitterly against Greece. If one takes this important Russian contribution to civilization into account, it is not surprising that there are many in the Soviet Union, especially among the studious youth, who do not want to cut off the Western roots of this culture but want to let them spread farther, bringing with them the life-giving lymph. To some extent it is the appeal of the same race and the same tradition to reinforce a unity and a common way of life. But it is also the pride of having contributed, with achievements of the highest scientific value and of exceptional historical importance, to the enrichment of a common civilization. There is, therefore, nothing more sterile and unnatural than to seek to isolate this people from the West, to forbid it contact with foreigners, to hinder and even forbid mixed marriages and to prevent members of the families resulting from such unions from living together.

12

The economic advances of the Soviet Union, its victories over its secular enemy Germany, the astounding triumphs of Soviet astronautical science, have revived the flame of Russian patriotism. This is a sentiment that the Soviet Union despite the anti-patriotic propaganda which it carries on in other countries, has taken great care not to crush and which it has indeed swelled to the mightiest diapason.

The Russian loves his land, to which he is attached with every fibre of his being, to the point where exile from his country is felt almost as a personal amputation. Nor is it possible to understand the Russian soul, with its fund of inexpressible melancholy, its sense of the beautiful and the infinite, the emotion that nourishes its romantic vein, if one does not associate it with the solemn and peaceful grandeur of the Russian countryside.

Every one of the salient traits of the Russian character reflects some aspect of surrounding nature. In the forests, on the plains and beside the rivers the Russian has conceived his songs which are an echo of the solitude which surrounds him. His immense capacity for tolerance comes to him from communion with the soil which teaches him to endure, to work and to help his fellows. From the familiar landscape, covered by the snows which paralyse life for six months of the year, comes his passivity when faced with forces greater than his own and his acceptance of the inevitable. The difficulty of reaction by a people immobilized by frost and thaw for so many months of the year, isolated among the woods and rivers, with very bad communications, makes it possible for the central power to abuse its force and to descend to arbitrary and violent methods.

Perhaps because of this modesty and simplicity of life, the Russian has never shown, or at least not up till now, that scornful nationalism which almost all of the Western peoples have sought to justify by futile theories of purity or superiority of race. Russian patriotism has been, up till now, a pathetic almost bashful sentiment, at times almost the expression of a Freudian complex, considering itself the victim of an unmerited lack of understanding. From that flows naturally, even if exaggerated, the reaction, the tendency to claim non-existing merits, as of the discoveries and inventions of others, or to proclaim itself the sole victor of the last war.

The Soviet government assures this people, so sensitive of its national honour, successes that flatter its pride. That is the surest means of winning popularity, whatever the conditions of discomfort in which the great majority is forced to live. But everything is accepted and endured in the name of the country, even as everything is pardoned to the most bloodthirsty tyrants if they have enlarged the motherland, while none of the rulers who have suffered defeats are spared.

In time of war, whatever may be the popular feelings against the régime, all will fight as a single man for the salvation and honour of the Russian motherland, even as they always did under tsarism. They will do so even more under a régime which has given the country a formidable war machine, of an efficiency such as Russia has never before known. No one may doubt the power of the new arms, after the spectacular successes of the Soviet astronauts. If any doubt remains, it is of the perfection in every detail of the immense organization that modern war demands. Though the advance has been overwhelming in many sectors, there is still much to be done in many others.

But perhaps it would not be prudent to stress the shadows in the picture. What must be remembered is that the nation has been launched and that nothing will now be able to stop its progress, guided as it is by men of formidable energy, competence and shrewdness. Pride in successes already achieved has multiplied its expansive force and confirmed the consciousness of the Russian that he is among the foremost ranks of the greatest, most cultured and best educated of peoples.

CHAPTER IV

Khrushchev and his Successors

1

IT may well be that the historian of the future will agree that the Soviet Union, which became a great industrial power under Stalin who rearmed it, extended its frontiers and made it the centre of a world system, reached the summit of its power under Khrushchev but also that under him it began to decline and that its decline was destined to grow more and more rapid.

The causes of this decline can only in part be imputed to Khrushchev's errors; for the most part they can be attributed to the nature of the régime which, compared with the progress of the Western democracies, has revealed the very serious defects of a state control dependent on a small oligarchy unsupported by popular consent and therefore subject to sudden crises due to the outbreak of clashes among cliques striving for power.

Khrushchev was the leading figure throughout the period 1953 to 1964, which will perhaps become known as 'the Khrushchev era'. Everything leads one to believe that its main trends will remain substantially unchanged since they respond to a clear appreciation of the basic interests of the country.

The transition from the Stalin era to the Khrushchev era was sudden and was accentuated by the dramatic revelation of Stalin's crimes. By this, Khrushchev wished to stress that one epoch had ended and another begun, more liberal and more humane in accordance with his temperament, but above all corresponding to the expectations of the masses which for the past twenty-five years had been subjected to the severest privations and sacrifices.

I met Khrushchev for the first time on October 21, 1958, at a reception in the Sovietskaya Hotel given in his honour by Marshal Amer, vice-president of the United Arab Republic. He had just returned from the Crimea, bronzed and rested. His thick-set body, his bull neck, his round head framed by a crown of snow-white hair, gave me the impression of a worthy village priest. He kept his hands crossed over his belly and listened, smiling good-naturedly, to his host's words, watching him all the while with cunning little eyes.

When he began to speak, it was in a quiet conversational tone as though explaining something or telling a story. He stressed his words with outstretched finger to give point to what he was saying, and changed his tone the better to express himself. Now and then he would spread his arms wide, smiling complacently, especially when he emphasized his words with one of his flashes of wit, which he himself was the first to appreciate. From time to time he gave the impression of searching for the right word or of trying to make himself clear; when his ideas flowed uninterruptedly and relentlessly he quickened his speech, raised his voice, as if ready to draw to a close, and then began again with greater impetuosity than before.

Seeing him so calm and smiling, I thought that his speech too would be facetious and uncontroversial. Yet rarely has he delivered a more scathing polemic against the West. His sarcasms were mainly directed against the United States and its policy of giving aid to the peoples freeing themselves from colonialism. 'The imperialists,' he said, addressing in the person of Marshal Amer all the African and Asian peoples, 'give you a penn'orth of aid and fleece you for ten rubles. They want your petrol, the diamonds of Africa and all your other minerals and products. Above all, they want to keep your countries under a merciless exploitation . . . The imperialists have plundered the peoples of Asia and Africa for centuries . . . They must restore to the Afro-Asian peoples all that they have plundered from them.'

One of the most successful pen-portraits of Khrushchev is that traced in 1959 by a Turkish journalist, Peyami Safa, in the Istanbul *Terciuman*. 'Khrushchev,' he wrote, 'is sixty-five. He is a peasant. He is short, fat and bald and moves like a bear. But he is not unpleasing. He looks sincere, gay and childlike. He often laughs till he cries. Sometimes he gets angry and then seems to lose all control of himself. But his character is quite the opposite of his physical appearance. The real Khrushchev is cold-blooded, calculating, terribly serious, cunning and hard-headed.'

2

This man owed his fortune entirely to his own efforts. Few of the great figures in the history of the world have risen from such humble beginnings. He comes from the poorest village of Russia, Kalinovka, in the Kursk district near the borders of the Ukraine, and from the poorest family of that exceedingly poor hamlet. He has himself told his own story:

'Before the revolution I attended only the parish school. I was very well instructed in the Bible; I was a diligent scholar and that is why sometimes I delve into my memory to drag out some biblical quotation in my speeches. Then, as you know, came the civil war. I spent three years at the front and then studied for three years at a workers' high-school. After finishing this school I went into politics. Some years later I attended a technical school then once more returned to politics. Now, as you know (he was addressing the French trade unionists in Paris on March 31, 1960), I am the president of the Council of Ministers of the Soviet Union. In our country that road is open to every worker, to every citizen, to every labourer.'

These are words which recall those famous words of Napoleon that every soldier carries a field-marshal's baton in his knapsack.

'I can tell you,' he declared on American television on September 27, 1959, 'that my father was an illiterate peasant, a serf. He was the property of the landowner and could be sold or even, as often happened, be exchanged for a dog.'

If one does not bear these origins in mind and does not remember that save for the revolution Khrushchev's fate would have been no different from that of his father and grandfather, despite his energy and intelligence, one cannot understand the fanaticism with which the young Khrushchev, as soon as he came into touch with the first communist propagandists, supported the cause of the revolution, to which he and men like him owe everything: freedom and power.

Nor can one find the key to this baffling personality, that of a hard man, intransigent and headstrong beneath the humorous and good-natured mask of a boon companion always ready for a jest, if one does not know how he rose from nothing to such boundless power as no other man in the world today possesses. To gauge the difficulties which he overcame, one must bear in mind that up to the age of twenty-seven, when he had already begun to attract attention by his war record in the Red Guard in the Ukraine and was developing his first political activities, he was still almost illiterate and that, though he has subsequently acquired a culture, even in literature, thanks to his prodigious memory, he has never learnt how to speak the Russian language correctly. He himself confessed this with that frankness which won him so much sympathy. One day during a speech to school-teachers he broke off, uncertain of the exact pronunciation of a word, and asked them if the word he had just pronounced was correctly accented.

'I admit that I am nervous all the time I am talking to you, because I know that I make mistakes in pronunciation and here I am addressing such strict judges. So I ask you, in advance, to be, let us say, indulgent. I do not want to blame my teachers. They were good folk, above all one mistress, Lydia Mihailovna, whom I will never forget. She spared no effort to make us cultivated persons. But obviously the surroundings in which I lived have left their mark.'

3

Khrushchev, like his predecessor Stalin and his successor Brezhnev, came from the ranks of the Party in which he had fought all his life. His rise to supreme power began on the day, shortly after Stalin's death, when he was appointed First Party Secretary. He thus inherited the post which Stalin had taken over on the death of Lenin and which he jealously held on to until the last day of his life. The Party is the absolute arbiter of the destinies of the country, because the discipline which binds its members makes it a reliable force at the orders of its commander. Neither Beria's police nor Zhukov's army has been able to prevail over it.

Khrushchev began his career when in 1924 he was elected secretary of the Party Committee in a section of the Yuzovka district, later renamed Stalino. A few months later and he was already president of the Party Committee for the entire district.

No one knew as he did the functioning of that formidable machine and the best way of making use of it.

When Malenkov resigned his post as First Party Secretary on March 15, 1953, Khrushchev succeeded him and his promotion was mainly due to the fact that no one expected that this man, so jovial and so moderate in his views, would ever become a serious rival. But once he had assumed power, Khrushchev gave leading posts to his closest friends, Frol Kozlov and Serov. The latter had been police chief under him in the Ukraine. Strong in the support of the Party he repeated the manoeuvre carried out with so much luck and skill by Stalin. Stalin too had been tried in the struggle and had had to force his way to the summit against men with an authority and prestige far greater than his: Trotsky, Zinovev, Kamenev, Bukharin. Furthermore, Lenin's testament, which had discouraged Stalin's election as Party Secretary, since it held him to be too crude, too intolerant and arbitrary, seemed to exclude him from being elected. None the less, the Party voted for him, for the simple reason that he was its arbiter. So too, Khrushchev's chances were not, at first, very brilliant.

Having eliminated Beria in 1953, he succeeded in February 1955 in forcing Malenkov to resign as Prime Minister, on the charge of wishing to give priority to light over heavy industry, in defiance of the immutable canon which gave preference to the development of industrialization and the strengthening of the armed forces over the improvement of the supply of consumer goods. Marshal Bulganin was chosen as head of government and shared the power with Khrushchev. With him he undertook the first official visits which brought them so much popularity abroad.

But the action which brought Khrushchev so much to the fore was his revelation of Stalin's crimes at the Party Congress of 1956. At that Congress he also introduced the policy of peaceful co-existence, which increased his popularity both at home and abroad. It was at this time that Leonid Brezhnev, who had previously been First Party Secretary in Kazakstan, was appointed candidate member (that is to say, member without voting rights) of the Presidium of the Party Central Committee.

In June that same year Molotov too was forced to resign as Minister of Foreign Affairs and was replaced by Shepilov. A few months later Shepilov relinquished this post to Andrej Gromyko. None the less Malenkov, as well as Molotov and Shepilov, remained in the Presidium. Thenceforward there was a group in the Presidium in opposition to the First Secretary. Almost all the first generation of the revolution, especially Molotov and even Kaganovich who, however, had always supported Khrushchev in his ascent, considered him unsuitable to high command. Only Mikoyan, Suslov and Kirichenko took his side in the Presidium. His supporters were definitely in the minority. The crisis broke out in June 1957. The manoeuvre by which he, when in a minority in the Presidium, urgently summoned the Central Committee, thanks to the support of the army, and had all his opponents condemned as an anti-Party group, that is to say dangerous public enemies, would have aroused the admiration of Machiavelli, so rapid was his reaction which was, furthermore, within a completely legal framework.

After the expulsion of the anti-Party group Brezhnev became a full member of the Presidium, while the advancement of Khrushchev was made more rapid by success. Towards the end of March 1958 Bulganin was forced to resign as head of government and Khrushchev took over his duties also, doubling the tasks of First Party Secretary and Chairman of the Council of Ministers. His position seemed unassailable, consolidated by the collaboration of friends who at that time seemed loyal, such as Anastas Mikoyan, First Deputy Premier, Alexei Kosygin, appointed Deputy Premier on May 4, 1960, and Leonid Brezhnev, three days later appointed President of the Supreme Soviet.

The fundamental difference between Stalin and Khrushchev was

Khrushchev's humanity. He liquidated none of his vanquished rivals. This humane policy, so exceptional in the millenary history of Russia, won him an increase of sympathy. This confirms the ever greater importance in Russia today of assuring the support of public opinion. To explain the rise of Khrushchev and to understand the force of his personality one must take into account, even more than the support of the Party, the methods used by him to ensure that support. He served the Party, defended it, strengthened it, increased its prestige and its popularity. He was the man of the Party, the man who, more than any other, incarnated its ideals by his intransigent fanaticism for the cause and by the formidable energy with which he ensured its success. This must never be forgotten in assessing the character of Khrushchev. He had the same intransigence in matters of principle, the same blind faith in the inevitability of communism, as Lenin or Stalin. But this would never have raised him to the leading posts in the hierarchy nor would it have been of any value to him had it not been acknowledged that he was tough. Thus the message of the Presidium sent to him on his sixty-fifth birthday was no mere flattery when it described him as 'the indefatigable fighter for the triumph of communism'.

It has been said that Khrushchev's empiricism led him to compromise with strict doctrinal rigour. Undoubtedly there have been criticisms of this nature. But in fact both Lenin and Stalin compromised far more than he, thanks to their authority as undisputed interpreters of doctrine. Not even Mao-Tse-Tung, who poses as supreme judge of the purity of the faith, ever dared to cast a doubt on the strict doctrine of Stalin. Khrushchev always took care not to lay himself open to such criticisms. More than once he hastened to beat a retreat and to eat his words when his policy aroused the criticisms of the Vestals of the Party. His realism often drove him to stretch the narrow limits of Marxist orthodoxy; for example, after Stalin's death, he abounded in promises of concessions to the peasants of the collective farms, but found himself unable to keep them all, lest he incur the censure of that Grand Inquisitor Mikhail Suslov, the rigid interpreter of the purity of the communist faith. As far as is known, Suslov, though criticizing him, stood by him to the end and supported his ideological theses against China, because Khrushchev, a consummate tactician, more than once professed that the Party should assume full responsibility for the decisions to be taken before he himself gave his opinion. This for example happened when it became necessary after the Bucharest Conference in June 1960 to take up a position in opposition to Chinese dogmatism.

By contrast with so many politicians who have come to the fore through intrigues and favouritism, Khrushchev made his way by the force of his exuberant personality. He, the Kalinovka miner, came to the fore because of his intelligence, his practical ability and common sense. Khrushchev has the background of a fighter, both in the Civil War and World War II. The responsibilities which he assumed, as a member of the Party Central Committee of the military council of the commander-in-chief of the south-eastern front during the battles for Kiev and Kharkov as well as in the defence of Stalingrad, are shown in the Soviet history of World War II.

Scarcely had the fighting ended when he devoted himself with his usual energy to reconstructing the Ukraine after the devastation of the war. In less than a year he changed the face of the country. In him, as is rarely to be found in a single person, the theoretician, the accountant and the dialectitian were linked with the builder and the organizer, since common sense always prevailed in his reasoning and suggested to him simple and practical solutions which all could understand. It was as a sound man who got things done that the people learnt to know him, to trust him and to realize that in the crystal clarity of his intelligence problems were simplified. Furthermore, he never left a job half done but gave himself no peace until he had finished it. He was a leader and an optimist, always gay and merry in humour, because he loved life, loved action, loved struggle, and devoted himself with all the overflowing energy of his nature to everything that he undertook. Yet he undertook nothing without turning over a thousand other projects in his mind at the same time.

The men of the Presidium, the members of the government and the Party leaders did not hesitate to give him precedence and urge him on, above all Kaganovich and Mikoyan. They valued the results that he was able to wrest from his subordinates. Kaganovich said of him: 'He is never in his office. He is always out and about, talking to people.'

4

Thus was born the indubitable popularity which he enjoyed. The Russians loved this man, in whom they recognized their qualities and their defects, even if his down-to-earth temperament, his peasant shrewdness and his colourful phrases, smacking of the soil, ended by exasperating the sensibilities of the rapidly growing intellectual class which today, reckoning graduates and the various types of specialists, amounts to more than sixteen million persons.

Perhaps Khrushchev's most striking characteristic was his acute intuition which was based on a remarkable sensitivity. His perception was immediate and drove him into action with irresistible impetus, since he was intoxicated by his own ideas. It would not be too much to say that Khrushchev has been a victim of two salient characteristics of his temperament; his impetuosity and his sensitivity. The first frequently led him to excess in words and actions; the second to sudden withdrawals when he sensed that he had gone too far. The result was a zig-zag policy, blowing alternately hot and cold, very different from the consistent, tenacious, unscrupulous policy of Stalin and the calculated, logical policy of Lenin always linked to reality.[1]

[1] The Italian edition of this book—published before Khrushchev's fall—contains the following assessment of his character:

Above all he is a man of great human warmth who seems to draw energy from his contacts with other men. Therefore he loves arguments; he loves long conversations with cut and thrust as in fencing. A sharp reply from his adversary arouses his respect and appreciation. This mental gymnastic, in which he excels, is not, however, a sterile game; he makes use of it to get to the bottom of problems and to sound out the reactions of his adversary. There is nothing of the bureaucrat in him. He does not isolate himself, as Stalin did, in an ivory tower. He is an extrovert, expansive and volcanic.

His humanity, comprehensive and almost paternal, is the mainspring of his popularity. Khrushchev has a welcoming, good-humoured smile. His face awakes an immediate sympathy. He has nothing of the arrogant haughtiness and the detached poses of a dictator. He seems a simple man, affable. He gives the impression of one who above all wants sympathy and understanding and with whom, at first sight, it seems so easy to come to an agreement.

He has a very lively sense of the comic and has the gift of bringing out in a few phrases, sometimes by a single word or even a gesture, the comedy or paradox of a situation. He has a jovial nature, likes good food and loves to laugh and to make others laugh. He laughs with his lips, his eyes, his whole person. His gaiety is infectious. The Kremlin receptions never have the boredom of official ceremonies. When he is present everything is vivid; he takes the centre of the stage, makes speeches, proposes toasts, tries to talk with everyone. For everyone he has a joke or a cordial or sarcastic word.

He is the real driving force of the Soviet Union. In a régime like the communist one, which excludes all private initiative, a tremendous effort is needed to prevent the masses from subsiding into inertia. And he is the man who knows how to get the maximum of effort from the people, because he knows how to convince them, arguing with them at their own level, amusing them with witty tales, making fun good-humouredly of fools and nitwits. He is a great actor who holds the attention of his audience for hours without boring it, arousing bursts of merriment by his sallies. Contact with the crowd electrifies him and makes his imagination sparkle with the fireworks of the most original witticisms. On the Stalingrad front he kept the morale of the troops high with his quips and speeches. His is the wisdom of Bertoldo, compounded of common sense and stuffed with proverbs. When he was at the technical school, Stalin, who had heard tell of him, once asked him point-blank: 'Give me your definition of communism.' 'Communism,' he replied, 'means a full belly, felt boots and a leather jacket.' The dictator burst out laughing and from that day kept an eye on him.

No head of government knows as he does the mentality of the masses.

There is more than one example of Khrushchev's impulsiveness, which shows how far he has gone beyond the limits of political convenience. The best-known is his indictment of Stalin, which aroused hostile currents of public opinion which had long remained submerged but which indubitably had an influence on his fall. Was it absolutely necessary to sully the name of the former dictator when the mud stuck to the régime itself, to the men who had worked with

There are few who know as he does how to discuss with them the burning questions of the moment, explain in the simplest and clearest way the problems to be solved. He is always on the move. In February 1959 he went to Tula, a little city south of Moscow, and spoke thus to the crowd.

'Our people has always been distinguished by its skill and its talent. Even long ago, when Russia was backward economically and technically, the Russian people made fantastic things. Our literature has many unforgettable pages about this. Do you remember the short story by the famous writer, Nikolai Leskov, which describes how a clever craftsman of Tula, Levska, managed to fit a thin horseshoe on the foot of an English flea? Leskov's description of the Tula craftsman is moving and wonderful. The story moves the reader and makes him proud of his people. But that, comrades, happened a long time ago when our people was still groaning under the tsarist yoke. The force of our people has now increased to such an extent that we will fit a horseshoe on capitalism by creating a communist society.'

The next day, another meeting and another speech. Khrushchev praised the increase in milk production which had more than doubled in five years. 'But meat production,' he said, 'hobbles a bit. The people of Tula have only caught the flea by one leg, at least for the moment.'

Meanwhile, between one speech and the next, he had spoken with the milkers and become aware that all was not going well at the collective farm which he had visited. He criticized sharply the defects and excesses, discussing them with the crowd and pointing out how often cows should be milked, how they should be fed and the best use to make of land lying fallow. Simple things like those old Hesiod taught in his poem about the land *Works and Days*. The statesman's words too became poetry since they taught the eternal laws of life and how to respect them.

This is how this poet, speaking at the third session of the Supreme Soviet on October 1, 1959, commented on the success of the Soviet scientists who had taken photographs of the dark side of the moon. 'In these days,' he said, 'our scientists have given their country an even more wonderful gift. They have paid their court to the Moon and she has been generous with her favours, allowing them to photograph the side which until now she has always kept hidden from the eyes of men.

'We are justifiably proud of our scientists who have persuaded the Moon to throw aside her veil, that relic of the past. Thanks to the advance of Soviet science, the Moon has put aside her veil, has begun to get into step with our own times and has shown her face to the Soviet scientists and to the Soviet people and they have offered to the whole world the opportunity of delving into the mysteries of that celestial beauty, naturally with her consent. We don't make a habit of sticking our noses into forbidden places.' This last sally was a sly reference to the U-2 flights.

Stalin and to the Russian people which had for so many years tolerated so long a sequence of infamies? The revelation shook the prestige of communism and it was also a terrible shock to the Russian people which, despite his crimes, had idolized Stalin, to whom it gave the merit of having created the might of the new Russia, of having saved it from the German invasion and of having restored the Empire, extending its bounds far beyond those reached under the tsars.

Equally excessive was his Canossa when he visited Belgrade in May 1955 in an attempt to bring Tito back into the communist fold. His gesture did not achieve the hoped for result, nor did it increase his prestige.

The withdrawal from Cuba, where he had imprudently set up missile bases, was precipitous and exposed him to Chinese criticism of not even having saved face.

Intemperate above all were his polemics with Mao. All the right was on the Soviet side, yet he weakened it by the violence of his personal attacks and by his intransigence in demanding the condemnation of his adversary. He thus gave an opportunity to the communist parties, which Stalin had always kept in strict obedience to Moscow, to act as arbiters between the two sides and to throw off their dependence on the Soviet Union. The monolithic block broke into fragments and no way has yet been found to restore its former unity. The Soviet Union has fallen from the high pedestal upon which Stalin had placed it.

5

To the personal errors listed in the twenty-nine charges in the letter in which the Party confidentially informed local organs and associated departments of the reasons for the dismissal of Khrushchev may be added the reasons inherent in the system, which has shown serious defects connected with both the agricultural crisis and with the crisis in planning.

Khrushchev started with one great idea: to make his country the most powerful in the world. He put his faith in the superiority of the Marxist system, based on planned state control, over the free market economy of the Western states. Had he not been taught that communism was the highway to the future, the swiftest way to advancement and prosperity?

The first years of the seven-year plan seemed to justify his ambitious hopes, in the same way as the first harvests in the virgin lands had seemed to justify his preference for extensive agriculture rather than the intensive system upheld by the anti-Party group. Those were the years, 1958 to 1961, which marked the apogee of Khrushchev's fortune and power. Soviet armed might was formidable. On August 26, 1957 Tass announced that the Soviet Union had successfully tested multi-stage inter-continental ballistic missiles. It was at once evident that the Soviet Union had a rocket propellant of exceptional power at its disposal; and, indeed, on October 4th the next year the first Sputnik was launched, followed on November 3rd by another Sputnik put into orbit. The Soviet Union believed that it had surpassed the military might of the United States and took advantage of this superiority to launch in November 1958 the famous Berlin ultimatum. The withdrawal of the Allied troops from the Western sectors and the transformation of Berlin into a free city were to have been the beginning of direct action to weaken the defence system of the West in the heart of Europe. But the attempt failed before the resistance of the Allies. The tension threatened to become worse; then Khrushchev received Eisenhower's invitation to visit America. To a realist like Khrushchev this visit offered a chance to judge the difference between the economic power of the United States and that of the Soviet Union. This definitely contributed to strengthen the Soviet Union in its policy of peaceful co-existence.

In the meantime the range of Soviet policy had been extended from the Middle East, where the Soviet Union had financed the construction of the Aswan Dam, to Africa, where it supported the pro-communist policy of Patrice Lumumba and to the American continent, where it supported the Castro régime and made Cuba a launching site for communist influence in Latin America. This policy of world irradiation, boldly pursued to its utmost limits, ended with Khrushchev's speech at the United Nations General Assembly in 1960, in which he set himself up as the champion of a crusade of the coloured peoples against the former colonizing powers with the aim of creating for himself a majority in the United Nations which would enable him to make that organization an instrument to support communist policy throughout the world.

6

Thenceforward, slowly, at first almost imperceptibly, the curve begins to descend. The agricultural crisis of 1963 and the abandonment in the same year of the seven-year plan reveal, on the one hand, the complete failure of the policy of cultivation of the virgin lands and, on the other, the chaos created in industry by a rigid planning system carried out with bureaucratic empiricism rather than on the basis of exact economic calculation.

These economic setbacks weakened the financial power of the state and compelled it to limit its military expenses, whereas America, under the energetic direction of the Secretary of Defence, Macnamara, again assumed an incontestable military superiority, thanks to which Kennedy was able to enforce the withdrawal of Soviet missiles from Cuba.

The check thus inflicted on Khrushchev's policy, despite the fact that the United States wisely abstained from making too much of it, exposed him to the criticisms of China which, not illogically, censured the contradiction between his policy of peaceful co-existence and his foolhardy actions which jeopardized its success. From then on, Chinese attacks redoubled in violence against Khrushchev's policy of détente, since this policy isolated China, was contrary to the revolutionary policy that the communist world has the mandate to press to the utmost in all countries freed from bondage to the capitalist powers, and rendered the Sino-Soviet Alliance of 1950 empty of meaning.

Never had Khrushchev's prestige sunk so low, never had been shown so evidently and so widely the discontent of public opinion, always extremely sensitive to every loss of national power and prestige.

7

On October 13, 1964 Khrushchev was summoned from his country house at Gagra in the Crimea to an extraordinary meeting of the Presidium of the Central Committee in Moscow. Khrushchev was surprised since, as First Party Secretary, it was his task to summon the Presidium. But the order was explicit. Not one of his many friends had warned him of the blow in store for him.

From the Soviet side there has been no definite information about the development of events. Those who had mounted the *coup d'état* had made sure of getting a large majority in the Central Committee. They repeated the manoeuvre carried out with such success by Khruschev in 1957, when the anti-Party group, which had a shattering majority in the Presidium, was placed in a minority in the Central Committee. This time too the arbiter of the situation was the Central Committee, which met on October 14th. Mikhail Suslov read a long report which formulated a number of accusations against Khrushchev. The reading lasted for five hours. Khrushchev replied, speaking for four hours in a tone, as far as is known, harsh and polemic, often insulting to his accusers, especially his former friends.

On October 15th, when Khrushchev became aware of the compact majority of the Central Committee against him, he asked to resign, giving as a reason his uncertain health and his advanced age. His resignation was unanimously accepted.

On October 16th Anastas Mikoyan, as President of the Supreme Soviet, had that body ratify the decision of the Central Committee and also dismissed Khrushchev from his post as Chairman of the Council of Ministers.

This, in outline, was the development of the crisis, which created great perplexity both at home and abroad, since the real reasons for the dismissal of Khrushchev remained undisclosed, although the principal causes were suspected from various indications.

Pravda, in an editorial on October 17th written apparently by Mikhail Suslov himself, charged Khrushchev with 'hare-brained schemes, immature conclusions and unrealistic activities . . . and unwillingness to take heed of science and practical experience'.

The ideological section of the Party, in its turn, immediately afterwards issued a number of explanatory documents in order to give directives to 'activists', Komsomol members and all kinds of propagandists. In the more important of these documents, of which seven hundred and fifty thousand copies were distributed, twenty-nine charges were made against the man who, until the day before, had been feared and revered. Some Western newspapers[2] have published these charges. They included errors and contradictions in agricultural policy, with especial reference to the cultivation of the virgin lands, to the abandonment of the former system of crop rotation, and to the excessive development given to the cultivation of maize; equal censure was directed against the 1957 orders for administrative decentralization, the reform of the planning organization, the favouring of light industry to the detriment of heavy industry, the criteria put forward for urbanistic development, and on the directives to the intellectuals, for a reform of the Party organization based on productive criteria rather than on a territorial basis; finally, they denounced Khrushchev's personal decisions in foreign policy, with especial reference to the Cuba crisis, the worsening of relations with Roumania, the polemics with China, the preparations for a conference of all communist parties, the sending of Adzhubey to Bonn and the grant to Nasser of the insignia of 'A Hero of the Soviet Union'. Other charges concerned his nepotism, his cult of personality, his lack of decorum in some of his public actions, the frivolity of some of his statements, and so on.

[2] The Moscow correspondent of *Paese Sera* published the list of twenty-nine charges, which he stated he had learnt from 'a most reliable source'.

All these charges, even though largely true, excite doubts that they were not the real reasons for Khrushchev's dismissal but merely *a posteriori* justifications intended as a smoke-screen to mask the real, impelling motive that forced Khrushchev's most trusted colleagues to take the harsh decision to remove him from power. All these men had been participants in his decisions and cannot impute the responsibility to him alone. They could not be unaware, when they made the decision to remove him from his high position, that sooner or later they themselves would be called upon to answer similar charges. Furthermore, they had been his friends; Brezhnev in particular was his 'favourite son', elevated by him to the summit of the hierarchy with an almost paternal interest. These are not men who plot a betrayal like the lurid characters of some popular tale. Everything leads one to believe that they acted against their inclinations. What drove them to this pass? Evidently the reason is one that cannot be revealed, and for this reason Suslov's report is not being published; and the reason it cannot be revealed is because to do so would be against the interests of the Soviet Union. Perhaps Russian prestige would be endangered as, for example, if the Soviet Union had had to submit to Chinese dictation. In this uncertainty, it only remains to make some conjectures based not only on the facts which preceded the crisis but also on those which have followed it and which have thrown a little light on its nature. According to the golden Roman maxim *Is fecit cui prodest*, the presumption is that the principal cause of the crisis must be sought for in a Chinese initiative. It is a fact that the main beneficiary of Khrushchev's fall has been Mao-Tse-Tung. To the people of his own country and to many in the outside world he appears the victor. This is true also of Chou-En-Lai who became the centre of all eyes in Moscow, eager to discern, especially during Brezhnev's speech on November 6th, signs of approval or disapproval. Mao had had the shrewdness to give the conflict with the Soviet Union the character of a personal controversy with Khrushchev, whom he had accused of betraying the Marxist ideals, in order to make the entire responsibility for intensifying the conflict fall upon Khrushchev and almost to give the impression that, once Khrushchev were removed, the controversy could be resolved. Khrushchev understood this and at Budapest in April 1964 stated publicly: 'The Chinese communists have spread their propaganda within our country and are trying to incite the people against me. But I pay no attention to these accusations.'

Perhaps he was mistaken in not paying enough attention to them, since evidently the subversive action by China continued and must have given Mao well-founded hopes of success, since he dared to predict, even to some foreign journalists, the imminent fall of Khrushchev. The Chinese communist party, when it refused the invitation to participate in the conference of communist parties in Moscow, prophesied that should the conference take place the Soviet Union would put one foot in the grave. What significance should be given to this dark threat? What were the currents inside the Soviet Union which Mao, according to Khrushchev's accusation, was trying to arouse against him? Evidently Mao, posing as the champion of Stalinism, tried to make use of Stalinist opinions. But what is the importance of these opinions? Is there a real possibility that they might be able to reassume control of the party?[3] It should not be underestimated that when Chou-En-Lai returned to Moscow for the anniversary of the Bolshevik revolution on November 6th he once again solemnly rendered homage at Stalin's tomb. This was not merely a formal act but a gesture intended to reaffirm a precise political viewpoint. Nor, perhaps, is the rumour unfounded that one of the conditions for an agreement laid down by Chou-En-Lai at Moscow in his talks with Khrushchev's successors was the rehabilitation of Stalin. Evidently a standard is to be raised again and a policy restored.

All this must be borne in mind when estimating the forces which have been pressing for a radical change in the policy of Khrushchev, both internal and external.

Naturally, the possibility that the Chinese pressure will prevail, whether exercised directly or through internal currents of Stalinist tendency, depends primarily on the authority that the new Soviet leaders enjoy, that is to say on the strength of their position. The leading post in the Soviet hierarchy, as is shown, among other things, by the order of the portraits of leaders on great ceremonial occasions, is held by the First Party Secretary. Who holds the Party holds the power. But to do that he must keep the Party under control, that is to say he must control its senior members. The neces-

---

[3] What part have these opinions or their exponents in the conspiracy against Khrushchev? Rumour has it that Mao was kept informed of the anti-Khrushchev currents in the Presidium by a deputy member of the Presidium, Viktor Grishin, president of the Soviet Trade Unions. It was Grishin who, on Mikoyan's order, led the Soviet delegation to the fifteenth anniversary of the foundation of the Chinese People's Republic at Peking on October 11th. He had two interviews with Mao, the first on September 30th and the second on October 2nd. Grishin, who talked privately with Mao, was told what Mao had said, a short time before, to the Roumanian Prime Minister, Maurer, namely that there could be no possibility of an agreement with the Soviet Union as long as Khrushchev remained in power. If this be true, it confirms that China was exercising the maximum pressure for Khrushchev's removal.

sity for a strong leader, surrounded by men linked to him by fear or interest, leads inevitably, after a more or less lengthy period of collective government, to the dictatorship of a single man, which ends by descending into the so deprecated cult of personality.

9

Who are the *dramatis personae* who have deposed Khrushchev and become his successors?

The First Party Secretary is Leonid Ilich Brezhnev, a Ukrainian, born in 1906 at Kamenskoe (Dneprodzherginsk). He is the son of a steel worker and he too began work in a steel plant at the age of thirteen. That did not prevent him taking regular study courses and he holds degrees in agricultural as well as metallurgical engineering.

Brezhnev's most striking characteristic is his absolute level-headedness. Accustomed to deal with concrete problems on the basis of figures and not with theoretical discussions, he loves practical and self-evident solutions. Conversation with Brezhnev is particularly pleasant, because this man has the gift, so rare among those who hold positions of command, of knowing how to listen and, with a spirit devoid of any sort of fanaticism or intransigence, to take into account the views of the man he is talking to, which he weighs with common sense, seeking to obtain clear and precise information which will allow him to make an objective judgment based firmly on facts. This man has a simplicity and courtesy which one expects from a gentleman of breeding, coupled with a human warmth that arouses immediate sympathy. Robust and elegant in person, Brezhnev is a cordial yet dignified man, natural and spontaneous; unlike the great personages who have preceded him in his high office, he does not like to assume commanding attitudes, he refrains from polemic attacks and intemperate language and even more from sarcasm and irony. He likes to reason, to convince, to consider. From the outset of his political career, which began in his youth, he has always been a mediator, a man used to unravelling the most complex skeins, whether it be a question of conflict of competence or of personal discord.

His good fortune began in 1939 when Khrushchev chose him to assist in the reorganization of the Ukrainian communist party. His earlier duties had fitted him for his task as leader of the political hierarchy at Kiev. Very soon after he had completed his studies he was entrusted with a provincial agricultural administration in the Urals and seven years later was appointed a member of the Regional Committee of Dnepropetrovsk. This modest *cursus honorum* within his own region gave him a knowledge of the men and affairs of the Ukraine. After the outbreak of war Khrushchev, who had been appointed military commissar, made him his assistant. He thus became, despite his youth, a leading personage to whom tasks of especial delicacy were entrusted. When the war was over he became head of the Moldavian Republic. After Stalin's death his star seemed obscured and he was relegated to the political administration of the army. But in 1957 he was summoned to take his place in the Presidium and from then on his rise was rapid and continuous. Khrushchev, who had appreciated his energetic, level-headed and prudent collaboration for almost a score of years, entrusted him with the very delicate task of administering the exploitation of the virgin lands, the result of which was to prove the correctness of the agricultural policy which he had caused to prevail against the opposition of the anti-Party group.

During the three years of Brezhnev's control, the harvests of the virgin lands maintained satisfactory levels, since the process of erosion had not assumed the disastrous proportions of the succeeding years. Thus, when he returned to Moscow in 1960, his prestige was high and as a reward for services rendered he was promoted to the presidency of the Supreme Soviet, succeeding Marshal Voroshilov. On July 19, 1964, by a decision of the Supreme Soviet, he was replaced in the presidency by Anastas Mikoyan and was appointed Second Party Secretary.

For many in the Soviet Union and also in the eyes of the world, Brezhnev is a new man. In the lower ranks, where he worked until now under the protecting shadow of Khrushchev, he has relied more on conciliation than on force. Will he have the energy necessary to maintain concord in the higher ranks of the Party and to check ambitions, which will not fail to be unleashed as has always happened in every crisis of changing the guard, at least until the new supreme leaders have consolidated their position, selected their immediate collaborators and taken the reins of the Party and the state firmly into their hands?

10

The man who with Brezhnev shares the responsibility of power, as President of the Council of Ministers, is Aleksei Nikolayevich Kosygin, a man of sixty and a typical specimen of the class of technocrats recruited from those men who have had the best training and are most in touch with economic reality, those men who hold in their hands the industrial power and the prosperity of the country. Of medium height, thin, pale and austere, Kosygin has the sickly appearance of a man who leads a sedentary office life. He is submerged in reports, tied to the labours and responsibilities which weigh him down and beset by problems that cannot be shelved, since he is at the centre of Soviet economic organization which receives from him its impulse and from him awaits its orders. The scale and multiplicity of problems has accustomed this economic dictator to order and clarity and above all to the calm which he needs to take well-considered opinions of decisive importance. He speaks little, listens patiently, impassible and always coldly courteous. Yet beneath this semblance of austerity and impassibility is concealed a warm temperament, rich in sympathy, as is often the case with Russians, which shines out unexpectedly in some words of warm-hearted agreement.

One is aware of a careful balancing of opposing ideas, a weighing up of men and facts, the search for ever more perfect techniques, since he is impatient of ready-made solutions; one senses in him a constant urge for the better, the goad of a continuous improvement, the torment of a man who knows that not everything is proceeding at the speed hoped for and planned.

At the age of fifteen this technician, this bureaucrat, began to take an active part in the events of his country, fighting in the decisive phase of the civil war. He then attended the Textile Institute at Leningrad, in which city he later directed an important textile enterprise. At thirty-four he was elected mayor of the former capital, his birthplace. Stalin appreciated his great technical competence and in 1948 appointed him Minister of Finance. Kosygin has also concerned himself with the development of light industry and in the supply of consumer goods. Appointed president of the Gosplan, he prepared and launched the seven-year plan. From 1960 onward he took part in the Presidium of the Central Committee, of which he was a member in Stalin's time.

The new premier has travelled outside the Soviet Union and has had frequent contacts with Western industrialists and economists, with whom he has compared views on his country's system and that of the West. His prestige is indisputable, both within the country and abroad. Everyone who has had the chance of talking with him has been struck by the exceptional technical competence, the mastery of figures and comparisons which emerge from his observations, always exact, clear and incontrovertible. His choice as Prime Minister shows the Party's intention to restore order to Soviet economy and give it back a regular and gradual rhythm according to the directives of a brain that loves practical measures, clarity and a sense of the possible. His co-operation therefore seems invaluable to Brezhnev, who finds in him an incomparable source of energy and a lever of extraordinary power to restore drive to the economic progress of the country. There is a true division of labour between Brezhnev and Kosygin; to the former politics and to the latter economics.

11

Anastas Mikoyan completes the triad, with an authority due to his long seniority in the higher ranks of the Party and the state. He is an Armenian, born in 1896, who owes to his race his typical physical characteristics and his acute intelligence, swift and flexible, thanks to which he has succeeded in holding a leading position not only in political intrigue but also in commercial affairs, which for a very long time were controlled by him with an almost exclusive authority and competence. One of Mikoyan's brothers is an aeronautical engineer, a designer of jet engines.

From his earliest years Mikoyan has devoted himself to revolutionary activity in his country. He is today one of the epigones of the generation that brought Bolshevism to power. In his adventurous existence he has run mortal risks, which he confronted with a courage not unmixed with cunning. Perhaps no one was as threatened as he in the last years of Stalin's rule, for the former dictator suspected a rival in every colleague to be suppressed before he became powerful enough to be of harm. It is therefore comprehensible why it was Mikoyan who initiated the denunciation of the crimes of the old dictator. It was he who set in motion that indictment of Stalin which Khrushchev amplified in his dramatic summary before the XX Party Congress and which reverberated throughout the world.

All these vicissitudes through which Mikoyan has passed unscathed have given rise to the impression that he owes his capacity for remaining afloat mainly to his ability for intrigue. There are many anecdotes current in Moscow which picture him as still enveloped by the incubus of the former dictator, as if he were still casting his threatening shadow over the Soviet Union. But this is to misjudge the personality of Mikoyan who has never hesitated to confront the most hazardous uncertainties whenever he considered that the vital interests of the Soviet motherland were in question. Thus he ranged himself with Khrushchev in the struggle against the anti-Party group, even though the group had a shattering majority in the Presidium. The truth is that this man, though moderate in language and policy, has remained the hard and intransigent revolutionary of his young days, firmly attached to the

Marxist ideology and a convinced champion of Marxist criteria, even those most evidently contradicted by reality. In his arguments in defence of orthodoxy he uses a caustic and brilliant humour which does not disdain the use of paradox. Perhaps this doctrinaire integrity, this invincible faith in the triumph of communism, despite his great experience, his many voyages abroad and his perfect knowledge of Western economic systems, explain the support which the Party has always given him and the high position that he now holds.

He is the Nestor of the government. He is perhaps the man who above all others discreetly and wisely exercises a prevailing influence on the decisions of the Presidium, even though his poor health often necessitates long and frequent absences from Moscow.

12

This picture of the Soviet hierarchy would not be complete without a word about the man who has acted as Grand Inquisitor in drawing up and justifying the charges which have led to Khrushchev's downfall. Mikhail Suslov is a spectre of a man, ravaged by tuberculosis; in his taut, sunken face, as if consumed by inner fires, one can read the austerity of a man who lives only for the thought concentrated in himself. I have never seen him smile.

Like most of the old leaders, he comes from a poor peasant family. He was born on December 12, 1902 in the little village of Shakovskoye in the province of Saratov. He owes everything to the Party, which was impressed by his severe and reserved temperament. He had already distinguished himself for his atheism and for his fervour as an activist. The Party maintained him during his studies, which strengthened his Marxist faith and made him the undisputed ideologist, the unyielding upholder of orthodoxy. He first attended the courses on political economy at the University and then those on Marxism at the Academy of Political Science. He is now teaching Marxism at the Moscow University.

Because of his idealogical rigour he became a protégé of Zhdanov, who introduced him into the secretariat of the Party Central Committee where he won the favour of Malenkov who had risen in Stalin's favour and was carrying out executive duties. Under the tutelary wing of Malenkov, who trusted him implicitly, Suslov soon became known for his severity towards anyone who infringed the purity of communist doctrine and morale. He thus became 'the Purger'. He began in 1933 by purging the Party sections in the Urals region and in 1934 those of Chernigov in the Ukraine. He became Second Party Secretary for the Rostov-on-Don region, where he liquidated officials and officers accused of anti-Stalinism. On the outbreak of war Stalin appointed him Political Commissar of the armies of the Caucasus and commander of the partisan units on that front. In the exercise of this task he proposed to Stalin the mass deportation of the Kalmuck, Circassian and Ingush peoples, which had collaborated with the Germans. Stalin approved the proposal and all these peoples were deported to Siberia.

After such a proof, no one was more clearly indicated than Suslov to 'liquidate the consequences of the war' in the Baltic lands reintegrated in the Soviet Empire. In 1944 Stalin sent him to Lithuania where, for two years, he carried out a reign of terror, imprisoning or condemning to death or deportation bourgeois or suspect elements.

On his return to Moscow, he took his seat in the Central Committee, of which he had become a member in 1939. In 1947 he was appointed Fourth Secretary and the following year Third Secretary of the Party, ranking behind Stalin and Malenkov. He at once distinguished himself by his intransigent attack on Tito, whose condemnation he demanded and against whom he inspired a bitter polemic in the columns of *Pravda*, which he edited in 1949 and 1950.

On Stalin's death he was promoted and, as Second Secretary, became Malenkov's close collaborator. But when Malenkov resigned as First Secretary, Suslov supported Khrushchev. In 1955, when he became a member of the Presidium, he backed Khrushchev against the anti-Party group.

When the Hungarian revolution broke out, Suslov was sent with Mikoyan to Budapest on October 30th, 1957 and this time too gave free rein to his ruthless severity. It was he who suggested that the Red Army intervene to suppress the revolt, he who suggested the appointment of Kadar and he who insisted that the rebellious students and workers be condemned.

Custodian of the purity of the faith, Suslov has fought for the monolithic unity of the communist bloc against all forms of deviationism, whether Tito's revisionism, Togliatti's polycentralism, Chinese dogmatism or the national currents yearning to free themselves from dependence on Moscow.

Khrushchev clashed with him several times in the Presidium debates. Many of Khrushchev's withdrawals may be explained by the criticisms levelled against him by this pitiless upholder of orthodoxy who will not admit any compromise between common sense or realism and the utopia of an anachronistic and discredited doctrine. In November 1962, in particular, he attacked Khrushchev in the Plenum of the Central Committee for the withdrawal from Cuba and defined him as 'the companion of Chamberlain' in a reference to the Munich 'appeasement'. In the controversy with China, he rigidly supported the Party directives on the defence of national interests. It is evident that for a long time past he had been collecting rich material for an indictment of Khrushchev, amassing details of activities not in accord with Marxist doctrine, on which he drew for his report against Khrushchev in the Central Committee. It is the destiny of every revolutionary movement to have its Fouquier-Tinville.

13

Another person who took a leading part in the deposition of Khrushchev, which recalls the analogous intervention of Marshal Zhukov in the struggle between Khrushchev and the anti-Party group, is Marshal Rodion Malinovski, who was invited by Suslov on October 13th to the meeting of the Presidium, to give evidence of the agreement of the armed forces to the dismissal of the First Party Secretary.

Tall, thick-set, as if hewn by an axe, Marshal Malinovski had always seemed docilely subordinate to the orders of his brother-in-law Khrushchev, who had appointed him to succeed Marshal Zhukov, the very popular hero of the last war, against whom Marshal Malinovski never concealed the passionate jealousy which so often sets the military leaders of an army against one another.

Malinovski had worked with Khrushchev on the Stalingrad front. Contrary to Zhukov, who aimed at making the military organism a force at the service of the state and totally divorced from politics, Malinovski supported in the Central Committee, of which he had been a member since 1952, the idea of the politicization of the armed forces, which he placed under the control of the Party. It does not seem that he was very popular in the army because of his acquiescence in Khrushchev's reforms of 1960, which reduced the effectives of the armed forces by more than a million men and reduced the budget allocations for military expenses.

Malinovski was born in 1898. He began his military career under the tsar and was one of the first to join the revolutionary forces, distinguishing himself in the campaign against the Whites.

After the precedents set by Zhukov and Malinovski, the support of the armed forces for one or another of the contestants in the struggle for power is now a factor which gives great importance to the influence of the military on political decisions. This will be the more efficacious the more decisive their contribution in the struggle between rival groups. It is in political situations of this kind that 'Bonapartism' has its origins.

Subordinate to these leaders who now hold the entire stage, there is a swarm of lesser figures, amongst whom it is not possible to discern those who, driven by ambition, favoured by circumstances or by internal strife, will succeed in seizing power and holding leading positions. For the moment two such men are in the public eye, which regards them as personages of the future. They are Podgorny and Shelepin, both of whom have come to the fore with Khrushchev's help.

Nikola Viktorovich Podgorny is an Ukrainian, born at Karlovka near Poltava in 1903. Stocky, jovial and energetic, he in many ways resembles Khrushchev. By the age of fifteen he was already working in a foundry and soon became noted for the revolutionary energy which led him to organize groups of young Bolsheviks. The Party took an interest in him. At the age of twenty he was attending a workers' school, whence he went to the Kiev Technological Institute where he graduated in engineering. He is above all a food industry technician. His inscription in the Party dates from 1930. The following year he became the director of a sugar factory, and in 1939 he became People's Commissar for the food industry in the Ukraine. During the war Stalin summoned him to Moscow to carry out similar duties in the central government. He then alternated between Moscow, Kiev and Kharkov, until Khrushchev appointed him his secretary in 1952 and a member of the Central Committee of the Ukrainian communist party. Thenceforward his rise was rapid. The next year he was Second Secretary and in 1957 First Secretary of the Ukrainian communist party. Thanks to Khrushchev he entered the Presidium in 1958 as a candidate member and became a full member in 1960. Though pushing him upwards to the highest posts, his old chief was not sparing of his criticisms and he was often derisive as he was publicly in 1962 at a meeting of the Central Committee which discussed the agricultural crisis and in particular the poor cereal harvests in the Ukraine. It is probable that these criticisms rankled, since in the debate against Khrushchev Podgorny appeared as one of his most vehement accusers. It may be that this attitude has increased his standing in the Central Committee, in which he was the rapporteur when it met in November 1964 for the first time after the fall of Khrushchev to discuss several of the more urgent reforms needed to correct the errors of the deposed leader, especially those concerning the organization of the Party and the circumspection of the industrial regions.

Alexander Shelepin, on the contrary, is only just forty-six. He is a southerner, a native of Voronesh on the Don. Having graduated in history, philosophy and literature, he early devoted himself to propaganda, especially among the young. In 1952 he was appointed to the First Secretariat of the Komsomol and won great popularity among young people. They responded enthusiastically to his appeal for mobilization for the work of clearing the virgin lands and for the colonization of Siberia. In 1958 he was promoted to preside over the Committee of State Security, better known by its initials KGB. He is a secretary of the Central Committee and is chairman of the committee for the control of the Party and the state. After Khrushchev's fall he became a full member of the Presidium.

The important tasks which he carries out have not only made him one of the leaders of the Soviet Union, but have assured him enormous support, especially among the young, as well as the control of some of the most delicate apparatus of the Party and the state.

15

In conclusion, it may be said that with the fall of Khrushchev a new generation has come to the fore, very different from the preceding one which was a generation of revolutionaries, of self-taught men, driven by the violence of their passions and their old hatreds to renew everything according to the canons of a doctrine imported from the West, which very few of them were capable of realizing how little it responds to reality and how slight is the possibility of putting it into practice. The young men who are now taking over the posts of command have a very different intellectual training from that of their elders, and their attention is centred on concrete problems of economic development and of technical advancement. They have one eye constantly fixed on the systems, the results and the scientific discoveries of the Western world.

Of especial importance in this new generation are the technocrats, that is to say the class of industrial and agricultural leaders who have to measure their achievements against reality, without paying too much heed to the formulas of an outmoded and obstructive ideology. The struggle between the technocrats and the Party is at the root of the economic and political development of the present-day Soviet Union. On its outcome depends the evolution of the régime and the future of the country.

It is to some extent a struggle between the present and the past, between reality and utopia. The intellectuals who are now emerging from the high schools, the academies and the specialized institutes in ever growing numbers are fully conscious of this secret and unrelenting struggle. The contrast can be discerned in the press and in literature; it is the conflict between a party bound to the interests of international solidarity and a technocracy which recognizes only the interest of raising the prosperity of the nation. The stronger national particularisms grow in the disintegration of the communist bloc, the stronger grows the policy of the technocrats, eager to place the organization of the country on a realistic basis in accord with economic laws which are ever nearer to those laws that assure the prosperity of the Western lands.

In order to estimate accurately the development of the situation, it is well to bear in mind that whereas the Party is a centralized organization able to control through its countless branches the whole nerve system of the nation, the technocrats may be considered as a class in course of formation, that is to say a force dispersed throughout the whole country, whose unity resides solely in its consciousness of common responsibility and in the attraction of certain dominating ideas which draw together all those who have to confront similar problems and pursue similar ends. It is now clear that the reaction to the systems of Khrushchev is to a great extent inspired by the necessity of reforming the system of production, which means that many innovations are dictated by the technocrats, whereas other reforms are wanted by the Party and yet others by the military.

16

Perhaps it is now possible to hazard some guesses on the future development of the crisis, both in internal and external policy. As a point of departure one can take the main directives of the Khrushchev policy which can, broadly speaking, be reduced to three: a more rapid development of the natural resources of the country (attempted by Khrushchev with his seven-year plan, the cultivation of the virgin lands, development of the chemical industry, etc.), an increase in and improvement of the supply of consumer goods, and the policy of peaceful co-existence.

In the organization of production, great insistence is made on the need for 'scientific planning'. In this the influence of Kosygin, who was president of the Gosplan, can clearly be seen. In the letter to the Party sections outlining the twenty-nine charges against Khrushchev it was stated that 'the main directives of the political economy will be maintained' but that 'the autonomy of management of industrial and agricultural enterprises will be accentuated'. This leads one to believe that, although no radical changes are en-

visaged, a movement is favoured in the sense supported by Libermann, Trapeznikov, Arzumanian, Vishenev and Leontiev, that is
to say that planning must be based on accurate economic calculation in which due heed is paid to interest on the capital invested,
adequate amortization and also profit, in order to put the enterprises
in a position to consolidate and develop their activities, vary their
production and, at least partially, to finance themselves. Czechoslovakia and Poland are already following this line, increasing the
powers and responsibilities of the directors of the enterprises. 'There
must be objective criteria,' said Brezhnev in his first speech on
November 6, 1964, 'for the correct application of economic laws.'

Brezhnev has also stressed the need to increase general living
standards by the expansion of light industry producing consumer
goods; but above all he insisted on 'the basic necessity of developing
heavy industry which assures the expansion of the whole economy
and supplies the needs of defence'. It is a fact that programmes based
on the priority of heavy industry have up till now reduced the expansion of consumer goods and that all those who have tried to
oppose this priority have been deprived of power. That was Malenkov's fate and that was Khrushchev's. One of the twenty-nine
points, specifically the fourth, castigates Khrushchev for having insisted 'on an excessive increase of the allocations for the production
of consumer goods', while point five accuses him of 'underestimating
the importance of heavy industry, where allocations were insufficient for the development of the Soviet Union as a leading
world power'.

The need for strengthening the defensive capacities of the country
has already been stated. This is the price that must be paid to the
military for the part it played in the deposition of Khrushchev.
Whether this increase in military expenditure is regarded as necessary to ensure that the Soviet Union is not outdistanced by America
or whether it is to garrison the Chinese frontier, which is almost
undefended for thousands of kilometres, is not yet clear. What is
clear is that this increase in military expenditure will contribute to
keep production of consumer goods low, since an ever greater part
of the national income will be destined for armaments.

For all these reasons it does not seem that it will be possible to
eliminate the real cause of the economic crisis that the Soviet Union
is now experiencing, which is too low a labour productivity. Khrushchev quite rightly, as Malenkov before him, realized the necessity
of raising the supply of consumer goods as the most urgent problem
for Russia, since only by assuring the working masses a higher
standard of wages and consumer goods is it possible to obtain from
them, whether in agriculture or in industry, a higher yield.

Other reforms concern the improvement of agricultural methods, the reorganization of the Party and the circumscription of the industrial regions. We shall refer to them in the chapters which deal with such matters.

17

There is, moreover, one fundamental point on which the Soviet leaders have hitherto remained silent, and that is the constitutional measures to regulate the transfer of power and thus avoid the long and difficult crises which up till now have accompanied changes at the summit of the hierarchy.

The Soviet Constitution, modelled on the laws of the democratic countries, includes a number of quite liberal measures which control the legislative, executive and judiciary powers of the state and grant a wide range of rights to the Soviet citizen. This impressive façade, however, conceals the overwhelming power of the Party, which substitutes its own will for that of the state, because all decisions are drawn up by the Party organs and the only thing left for the state is to put them into force. The situation is similar to that in many Western states, in which the party apparatus establishes programmes and imposes them on its representatives in parliament or in the government. But in the Soviet Union the situation is incomparably more grave since there is only one party to make the decisions and, within it, there is a single man, or a restricted group of men, who decides for all. The debates are hermetically secret and differences of opinion cannot transcend the limits ensured by the unity of the controlling group. There is no control by the press or by public opinion, which in the democratic countries intervene and complete to assure the rejection or acceptance of one or another thesis.

Let us take the typical case of the discussions to increase cereal production which took place after the death of Stalin. Khrushchev succeeded in having the principle of extensive cultivation accepted, involving the exploitation of the virgin lands. The group afterwards known as the anti-Party group only because it was defeated held that the cultivation of the steppe would lead to disaster. Events have proved it right, but that has not prevented its exclusion from the Party.

The real reason for the concentration of power in the hands of a single man, or a small group of men, is to be found in the measure adopted by the X Party Congress which forbade opposition viewpoints within the Party. But when is a difference of opinion an opposition viewpoint? When does a group which upholds a point of view different from that of the Party Secretary become an anti-Party group? There is no provision. Everything, therefore, depends on the judgment of the leader. Nothing remains for those in opposition save recourse to a *coup d'état* to rid themselves of the head of government. But a *coup d'état* cannot become a normal method of assuring the transfer of power from the ruling clique to the opposition.

In the Yalta *aide-memoire* of August 1964 Togliatti wrote: 'The problem to which the closest attention should be given . . . is to overcome the régime of restrictions on, or suppression of, democratic and personal freedom which was set up by Stalin' and he hoped for a return to 'the Leninist norms which assure, both within the Party and outside it, a broad freedom of expression and debate.' But it was Lenin who, in March 1921, approved the prohibition to hold opposition viewpoints within the Party and in this way gave Stalin his most efficient instrument to obtain the condemnation or suppression of all his rivals.

It is therefore difficult to see how democratic freedoms can be restored in a régime based on a highly centralized party and controlled by the will of a single man or a small group of men. It must be added that even the Party leaders have a somewhat narrow freedom of action, since they are hemmed in by Marxist doctrine within whose limits they must make their decisions if they do not want to expose themselves to the charge, so frequently repeated, of betraying the sacred principles. Perhaps when we have more knowledge of the details of the crisis that has swept away Khrushchev, we will be able to appreciate the dramatic struggle made by him to ensure the prevalence of realistic solutions against the absurd limitations of the ideology. These not only exclude every heterodox conception within the Party but with even greater reason exclude the plurality of parties, freedom of the press and information, and the free discussion of ideas. In his speech on freedom of thought and expression on March 8th, 1963 Khrushchev did not hesitate to say that whenever such freedom was granted the intellectuals 'would try to speak against the achievements of the revolution'. In other words the grant of democratic liberties would give the people the power to overthrow the régime.

None the less, something is afoot. After Stalin, who had set up a personal dictatorship, there was a return to 'collective leadership' within the Presidium. But Khrushchev weakened the authority of the Presidium, referring its decisions when they were unfavourable to him to the Central Committee from which the Presidium took its orders. In October 1964 the manoeuvre was repeated, so that the Central Committee seems to have acquired the authority of a Supreme

Court of Appeal. Does this mean that it regards itself as continually controlling the Presidium and claiming freedom of opinion and upholding the right, common to every democratic régime, of deciding between majority and minority? That should be the logical outcome; but it is doubtful if the other Party leaders, at any rate as long as they remain united, would agree to an evolution which would have inevitable repercussions in the lower ranks of the Party and would shatter its monolithic discipline. The forecasts, therefore, cannot be other than pessimistic.

18

In the foreign political field what interests world opinion is whether the fall of Khrushchev will or will not slow down that policy of détente of which he was the principal and firmest supporter. It is true that the new Party leaders have not criticized this policy and have even wanted to reassure the Western governments on the continuity of the policy of détente, as appears from the explicit statements of Soviet ambassadors in the more important capitals. Mikoyan and Kosygin have taken advantage of the election of President Johnson to send him a message of greeting which assures him full Soviet co-operation in trying to develop relations between the United States and the Soviet Union in the interests of the Soviet and American peoples and in the interest of strengthening universal peace. Then came Brezhnev's declaration, in his policy speech of November 6, 1964, in favour of peaceful co-existence with all countries regardless of their social systems and of developing economic relations with all countries. 'The Soviet people,' he said, 'sincerely hopes that the present international slackening of tension will continue.'

Kosygin was no less explicit when speaking on November 19, 1964 to a group of American businessmen. He defined peaceful co-existence as 'an immutable principle of Soviet policy' and expressed the desire to see commercial relations develop between the Soviet Union and the United States.

Certainly there has been no lack of discordant voices, such as that of Marshal Malinovski who, in his message to the armed forces during the review on Red Square on November 7th, declared that the Soviet communist party, faced by the threat of military adventures by the imperialists, is showing a constant solicitude for the strengthening of the defences of the Soviet Union and is giving its army the most modern arms. The Soviet armed forces, he went on, are ready, together with those of the other communist countries, to defend the freedom and independence of the Soviet Union and all the communist countries from any aggressor, since it is well known that the imperialists, under the leadership of the United States, are stubbornly opposed to international lessening of tension and do not renounce their plans for military adventures. At the Kremlin reception the old Marshal reiterated this in an attack on the American Secretary of Defence, Macnamara, but the Soviet press censored this part of his speech.

Grishin, also a member of the Presidium, has made himself the mouthpiece of similar accusations against American imperialism, echoing the theses of Chinese polemics.

Evidently there are currents, whose importance it is hard to assess, pressing for a policy alignment with Peking. What does China want? She wants a slowing-down of the policy of peaceful co-existence and, if possible, its abandonment, the withdrawal of the Soviet Union from the West and its support in the so-called front against the imperialists. Mao's message to Brezhnev and Kosygin, while it reaffirmed 'the eternal and unbreakable friendship between the Chinese and Soviet peoples' looked forward to 'the renewal of the common struggle against imperialism led by the United States'.

The price of reconciliation between the two countries is, in fact, a reversal of Khrushchev's policy. Peking will not give up the basic directive of its policy. Experience confirms this beyond the shadow of a doubt. Every time that Khrushchev tried a reconciliation with China he had to pay by a stiffening towards the West. This explains the sudden variations of his policy, especially at first, with its disconcerting alternation of friendly gestures and intransigence.

It may be asked how far will Mao's pressure be successful. Now that Khrushchev, who was his most serious rival because of the authority which he enjoyed, has been eliminated, it will seem to him far easier to exert pressure on men still not consolidated in power. From what has emerged from the talks between Chou-En-Lai and the new Soviet leaders, the latter have put up a firm resistance to Chinese pretensions on all essential points. They have given way on the summoning in December of the union of communist parties, they have recognized, as Brezhnev said on November 7th, that 'Taiwan (Formosa) must be reunited with the Chinese People's Republic' and they have condemned 'the provocations to the Democratic Republic of Vietnam'. But as far as we know, they have not gone any further, well aware that every concession is dangerous because the first will inevitably lead to others. What exactly have been Mao's pretensions? It has been said that he does not consider the dismissal of Khrushchev as enough but has also asked for that of his closest collaborators, whom he regards as equally responsible for his policy. It is not, it is true, a question of the replacement of men but of a change of policy. Now it is indisputable that the Khrushchev line, without the polemical and personal idiosyncrasies of the former leader, is fully in accord with Soviet interests. It is not without apprehension that the Soviet Union sees growing on its frontiers a hegemonic power which claims a good part of its territory and which has for years pursued in Asia a policy of the most un-bridled imperialism. It is evidently in the Soviet interest to call a halt to the expansion of this threatening neighbour, which con-stitutes a danger to the security of the Soviet Union. This explains why Mikoyan hastened to reassure Mrs Indira Gandhi, Minister of information in the Indian government, of the continuance of Soviet friendship, since such friendship 'is not a piece of merchandise that the Soviet Union may give away in exchange for the friendship of another country'.

The talks with Chou-En-Lai therefore ended with an anodyne communiqué. All that the new régime seems to have obtained is a truce to polemics. For how long? In the meantime China will con-tinue to strengthen her influence in the communist parties and hasten the process of scission already evident in the old parties of the Moscow obedience. These are signs of a policy boldly aiming at assuring China leadership of the communist world.

All in all, it does not seem that the new régime can deviate widely from Khrushchev's directives. The future will tell whether the sacrifice of Khrushchev was really inevitable.

CHAPTER V

The Schools

1

THE masterwork of the Soviet régime is its school organization. In the first days of the revolution Lenin, with prophetic vision, stated that everything must begin with the schools. 'Give me a fulcrum,' Archimedes said, 'and I will move the world.' The Soviets have found the point to place the lever and have lifted their country to incredible heights. All their progress, not only scientific and technical, but also economic, political and military, stems from the schools, because without the education of the masses and the formation of cadres the industrialization of the country, the development of agriculture or the power of the new arms and of the army capable of handling them was not conceivable.

The elimination of illiteracy and the specialized education of all citizens has made possible the exploitation of all the talents available and their utilization for the advancement of the country. That is the great force which has remoulded Russia. The first lesson which the communist world has to teach the West is that the secret of progress lies in the development of the schools, because the power of a country is in the multitude of its scientists, its technicians and its intellectuals.

In tsarist Russia seventy-five per cent of the people were illiterate. Its school population did not reach ten millions, of whom only 127,000 went on to higher educational institutes. To these, moreover, women were not admitted. It was the most backward country in Europe; today, if one is to judge from the number of students, it is without doubt the most progressive in the world. One can well speak of a cultural revolution which has taken place within a span of forty years.

At first the difficulties to be overcome appeared insuperable. The population of Russia was in great majority peasant and lived for six months of the year in the rigour of a glacial winter and for two months of thaw in mud up to the knees. The nomad peoples of Central Asia, backward Moslems, were suspicious of any non-Moslem culture. Some of the Mongol or Mongoloid peoples in

Eastern Siberia and in the Far East had no system of writing and did not even have an alphabet. To this must be added the immense distances, the shortage of teachers and of text-books.

All these difficulties were overcome in one of those bursts of energy of which only peoples who have just carried out a revolution seem to be capable. Illiteracy has disappeared on all Soviet territory. The school attendance has now risen to thirty-five million students. According to the last census in 1959 more than forty-five million persons have now had a secondary education; there are about thirteen and a half million specialists and about four million who have had higher education. Women attend all schools from the lowest to the highest in about the same percentage as men.

These are indisputable merits of the régime and a source of shame for so many democratic governments which prate about social reform yet show themselves incapable, in conditions undoubtedly more favourable than in Russia, of healing the sore of illiteracy which is the primary cause of backwardness, unemployment and pauperism. The correspondent of *Il Popolo*, Roberto Savio, when visiting Uzbekistan, was asked by the secretary of the Tashkent Scientific Institute how it was that Italy had not yet succeeded in solving the question of illiteracy in the south or that of the lack of classrooms. If the West does not tread the same path as that already trodden by the Soviet Union, it will be impossible for it to regain the ground that it is losing. The Americans are beginning to be aware of this and are worried by the 'Russian achievements in the decades to come' in the words of Prof. Jerome Weismer of the Massachusetts Institute of Technology.

2

Lenin's basic idea, when tracing the outlines of the Soviet scholastic organization, was that it was not possible to create a state of proletarians if the people were not provided with the cultural preparation indispensable for carrying out the tasks entrusted to them. In order to build socialism it was necessary to begin by transforming the masses through education. To go on relying on a tiny minority of intellectuals to fill executive posts would inevitably mean to create a new bourgeois class. The need to make culture the patrimony of all citizens was, moreover, implicit in the concept of the socialist state.

It was first of all urgent to form a general staff of executives and above all of technicians. On the morrow of the October revolution Lenin noted the lack of engineers, of agricultural specialists and of scientists. Such specialists must come from the ranks of the workers and peasants. On this point Lenin was unshakeable. But the workers and peasants were only illiterate or semi-illiterate raw material. He did not let that worry him. He wanted to prove that the antithesis of intellectual and manual labour was a mere prejudice, so that the field-workers and mechanics could be transformed into excellent administrators and executives.

With a gesture of true revolutionary audacity, he admitted to the universities all who asked, even though they were without the necessary academic qualifications, provided they came from the working class. So ordered the decree of August 2, 1918. School fees were abolished. Women were admitted on equal terms with men. There were no entrance examinations, nor were the candidates asked to show any certificates. Any teacher who tried to transgress this decree was to be brought before the revolutionary courts. The People's Commissariat for Education was given the task of supervision and of seeing that everyone who wanted to study should have the chance of doing so. 'Preference,' Lenin said, 'must without question be given to the poorest peasants or the proletariat. They must be given grants on a generous scale.'

To encourage the workers to create a culture for themselves, he organized three-year preparatory courses to enable them to go to the universities and other higher institutes. Thus, in February 1919, the first Workers' Faculties, or *Rabfac*, were created, which gave to those who attended them regularly the right to enrol in the universities or higher educational institutes with priority over all others. Culture was put within the reach of all and became the patrimony of the people, not formally as in most of the democratic states but actually by means of suitable and practical measures. It was the miracle of a human mass, still crude and primitive, which had till then only the most rudimentary notions of manual tasks, stretching their intelligence and their will to overcome the most difficult trial to which the revolution had called it, namely to become the intelligentsia of the new state. It was at the price of such sacrifices and such efforts that a people proved itself worthy of a better destiny. Bolshevism opened the way to all, but made no concessions to anyone; no rights were granted which were not a recognition of merit painfully achieved. This gave the lie to the too facile expectations of those who saw in the communist revolution only the realization of the maxim: Get up that I may take your seat. From that point of view the Bolshevik revolution became the replacement of a ruling class of aristocratic-bourgeois origin by a ruling class of proletarian origin. The means for carrying out that replacement was the school.

It might well be asked: was it absolutely necessary to destroy the whole ruling class of the old régime to obtain this result? Would not the scholastic revolution carried out by Lenin have been enough to open the way to the higher grades of education to the proletariat and to put its representatives into posts of command? China has followed this second way in order to make use of all available elements, which it has forced to participate, under surveillance, in the revolutionary process. Undoubtedly the Soviet precedent has been of value, to prevent falling into similar errors and to conserve all its forces.

But Lenin wanted a clean break with the past. In order not to prejudice the revolution all Soviet citizens must be made potential executives. The equality preached by communism would not have become a reality, but it would have been empty words if it had not assured to everyone not merely theoretical rights but identical and practical chances of making the best of their opportunities. All therefore should not only have the right but also the obligation to go to school. The idea of a crusade against illiteracy was born. The spread of education must seal the rebirth of the Russian people and become the foundation of the power of the state. Lenin never tired of repeating that the first and irreplaceable factor of wealth is man with his creative intelligence. He must be armed with all the most advanced discoveries of science. A heroic effort was therefore demanded of the revolutionary generation. The people accepted it, took upon itself the formidable task and furnished the country with a ruling class of proletarian and revolutionary stamp. Some of the present members of the Presidium come from that first summons. Their studies were hasty and summary, but experience has completed their education far better than any school could have done. The epigones of the revolution, who have become heads of industrial enterprises or great administrative departments, retain the stamp of their worker or peasant origin; they are brusque, stunted, but energetic, self-willed and realistic. They are the backbone of the régime.

If the formation of a ruling class, political, administrative and economic, was the foremost necessity in Lenin's time, another need, no less urgent, became apparent as soon as the industrialization of the country began under Stalin. This was the need for ever greater numbers of technicians, specialists, directors of collective farms. This executive had also to be recruited from the people, because that inherited from the former régime and still available was totally inadequate.

Naturally it could not be claimed that the sacrifices and efforts of the revolutionary epic should be prolonged indefinitely. The new generations must have an easier life. So the first haphazard formation of the earliest cadres was succeeded by a regular and continuous organization which took account of the limited time at the disposal of adults to perfect their studies. In addition to their work in the factories and in the fields they would have to spend supplementary hours at evening classes or on correspondence courses. Only thus was it possible to select from the best of the workers and peasants the mass of technicians required for the fulfilment of the first five-year plan, which needed about 75,000 engineers and 100,000 technicians for industry as well as 40,000 agricultural specialists, whereas there were available only about 20,000 technicians for industry and 11,000 for agriculture. The second five-year plan demanded another 340,000 engineers and 900,000 technicians.

3

There were three demands which the scholastic organization had to meet; the first and most immediate was to create political and administrative cadres, the second, a short-term need, was to form technical cadres for economic development, while the third, which was to be the foundation of cultural rebirth, was to provide a nursery for the growth of these executive elements and consisted in teaching the entire population to read and write. There was also a fourth, more and more important as the economic exploitation of the country proceeded, which was to train skilled workers, both industrial and agricultural. This last, as will be seen, became the basic aim of the recent scholastic reforms.

The struggle against illiteracy has remained an epic event in the annals of the Soviet Union. On December 26, 1919 Lenin signed the famous decree which fixed the objective of 'giving to the entire population of the republic the chance of consciously participating in the political life of the country'. But where to find the army of teachers needed to translate this revolutionary reform into practice? The Soviet government mobilized all its citizens with a certain degree of education and conscripted them as teachers. Three- and ten-month courses were organized for adults, semi-illiterates and illiterates respectively. Many were the objections. There were arguments about the timeliness and the possibility, but Lenin was inexorable and his orders prevailed.

It was inevitable that at the beginning the qualifications of this improvised teaching body were somewhat scant. But by 1940 it greatly exceeded one million teachers and by 1956 it had reached one million seven hundred thousand. Today there are about two million teachers. With their number the quality of the teachers has also improved. How? By raising their status and above all by paying them well. That was Lenin's order. In 1923 he wrote:

'The teacher must be granted a better position amongst us than he has ever had in the past or than he has now or than he can ever hope to attain in a capitalist society . . . In order that this may be we must work systematically, untiringly and tenaciously both for his spiritual advancement and to prepare him, from all points of view, for his great mission. Above all, above all and once again above all, we must work for the improvement of his economic well being.'

These are words to be pondered. It is in schools that citizens are formed. They will turn out as their masters have formed them. Therefore the corps of teachers is the corner-stone in the edifice of state. It will do its utmost, to the extent that the state recognizes its merits, not only morally but financially. But this, the primary social reform, is far too often forgotten and passed over in favour of other more costly and demagogic reforms.

On July 19, 1920 an Extraordinary Commission was founded for the abolition of illiteracy throughout the Soviet Union. Lenin said to the People's Commissar for Education, Lunacharski: 'The day will come when we shall have only two great People's Commissariats: Economy and Education.' The paradox contained much truth, because economy can only advance if education provides technicians and specialists.

But the principal aim of the reform and the reason for its urgency was 'the education of a generation capable of finally introducing communism' as was stated in the preamble to the programme prepared by Lenin and approved by the VIII Congress of the Soviet Communist Party in March 1919.

Thus illiteracy was rooted out. I wanted to see for myself the results of this scholastic reform in two regions which, for different reasons, I considered offered the greatest obstacles to its fulfilment: Uzbekistan and Yakutya. The first is a Moslem country, where up to the last war women still wore the veil and where the influence of the *mufti* and the *ulema* lasted longest. I visited Tashkent, Samarkand and Bukhara; this last especially because it had been for centuries the most active centre of Moslem culture in all Central Asia. I expected to find there a people in rags and ravaged by trachoma, as travellers had described it up to a few decades ago. To my surprise I found the schools thronged with healthy boys and girls who obviously attended them gaily and willingly. The young students all wore clothes of clean, freshly-ironed cotton. There were no signs of trachoma or other infectious diseases. How had it been possible, I wondered, to induce one of the most backward and fanatical Moslem peoples to send its children to the state schools? The answer was to be found in the many advantages which the state guaranteed them. Apart from the chance of obtaining higher wages through education and going on to the universities and technical colleges, the schools provided hot and plentiful meals, clothing and medical attention; free transport was organized for those who lived at a greater distance. Furthermore the school authorities took an interest in the home life of the students and intervened in favour of the poorer ones by drawing from a joint fund partly contributed by the state and partly by agricultural co-operatives, factories and the like.

I got a similar impression of the schoolchildren in Yakutya, the district nearest to the Cold Pole. In Yakutsk all the houses are of wood, but the schools are of brick and in the city itself, developed during the Soviet régime, there are thirty-four of them. Many pupils come into the city from the surrounding countryside, in winter on sledges and in summer by boat when the river Lena rises. Some of them belong to mixed Russian-Yakut families and the beauty of this type of cross is as great as its robustness. Undoubtedly it is a sacrifice for families to keep their children at school when they are old enough to work, but the sacrifice is compensated for by the benefits which they receive. As far as I could find out, the children have a passion for learning. They are healthy, well-dressed and cheerful. In the villages the best kept and most welcoming building, often with some artistic pretension, is the school. The state has given priority to the construction of school buildings over that of houses. The teaching is varied, pleasant and interesting. The teachers often take the children to visit civic monuments and museums. Of these last every city of importance has one. All are well arranged along similar lines and exhibit geological specimens, fossils and the archaeological and artistic treasures of the region. The teacher makes use of them to explain the events of nature and of history, interpreting them according to the precepts of materialism. The children become used to regarding the museum as a collection of useful facts and a source of living impressions and not, as with us, a cemetery of vanished worlds.

The Soviet claim to have abolished illiteracy is almost literally true. From the census of January 15, 1959 it appears that the number of illiterates between the ages of nine and forty-nine was 1,929,000, that is to say $1\frac{1}{2}\%$ of the whole population.

4

The progress of school organization is shown by the following figures of pupils in the elementary, secondary and professional-technical schools and in the universities and colleges:

Year	Elementary schools	Secondary and technical schools	Universities and colleges
1914-15	7,900,000	35,800	112,000
1932	21,400,000	723,700	504,400
1940	32,900,000	840,000	541,000
1945	26,900,000	938,000	490,000
1948	33,200,000	1,094,000	1,032,000
1950	35,700,000	1,298,000	1,247,000

The Soviet Union has 766 higher educational institutions attended by a number of students roughly four times as many as the total number of students who attend similar institutions in England, France, Federal Germany and Italy, though the combined population of those four countries is approximately equal to that of the Soviet Union. In 1958, 94,000 engineers graduated from the Soviet universities; from the American universities 35,000

To sum up: whereas Soviet society aims at exploiting all human skills, in the Western world too large a part of them remains inactive. The real danger of the West being outdistanced by the Soviet Union is in the difference, which grows greater year by year, between the numbers of the cultural élite. In the contest of progress the Soviet Union has a larger number of well-trained effectives and a widely recruited general staff chosen from the growing number of young scientists, more and more perfected for scientific research. Even more than in arms, there is power in this formidable number of intellectuals, in this syndicate of brains, among the most gifted in the world.

It should be noted, and this proves how deeply the scholastic reform has penetrated, that the highest percentage of persons with degrees or certificates of higher education, is not to be found among the Great Russians or the Ukrainians, the two dominant nationalities of the Soviet Union, but among the minorities of Transcaucasia. Whereas the Great Russian percentage of students is 19% and Ukrainian 17%, the Georgian percentage is 38%, the Armenian 21% and that of the people of Azerbaidzhan 21%. These figures show the rebirth set in motion by the Soviet régime in the course of scarcely four decades among peoples who at one time were the most neglected by the central government.

Naturally the cost of a scholastic organization on such a scale is proportionate to the impressive results which it has attained. The grandeur of Lenin's idea is matched by the profusion of means to translate it into reality. That is the real secret of success. To specify

how much the Soviet Union spends on education is not easy, because the collective farms, the industrial establishments and the
trade unions all participate in the expense. An approximate idea of
the total has been given by a member of the Presidium, M. A.
Suslov, who stated at the IX Congress of the Italian Communist
Party on February 2, 1960 that a third of the outgoings of the Soviet
budget is devoted to education, culture and social assistance, which
amounts to about two hundred and thirty milliard rubles, equal to
twenty-three milliard dollars in 1959.

5

From the time of Lenin, the school organization has been the
theme of impassioned debates in which the leading figures of the
régime have taken part. The basic principle is that the schools must
be the forge of communist man; but at the same time they must
serve an essentially practical end, which is to create units of maximum productivity, whether they be executives, technicians or
specialists. It has therefore constantly oscillated between these two
poles, between the political and the practical nature of the schools.
According to which tendency has been predominant, they have
passed from one experiment to another without having yet found a
final solution.

In March 1919 Lenin outlined a scholastic organization which
was approved by the VIII Party Congress. Following his general indications his wife, Nadezhda Krupskaya, collaborated in drawing up
the first school regulations, published in 1920. Two courses were provided for: an elementary course of four classes and a secondary
course of five. Only the first was obligatory. The teachers were to be
inspired by the idea that the Bolshevik revolution had initiated a
new phase in the history of the human race, in accordance with the
scientific law of historical development formulated by Marx.
Materialism therefore became the basis for the education of youth,
which must be given a mainly scientific education.

The results of experience, based on such criteria, were not, generally speaking, satisfactory. There were complaints about the excessively doctrinal character of the schools. These criticisms were especially levelled at the five-class secondary schools. The education
that they gave was considered of little value for young people
destined to work in the fields or the workshops; they lacked knowledge of any practical trade. It was, in fact, a school for white-collar
and not for manual workers. But Krupskaya defended the task entrusted to the schools with drawn sword. A good general education,

she said, was necessary to create the new consciousness of man; it was not enough to be a mere instrument of production.

The idea of dividing the school organization into three phases was then put into force:

—the first phase of four classes was compulsory;
—the second of three classes, polytechnic in character;
—the third phase, of two classes, was to prepare young people intending to go on to the universities or higher educational institutes.

The idea was that the first two phases would be sufficient for the general education of the future workers and peasants while those who set their sights at academic honours should take the third.

However, as was to be expected, it was found that the majority of the students aimed at continuing their higher education and therefore wished to attend the third phase reserved for those preparing to enter the universities. The state could not oppose such a tendency because of the honour in which it had always held the criterion of equality. Therefore the idea prevailed of organizing a school for all, made up of a first course of four years, a second of three and a third, also of three.

The reason why the Soviet state, before the war, ended by choosing the ten-year system was to impart a sound cultural background to the maximum possible number, that is to avoid the creation of semi-illiterates who left their elementary schools with vague and superficial ideas that only enabled the pupil to spell with difficulty and to read comic strips.

But not even experience of the ten-year system was conclusive. It revealed itself as a factory of misfits because all the young people burdened with a scholastic apprenticeship lasting for ten years wanted, not unnaturally, to go on to the universities. This was not possible in practice because the universities could not absorb so large a number of candidates, nor were there enough executive posts for so huge a number of future graduates. On the other hand there was a grave risk of seeing the fields and workshops deserted. As production developed there was a greater and greater shortage of workers.

As can be seen, even democratic reforms have their limits.

A report by Khrushchev in September, 1958, set out with his usual clarity, surveys the situation and lays down the main lines of the reforms to be put into practice. The result was that only one-third of the students who completed their secondary education could pass on to higher education.

The figures given by him show that in 1958 about 450,000 new students were enrolled in the universities while another 800,000 released from the secondary schools were forced to work in the workshops or in the fields. But many of these 800,000, excluded from higher education by the lack of posts, did not resign themselves to sink into the mass of manual workers, especially if they were from families which formed part of the new bourgeoisie. These misfits therefore remained idle, living on their parents while waiting to have another try at the entrance examination to a higher educational institution. The number of these 'parasites', as they were called by the authorities, grew from year to year. In 1957, that is to say on the eve of the school reforms, they were estimated at about three million. Of the 450,000 who had enrolled, half attended the normal day classes and the other half attended evening classes or took correspondence courses.

Khrushchev recognized the failure of the ten-year educational system. 'It would be quite out of place,' he said, 'to keep the complete general and compulsory secondary school system in the form in which it has been until now.'

The chimaera of equality must therefore be renounced. Only some of the students could be allowed to continue their studies and be trained to hold executive posts; the others, that is to say the great majority, would have to resign themselves to lesser posts in the countryside or in industry. Reality, with its iron exigencies, again triumphed.

In the discussion which preceded this reform, this renunciation of the sacred principles was unanimously passed over in silence. The argument prevailed that the ten-year system was not a people's school, that is to say it was not suitable for a nation of workers. It had been beguiled by bourgeois influences and ideals, whereas it was necessary to create from scratch a school system that reflected the needs and the ideals of the new world which had arisen from labour and for labour. Above all, the schools must fulfil the needs of the country, which needed less executives and more specialists. A radical transformation of its structure was therefore necessary to avoid the greater inconvenience lamented by all, namely that the students released from ten years of school were in a state of mind to devote themselves to intellectual pursuits and were unwilling, after so long a cultural apprenticeship, to assume the burden of manual labour in the factories and on the farms.

The sharpest criticisms were made by Khrushchev in a speech to the Congress of Communist Youth (Komsomol) in April 1958. He openly condemned the petit bourgeois tendencies of many students. 'Boys and girls,' he said, 'at the end of their ten-year schooling are unwilling to work in workshops, in the factories, in the kolkhozes, and in the sovkhozes. They consider such work as a personal insult. This princely and scornful attitude towards physical labour is also shown in many families. When a scholar does not study his parents say to him: "If you don't study you will not be able to go to the university and you will end up in a factory as a common workman."'

In fact, logic was on the side of the students. The ten-year school prepared them for the university. To forbid them entrance at the very moment when they were on the threshold could not but create considerable resentment. What use, then, was the general education given them for the past ten years? Was not so prolonged an intellectual effort excessive if at the end they could not make use of their intelligence but only of their hands which had not been trained for any trade? The incongruity lay in the fact that it was everyone's right to have a secondary education but it was not everyone's right to have a higher education. The logic was on the side of the parents who encouraged their children to study in order to better themselves. The utopia was in the mirage of setting up an impossible equality founded on the sophism that every difference between intellectual and manual labour had been abolished.

It was, however, surprising that whereas in fact the principle of equality had been sacrificed, the preamble to the law sanctioning the educational difference between workers and executives contained this statement: 'The Marxist-Leninist doctrine, confirmed by the practical experience of the Soviet Union in the building of communism as well as by the experience of the other socialist countries, has given the lie to the bourgeois legend about the inevitability of the existence, for all time, on the one hand of a grey mass of men destined to subservience and to heavy physical labour and on the other of a handful of men called by nature herself to think, to direct, to develop science, technology, literature and art.'

But surely it was just this distinction between these two categories that the scholastic reform was putting into force.

It was said that the major defect of the ten-year system was that it was divorced from life. 'The students know nothing of productive work,' stated Khrushchev in 1958. 'Society does not know what to do with these young people filled with vital energy, and consequently both they and their parents feel dissatisfied. The more we advance, the more this state of affairs is worsening instead of improving.'

The stress was therefore shifted to the need to create a skilled labour force. The secondary schools must produce skilled workers. But surely this compromises the training of the students destined for the universities, that is to say the creation of a sound and well-based general knowledge such as is indispensable for the flourishing of science, letters and the arts? That was the doubt which assailed many who took part in the discussion. Culture is theory, the enrichment of ideas, good judgment; if one passes from theory to practice one enters a quite different field, strictly limited and with very precise aims, very far from the unconfined horizons of knowledge.

An ingenious formula devised by Zelenko, chief of the Central Direction of Labour Reserves, was considered to have bridged this gap. It ran: 'Labour plus study for the masses; study plus labour for those destined for the universities.' But a concept like this only displayed more openly that difference between the masses and the pre-destined elect which, as has been said, was in contradiction to the principle of communist equality.

The practical concept prevailed. The secondary schools were for training workers. And since a young man, who has been studying up to the age of seventeen, brooks with difficulty the discipline and effort of manual labour, the term of compulsory school attendance was reduced from ten to eight years. Furthermore, students from the elementary classes had to be trained in the trades which would be entrusted to them, either in the fields or in the factories, when they had completed their studies. The preamble to the law of December 24, 1958 on the scholastic reform stressed that 'the accelerated development of the mechanization, the automation and the chemicalization of production, the wide application of electronics, the use of mechanical brains, the ever more widespread application of electrification and other conquests of science and technology, are radically altering the character of labour. The duties of the workers in the factories and collective farms are becoming ever closer in essence to those of the engineers, the technicians, the agricultural and other specialists. Workers of socialist production must be able to use up-to-date machinery and high precision tools; they must understand the practice of calculation and the use of complex technical drawings.'

From these premises flowed the necessity of splitting up secondary education into a vast echelon of specialized schools, always with the aim of training the labour force, that is to say the executants and not the executives. Though, the preamble went on:

'The statement that in a communist society physical labour would cease to exist is wrong; the gigantic technical advances made will immeasurably lighten physical labour, though it will continue to exist. . . The Soviet secondary school is called upon to train skilled men who know well the basic principles of science and are at the same time capable of systematic physical labour . . . Today, in certain cases, increased production is being slowed down by the insufficient technical training of some workers.'

The schools were subordinated to the needs of the seven-year plan. It was no coincidence that the school reform was approved at the same time as the plan. The schools must provide the specialized labour force and yield the high level of production needed for the fulfilment of the plan.

The law on school reform makes it compulsory for all children who have completed their seventh year to attend eight school classes, that is to say four elementary and four devoted to general and poly-technic training, known as 'the lesser secondary'. At the end of the eight-year period, which is free and compulsory, all students must go on to productive work combined, in various ways, with their studies. The compulsory education, spread over a period of eight years, is such as to lay a firm foundation on which to build a wider and more varied culture. Active productivity plays a large part in the eight compulsory classes. From the very first the children are taught to make little cardboard models, to design in clay and plasti-cine, to cultivate plants, to bind books, until they are able to work at a trade in the school classrooms.

Preference is given to the teaching of scientific subjects, especially mathematics and physics.

7

The Soviet state takes special care of young children from a very early age. In 1959 about three and a half million children were being taught in crèches and other pre-scholastic institutions at a cost of ten milliard rubles, equivalent to one milliard dollars. The seven-year plan provided for a tenfold increase in the number of such in-stitutions, the need for which is especially felt in a country where all women work. Farms and factories are encouraged to set up within their own ambient crèches and kindergartens. For similar reasons a great impetus has been given to the teachers' training colleges, which will be able to train two and a half million students by 1965. There is an evident tendency for the state to take over the care of children from their parents in order to concentrate them in its own institutions and to supervise their training unhindered by any outside influence. Communism sees in every human being a producer to be trained in order to increase his efficiency to the maximum.

Little by little as one passes from those children born during the war, and therefore fewer in number, to those born in normal years after the war, the school population increases. But plans have already been prepared for the education of this numerous population of future students. It is an example of planning that all governments should imitate.

8

As soon as the eight compulsory classes are over, the young people leave school for work; but they are given the most ample facilities and the maximum encouragement to go on with their studies whilst carrying on with their jobs.

In the school year 1960-61 the number of students enrolled in the upper secondary schools was 2,395,000 which rose to 2,600,000 in the school year 1962-63. There were four possibilities open to them: evening classes or correspondence courses, day schools for professional training, schools for technical-professional training, and specialized secondary schools for the formation of technicians destined to complete their education in the universities or other centres of higher education.

There is an evident preference for the evening schools and correspondence courses. The government has devoted the closest attention to them in order to make them as efficient as possible, with the aim of making them as soon as possible the universal secondary schools. These make it possible for those who work during the day, whether factory workers or peasants, to complete their professional education. The courses last for three years. This type of school, whether evening school or correspondence course, has become very popular. The greater number of Soviet specialists have been trained by them. The system has been spreading for about thirty years. Today it is estimated that 1,400,000 young people attend such schools without interfering with their daily jobs.

This is undoubtedly an urge for advancement that does credit to the Soviet people.

The correspondence schools especially have developed throughout the country, spreading outwards till local centres have been created for the guidance of individual students. At the beginning, at each of these schools thousands, even tens of thousands, of students enrolled for the courses. Almost all of them were in the big cities. But the popularity which they achieved induced the government to arrange that every higher grade school should set up evening class sections and correspondence sections. Their courses are exactly similar to those of the day schools. Once given this initial impulse, the organization has developed spontaneously, each school competing with another in increasing its network of sections. Some of them have been set up in the countryside near the collective farms or isolated factories.

The correspondence schools make use of radio and television, for almost all Russian families have sets. But generally speaking the evening classes are more popular than the correspondence schools.

Obviously an uncommon degree of endurance is needed to assume the burden of study after the fatigue of everyday work; but the young worker or peasant is assisted and given every facility, by explicit government order, by the directors of the enterprise where he works. They must spare him nightwork and overtime and grant him all the exemptions prescribed by law. This lightening of his everyday task without doubt stimulates enrolment for the courses.

At the end of the three-year period the student gets a certificate from the higher secondary school which opens the way to various institutes of higher education.

The day schools for professional training also have a three-year course. Enrolment in these schools is limited for each of the subjects taught according to the number of posts estimated to become available at the end of the course. The local soviets therefore keep the schools informed of their requirements in order to avoid unemployment or a shortage of well-trained men for each trade or productive activity.

In the day schools too education alternates with work. The industrial enterprises and the collective farms are both obliged to assist in the practical training of students, making them work either in the general departments or in the specialized departments according to the shifts arranged by the school. As his skill increases the student receives a certificate which sets his wages scale.

At the end of the course the students are able to enrol in one of the institutes for higher education.

The technical-professional schools have a completely different character which, as their name implies, provides for the qualification of the workers and are therefore diversified according to their specialized needs. Naturally these schools pay especial attention to regional requirements and keep in close touch with the enterprises, whether agricultural or industrial, to which they send skilled and qualified workers. The prevailing tendency is to group the types of specialization by sections in order to avoid wastage of effort in the multiplicity of too detailed courses. Indeed advances in technique require a general knowledge of the new processes which tend to extend to all industries: automation, mechanization and the like, all of which demand a thorough knowledge of electrotechnics, radiotechnics and electronics.

The qualifying courses last, according to their importance, from one to three years. The student devotes half his time to productive work, for which he is paid, and the school which provides his services must assure itself of an adequate financial reward as if it were a productive enterprise. The courses at these schools do not give right of access to higher educational institutions.

The technical schools, the so-called specialized secondary schools, are however intended to prepare executive cadres and are a preliminary to the universities. The duration of the course is from three to four years. For certain types of specialization they grant diplomas which permit the exercise of certain professions, similar to those granted by the institutes of higher education. Such, for example, are dentists, veterinarians, pharmacists and the like. In these schools too, though advanced theoretical training prevails, the students must obtain working qualifications by labour in the farms or workshops attached to the school. Special correspondence study sessions are organized in association with these schools with the result that, by the end of 1965, the enrolments for correspondence courses are expected to be double those for the normal course.

Finally, the courses organized by the main industrial enterprises are acquiring a growing importance. These aim at preparing those of their workers who have been to evening classes or taken correspondence courses for the entrance examinations to the universities or other higher educational institutes. It is in fact laid down in the school reform law that due heed must be paid to the recommendations of the directors of the enterprise in which the candidate has been working. Such a recommendation will be the more valid the better the preparation of the young candidate has been. These preparatory courses last eight or nine months and are held either in the enterprise itself or at some higher grade school. The popularity of such courses has encouraged the schools to increase their number. For example, the Institute of Mining at Moscow has organized a good sixteen preparatory study centres in the Donbass and Kuzbass districts. They are attended by nine hundred young miners, who are in this way preparing for their admission to the Institute.

9

The variety of the secondary schools and their countless welfare services, whether sponsored by the government or by the enterprises, is of valuable assistance to all workers who want to improve their education and thus find the way to better paid jobs with greater responsibility. This is healthy, intelligent and dynamic democracy which all countries, whatever their régime, would be well advised to imitate.

As can be seen, the main task of the school reform law is to sort out the students, at the end of their eight years compulsory education, into those intended to become workers and those destined for positions of command. The difficulty is to establish fair and equal criteria for all, on the basis of which to make the selection. Logic and justice would have it by merit alone. But that is not the prevailing criterion. Khrushchev said in 1958: 'The system, in force up to a short time ago, of creating privileged conditions by the admission into higher educational institutions of those who have won gold or silver medals has complicated the situation more than ever. There have been cases proved where pressure has been put on the teachers by parents who want their children to obtain such medals.'

But surely in such cases it is enough to punish those who have exercised such pressure and those who have yielded to it? A strong government like that of the Soviet Union surely does not lack means of prevention and repression? The reality is quite another thing. It appears clearly from Khrushchev's statement that social classes have once more been created. Those who belong to the upper class fight tooth and nail for their children too to belong to it. The resistance of a ruling class, above all one as new, unscrupulous and dynamic as this one is, ends by convincing any government that it must rely on just such a class because it holds in its hands the reins of administration and the economy of the country.

There is no doubt that one of the aims of the reform was to weaken these upper cliques. Two expedients were therefore devised; on the one hand the obligation for all young people to take a job at the end of their eight-year schooling. All students are therefore sent to work in the factories or the fields. On the other hand special norms were established to facilitate the entry of the workers into the universities and institutes. There are, it is true, competitive examinations but it is laid down that heed must be paid to the observations of the Party, of the trade unions, of the Komsomol and of the directors of the industrial and agricultural enterprises. Every candidate must have these political references. Other regulations, published in April 1961, prescribe that priority must be reserved for outstanding workers, world war veterans, officers demobilized in 1960, workers who have completed two years of labour and who have had favourable reports or have worked in the sector in which they intend to specialize after their enrolment in the university or other institute of equivalent standing.

In short, it is intended to open wide the gates to workers desirous of obtaining executive posts by giving primary importance to practical experience acquired in the exercise of a trade. In this way, practice is elevated to the same plane as theory. In putting forward so novel a criterion the Soviet régime is undoubtedly recalling the experience of the revolutionary period when the cadres of the old régime were replaced by working-class elements, badly trained if you will but dynamic and constructive, who proved themselves to be able leaders and organizers and to whom the powerful structure of the Soviet state is due. At that time there were impelling motives, proper to a period of social convulsion. But in a socialist state, based on the principal of the most absolute equality, preference for one group rather than another is a proof that such equality does not in fact exist.

Let it be quite clear; there is no reason to criticize, indeed there is every reason to praise, the government for encouraging the efforts of the workers to rise to positions of command. The idea of devoting the secondary schools to the training of technical craftsmen is new and bold, as is the criterion of associating work and study. The Western democracies have every interest in closely following such experiments, because they too have to face the problem of a shortage of qualified workers and technicians in an epoch in which new industrial processes demand both one and the other in ever greater numbers. No less evident is the need to bring the working class closer to the ruling class, to infuse new blood into the latter, and to facilitate the flow upward of persons gifted with character and intelligence. In fact it requires an energy out of the common to surmount the barriers of culture when the whole day has been devoted to manual labour. The directors of enterprises and the government must therefore put into force the best possible methods to assist such efforts, as the Soviet Union is doing. Anyone who emerges from the anonymous mass has proved himself a real force and it is a good thing to make use of him. The secret of the vitality and progress of a healthy democracy is in this process of osmosis and endomosis between classes and it is to be encouraged in every way.

But if the interests of the state and the enterprises in facilitating access to higher education for workers be justified, this does not justify these facilities becoming a privilege for some to the disadvantage of others. Culture cannot be the monopoly of a bourgeois class, nor of a proletarian class. It is especially obnoxious that the choice of students to be enrolled in the universities or equivalent institutes be governed by political influence, that is to say by recommendations of the Party, the trade unions and the Komsomol. Regulations of this kind are incompatible with the most elementary criteria of equality and justice. There is no really democratic state which could admit such partial interventions. What hopes of admission to the universities have those students who make no secret of holding religious, political or philosophical convictions disapproved of by the Party? To exclude them means to sacrifice the most straightforward characters and to encourage hypocrisy. The fact that the school reform law has introduced a political directive so little egalitarian leads one to believe that the Soviet state still feels the need, after forty-five years of existence, to discriminate between favourable and hostile elements, that is to say that it still fears the prevalence of opinions that it distrusts and which it seeks to check by limiting their influence.

Nor can it be seen clearly what value these directives ordained by Khrushchev can have in practice. This doubt is mainly concerning the value of the norm that forces all students to work at a trade after completing their eight-year schooling. It is easy to foresee what will happen. Sons of good families will find some way, by influence or recommendation, to be assigned to light work, so that they may continue their studies in comfort and prepare for their examinations in advantageous conditions over those employed in heavy daily manual labour. There are some schools, camouflaged as specialized schools, that exist especially for the preparation of young people who wish to enrol in the universities or institutes of higher education. Such are the Suvorov and Nakhimov Academies, schools reserved for the children of high officials, who are given a military training; there are also foreign language schools for the children of highly placed bureaucrats or Party leaders. These have been founded in recent years at Moscow, Leningrad, Kiev and the capitals of the federated republics. They accept pupils who already have a rough knowledge of some foreign language which they have learnt at home. It is clearly not an easy task to uproot a 'bourgeoisie' embedded in positions of command and determined to defend them by every means in its power.

This Soviet bourgeoisie has also succeeded in having a clause inserted in the 1958 school reform law which ensures that not less than twenty per cent of the places in the higher grade institutes be reserved for those who have completed their secondary schooling but who have not worked in industry. The children of bourgeois families who, previous to the reform, held sixty, even seventy, per cent of the places available now compete for this twenty per cent. There is always a large percentage of students who have finished their eight years compulsory education and who do not intend to complete the period of labour in the workshops or fields prescribed by law, and who have therefore no possibility of acquiring higher education. To avoid the danger that these might swell the army of parasites, the federal republics have published decrees 'for the intensification of the campaign against those who abstain from socially useful work and live an anti-social and parasitic life'. Such young people are threatened with compulsory residence orders and directed labour for from two to five years. This means the imposition of forced labour.

10

The Soviet school system culminates in the University of Moscow, with its pinnacles and tall towers enthroned like a cathedral on the Lenin hills which dominate the city. It is the citadel of culture and one of the great achievements of the régime. Here are gathered the cream of the cream of the men of learning and here are reviewed and debated the most important problems of culture.

From the time of its foundation in 1755 by the efforts of the great scholar Lomonosov, whose name it bears, the University of Moscow has been the cradle of the Russian ruling class and the most active instrument of the diffusion of knowledge. It was, at first, situated on the Red Square facing the Kremlin, as if to oppose the power of force by the power of the spirit.

In 1959 the student body numbered about twenty-two thousand. Of these, fourteen thousand attended the day courses, four thousand six hundred the evening courses and three thousand five hundred took correspondence courses. Those enrolled in the correspondence courses are scattered throughout the whole territory of the Soviet Union and come to Moscow twice a year for the examinations.

The teaching body is made up of 1,948 teachers and 879 assistants, technicians to whom is entrusted the care of the scientific equipment. This is placed at the disposal not only of the teachers and students but of countless aspirants who, having completed the university course, wish to specialize in some specific scientific field. This equipment is very comprehensive and up-to-date and serves the several thousand post-graduates who attend the university. Amongst them are hundreds of members of various academies, from the Academy of Sciences to similar institutes existing in the federated republics.

The University of Moscow has fourteen faculties, with two hundred and fourteen chairs. They have at their disposal two hundred and fifty laboratories and a hundred and sixty-three special study sections. Four institutes for scientific research form part of the university: mechanics, nuclear physics, astronomy and anthropology. The university has founded eight centres for practical scientific studies where the students can carry out scientific research. It also has three museums: geological, zoological and anthropological, as well as botanical gardens and five astronomical observatories.

University instruction is free. Furthermore, the greater number of students receive state grants; if the student gets good marks the grant is increased.

The courses last five years, with the exception of the physics courses which last five and a half.

The university curriculum is of the widest sort. The student of any subject has to have a wide general knowledge embracing every subject kindred to his study to enable him to get a firm grip on an entire sector of knowledge. The graduate thus acquires a rich cultural background which allows him to go on, independently, to further studies and research. During his university courses he trains himself by collaboration with his instructors in their scientific researches. This creates the best possible atmosphere for the ferment of ideas, thanks to the communion of interests established in these forcing houses of learning. The Soviet Union has thus been able to form a valuable reserve of specialists, research students and inventors imbued with the maximum of enthusiasm and driven to express themselves by original work. The student leaves the university as an expert in laboratory work, aware of the most recent investigations and therefore ready to launch out for himself, using the goals attained by his instructors as points of departure.

Everything is systematically laid down in a study plan to which the student must rigorously adhere. The plan lays down the lectures he must attend, the seminars in which he must take part, the practical work to be carried out in industrial or agricultural enterprises and the laboratory experiments. The seminars integrate the regular course laid down in the lectures, leaving to the student the choice of subjects with which he intends to integrate his training.

There are two examination sessions; in January and in June. When presenting themselves for examination, the students follow the order of subjects laid down in their plan of studies. Anyone who does not present himself for examination loses his state grant for the whole term.

The penultimate year is devoted to practical work. During this year the student continues his course either at evening classes or by correspondence. When it is over, he returns to the day classes and prepares, on the basis of the practical knowledge he has acquired, his doctoral thesis, in which he must prove not only the solidity of his theoretical and practical training but also his originality in envisaging practical solutions, the fruit of his studies and research.

By the serious nature of its studies, the authority of its teaching body, the strict nature of its research and the progress achieved in many branches of knowledge, the University of Moscow enjoys the highest prestige throughout the world. Students flock there from all countries, as at one time to the University of Bologna. Cultural centres like Moscow add prestige to a régime and splendour to an epoch. The cities in which these centres of learning have their seat become capitals of world culture. It was thanks to institutions of this sort, and especially to the Library and the Museum, that the Ptolemies assured Alexandria for many centuries her place as the controlling centre of world culture. The authority of such centres is solely due to the high level of the teaching staff. The Moscow University enjoys especial fame for the teaching of mathematics, physics, biology and, in general, all the natural sciences. Many of the learned men teaching there have achieved world-wide fame.

In 1959 five hundred foreign students from about fifty countries attended the University of Moscow. Today the foreign students attend the Friendship University founded especially for them. Of even greater interest is the attendance of more than three hundred post-graduates from foreign universities.

In building the new university on the Lenin hills the Soviet has clearly been inspired by American models. Has it succeeded in surpassing them? It is worth while quoting the opinion of the correspondent of the Christian Science Monitor, Nate White, in an article published in July 1960 after a trip to the Soviet Union. He says that the lecture rooms are excellent and the dormitories luxurious. The student has every up-to-date comfort. The study rooms are vast and the libraries abundantly provided with carpets. Moscow University can challenge comparison with Columbia University, but it is not so large nor has it as many departments of specialized instruction. Nor can it be compared, in size or in specialization, with the University of California or of Michigan, or the Northwestern or the University of Chicago.

It is clear, however, that the importance of a university is due to the reputation and quality of its teaching rather than to the size and convenience of its premises.

11

In the Soviet Union there are thirty-nine universities with three hundred faculties and two thousand chairs, as well as about eight hundred institutes of higher education attended by more than two million two hundred thousand students in all.

The universities differ from the institutes of higher education by the greater number of courses that they give, by the mainly theoretical nature of their teaching and by their aim of training learned men, researchers and teachers. The higher educational institutes devote themselves to strictly limited sectors for the training of highly skilled technical specialists. The interest in creating more and more specialized faculties and institutes is such that in engineering alone there are one hundred and eighty-two specialized centres and the Higher Institute of Power at Moscow is able to confer degrees in nine special subjects and twenty-four sub-subjects.

In the higher institutions too study alternates with practical work, which is carried out either in the laboratories or the industrial enterprises of the institutes themselves, or in autonomous factories. The student acquires a technical qualification and may then expect first subordinate and later responsible positions. Only at the end of his apprenticeship is he allowed to present his thesis for his doctorate, which must prove his capacity for organization and initiative.

About half of those enrolled take the correspondence courses. Anyone may enrol for them without an entrance examination. The tuition is exactly the same as for the normal courses. The degree conferred on those enrolled in the correspondence courses is equal in every respect to that conferred on students attending the normal courses.

The state aims at making these correspondence courses and evening classes universal. In order to encourage their diffusion and make them more and more convenient, a system of follow-up assistance to the students enrolled has been organized through consultation centres, to each one of which a specific group of students is assigned. Inspectors are appointed to maintain personal contact between students and teachers, to clear up uncertainties and correct false impressions. They are at the beck and call of the students, provide them with textbooks and, in fact, carry out the duties of a university assistant, forming a link between the student and the professor.

12

What considerations should prompt a detailed examination of the Soviet school organization in the light of the first results of the reform?

It should be recalled, first of all, that the eight-year school period became compulsory in 1962. At that time, however, the school organization was insufficient to cope with the increased number of students, nor were the laboratories attached to the schools sufficient to train the children in a trade. In many centres, therefore, the schools function in three shifts, the last of which, given the shortness of daylight in the Russian winter, takes place by electric light or, often enough, by the light of oil-lamps.

Boarding schools, to which the state attributes so much importance for the training of the new communist man and which help to facilitate the access of the sons of peasants and workers to higher education, are still very few.

The evening classes are likewise insufficient. These deficiencies are mainly the fault of the governments of the federated republics, on which the control of the higher educational institutes has also devolved.

There are considerable differences of opinion on the suitability of making young people break off, after the compulsory eight-year schooling, and take up a trade. It has been noted that when they resume their higher studies they show serious gaps in their training and a reduced capacity to adapt themselves to the intellectual effort that the difficult training requires. The academician Sobolev in the review Yunost (no. 6, 1962) states that the examining commission of the University of Novosibirsk remarked that the young people who had interrupted their studies at the end of their compulsory schooling had only a limited and superficial knowledge which made it difficult for them to follow the mathematics and physics courses, for which an effort of concentration was necessary. These young people did not seem to be able to accustom themselves to any systematic activity, such as that required by creative work. Similar comments have been made by the academician Kuznetsov on the results achieved by the students enrolled for the courses in biology, chemistry and physics. Even blunter was the opinion of the academician Nesmeyanov that attendance at day classes is necessary for advanced studies; the evening classes and correspondence courses make a poor substitute for regular study.

Many criticisms have been levelled at the criterion which is at the base of the reform, namely that of associating labour with study. In this way, the criticisms claim, no one can work or study properly. It imposes an excessive burden on the children which affects their health during a delicate period of physical and mental growth. In most cases the work that the student does during the compulsory eight-year course is a mere pretence because of the lack of well-equipped workrooms and the scant attention both of teachers and pupils. It is also claimed that by making labour obligatory an effect exactly contrary to that intended is achieved, that is to say that instead of inculcating love of physical work it makes the students loathe it.

The young people enrolled in the evening classes or correspondence courses must devote ten hours a day to work and study and therefore have to renounce sport, amusements, reading, the theatre, music and all that makes life rich and gay. It is not only the teachers at the higher institutes who complain of this burdensome association of work with study but also the directors of the enterprises who, driven by the need to fulfil quotas for the general plan and, if possible, exceed them, look askance at the student workers who cannot give to their work the effort demanded from the rest of the employees and who create a slackening of the productivity of the enterprise. In fact it cannot be said that the aim pursued by the régime, and in particular by Khrushchev, to facilitate access to higher educational establishments for workers and peasants has been attained, just because of the excessive overburdening imposed upon those who aspire to it. An increased apathy has been noted among the students at the evening classes and of the correspondence courses and a lack of progress which often compels them to repeat their classes. In fact the inflow of young peasants to the higher agricultural institutes, or even to the agricultural schools, has been very small.

These criticisms are by now widespread and have even been echoed by the leaders. It cannot, therefore, be said that the results of the reform have been all that was hoped; it has been suggested on many sides that the criteria should now be re-examined on the basis of experience.

What no one dares to mention is the damage and irritation caused by the priority granted to communist, that is to say political, education at the expense of scientific education. In all schools there are courses on 'the fundamentals of political knowledge' and on 'social science'. In the higher-grade schools there are also courses on 'the fundamentals of atheism'. The practical application of this teaching is by means of lectures which the students are asked to give to workers and members of the kolkhozes.

But despite these darker aspects, the merits of the present school organization are far from lacking and are incontestable.

First and foremost, study is taken very seriously in the Soviet Union. Perhaps in no other country do the teachers devote themselves to their job with such enthusiasm, nor do the students take such pains to profit by it. In no country are academic titles so much used, or honoured by so much prestige. The title of doctor is not won merely by graduation after university studies, but only after a long scientific apprenticeship during which the student must have given proof of his worth by research and publication which qualify him to present a thesis for his doctorate. The Soviet university student lives a life of monastic austerity. He maintains himself during his studies on the stipend granted him by the state. The state does not want to spend money uselessly and, therefore, at the first signs of slackness strikes him from the rolls. Whoever is thus struck off has no further prospects and is forced to go into a factory or the fields and must content himself with the meagre wages paid to those who do manual work. The student is therefore continually goaded by a lively sense of personal responsibility. He knows that he must win the first and hardest battle of his life, in fierce competition with his fellows, equally resolute to contest the prize with him. Therefore in the Soviet universities there is an atmosphere of intense fervour, quite different from the *vie de bohème* which still predominates in many Western universities.

Soviet teachers devote themselves exclusively to teaching and scientific activities. Their pay is among the highest granted by the state. They also enjoy very great prestige. The state, the public bodies and the great enterprises frequently refer to them for advice.

The Soviet Union, which has renounced every religious belief and every form of idealism, expects from the advance of knowledge confirmation of the materialist conception fundamental to its doctrine. Science takes the place of faith. And it is with the enthusiasm of neophytes that this cult of science is practised. Universities and institutes of higher education, in addition to being teaching centres, are research centres. Half of the researchers of the Soviet Union work in the higher grade schools, combining teaching with scientific work, in such a way as always to be abreast of the most recent advances in science and experiment. The students collaborate with the teachers and share with them their passion for research. There is a growing tendency to merge the institutes of higher education with the institutes of scientific research which prepare the university graduates who aspire to become doctors. Almost all the higher schools are associated with vast industrial complexes whose activities they follow, whose problems they study and to which they suggest solutions. Science is allied in the most practical way with technical production. Thus projects, innovations and improvements come from the schools. In the Archangelsk Forestry Institute, for example, the students have inaugurated the technical reforms suggested by the timber industry. The students of the Khabarovsk Institute of Railway Engineering have provided the Far Eastern Railways with twenty-two projects, all applied successfully. Six of the originators immediately received offers of employment.

It is estimated that in the course of one year the schools have carried out research on thirty thousand problems, some of them set by the regional economic councils and the industrial enterprises. The value of this collaboration induces the economic councils and the large enterprises to donate the necessary equipment to the schools, provide them with instructors, and finance studies and experiments. Thus the siderurgical plant at Magnitogorsk, in collaboration with the Institute of Mineralogy and Metallurgy in that city, has put five research centres into operation. The institutes of scientific research are also accustomed to conclude agreements with the enterprises for the study of specific technical problems. In 1963 the total number of such agreements involved payments by the enterprises of eight hundred million rubles.

The stress is shifting more and more from pure theory to practical application. The academician A. N. Nesmeyanov has summed up this tendency by saying: 'The most important thing, in life as in science, is to know how to apply one's knowledge.'

Consistent with this tendency is the idea, which is growing, of transferring wholesale many of the professional schools and higher grade institutes into the framework of the factories and collective farms, because the teaching centres must serve production and can carry out their task better by being in direct touch with the productive factors for which their teaching is intended and for which their aid is of use.

Certain dangers of this stress on practice have already been noted. There is a risk of transforming the eight-year schooling into a school of arts and crafts and the higher secondary training school into a sort of apprenticeship.

Moreover, whereas the combination of study and practical work is justified in technological subjects and especially in engineering, it is hard to see what importance it may have in the training of anyone who intends to devote himself to subjects of mainly theoretical character such as mathematics, physics, chemistry, biology, medical science and especially letters and the arts, philology, philosophy, law, journalism, languages or political economy. But even from these last a period of practical work is demanded. For example, students in the first year of Russian history, language and literature or of economics, work during the day and attend evening classes or study correspondence courses. This work, which is compulsory during the first year, has nothing to do with their future profession; but it is believed that it allows them to acquire the habit of working and gives them experience of life. All this one is permitted to doubt.

Clearly a revolutionary order of this nature can only be carried out in a country not bound by the tradition of classical studies, a country which has broken with the past and which looks only to-

wards the future. The motivation of all those who took part in the
debates on the school reform was to take full account of present day
needs and of provision for the future education of young people.

In a milieu of humanist culture, as is the greater part of the
Western world, the Soviet system would have to be adapted to
differing needs and subjected to suitable modifications. But some of
its fundamental directives, which respond to the spirit of the times,
would be worth retaining, even if merely not to lose ground before
the undeniable advances of the Soviet people in the fields of science
and technology.

One of the most striking results of Soviet educational policy is the
ever greater prominence taken by persons from ethnic groups which
were until now deprived of strong distinctive character and which
ran the risk of disappearing in the melting pot of races that makes
up the Soviet world. The instruction given them in their own
languages has created a national consciousness in many of these
groups. The Soviet Union has within it more than a hundred peoples
of differing origin and differing languages. Only now have the
greater number of these an opportunity to develop their own talents
and show their originality, not only in technology and the sciences,
but in letters and the arts. At Tashkent I went to a musical show
composed by Uzbeks, based on Uzbek legends, and played by Uzbek
actors. A young world enters history or rather re-enters history. The
Soviet government and the communist party assist the cultural
efforts of these ethnic groups with the aim of binding them ever
more closely to it by the influence which the dominant ideology and
Russian models exercise in inspiring the nascent art-forms and
literature of all these peoples. What happened in the West nineteen
centuries ago when Celts, Iberians, Teutons and Britons began to
emerge as a part of, and by the influence of, Latin civilization is
being repeated here.

Poetry, narrative, theatre and dance are the first forms in which
the creative ability of a new people is shown. In Russia the writers
are a privileged body because of the broad interpretation given to
authors' rights. Every city, even if only of minor importance, has
its own theatre, even as Rome built amphitheatres and circuses
everywhere. The dance, one of the most expressive Slav art-forms,
has been widely diffused by the Russians, encouraging the innate
tendency of all young peoples to translate their feelings and their
ideas into gesture and rhythm.

In the immense territory of the Soviet Union books circulate in
millions of copies. The peoples of the Union, though differing among
themselves, are being drawn closer together. There is a vast surge of
reciprocal influences. The peopling of the vast spaces of Siberia fills

a void existent for centuries. The world which is rising there, rich in cities, in industries, in schools, accepts and harmonizes the ideas that flow in upon it from all sides, from Europe, from India, from Islam and from China. Institutes of oriental languages and civilization multiply, especially in Central Asia and Siberia, and carry out a valuable work of collection, study and publication of works of every origin. For centuries the great centres of Western, Chinese, Islamic and Indian culture were kept apart by the deserts of Central Asia and the nomad world, warlike and plundering, which intervened like a barrier between the settled societies where high civilization flourished. Today this centre of the Asian continent, which has remained so long inviolate, is beginning to open to all these life currents and has become the crucible of new peoples and civilizations.

Most of these peoples, whether of Turkish or Mongol race, have shown aptitude for the exact sciences, especially for mathematics, similar to that which made them famous in the centuries of their splendour. Thus the circle of elements that contribute to the advance of knowledge is being widened.

According to Soviet forecasts the present thirty million pupils of the eight-year compulsory schools will become forty-five million in 1965. The specialists with higher education will therefore increase proportionately to four and a half million. The seven-year plan forecasts that, during its term, the number of those taking degrees will be two million three hundred thousand.

Thus strengthened by its executive cadres and its technicians, the Soviet Union is preparing to increase the exploitation of its resources until it achieves world primacy.

CHAPTER VI

Higher Scientific and Technical Education

1

THE first application of scientific education was in the field of geological prospecting, which is the basis of industrial progress.

Thanks to the technical cadres formed in the schools, the Soviet Union has been able to go on to locate and exploit its immense natural resources.

The inventory of this wealth was begun in tsarist times but with insufficient means, fragmentarily and in very limited areas. The Soviet Union has continued it with a superabundance of means, systematically and over its whole territory.

The new hero of the régime is the geologist, the discoverer of the country's treasures, the technician provided with the arms of science and with perfected instruments, who explores the land foot by foot and sounds the entrails of the earth. Often he presses onward into the *taiga* or the tundra where human foot has never trod. He uses the most modern methods of geological prospecting and the most modern techniques, such as gravimetry, seismometry and aeromagnetic relief maps. All are aids for locating mineral deposits. Studies are based on the stratification of the earth-crust, and from these studies tectonic and stratigraphic plans are drawn up which aid the researches of the geophysicists.

Siberia alone has fifteen geological-geographical institutes. Each of them plans its researches in the area of its jurisdiction, organizing on-the-spot investigations so that no section of the country is left unexplored.

In this way were found the enormous oil reserves between the Volga and the Urals, the almost inexhaustible gas deposits south of Bukhara, the colossal iron ore deposits in the Kustanai region and in the Angarà-Ilim district and the great diamond-bearing area of Yakutya. It is as if the Soviet geologists had made a gift of fabulous riches to the Soviet Union, the like of which no one before had even suspected.

One of the greatest results of these systematic researches is the discovery that valuable mineral deposits exist even in the zone of eternal ice. Thus were located the coalfields of the Pechora basin, the Tunguska and the Lena, the gold-bearing terrains of Yakutya and the copper ores of Kunrad and Dzhezkazgan.

The order to extend prospecting over the whole area of the country was given by Lenin who wished to verify all the productive resources of Russia, not only agricultural and forest but mineral and hydrological as well. He ordered not only the geological exploration of the country but also the study of its flora and fauna. The decision of the Council of Labour and Defence on August 24, 1920 to 'explore the magnetic anomaly of Kursk' was a historic event. This brought to light the rich iron ore deposits of that region.

To carry out Lenin's orders more than fifty thousand persons, including ten thousand engineers and technicians, took part in the systematic prospecting of the country. Every year an average of six hundred geological expeditions are organized and provided with land, sea and air transport, including helicopters, to reach the most inaccessible regions.

Thanks to the work of these researchers the academician D. V. Nalivkin was able to compile the geological map of the Soviet Union which was published in 1956 and won him the Lenin prize. Thenceforward the discoveries have gone on, some of them of fundamental importance like that of the methane-bearing deposits of Uzbekistan which was followed by other discoveries of the same gas, either nearby or in more remote areas. It often happens that the exploitation of a mine is followed by the discovery of others of even greater importance. The territory is immense and it is not impossible that sensational discoveries are still to come. For example it is believed that the oil-fields of Central Asia and north-west Kazakstan are not less rich than those of the Middle East, whose reserves amount to three-quarters of the total reserves of the capitalist world. Similarly, after the discovery of the diamond-bearing deposits in Yakutya, other fields were found in the Urals, in the Ukraine, in the Pechora basin and in Siberia.

Between 1928 and 1945 the Soviet Union spent 23,600 million rubles on scientific research, a great part of which was devoted to prospecting. In the 1950 budget a figure of 5,600 million rubles was set aside for scientific research, together with a contribution from the funds of the industrial enterprises amounting to another 2,500 million, making a total equivalent to 810 million dollars.

2

The supreme authority for the study and exploitation of these resources comes from the institutes of scientific research. The Soviet Union has created a dense network of such study centres, which have a personnel of three hundred and fifty thousand persons. Some of these experts are pure scientists, such as mathematicians and astronomers, others are practical men such as inventors and researchers; lastly there is the highest category of all, nuclear physicists, biologists and the like. All have an abundance of laboratories, museums and scientific work centres which are among the best-equipped in the world. This hierarchy of scientists is entrusted with the task of advancing the progress of the country, not only cultural but economic, military, hygienic and social.

The research institutes for industrial production are worthy of special mention. There are over a thousand of them and they are dependent on the sovnarkhozes, that is to say on the departments that preside over the economic development of individual regions. These institutes are centres for invention and design and are completely independent of the productive enterprises. The sovnarkhozes have their own technical consultants who see to the detailed study and planned execution of the directives given them. They also suggest new technical methods and new methods of production. Some of these research bodies, for reasons of convenience, are near the great industrial plants but they keep their complete administrative and financial independence. They obtain their financial resources from the state budget, from the funds of the sovnarkhozes and from payments received from individual enterprises for contracts of service. These too have, as has been said, their own research laboratories and technical departments. Very well equipped 'problem laboratories' have been built, each with a highly skilled staff to assist the experts and students in their search for the answers to the most difficult scientific problems.

Lastly, the inventive skill of the workers is stimulated by prizes for those who suggest useful innovations and improvements. It is estimated that millions of such proposals are winnowed each year by special factory committees. The worker can even appeal to the Society of Inventors in order to get a better reward.

3

Over this immense ferment of study and research presides the controlling organ of all Soviet culture, the Academy of Sciences, which is the brightest star in the constellation of its fellows in the individual federal republics. All these academies follow similar working methods and are organized along similar lines, developing the tasks assigned to them either directly or through the scientific institutes created by them, which are the specialized organs in sectors of particular interest.

Of equal importance is the Academy of Agricultural Science.

Little by little as more importance is paid to the development of one or another region, the network of cultural organizations is extended. Thus, by decision of the Council of Ministers in May 1957, a Siberian branch of the Academy of Sciences was founded in Novosibirsk. A picturesque spot in the heart of the forests was chosen for its site. This new centre, Gorod Nauki, has thirteen research centres, a university, living quarters and services; it is a city of science extending over eleven hundred hectares. Among the problems entrusted to this complex are those connected with terrestrial magnetism, the ionosphere and the propagation of radio waves. The personnel numbers 2,658 teachers including eleven academicians. The new city is intended, among other things, to train an élite of young experts.

Similarly, in Kazakstan, which is one of the great mining centres of the Soviet Union, there is an Academy of Sciences with five dependent institutes and twenty laboratories scattered through the more important mining areas. Both the Academy and the institutes devote their activities to research and the study of the mineral resources of the region. Thanks to their prospecting work more than three hundred and fifty metal-bearing deposits have been found, some of them of rare metals.

The academies do creative and original work of real value. They are the scientific framework of the Soviet Union and the great organizing force of progress and civilization. They have very close links with the universities. The Moscow Academy of Sciences sends to the Moscow University certain of its more famous members even as it, in its turn, welcomes many of the leading university teachers among its members.

The academies give scientific advice to the state executive and expect from it the order of priority established by the government for the study of the problems entrusted to them.

It is due to this formidable organization that the Soviet Union has come to the fore in many scientific and technical fields, has been able to make its army one of the most powerful war machines in the world, has taken the leading place in missile construction, space science and astronautical techniques, has carried out an intense industrialization of the whole country and has changed the climatic conditions of vast areas by a bold irrigation technique.

4

Professor V. Yepelov, teacher of mathematical physics at the Leningrad Polytechnic Institute, in a press interview in December 1960 revealed how the young generation of Soviet experts is being formed. It is to its work that Soviet nuclear physics and electrotechnics owe the leading place which they now hold in the world. 'Let us see,' he said, 'what sort of schools have produced the greatest number of leaders in nuclear physics, electrotechnics and electrical engineering. The Leningrad Polytechnic Institute must certainly be considered as one of the best. This is now a historical fact. Men of science of world fame, such as the academicians Alikhanov, Kondratev, Kikoin, Semenov, Kostenko and Khariton and the professors Efremov, Valter and others, have come from this institute. Why should this be? The Leningrad Polytechnic Institute has excellent laboratories with first-class equipment. The students listen to the lectures of leading scientists and work with them during their third year. I know, for example, that the academicians Alikhanov and Skobeltsyn have made many discoveries in the Institute's laboratories; and the students worked with them. All the professors live near the Institute, as do the students who have rooms in a nearby dormitory. The institute run by academician Yoffe is just on the other side of the street and that run by academician Semenov is quite near. The most important thing is that the students have the chance to watch the most recent procedures every day and every hour and can get their knowledge directly from the lips of the professors.

'The scientists, for their part, are genuinely interested in getting to know their students well and in distinguishing the most able amongst them. In the majority of cases,' Yepelov declared, 'our best work has been produced by young people who have already become experts, since a young person is formed by great responsibilities and not by trivialities.'

The sort of responsibility and initiative left to the younger scientists and even to the students is specified by another eminent personality, Professor D. Blokhintsev, Director of the Institute for Nuclear Research. 'Davidov and I,' he said, 'studied under Igor Yevgenyevich Tamm. He was a real master in the best sense of the word. He was always ready to help us. But to do that we had to go to him with our ideas, our projects and our problems. He guided us with advice and criticism. It would have been silly for us to wait for him to give us plans already complete and perfected.

To sum up: the great progress of Soviet science is due to two factors, the very advanced equipment of the universities and the close communion between teachers and students, both the one and the other gripped by a single passion—the quest for knowledge.

The progress made in the exploration of cosmic space and astronautical technique has also been due to the studies in the universities and higher educational institutes and research centres, beginning with the Academy of Sciences. All these bodies are interested in the solution of the countless problems raised by space exploration. 'The alloys of which the hull of the space-ship *Vostok* (in which Gagarin made his first space flight) were made,' wrote *Izvestia* on April 17, 1961, commenting on that epic enterprise, 'the fuel that launched it into the cosmos, the computers that determined its trajectory and all the rest of the equipment were the factors which, taken as a whole, made that magnificent technical achievement possible.' The newspaper quoted only a few of these factors. It must be remembered that the space-ship was composed of about three hundred thousand parts which had to work with absolute accuracy. Thousands of researchers, inventors, technicians, scientists, mathematicians, studied the details of this remarkable construction. Their efforts were co-ordinated by a group of exceptionally intelligent men, gifted with encyclopaedic knowledge, who had drawn up the master plan and allocated the parts. The exceptional number of brains ready to undertake such difficult tasks, trained to make use of the most complicated equipment and to work in team spirit on the vastest scale, is much to be admired.

Even more important than the construction of the space-ship was the operation of the launching pad. The ship must move in an accurately planned orbit, must pass through the atmosphere in a precisely calculated manner lest it catch fire. Its navigation must be accurately controlled both in flight and on landing. An error of calculation could mean a deviation of tens of kilometres from the prearranged landing site and lead to disaster. There were also biological, physiological, hygienic and nutrition problems which had to be carefully investigated. This immense mass of difficulties was faced and overcome in record time.

It would be possible to say similar things about irrigation techniques, the web of great catchment basins and the gigantic hydroelectric power stations. The Moscow Institute of Hydraulic Design is one of the great centres for the planning of such works. It planned the Volga-Urals canal, four hundred and fifty kilometres long, twenty-five metres wide and seven metres deep. Two pumping stations raise the level of the water by forty metres. Eight million hectares of pasture land and one million hectares of ploughland can be irrigated. Other projects forecast whole rivers passing in tunnels under mountain chains. We have already mentioned the project for the reversal of the courses of the Pechora and Vychegda rivers from the Arctic to the Caspian by using the bed of a third river, the Kama. Three immense reservoirs will collect the waters of the rivers and together will cover an area of fifteen thousand five hundred square kilometres. Thanks to this immense mass of water the level of the Caspian, which has fallen two metres below the average in recent years, will again be raised.

Geological, meteorological, biological and glaciological studies of the Arctic coastline have made it possible to organize navigation along the northern seaway, following the course of the North-East Passage. Navigation is regular in the fine season and there are ports and airports under the control of a general administration.

CHAPTER VII

Industrialization

1

THE most remarkable achievement of the scientific and technical progress of the Soviet Union has been its industrialization. The merit should undoubtedly be given to Stalin. He was, it is true, inspired by Lenin's directives but it was he who laid down clearly the planned lines of a continuous process, who created the organization, procured the means, initiated the series of five-year plans. It was under him that the two great leaps forward in industrial production took place, the first from 1928, the date of the first five-year plan, till Russia's entry into the war, the second from 1948, that is to say from the period of renewal followed by the rapid reconstruction of the war damage, up to the time of his death. In the first period, from 1928 to 1940, the value of capital equipment, machines and plant, increased tenfold, rising from 8.5 milliard rubles to 84.8 milliard rubles. In the second, production itself almost trebled, reaching 240 milliard rubles, a value thirty times greater than that at the commencement of the first *pytiletka*.[1]

In boasting of this formidable progress, the Soviets are apt to minimize the productive efforts of tsarist times. But it is a fact that the foundations of Soviet industry were laid by the tsars and some of their shrewd and energetic ministers.

The first Russian industrial enterprises date back to Peter the Great, who called on German, English and Dutch technicians to organize them. Modern industry, however, only made its appearance in Russia in the second half of last century, mainly thanks to Witte, who also called on foreign technicians and capital. This last amounted, before the revolution, to the value of 1,168,500,000 dollars.

There were five centres where industries of primary importance were developed: the capital, Petrograd, with heavy industries, Moscow with textiles, the Donetz coalfields or Donbass, the Ukrainian iron and steel centres and the Baku oil-fields.

[1] Harry Schwartz; *Russia's Soviet Economy*, Prentice-Hall, Inc., 2nd edition, 1961.

For more than half a century progress was exceptionally rapid and successful. If Soviet industry can boast of expanding with a rhythm which is amongst the most rapid in the industrial world today, the industrial growth of tsarist times was in no way different. The American economist Harry Schwartz recalls that between 1885 and 1889, and later between 1907 and 1913, the average rate of increase, often exceeding 8%, surpassed that of any other country, including the United States, Great Britain and Germany which were the leading industrial powers of the time.

The Soviet régime has made use of these foundations to industrialize the whole of Russia. The exploitation of its resources proceeds on so vast a scale that it cannot be paralleled in any other country. America, which has made the colonization of the Far West legendary, has long been overtaken by the transformation of the vast expanses between the Caspian and the Pacific. The centre of gravity of Russian economic power is moving eastward and southward. The effort is above all concentrated in Siberia, in Central Asia and in Kazakstan, which reveal almost inexhaustible riches. The directives for this development were given by Lenin. In opposition to Bukharin, who insisted on the priority of agricultural development, Lenin opted for industry. Many reasons, not all of them economic, justified his preference. The strength of the revolution was in the workers. The peasants had maintained a wavering, egoistic and suspicious attitude, similar to that of all rural populations. The countryside was, moreover, over-populated and it was necessary to reduce the human burden on the soil by transferring some of the peasants to the factories. Lenin supported the idea of distributing the factories equally throughout the country. He therefore smashed the narrow framework of the industrial concentration of tsarist times and gave orders that industry must be developed on the actual production sites of new materials and in the most densely populated cities.

Trotsky was a faithful interpreter of Leninist ideas and used them as a basis for a programme of country-wide industrialization imbued with the idea of the predominance of heavy industry. Stalin had him attacked by Bukharin with the accusation of wanting the super-industrialization of the country; but, once Trotsky was eliminated, the dictator took over his programme, applied it rigorously and set up a directive which has prevailed until now and which Khrushchev too made his own.

The keystone of the economic development of the Soviet Union is electrification. On this point too Lenin was farseeing and put electrical potential in the leading place. This would provide an unlimited quantity of low-cost power, a prime condition for a development of productive activity which would give Russia an absolute advantage over all the other industrial countries.

Lenin's successors gave second place to the exploitation of the mineral resources, equally unlimited, of the country.

The combination of these three factors, low-paid labour from the countryside, cheap electrical power in almost unlimited quantity and raw materials of all kinds, easily produced and almost inexhaustible, explain the miracle of the rapid Soviet industrialization under the leadership of excellent technicians trained in the Soviet schools.

The opinion current in the Soviet Union is that only from a greatly developed industry, especially electrical, chemical and mechanical, can be expected an improvement in agriculture with an expansion of the cultivable area and increased yields. Khrushchev put on the same plane as the electrification of the country wished by Lenin the 'chemicalization of the economy', regarded as the keystone of an abundant agricultural production and a wide distribution of low-cost consumer goods.

2

These ideas and programmes have been growing more definite and developing side by side with Soviet technical advances. However prophetic was Lenin's vision in stressing the development of electrification as the lever of economic progress, the aims that he set himself were extremely modest. They were set out in the famous GOELRO (State Commission for Electrification) plan drawn up in 1920 which aimed at the construction of local power stations at Volkhov and on the Dnieper for the production of 8,800 million kwh. But by 1959 the Soviet Union was producing 264,000 million kwh., even though almost a half of the electric plants had been destroyed in World War II, with a consequent loss of five million kw. of installation. Reconstruction was, however, very rapid. By Stalin's death electric potential had tripled since the end of the war.

The seven-year plan provides for the doubling of the 1959 figure, increasing production to 500,000 million kwh. In this way every centre, whether industrial or agricultural, should have ample power at its disposal.

But this is only regarded as a departure point, since the twenty-year plan drawn up in 1960 aims at increasing the production of electrical power to 2,300,000 million kwh. by the creation of power stations whose total output should increase as follows:

Year	Million kw. of installed power
1965	121
1970	190
1975	300
1980	480

How far has this impressive programme been fulfilled? In 1960 power stations were being built on the Kama, the Volga, the Dnieper, the Ob and the Angarà. Those at Irkutsk, Novosibirsk, Ust-Kamenogorsk and Atar-Bekyan were already completed. The gigantic plant at Stalingrad (Volgograd) on the lower Volga was almost completed and the first part of the hydro-electric station at Kaunas (Kovno) on the Niemen. The Irtysh dam for the Bukhtarma power station is nearing completion. Two great power stations even more powerful than those at Stalingrad (Volgograd) and Kuibyshev on the Volga have been built at Bratsk on the Angarà, with a potential of four and a half million kilowatts, and at Krasnoyarsk on the Yenisei, with a capacity of six million kilowatts. This last, the largest in the world, was opened on March 25, 1963.

No less vast is the construction programme of thermo-electric power stations. There are some dozens in construction with a capacity of three hundred and even six hundred thousand kilowatts each. In 1960 the thermo-electric station of Tom-Usinak with a capacity of 1,300,000 kw., that of Nazarovo of 1,400,000 kw. and that of Staro-Beschevo in the Donbass (Ukraine) of 1,500,000 kw. were being built.

The seven-year plan provided for the building of another forty large power stations in the Urals, the Baltic republics, the Ukraine and Transcaucasia.

This electricity is at very low cost. One kwh. produced by the Bratsk power station costs six-tenths of a kopek and one kwh. produced by the Krasnoyarsk power station costs half a kopek. The same may be said of the thermo-electric power stations which make use of Siberian open-cast coal.

3

A somewhat similar report may be made on the exploitation of mineral resources. The development of the Soviet iron and steel industry is shown by the following figures:

	Tons of Pig-iron	Tons of Steel	Tons of Rolled-strip
In 1913 Russia produced	4,641,000	4,051,000	3,500,000
From 1960 production has been	—	64,900,000	50,300,000
1961	50,900,000	70,700,000	55,200,000
1963	58,700,000	80,000,000	62,000,000
It is estimated that by the end of 1965 production will have risen to	65,700,000	89,300,000	69,300,000

Today Soviet production of pig-iron and steel is already twenty per cent of world production.

The first siderurgical centre, founded by the initiative of Witte in the Ukraine in order to make full use of the Donbass, that is to say the coal-fields of the Donetz basin, has a productive capacity of twenty million tons of steel. But by Lenin's time there was a pressing need to create a second iron and steel industry in the Urals in order to exploit the iron ore deposits scattered over the eastern slopes of the chain. The ore is worked near the mines, in the centres of Perm, Nizhni-Tagril, Sverdlovsk, Ilatust and above all Magnitogorsk which gets its ore from the Magnitnaia mountain, and finally at Orsk. They make use of the coal from the Kuznetsk coal-fields in Western Siberia.

Kazakstan is the seat of a third great siderurgical centre founded by a decision of the XXI Party Congress to exploit the iron ore deposits of the region and make use of the immense Karaganda coal-fields. Here a first blast furnace has been erected.

According to the seven-year plan the Kemerevo plant in Western Siberia and the Taishet plants in Eastern Siberia near Irkutsk will soon come into operation.

In the centre of European Russia the Ukrainian iron and steel complex is being reinforced by new plants. In 1960 a blast furnace, the largest in the world, was put into operation at Krivoi-Rog, while the production of the plants of Novo Lipetsk and Nova Tula is being accelerated.

Despite these developments in European Russia, the Ural centres, Siberia and Kazakstan are rapidly increasing in importance. In 1960 they provided 39.6% of the pig-iron and 45.5% of the steel produced in the Soviet Union.

Siderurgical technique is very advanced as a result of new processes tried out in the Ukraine with gas fuel, especially oxygen, for the fusion of steel, with a consequent saving of coke and an increase in production.

4

Non-ferrous metallurgy is also expanding rapidly, thanks to the abundance of bauxite, copper, magnesium, nickel, cobalt, wolfram, molybdenum, tin, gold, silver and platinum. The main centre of the metallurgical industry is the Ukraine, which is now modernizing its plants; but the industry is also developed in those districts where large metalliferous deposits have been found, in Transcaucasia (Georgia, Armenia, Azerbaidzhan), Central Asia (Uzbekistan, Tadzhikistan), Kazakstan (copper, lead and zinc) and in Kirgizia.

As can be seen Lenin's directive to expand industry over the whole country is being systematically put into operation. The idea of exploiting industrially the natural resources on the actual production and extraction sites has given a clear predominance to the Ukraine and to the mineral-bearing zone that extends from the Urals to the Altai mountains across the lowlands of Kazakstan that link those two mountainous areas.

The great southern plains beyond the Ukraine which make up Moldavia and the southern strip of the Russian federal republic are swarming with industrial centres. The population is about sixty million inhabitants. It is one of the richest areas in the world, not only because of the abundance of coal, oil and iron ore but also because of the fertility of the *chernozem*, or black earth, and because of the enormous masses of water which pour into the Black Sea and the Caspian, providing electric power, good means of navigation and the possibility of irrigating immense arid, or semi-arid, expanses.

Since the inauguration of planning, the zone of the Urals, the other great zone of industrial concentration, has seen its population doubled. In the cities it has tripled or quadrupled. Magnitogorsk, with about three hundred thousand inhabitants, did not figure in the 1926 census at all. The mining centre of Kameno-Uralski has risen from five thousand inhabitants in 1926 to a hundred and fifty thousand. Sverdlovsk is called the Pittsburgh of the Urals because of its thirteen hundred factories.

Like the Ukraine and the Urals, Kazakstan too bases its industrial development on the exploitation of the three fundamental raw materials, coal, oil and iron, as well as on non-ferrous metals. Because of this industrialization as well as the agricultural colonization of its northern areas its population has more than doubled since 1926; a third of it is in the cities, almost all of which were founded after the revolution.

Perhaps the greatest promise for the future is the industrialization of Siberia. Not for nothing is it called 'the gem of the world'. It has incalculable wealth of gold, diamonds, platinum, iron, aluminium, nickel, copper, tungsten, molybdenum, cobalt, graphite, mica and asbestos. For the moment the main effort is concentrated in the triangle Novosibirsk-Krasnoyarsk-Irkutsk straddling the great rivers Ob, Yenisei and Angarà which provide hydro-electric power, while the Kuzbass region provides coal and the districts a little to the south iron ore. A crown of industrial cities has arisen around these mines: Kemerevo, Stalinsk, Barnaul. The capital of Western Siberia, Novosibirsk, has increased from a hundred and twenty thousand inhabitants in 1926 to more than six hundred thousand today. Built on the last outcrops of the Altai, facing the boundless *taiga*, Novosibirsk is considered the Chicago of Siberia.

At the end of April 1918 Lenin, while tracing out a 'scheme for a plan of scientific and technical work', paid great attention to the exploitation of Siberia, with especial reference to its enormous potentialities of water-power. It is estimated that the hydro-electric potential of Siberia is more than a half of the whole potential of the Soviet Union, while Siberian thermo-electric potential is four-fifths of the total Soviet reserves. Technicians calculate that the complete exploitation of both these sources of power would produce a potential exceeding that of all the electric power stations now existent in the world. The Soviet Union has not wasted time. A chain of enormous hydro-electric power stations has been planned and some of them have already been built.

Despite the immense hydro-electric potential, priority will be given, at least in the first phase, to thermic plants, not only because they can be put into operation more quickly but also because the coal reserves of Eastern Siberia amount to the astronomical figure of 6,800 milliard tons, thus exceeding the total coal reserves of all the capitalist states. They are sufficient to cover the entire fuel requirements of the world for more than a thousand years. Also the extraction costs are the lowest in the world. It is enough to point out that the cost of extraction in the Krasnoyarsk region is close to that of natural gas. One of the largest thermo-electric power stations in Europe is now rising at Nazarovo, with a potential of one million two hundred thousand kw. A line of cable-cars transports the coal directly from the mines to the boilers.

A six hundred kilowatt electric grid is in project, from the Yenisei to the Urals, a distance of two thousand kilometres, so as to link the Siberian power stations with those of European Russia. Low cost Siberian power will thus become available to the industrial plants in the Ural region. This will also gain an advantage from the time-zone differences between Siberia and Europe, since it is night in the former when it is still evening in the latter. Eventually it will benefit from the differing water levels of the European and Siberian rivers at certain seasons.

Recent prospecting has revealed that the Angarà basin not only has a rich hydro-electric potential but also possesses iron ore deposits estimated at 4,500 million tons of haematite.

The abundance of raw materials and power permits the creation of a range of industries on a vast scale. Other than the siderurgical centre of Taishet, factories are being planned for non-ferrous metal working and for the production of synthetic materials, including artificial fibres and plastic goods. Special importance will be paid to electrometallurgy, electrochemical processes and petrochemicals for the production of fertilizers and artificial rubber, as well as coke by-products. The light metal industries will also be greatly developed: aluminium, titanium and magnesite, which require a great consumption of electricity. The chemical industry will make use of the petrol refineries at Kritovo in the Krasnoyarsk region and Angarsk, fed by the Bashkirya oil-pipeline.

Furthermore, the saline depression of the Angarà-Lena is an inexhaustible source of saline solutions from which are obtained chlorites, potassium salts, magnesium and borax.

Thus the process of industrialization is expanding over wider and wider territories, reaching to Transbaikalia and the district of Chita, that is to say the lands inhabited by the Buriat Mongols on the borders of Outer Mongolia. Irkutsk, which is the greatest city of this great area, has already become a great industrial centre. In the same zone the industrial centre of Angarà-Usolye is developing, with factories for mining machinery, electrical equipment and building materials. The Angarà petrol refinery is in operation, as also the Irkutsk aluminium plant. In the Baikal district several open-cast coal-mines are being worked, as well as gold-mines; there are also wood and cement factories, mica-mines and plants for the processing of their products. A cellulose plant has been planned, as well as a factory for the production of fire-resisting materials at Polovinkino, a textile plant at Zima and factories for the processing of asbestos and the like.

The plans referred to above have been inspired by the directive to push the industrialization programme more and more eastward. Ulan Ude, the capital of the Buriat federated republic, has very large railway workshops. More to the east, Chita, a city entirely inhabited by Russians, has many metallurgical plants and factories for food products and wood processing. The whole region is rich in ferrous and non-ferrous metals: gold, tin, tungsten and lead.

In the Soviet Far East the main terminals of this chain of industries, which stretches from one end of the Soviet Union to the other, are Khabarovsk, Komsomolsk and Vladivostock. The population of these three cities is almost exclusively employed in industry. They are very modern cities, with parks, gardens and monumental public buildings which give the peoples of the Far East their first magnificent glimpse of Soviet power. This region has very fertile soil and is rich in iron ore and coal. It is, therefore, an area destined for rapid colonization.

6

The rhythm of Soviet industrial production as a result of the plans can be seen from the following annual percentages of growth since the war:

Capital goods	1946-1950	1951-1955	1956-1958
Electricity	16.06	13.29	11.03
Coal and lignite	11.82	8.42	8.21
Oil	14.34	13.29	16.86
Steel	17.28	10.66	6.62
Cement	40.76	17.14	13.99
Consumer goods			
Paper	30.02	9.32	5.70
Cotton textiles	19.24	8.65	—0.99
Woollen textiles	23.69	10.21	6.30
Leather shoes	26.37	6.15	9.08
Raw sugar	40.25	6.25	16.45

It is evident that, even in the Soviet economy, the law of decreasing rates of progress operates. It is noteworthy that the rate of increase in industrial production which was, according to Soviet statistics, 10% in 1959-61 fell to 9.5% in 1962 to 8.5% in 1963 and to 7.8% in 1964.

Not a day passes without the news that some great undertaking has been completed. The *Ekonomicheskaya Gazeta* of November 4, 1960 printed a calendar of the work completed from November 1, 1959 to November 1, 1960 and pointed out that in this period orders had been given for the construction of 1,130 large plants and that, according to the seven-year plan, there would be others the following year. Riffling through this calendar the most important orders were for: high potential blast-furnaces, gas pipelines several hundred kilometres long, hydro-electric power stations, large diameter tube factories, electro-welding plants, factories for the construction of rails, steelworks, rolling mills, sugar factories, cotton mills, tractor factories, new mines, metallurgical centres, electrical transmission lines, construction of catchment basins and irrigation canals, production of high power nuclear reactors, oil drillings, automatic motor car assembly lines, phosphate factories, cable factories, synthetic rubber factories, factories for cellulose, paper and artificial fibres, petrol refineries, aeroports, tanker fleets and dry-cargo vessels, and so on.

7

These immense plans require enormous resources in manpower and capital.

The flow of workers from the countryside to the cities was particularly intense in the initial phase of planning, which to a great extent coincided with the period of land collectivization. This is shown by the following table:

Year	No. of persons leaving the countryside
1927	472,000
1928	1,062,000
1929	1,392,000
1930	2,633,000
1931	4,100,000
1932	2,719,000

Whereas the 1926 census showed an urban population of 26,300,000 that of 1959 showed 55,900,000. The increase is the more remarkable in that in the meantime the urban birth rate had fallen to the point of reaching —6.5 per thousand in 1930 and —9.9 per thousand in 1931.

From the first *pytiletka* in 1928 to the death of Stalin in 1953, the urban population rose from 26,300,000 to about eighty millions. From 1953 to 1961 it increased by another twenty-eight million, while the increase in the countryside was only one million.

Immediately after the war the working population increased rapidly, so that recruits for industry rose from nine and a half million in 1945 to 19,841,000 in 1958 with an average increase which, during the five year period 1945-1950, was about 8.3%. But it decreased rapidly in 1957 to 3.6%, only to rise again in 1958 to

3.7%. It seems that this increase was in great part due to a rise in the birth rate of the urban population, since the Statistical Annual of the Soviet Union for 1956 shows that in that year the personnel of the collective farms not only did not diminish but even slightly increased. It made up 37.7% of the working population, whereas the percentage in the previous year had been 37.5%.

According to the data given by the Central Statistical Bureau in Moscow the population of the Soviet Union in December, 1963, was divided as follows:

117 million inhabitants lived in 1,763 cities and 3,255 industrial centres;
108 million lived in 700,000 rural districts.

A special organization called the Orgnabor (Labour Organization) is entrusted with the recruitment of workers on short-time contracts. The manpower thus recruited is mainly unskilled and employed on construction work. From 1923 to 1940 this organization recruited annually from two-and-a-half to three million workers on the basis of contracts agreed with the collective farms. Today, rather than recruiting which has become difficult, the Orgnabor is concerned with transferring workers from areas in which there is a superfluity of manpower to others where there is a scarcity, more especially from one city to another. In fact, whereas in 1950 only 28% of the workers recruited by the Orgnabor came from the cities this percentage had doubled by 1953, amounting to more than 56%, and in 1958 reached 74.3%.

But in the years 1959, 1960 and 1961 the flow of manpower from the country quickened, especially, or so it seems, from the collective farms, and assumed a rhythm that has been noted, not without a certain preoccupation, by the Party Central Committee in its session of March 1962.

It is an uncontestable fact that there is a shortage of manpower, even though much use is made of women. When, however, Soviet propagandists stress as one of the great achievements of communism that it has made unemployment impossible by the assurance of work for all, they pass silently over the reality of the situation, which is that on a territory of more than twenty-two million square kilometres there is a population of two hundred and twenty-five millions with a density of ten inhabitants per square kilometre compared with the population density of the Western European countries which is nearly two hundred per square kilometre. The truth is that the Soviet population is numerically insufficient to exploit the immense resources of its territory and that the industrialization of the country would have been even more rapid if it had had greater manpower resources.

This situation is aggravated by the squandering of manpower which is so common a feature of Soviet industry and agriculture.

The burden of excess personnel is almost always very heavy when compared with that in similar productive activities in the West administered by private individuals. But in the West too this tendency towards excess of manpower is often to be found in nationalized undertakings.

There should also be noted the pressure exercised by the inhabitants of a city to get work on the spot so as not to have to move from their homes. This local resistance makes a rational distribution of manpower between the western and eastern zones more difficult.

Finally there is a tendency for the factories to exaggerate their manpower demands even though in most cases they lack adequate housing and facilities. A system of control by the local soviets over the manpower requirements of the factories has been set up.

It can be seen from Soviet statistics that the personnel engaged in industry has increased between 1945 and 1958 as follows:[2]

1945	9,508,000
1945-1950	14,144,000
1950-1955	17,367,000
1956	18,457,000
1957	19,120,000
1958	19,841,000

The great leap forward was during the five years after the war, with an annual increase of 8.5%. In 1957 the increase was 3.6% and in 1958 3.7%.[3]

According to the thesis on the seven-year plan put by Khrushchev to the XXI Party Congress, the number of those engaged in industry and building should increase on an average by about 3% per annum during the seven years of the plan's fulfilment.

It is estimated that as a result of the automation and mechanization projects laid down in the seven-year plan there will be a manpower saving of about a hundred thousand workers in the metallurgy and machinery industries and of four hundred and thirty thousand in the consumer goods industries. It is believed that other reductions may be obtained by the use of oil and gas instead of coal as sources of power.

[2] *Narodnoe Khozyastvo S.S.S.R. Statisticheskii Sbornik 1956; Narodnoe Khozyatsvo S.S.S.R v 1956 godu, Statisticheskii Ezhegodnik 1957; S.S.S.R. v tsifrakh, Statisticheskii Sbornik 1958.*

[3] Sergio D'Angelo and Leo Paladini; *Khrushchev's Challenge, op. cit., p. 23.*

Lastly it must not be forgotten that the period of fulfilment of the seven-year plan coincides with the call-up of the classes born during the war. To increase the availability of manpower there has been a demobilization, partially suspended, of a million and a half men serving with the colours. Furthermore, it has been made compulsory for all students, at the end of their eight-year compulsory schooling, to devote themselves to productive work.

8

If the recruiting of manpower is today one of the greatest difficulties of the industrialization of the country, the great problem at the beginning was to assure the capital to finance it. The tsarist government had obtained capital to a great extent by means of credits from the Western powers. But since the new régime refused to recognize such debts, it cut off all hope of financial credits from abroad. It only remained to extort them from the people, despite the general misery after the civil war. These were the heroic years of the first five-year plan.

Soviet economists stress that this was an unprecedented experiment, since it was necessary to create an immense and complex economic organization by the use of national capital. Lacking any industrial production for export, the funds for the acquisition of plant and machinery as well as funds to cover the enormous establishment expenses had to be obtained by the sale of agricultural produce. This was wrested from the peasants at derisory prices and resold at extortionate profits, or was exported, subtracting it from the already meagre home consumption.[4]

When industrial development made possible a vast city proletariat, it was the burden of investment which weighed them down, either because of their insufficient remuneration or by the imposition of forced loans, which reduced their already modest wages. Taxation too was another form of wage reduction since, as the ownership of goods productive of income is not permitted, the only revenue to be taxed was wages, grants and pensions.

In fact investment capital was squeezed out of the consumers through the excessively high cost of all consumer goods. Investments

[4] In his speech to the Plenum of the Central Committee on December 9, 1963, Khrushchev accused Stalin and Molotov of having sold grain abroad 'even when the people were dying of hunger . . . Yes, comrades,' he said, 'it is a fact that in 1947 in many regions, for example in the district of Kursk, the people were dying of hunger. It was just at that time that they were selling grain abroad.'

represented, broadly speaking, twenty-five per cent of the national income. But it is estimated that in the five-year period 1923-1927 28.5% of the national income was earmarked for investments. Thenceforward progress has been constant in the rapid and continual production growth, thanks to massive doses of investment capital.

Early in 1962 the Central Statistical Office of the Soviet Union published data on Soviet investments from 1918 to 1960, calculated in milliards of new rubles, valued at 1.11 to the dollar.

These investments include those made by the state, by the co-operatives and by private persons for the purpose of house-building.

The advance of total investments has been:

Year	Total investments (in milliards of new rubles)
1918-1928	4.1
1928-1933 (first five-year plan)	7.4
1933-1937 (second five-year plan)	16.8
1938—June 30, 1941 (third five-year plan, interrupted by the war)	17.6
July 1, 1941-1945 (War period)	17.7
1946-1950 (fourth five-year plan)	42.0
1951-1955 (fifth five-year plan)	79.2
Sixth five-year plan (interrupted):	
1956	22.9
1957	25.8
1958	30.0
1959	34.0
1960	36.7
Total	334.2

According to the Central Statistical Office of the Soviet Union another 40.1 milliard new rubles should be added, of which half were spent on geological research, public building projects and re-afforestation and the other half on acquiring breeding stock.

It is not easy to control the accuracy of these figures, especially those concerning the first years. We have already referred to the errors of calculation shown by leading Soviet economists in the Soviet official figures, above all because of the need to take into account the prices current at the time to which the investments refer. It is clearly of interest to give maximum figures in order to show, by comparison with those of the main industrial countries, the high rhythm of investment increase in the Soviet Union. The Central Statistical Office in fact arrives at the conclusion that in the decade 1951-1960 investments in the Soviet Union increased by 231% whereas the increase in the United States was 21%, in Great Britain 64% and in France 63%. The very much higher annual percentage of increase in Western Germany, Japan and Italy are passed over in silence.

However, the rhythm of the annual increase is impressive. To the figures from the Central Statistical Office given above, the following data may be added. In 1961 state investments alone amounted to 32.5 milliard new rubles, not including investments by the enterprises, by co-operative or private interests. In the years 1962-1965 the state investment programme amounted to 106 milliard new rubles.

If instead of total investments we consider only state investments, it may be seen that these have progressed as follows:

Year	Milliard new rubles
1956	19.1
1957	21.6
1958	24.5
1959	27.4
1960	30.8
1961	32.5

It is interesting to see how the total investment of 334.2 milliard new rubles has been allocated in the period 1918-1960. It is as follows:

	Milliard new rubles	Percentage
Capital industry	117.3	35.1
Consumer goods industries	16.3	4.9
Agriculture	48.0	14.4
Transport	34.2	10.2
Private building	71.0	21.2
Public building	47.4	14.2
	334.2	100.00

To complete the picture it is worth while examining the allocation of the 117.3 milliards assigned to heavy industry. It was allocated as follows:

	Milliard new rubles
Iron and steel	11.6
Chemical industry	5.4
Oil and gas	15.2
Coal	13.2
Hydro-electric and thermo-electric plants	14.5
Machinery	21.4
Building equipment	13.7
Others	22.3
	117.3

In the first two years of the seven-year plan the construction of 3,700 large industrial plants was undertaken.

From the official Soviet statistics it can be clearly seen that whereas 35.1% of the total investments was allocated to capital goods, only 4.9%, that is less than a seventh, was set aside for the industrial production of consumer goods. The data given are a mathematical proof that the high rhythm of industrial increase was obtained by restricting as far as possible the level of consumer goods. This is a policy that only a dictatorship can permit itself, but certainly not a democratic state which places the interests of its people above all else.

Rapid capitalization increased the growth of the national income at least thirteen times between 1913 and 1956. If the statements of the Soviet statistical institutes are accurate, this growth has quickened from 1946 onward, when the national income was only four times greater than in 1913. In ten years therefore it has more than trebled.

9

According to the thesis presented to the XXI Party Congress by Khrushchev, the fulfilment of the seven-year plan should have increased industrial production by 80% and agricultural production by 70%. In this way the Soviet Union would cover, in its view, a half of the gap that separates it from the pro capite production of the United States and be sure of catching it up after another five years, that is to say in 1970.

The seven-year plan for industrial production hinged basically upon three factors: development of sources of power, development of the iron and steel industries and the chemical industry.

The following increases in power sources were forecast:

> Oil production to be increased from 100 million tons in 1956 to 240 million tons in 1965, rising to 400 million tons in 1972.
> Natural gas from 150 milliard cubic metres in 1963 to 1,500 milliard cubic metres in 1972.
> Coal to six hundred million tons in 1962.
> Thermo-electric power stations. Their potential will be raised from 52 million kw. in 1958 to 110 million kw. in 1965. The plan forecast, *inter alia*, the construction of seventeen large gas-fuelled power stations with a potential of 11.4 million kw. Others will use coal and mazout.
> The iron and steel industry is to reach the following levels in 1965:

	Million tons	
Pig-iron	65-70	
Steel	86-91	to be raised within twenty years to two hundred and fifty million tons
Rolled strip	65-70	

Not less than two-thirds of the investments set aside for the iron and steel industry and not less than 60% of those intended for the non-ferrous metal industry will be employed to develop or modernize existing plants, since it is from this improvement that the Soviet Union expects for the most part an increase in production.

The seven-year plan assigns to the chemical industry a hundred milliard old rubles, equivalent to about ten milliard dollars, for the production of synthetic fibres, plastics and fertilizers.

10

The plan was inspired by the order to give priority to the production of capital goods, that is to say heavy industry, which, as was said in the Party programme at the XXI Congress, was 'to guarantee the development of the productive forces and the strategic reserves of the country'. Therefore, the document adds, 'heavy industry must advance sufficiently to assure, on the basis of technical progress, an increase of those sectors of the national economy that provide consumer goods'.

But even though the production levels fixed by the seven-year plan have been reached and even exceeded in many sectors, these levels have not everywhere been attained, and as Khrushchev stated to the Plenum of the Party Central Committee on November 19, 1963: 'The quotas for the production of electric power, gas, synthetic resins and fibres, plastics, turbines, locomotives, rolling stock and equipment for the oil industry have not been reached.' The most serious deficiency was revealed in the development of the chemical industry to which Khrushchev has attributed fundamental importance for the economic progress of the country.[5]

The fulfilment of the plan has therefore been postponed and a two-year plan for 1964 and 1965 has been adopted, after which there will be a return to the traditional system of five-year plans, within a twenty-year programme. In the two-year plan the production quotas to be reached in 1965 are, as regards the main sectors, as follows:

Oil	240 million tons
Coal	553 million tons
Electric power	508 milliard kw.
Pig-iron	65.7 million tons
Steel	89.3 million tons
Rolled strip	69.3 million tons
Fertilizers	35 million tons
Tractors	700,000 units to be produced within two years

The plan aims at developing the so-called 'progressive' industries, that is to say the chemical industry and the production of gas and electric power.

Consumer goods must be increased by 14.5% and houses built for fifteen million persons. Eight milliard rubles have been earmarked for building construction.

In the two-year period eight thousand five hundred kilometres of oil pipelines and five thousand five hundred kilometres of gas pipelines will be built. Financial investments amounting to 2,088 million new rubles, equivalent to about 2,300 million dollars, in 1964 and 2,743 million new rubles, equivalent to more than three thousand million dollars, in 1965 have been allotted to the chemical industry. These are relatively modest quotas compared with the allocations planned in the next five-year plan, at the end of which 42,000 million rubles will be invested. Logically, the foundations for future development will be laid in these first two years, which provide for the construction of two hundred new plants, of which fifty-eight are for fertilizers, and the modernization of more than five hundred plants. Chemical production is to increase by 17 to 19% annually.

In these investments 10.5 milliard rubles are included for the production of fertilizers. This must increase from the twenty million

[5] 'Vladimir Ilich Lenin,' he said to the Central Committee on December 9, 1963, 'said these winged words: "Communism is all power to the Soviets plus electrification of the whole country." If Lenin were alive today he would undoubtedly say something like this: "Communism is all power to the Soviets plus electrification of the whole country plus the chemicalization of the national economy." '

tons produced in 1963 to 70-80 million tons in 1970. Insecticides and weedkillers must be increased by seven and a half times the 1963 production.

Khrushchev has observed that Russia has a leading place in the world for reserves of potassium salts, sulphates, gas, etc., and has everything for a flourishing chemical industry whose main centres will be in White Russia, the western Ukraine and Kazakstan.

Amongst its other aims the chemical industry must in the seven-year period 1964-1970 increase its production of the following products:

Synthetic fibres from 310,000 tons to 1,350,000 tons;
Plastic materials and synthetic resins by six or seven times the 1963 production till it reaches a figure of 3.5-4 million tons;
Tyres from 22.5 million to 44 million.

'Perhaps,' remarked Khrushchev, 'we shall have to diminish for a certain period the tempo of development of other industries.' He then specified that he was referring to heavy industry.

11

'Our people,' Khrushchev said in his report to the Party Central Committee on December 9, 1963, 'has created, under the direction of the Party, a first-class heavy industry.' It is in this very industry that Soviet productive technique has made its greatest advances, so that in many sectors it is now one of the best in the world. This is mainly due to innovations in the iron and steel industries and the vast scale of the hydro-electric power stations, like that of Bratsk which has no equal in the world and which will in its turn be surpassed by the power station at Krasnoyarsk on the Yenisei. The Soviets take as a comparison Gran Coulée, which is the largest hydro-electric power station in the United States, with a potential equal to only half that of Bratsk.

No less striking successes have been achieved by Soviet engineers in the construction of huge turbines, motors and machine tools.

Italian technicians, who have visited both American and Soviet plants, say that in these sectors Soviet technique is in advance of American.

Similar appraisements have been made by the financial editor of *The Christian Science Monitor* who has expressed himself very unfavourably on the Soviet agricultural situation. He declared himself to be of the opinion, after discussions with American, British, French and German economists, that 'Soviet superiority in the production of heavy machinery and machine tools would be evident within five years'.

He wrote this in 1960. The same journalist quoted the opinion of Prof. Seymour Melman of the Industrial and Mechanical Department of Columbia University who, on his return from a visit to the Soviet Union in 1959, declared that 'machine tools are mass produced in only one country in the world, the Soviet Union'. In a BBC broadcast on November 1, 1959 he specified that in the Soviet Union, which he recently visited, he found that 'the mechanization of the machine-tool industry, the specialization of the factories, the standardization of parts and the use of mass production techniques were being energetically exploited as the basis of the present economic plan'.

It has already been said that not all sectors of Soviet industry produce so favourable an impression. Many factories leave much to be desired for the slowness of their work-rhythm and their out-of-date machinery.

The consumer goods are very poor in quality and are of old-fashioned design. Where there is competition the producer takes the greatest pains to interpret, guide and, if possible, anticipate public tastes by the constant search for novelty, refinement and practical advantage. But where the economy is state-controlled, the sole preoccupation of the director of the enterprise is to carry out the plan imposed on him, without assuming the responsibility of introducing novelties, which involves risk, increased expense, modifications in machinery and processes. The American writer Nate White says: 'The choice is very limited. The goods are inferior, of atrocious quality, in very poor taste and extremely high in price.'

12

Attempts are now being made to eliminate these faults by modernizing the factories, introducing large-scale mechanization and automation, training the personnel and increasing the minimum wage. The Party programme of the XXII Congress says: 'Total mechanization will bring about the elimination of manual labour both in main operations and in subsidiary ones.' The programme has issued its directive that industries be distributed over the whole territory in order 'to assure the organic development of regions and the specialization of their economy, and to avoid an excessive concentration of population in the great cities'. For this reason the development of industry will be intensified 'in the zones east of the Urals, which possess incalculable wealth, raw materials and sources of power'. All these industries will be co-ordinated. For example the Kuschuk sulphate factory, created in the Kulunda steppe in the Altai region, will produce the sodium sulphate for the paper and cellulose factories of the Krasnoyarsk district and Irkutsk; it will also produce varnishes, mineral fertilizers and caustic soda for the leather and soap factories. Similarly, the artificial rubber factory at Krasnoyarsk will operate on the wood alcohol produced by the electrolytic factories in various parts of Siberia.

Taken as a whole, the exploitation of mineral deposits, the network of electric power stations and the deployment of industrial centres will be concentrated east of the Urals, in a strip which includes the central part of the Ural chain from Chelyabinsk to Magnitogorsk, with its pivot at Sverdlovsk, descends as far as Novosibirsk, including the zone of the Altai, goes on to Krasnoyarsk and then broadens out to Minusinsk, to include the rich Tom basin with the centres of Tomsk, Kemerovo, Leninsk-Kuznestki and Stalinsk, and ends at Irkutsk, including the affluents of the Angarà from Taishet to Bratsk. It is a zone of immense economic value, a sort of Po valley or Rhineland multiplied many times. Here the cities swarm, because resources abound, beginning with mineral resources. The cities grow like mushrooms. In the course of a few decades little villages have become industrial centres: Chelyabinsk, the centre of the coal-fields on the eastern slopes of the Urals, Sverdlovsk with its timber and non-ferrous metal industries, the Orenburg region with its copper mines, the Perm region with its oil refining. In the centre of Western Siberia is Novosibirsk, which is scarcely seventy years old and is already a metropolis with machine factories which make the largest turbines in the world. It has already been surpassed by Krasnoyarsk farther east, which is the centre of an immense area, fertile and rich in minerals. New cities are being added to the old centres, in a constant contest to exceed one another and attract more and more immigrants; such are Nokhodka, Angarsk, Gubkin, Divnogorsk, Almetyevsk, Pubtsovsk, Raichikhinsk, which one will soon hear of as industrial centres.

This band of industrial concentration, which reaches from the Urals to Lake Baikal, follows the line of the Trans-Siberian and forms the backbone of economic Siberia. The main lines of aerial communication follow the same general direction and link the many cities that spangle it. Gradually this band tends to widen both northward and southward and little by little as it expands, branch lines leave the Trans-Siberian for the more distant centres. Perhaps in the future a new Trans-Siberian, parallel to the present line, will be necessary to connect up the present system of so many radial lines.

The impulse has been given and the transformation of Russia is proceeding on a gigantic scale. The mass of investments grows from year to year. There is no doubt that, as in every process of industrialization, so too in the Soviet there will be an inevitable slowing down when even greater volumes of production are reached. But by that time the great internal market will be opened as also that of aid to the underdeveloped countries, which will maintain the high production levels. In a word, a formidable machine has been created which is being continually perfected and whose potential is above all determined by the inexhaustible natural resources of by far the richest country in the world.

This machine has been for the most part built in the post-war period. From it the Soviet Union anticipates world leadership, not only economic but also political and military. It is logical to think that it will not run the risk of seeing it destroyed by nuclear conflict. Khrushchev often said that in a nuclear war Russia would be less exposed to the danger of destruction than the Western countries because of her immense size. But it is not necessary to belong to the Intelligence Service to foresee that in the event of a nuclear war missiles with nuclear warheads would rain down on the strip of territory along the Trans-Siberian line because, once the spine of the country had been broken, Soviet power would be paralysed.

The industrial potential of Russia, while it increases her military power, is none the less a remora to hold back the threat of conflict.

PART III

THE ELEMENTS OF WEAKNESS

CHAPTER VIII

Marxist Ideology

1

IN the preceding chapters the factors of the wealth and power of the Soviet Union have been discussed. Official propaganda from Moscow attributes Soviet successes to Marxist ideology, which it claims to be the force which has revived the country and which is destined, similarly, to revive the world, since the Russian achievements will be the proof that the social, economic and political organization based on Marxism has, by comparison with capitalism, the threefold advantage of intensifying productivity, raising the workers' living standards and putting an end to their exploitation. It has been seen, however, from a comparison between communist and capitalist countries, that in the former productivity is considerably lower and the scale of wages and the supply of consumer goods are also lower. Regarded in its practical application, the Marxist ideology is not a stimulus but a brake, because it slows down effort and retards the processes of production. All this will be shown in the chapters that follow.

By this there is no intention of denying certain merits of Marxism. It has been a powerful leaven, especially for the human emotional feeling which it has inspired. Certain of its statements, conclusions and forecasts have turned out to be true; others are clearly false, either superseded or denied by reality. As time passes, the more it shows its inability to adapt itself to a reality that is changing rapidly under the drive of technical processes which could not be foreseen in its times.

The principal merit of Marxism is its criticism of capitalism, of which it has stressed the injustices, the excesses, the tendency for the amassing, concentration and monopolizing of wealth, resulting in social inequalities. If some prophesies have not proved true to the extent forecast by Marx and Engels, this is due in great part to the efficacy of Marxist criticism which has aroused corrective and balancing forces.

This critical influence continues to act as a ferment, in the same sense as the Christian Socialist doctrine, to drive the capitalist régime towards those social and economic reforms which permit a more equal distribution of wealth and a more rapid ascent of the lower classes towards living standards which permit the full exploitation of individual capacities.

But when one passes from the destructive criticism to the constructive programme of Marxism it is hard to hide the perplexity aroused by its application in the communist countries, the more so as they are all still in the first phase forecast by Marx and called by him 'socialist'.

Engels has written that the proof of the pudding is in the eating. Therefore the best way of judging Marxism is to see it in action. It is worth while to find out what is the present exegesis of Marxist doctrines in the communist countries, what part of them has up till now been applied and with what results; what reaction have these results aroused in the public opinion of the most developed of them, the Soviet Union.

It must be acknowledged at once that formal homage to these doctrines is absolute. Officially, Marxism integrated with Leninism is the foundation of Soviet society. The schools prescribe its teaching in all classes, up to the universities and the higher educational institutes, whatever be the faculty or the technical speciality chosen by the student. The Marxist-Leninist doctrines must be taught within the framework of the 'materialist conception of the world and of life as a basis for a real knowledge of the physical world', as is stated in the preamble to the school reform law of December 24, 1958.

The interpretation of Soviet men of culture, especially of the economists, is extremely wary and not far from the formulas of Marx, Engels and Lenin. Till recently these writers were more apologists than interpreters. It was impossible to find in their writings the slightest trace of critical spirit and still less of originality of ideas.

Now some economists, such as Liberman, Traperinkov, Arkumanian, Leonhev and others are trying to introduce new conceptions but they are meeting with the opposition of the conformist writers for whom 'Marxist political economy is the only scientific political economy'. In fact we are more in the field of faith than of science. The reasoning of these writers follows the safe path of quoting the sacred texts. In fact the sole valid argument, as will be seen, is the *ipse dixit*. Soviet writers, following the example of Lenin, begin by denying that the political economy of the Western world is a science, since, they say, it reflects the interests of the bourgeoisie. As good communists, they deny the existence in the West of that freedom of thought which is inconceivable in the Soviet Union.

176

2

In all the communist countries Marxism is being canonized. To understand the inescapable forces that drive them, one must begin with the dogmatic assertions made by Lenin on Marx's teaching. When Lenin set communist propaganda in motion, the ideological bases of Marxism had been subject to intense criticism by Western sociologists and economists, even as its aims had been subjected to radical revision by the Socialist International. The lack of foundation of certain of its postulates is demonstrated by a copious literature which can be summarized in the lapidary definition of Karl Marx's *Kapital* by Keynes as a text scientifically mistaken in its economy, not only out of date but without interest and without possibility of application in the modern world,[1] a definition which resembles that cruder one of Bakunin who accused Marx of 'perpetual theoretical insanity'.

Despite this process of revision Lenin swallowed the diagnosis of capitalism made by Marx and Engels hook, line and sinker and accepted its planning postulates wholesale. Undoubtedly he was not unaware of the criticisms of Western writers or of the reduction in Marx's programme made by the Socialist International. Both one and the other were well-known in Russia, as appears from the polemics between Bolsheviks and Mensheviks.

But why did Lenin, instead of drawing attention to the weaknesses of the system, make himself the surety of its scientific truth and thus break away irrevocably from Western Marxism? The hypothesis suggested by his whole attitude is that he, solely dominated by the need to loose the revolution against the established order in Russia, thought it indispensable to base his propaganda on an irrefutable faith. It is enough to look at the typical form of organization given by him to the communist party, conceived as the advance-guard of the proletariat and as a force made up of men blindly obedient to every order of their leaders, to realize that the word as spread by him must be presented to the masses as the last word in science, and therefore capable of imposing itself on will and intelligence alike and capable of replacing every earlier faith and conviction. To make *tabula rasa* of the ideas of the past and assure uncontested dominion for the new doctrine, he had to accept it as a whole in order not to crack its monolithic unity. Hence his aphorism, repeated by Khrushchev, that 'Marx's ideas are omnipotent because they are true'.

The same exigency continues to exist in our own days, because

[1] See *Essays in Persuasion*, New York, 1932.

only in the name of absolute truth, which heralds new times and will install a régime of justice and prosperity for all, is it possible to arouse the imagination of the masses and force them to revolt against existing conditions. Therefore any revision of its postulates is impossible, since it would weaken this faith. The tragedy of the communist parties is that they drag along behind them the dead weight of an archaic doctrine, falsified by reality and swarming with errors.

Lenin was not, however, so blind as not to see the weaknesses and above all the shortcomings of Marxism. Under a formal respect for the teaching of the Master, Lenin began a cautious, secret work of integration and adaptation of the doctrine to reality. The restoration of the venerable edifice has been carried on with greater or less freedom of modification according to the authority of whoever undertakes it. Lenin, strong in the prestige of having ensured the triumph of communism by the October revolution, did not meet with overpowering difficulties in making his innovations seem like logical developments of Marxist postulates. There was, therefore, a continual oscillation between the need to accept the basic principles of the system unreservedly so as not to weaken its validity and the no less imperious need of casting out those sections which no longer stood up to criticism and of correcting in practice certain of its postulates, such as the basic theory of value and surplus-value. We shall see to what expedients Soviet planning has had to go in order to pay due heed to the productivity of capital, which was denied by marx.

Lenin had given a clear warning against the danger of transforming the Master's doctrine into inviolable dogma. In a report in Volume IV of his works, he warns: 'We do not in any way consider the theory of Marx as complete and inviolable.' Elsewhere, in Volume VI, Lenin goes on to say: 'To continue to defend the old solutions of Marxism means to pay attention to the letter but not to the spirit of his teaching; this means to repeat parrot-fashion the old conclusions without being able to adapt Marxist methods to a new political situation.'

Once the principle that 'Marxism is not a dogma but a guide to action' had been established, Lenin freely availed himself of the faculty of interpreting it, developing it and adapting it to reality. Therefore it is not without reason that the Soviet people speak of Marxism-Leninism, but, in their view, Marxism represents the theory and Leninism the practice, thereby making it clear that Lenin remained within the framework of the most orthodox teaching. Stalin openly stated that Leninism is the development of Marxism, which is considerably more exact.

Stalin claimed similar powers to his predecessor by maintaining, at the XVIII Party Congress in 1939, that one could not expect to find an answer to all problems in Marx, Engels and Lenin, but a solution inspired by the general principles of communism must be sought for.

This was the thesis upheld by Khrushchev against the Chinese dogmatists at Bucharest in June 1960.

But whereas Lenin's authority as an interpreter of Marxism was contested by no one, the same cannot be said of his successors. Yugoslav revisionism rebelled against Stalinist conceptions; Chinese dogmatism has rebelled against the thesis of Khrushchev.

The meaning of these dissensions is clear; the more and more evident revelation of the cracks in Marxist ideology. This does not mean the test of reality. The crisis through which communism is passing lies in the impossibility of reconciling fidelity to the basic principles of Marxism with the necessity of an evolution that inescapably forces it to depart even farther from those principles. What else is Yugoslav revisionism than the revolt of common sense against Utopia? What else is Chinese dogmatism if not the rigid adherence to formulas which perhaps are applicable to a primitive economy like that of China today or like that of Russia at the time of the Bolshevik revolution, but which certainly no longer correspond to the present development of Soviet economy?

Moscow is therefore forced to fight on two fronts. The struggle it is carrying on is born of a crisis of authority, a crisis aggravated by various factors which have bewildered public opinion and aroused reactions. It is enough to recall the transition from the Stalin phase to the Khrushchev phase, with the change in spirit and in methods, the revelation of Stalin's crimes, the uncertainty of a directive wavering between the principle of national ways to socialism and a return to the most rigid conformity of methods.

Caught between two fires, Soviet doctrinaire interpreters have ended by acting with the greatest possible prudence and displaying on all occasions the most scrupulous respect for orthodoxy. It is better to remain tied to traditional moorings than to make experiments and run the risk of being exposed to accusations of heresy by fanatical upholders of the letter. The prevailing policy is therefore: wait and see. In this way it hopes not to aggravate the crisis, which is in reality incurable.

The Soviet Union can prolong indefinitely this experiment because it has immense resources which permit a formidable deployment of power. But in all the other communist countries the influence of the ideology is paralysing. None of them can stand up to comparison with capitalist countries of similar size, population and natural resources. The superiority of the Western world lies in the free evolution of reality which does not allow itself to become imprisoned by any kind of formula. All the Western political parties are inspired by very wide principles which are more like guiding lines than rigid precepts. Marxism, on the other hand, lays down impassable limits and fixed aims which must be achieved; it prescribes radical transformations which must be made and mortgages the future with bills of exchange which, however often they be extended, must at some time be paid. It is, in a word, the prisoner of its own principles. Thus it is preoccupied with prophesying the imminent collapse of a capitalism that is more thriving and vital than ever before, and promises the advent of an integral communism which fades more and more into the mists of the future since it is unrealizable, and which systematically excludes certain natural and logical solutions since they cannot be reconciled to its principles. This conformism to the thinking of a man who lived a century ago, in historical conditions completely different from those of today, is one of the most mortifying and incomprehensible phenomena of human intelligence. One might say that millions of men are incapable of looking at reality with their own eyes or of reasoning with their own brains, but are forced, whenever confronted with any new problem, to consult the canonical texts of Marxism as if they were some sort of Sibylline books. How long such a practice can endure is difficult to foresee; but the day when it is abandoned will see the crisis sharper than ever. In vain some of the Soviet exegetists, like Preobrazhenski, try to distinguish between the immutable aspects of Marxism, which will be developed and completed, and those which will be replaced by new elements. Such a distinction has no sure foundation because the Marxist doctrine is, as the communist theoreticians never fail to point out, a monolithic whole which must be accepted or rejected as a whole. If everything that Marx wrote is not to be recognized as inviolable, what part is to be saved? The only thing left to do is to hold fast to Lenin's aphorism: 'Marx's ideas are omnipotent because they are true.'

3

Even if it may be possible to block the evolution of an idea, it is not possible to halt the evolution of reality. Therefore many of Marx's theses have fallen by the wayside, despite the last stand made by communist theoreticians, since they have been clearly falsified by facts.

Such is the case of the Marxist law of 'absolute pauperization' of the proletariat under a capitalist régime. The first refutation of this so-called law was taking place in those very years in which Marx published the first volume of his *Kapital*, which coincided with the rise in wages in the industrial countries beginning with England, while at the same time prices diminished. The rise in wages continued for thirty years till it amounted to 15%, whereas prices were reduced by 45%.

Despite the isolation in which it is kept, the Soviet public knows very well that the living standard of the workers in capitalist countries is far higher than that of the workers in the communist countries. Even if one limits the comparison to the United States and the Soviet Union, it is well known that the average wage of the American worker is four times greater than that of the Soviet worker. It has therefore been found necessary to suppress from Soviet texts of political economy the Marxist law of the 'absolute pauperization' of the proletariat in a capitalist régime. Furthermore, Mikoyan at the XX Communist Party Congress held in February 1956 exposed the falsity of this law. From that time communist theoreticians have restricted themselves to speaking of the 'process', that is the 'tendency' towards this, although reality has also shown how false is this thesis with which they have sought to hide the baselessness of the Marxist law.

In the Soviet tract *Fundamentals of Marxism-Leninism* published in November 1959 the writer says that the pauperization of the working class is 'a tendency shown in various ways which is capable of modifications and divergences in individual capitalist lands'. The conclusion therefore is: 'Only slanderers and falsifiers can assert that the tenor of life for the workers in the capitalist states must be, according to the theory of Marx and Lenin, lower than that, for example, at the turn of the century.'

Despite these evident refutations Soviet propaganda continues imperturbably to insist on the correctness of the Marxist diagnosis. In particular, Khrushchev during his visit to America affirmed that for a hundred years, that is from the time when Marx described the dynamics of capitalism, the situation has remained unaltered and the misery of the working proletariat has been increased, certainly not alleviated. Therefore, he concluded, nothing can save capitalism from the fate that awaits it from the inevitable outbreak of revolution.

This shows only too clearly how impossible it is for communist propaganda to renounce any of the premises on which it bases the inevitability of communist revolution. It must continue to support the thesis of the progressive pauperization of the proletariat because only in this way can it justify the intensification of the class struggle which must lead to the communist revolution.

4

Marx not only predicted the progressive impoverishment of the working class, but also the progressive proletarianization of the middle classes, the bourgeoisie, and that more and more bourgeois would fall into poverty and go to swell the growing ranks of the proletariat. Thanks to this general weakening of the bourgeoisie the disproportion of forces would become such as to facilitate the ultimate triumph of the revolution. Therefore the study of the bourgeoisie in the capitalist countries and especially of the lower middle classes in whom they see the natural allies of the proletariat is of especial interest to Soviet theoreticians. The political and economic reviews of the Soviet Union analyse in detail the numerical strength of the bourgeoisie based on the official statistics of the individual countries which publish such data. From these reviews it seems that at the beginning of the last decade there were:

In France 737,000 artisans, each of whom employed not more than five paid workers, and 1,275,000 retail traders, each of whom employed not more than two workers. All in all the French lower middle classes (*petit bourgeoisie*) comprised more than two million families;

In Italy, according to 1951 data, a million and a half small traders, artisans, shopkeepers, innkeepers, carriers, and the like;

In the towns of Federal Germany 1,600,000 lower middle class families in 1950;

In the United States 4,600,000 families belonging to the lower middle classes.

All in all it appears from these figures that the lower middle classes make up about 15% of the French population, 12% of the Italian, 11% of the American and 15% of the Federal German. To these must be added those who enjoy only a modest income: smallholders, public and private employees, craftsmen and the like. In this way one reaches a comparatively high percentage which shows the continual flow from the proletariat to the bourgeoisie, contrary to Marx's forecast which postulated a flow in the other direction, from the bourgeoisie to the proletariat.

The Soviet press does not contest the fact of this movement from below to the lower middle classes but tries to maintain, notwithstanding, the accuracy of Marx's thesis by pointing out that the percentage of national income represented by the contribution of the lower middle classes tends to diminish while that from the great industrialists tends to increase. In this way the problem is no longer that considered by Marx, since he wished to show that the ranks of the future revolutionaries would be increased and those of the bourgeoisie thinned out; whereas the opposite is true, especially taking into account that the figures quoted in the Soviet reviews are about ten years old. In the meantime the national incomes of almost all the Western states, including Federal Germany and Italy, have almost doubled and the movement upwards from the proletariat to the bourgeoisie has been accelerated, as is shown by the purchases of cars, electrical household appliances and the like in ever growing quantities. It may incidentally be observed that those who form the lower middle classes, that is to say the small shopkeepers, artisans, smallholders and the like, would immediately be liquidated since the exercise of such activities plays no part in a communist régime and therefore it does not seem possible, on pain of suicide, that the communists should find allies in these victims so designated by the partisans of revolution.

Soviet writers recognize that, contrary to the simplified Marxist conception of two classes struggling against one another, wide differentiations of classes and sub-classes are being formed in the heart of capitalist society. The most prominent of the Soviet economists, Academician E. S. Varga, in a lecture on the evolution of capitalism given in December, 1959, stressed that the new techniques of production favour this selective movement, since they tend to reduce the employment of unskilled workers and stimulate the increase of those 'technicians who control the whole process of production by their handling of machines'. Varga also recognizes that 'there is an ever larger bureaucratic class in the world of labour (that is to say in the trade unions, the workers' co-operatives and the workers' parties). This bureaucracy is not made up of wage-earners but of salary-earners. Today these make up a third of the personnel of the factories and this percentage will continue to increase until it exceeds the number of wage-earners. . . . This is a fact of great political importance,' Varga admits, 'because it is a new bourgeoisie in course of formation which tends to make common cause with capitalism.' This admission is of great importance. Varga, in other words, recognizes that even numerically the bourgeoisie is destined to exceed the forces of the proletariat as a result of new economic and technical conditions. We are therefore at the reversal of the tendency forecast by Marx. What then remains of the prophecy, repeated so often and so proudly, that the collapse of capitalism is imminent, if one is forced to recognize this continual blood transfusion into the forces of the bourgeoisie?

Despite the refutations of reality, it is indispensable for propaganda reasons to insist that capitalism is incapable of evolution and is unable to eliminate some of the grosser abuses that stained it in its initial phases. Marx claims that these abuses can only become worse until they make the conditions of the proletariat unbearable and drive it to revolt.

Let us take as an example a long article in *Sovetski Flot* of January 16, 1960 which is evidently intended as a catechism for the Red Fleet crews. It begins by stating that 'the present era is the era of the fall of capitalism and the consolidation of the socialist system' because capitalism is a régime exploiting and arbitrary, a régime rotten to its core. The author especially attacks Averell Harriman for having said: 'Our economic system has little in common with the old Marxist conception of capitalism and we should do well to abandon such an expression.' The Soviet article asks: 'Has there really been a transformation of capitalism? Has its nature changed?' and replies that so startling a change has not taken place, nor can it ever take place, because it forms no part of the 'laws of social development discovered and elaborated by the classics of Marxism-Leninism'. This is surely a curious way of confuting facts that do not square with the theories of Marx and Lenin. On the other hand the author finds no better argument for his thesis than to quote Khrushchev's words in reply to a statement similar to that of Harriman made by Cabot Lodge. 'I see no difference,' said the Soviet Premier, 'between the capitalism of which Marx writes and the capitalism of which Lodge speaks today.' The best expedient of propaganda is to deny the facts, after which every serious polemic becomes impossible. But reality is not annulled by denying it. The facts cited by Harriman, Cabot Lodge and American economists prove the transformation of capitalism mainly because of two factors: the broadening of the middle classes and the advent of technocracy at the head of the great industrial enterprises.

It is estimated that there are about fourteen million shareholders in the United States. The tendency of the Western world to increase the number of shareholding workers is looked on by the Soviets with much apprehension and suspicion, because it opposes to the theoretical collective right of the communist worker to own the means of production the effective right of the Western worker to individual ownership of a freely negotiable portion of such means. The *Sovetski Flot* is very sarcastic about this tendency: 'The sale of shares to the workers is only a mask adopted by the imperialists to conceal their dominant position,' and recalls Khrushchev's words: 'When there is a crisis, the real owners seize these shareholders by the scruff of the neck and throw them out of the enterprises in which they hold shares. The shareholder becomes unemployed, one of the army of more than a million unemployed.' Though denigrating the fact, Khrushchev is forced, as we have seen, to admit it. What he does not explain is why, if shareholding by the worker is a fact of no significance, it has won so much favour and is developing so rapidly in the more progressive industrial countries.

The *Sovetski Flot* also contests the other fact stressed by American writers that bourgeois society is being transformed into a 'society of executives' and that its leaders are no longer persons who owe their positions to accumulated or inherited fortunes, but to technicians who have risen to the control of enterprises because of their greater skills. This is true democracy. The fact is not denied, but every attempt is made to minimize it by saying that these executives do the will of the capitalists and eventually become capitalists themselves.

6

When Marx and Engels, in the Communist Manifesto, inaugurated communist propaganda and the international organization of the workers' movement in the struggle against capitalism, no state existed which was based on the principles put forward by them as valid, and which in practice showed the superiority of the régime that they desired over the abuses and faults they so vehemently attacked. But today, even though integral communism as wanted by Marx and Engels has not been put into operation, there none the less exist a certain number of states which have overthrown capitalism and installed a régime inspired by Marxist principles. Therefore the validity of the new régime may now be judged from the results of its application rather than from textbooks. It is especially interesting to find out if the new régime has succeeded in eliminating the evils imputed to capitalism by Marx and Engels or whether it has worsened them and to what extent.

It is worth recalling, for the sake of greater clarity, that Marx in his *Criticism of the Gotha Programme* of 1875 forecast a phase preparatory to communism which in later writings he called 'socialism'. Lenin adopted the idea that the transition from socialism to communism must take place in two periods. The Soviet Union and the countries of the Eastern bloc are still in the preparatory phase; therefore the Soviet Union has adopted the name of the Union of Socialist Soviet Republics.

This preparatory or 'socialist' phase is marked by three factors: dictatorship of the proletariat, state ownership of all means of production, planning. Between these factors there exists a relationship of cause and effect. The dictatorship of the proletariat implies the elimination of all other social classes. These will in part be physically liquidated, that is suppressed by violence or forced to leave the country, and in part be eliminated socially and economically by the confiscation of all their goods. Forfeiture to the state of sources of production imposes on the state the need to administer them, which it does by means of planning.

It is not possible to put any one of these innovations into operation without involving the other two. It is an illusion to think of partial reform; either the three factors are accepted as a whole or none of them is put into force.

The essence of the new régime installed in the socialist bloc is the substitution of state capital for private capital offered spontaneously by the public which receives from it a commensurate reward in the form of interest or profits.

But where does the state get this capital? The popular view is that the state expropriated it from the wealthy classes. This was true only at the beginning. For Russia had very modest capital resources compared with those of the Soviet Union today. Almost the whole of this immense amount of capital has been extorted from the working class, that is the workers and peasants, in the form of low wages, which means unpaid labour, forced loans never repaid and fiscal charges. Only by force can such an extortion of wealth be carried out. Therefore the only way to achieve it is revolution.

The Soviets stress that in a communist régime the means of production belong to those who work. That was the central theme of Khrushchev's propaganda. In his speech on the American radio-television on September 27, 1959, during his visit to the United States, he said: 'The Soviet Union is a workers' state. We have no capitalists. Our factories belong to the people. The soil with all its riches belongs to the people.' The sophism is clear. Neither the factories belong to the workers nor the land to the peasants but both one and the other belong to the state, which is an entity quite different from the workers.

7

The truth is that Marxism has never succeeded in specifying clearly who should be the proprietor or administrator of the sources of production once they have been collectivized. Must it be a 'social' or a 'state' ownership? Marx, Engels and Lenin have oscillated between one and the other, because of the difficulty of admitting the transfer of ownership to the state, seeing that the state itself must be abolished after the abolition of class.

The Communist Manifesto says: 'The proletariat will use its political supremacy . . . to centralize all instruments of production in the hands of the state, that is of the proletariat organized as the ruling class'; so that since the state must wither away, it is specified that all production will be 'concentrated in the hands of a vast association of the whole nation . . .'

Two problems then arise; when is the liquidation of the state to take place? And what is meant by 'a vast association of the whole nation'?

Marx, Engels and even Lenin himself in his revolutionary period have held very changeable and nebulous ideas about these two problems.

When must one proceed to the liquidation of the state? Engels in Anti-Dühring gives the impression that it must take place as soon as the proletariat has triumphed in the revolutionary struggle. 'The proletariat,' he writes, 'takes possession of the powers of the state and immediately transfers the sources of production to state ownership. By this action it puts an end to its own existence as a proletarian class, eliminates all differences and class-antagonisms and also destroys the state as such. . . The first act whereby the state represents the whole of society, that is to say taking possession of the means of production in the name of society, will be its last act as a state. The intervention of the power of the state in social relations becomes superfluous in one sector after another and finally ceases to exist. The government of individuals is replaced by the administration and the control of production processes. The state will not be abolished but will end in being non-existent.'

The experiment of the Paris Commune led Marx and Engels to believe that it was necessary in the event of revolution to hasten the destruction of the state. It was not enough to take possession of the machinery of state and use it for their own ends. This criterion was stated in the preface written for the 1872 edition of the Communist Manifesto.

This was stated with greater precision in 1875 with the Criticism of the Gotha Programme, in which Marx declared that 'between capitalist society and communist society is the period of transformation from the one to the other'. During such a transitory phase 'the state cannot be other than the revolutionary dictatorship of the proletariat'. In other words the proletariat, having assumed power by a revolution, assigns to the state the expropriated sources of production and entrusts it with the task of organizing a communist society. How long is this transitory period to last? On this point also no definite pronouncement is made, and interpretations differ considerably.

The fact remains that the dictatorship of the proletariat, or better the dictatorship of the proletarian state, only represents a transitory phase, since all Marxist authors are in agreement that the state must disappear.

The final aim is to entrust the administration of the sources of production to a state body, or to a number of state bodies, but deprived of coercive powers. This is the essence of communism. But when one tries to clarify what this body that is destined to succeed the state shall be, neither Marx nor Engels provides any valid criterion. Engels proposed to the Congress of Unity of Gotha that in place of the state one should speak of a *Gemeinwesen*, which is equivalent to the French *commune*. But his proposals were not accepted.

Can it be maintained that state capitalism, that is to say state administration of the sources of production, responds to the fundamental concepts and aims of Marxism? Clearly not, since the abolition of the state with its coercive powers is a pivot of the doctrine upon which Marx and Engels have insisted with remarkable energy.

'Not a single book,' said Lenin to the XI Party Congress in March 1922, 'has been written on state capitalism as it exists in a communist régime. It did not occur even to Marx to write anything on the subject and he died without leaving a single precise statement or irrefutable instruction. This explains why we must get out of our difficulties by our own efforts.'

This also explains why state capitalism is one of the most controversial points for discussion among Marxists themselves. Engels declared himself hostile to state capitalism as a permanent régime[2] because 'the modern state, whatever be its form, is essentially a capitalist machine . . . the more producers it absorbs . . . the more citizens it exploits'. This is completely in accord with his premises. One cannot, without falling into flagrant contradictions, arm with fresh and formidable powers that state organization in which one sees the source of violence, of arbitrariness, and of social inequalities.

Lenin too, when writing his *State and Revolution* in 1917, took a somewhat diffident attitude towards the state. This publication shows the influence of Bukharin who, in an article entitled *The Robber State*, pointed out the danger of the state becoming a collective capitalist, in which case the workers would be even more ex-

[2] Friedrich Engels—Karl Marx; 1878, *Selected Works*, Volume II.

ploited than before. Therefore Lenin insisted on the destruction of the state, though affirming that its powers should be exercised 'for an entire epoch' during the régime of the dictatorship of the proletariat. Such a régime should be ready to transfer to the workers the administration of the state and of production.

These ideas reflect the principle stated by him in the project for the Party programme drawn up in 1910, and specifically in para. 8, in which it was said that the trade unions 'must concentrate in their hands the entire control of the whole of the national economy'. This was the conception of Karl Kautsky, namely that the participation of the workers in fixing the aims of industry and the conditions of work must be made clear through free trade unions in a democratic society. To Kautsky the essential thing was that the will of the workers prevail, since it was for their benefit and to affirm their complete liberty that the collectivization of the sources of production was arranged.

However, the problem of reconciling the collectivization of the sources of production with respect for democratic freedoms has not been solved. Perhaps it is insoluble, because the two exigencies appear irreconcilable. Logic demands that collectivization of the sources of production leads inevitably to state capitalism. This is the way followed by the Soviet Union. But is this way in accord with the postulates from which Marx and Engels started when they denounced in the harshest manner the excessive powers of the state from which they wished to free the working classes? Juarès has said: 'Socialism is not nationalization.' The fact remains that once on the road to state capitalism there is no turning back.

It is therefore not surprising that the revisionist critics rail against a course which leads, not to the liquidation of the state, but to its omnipotence, and denounce such a course as a deviation from the essential principles of Marxism. Thus Kardelj in his speech on December 6, 1956, in which he specified his points of divergence from Soviet Marxism, stated that 'to have recourse to an ever more energetic strengthening of the state in economic and social affairs in a socialist country is not the right road towards a complete liberation of the forces of socialism. . . . It is not possible to speak of a perfect socialist system, let alone communism, as long as the state as an instrument of force is the main factor in economic relations.' This hampers the 'advance of specific democratic forms corresponding to basic socialist economics'. Statism 'separates the masses from power' because it is 'in conflict with the elementary interests of the working classes and prevents them from exercising an influence on the control of basic social relations'.

Kardelj declares to be absurd 'the conclusion that it is possible to establish socialism without the working class and even against its will' and upholds the necessity of organizing workers' councils, thus 'transforming the sources of production under state ownership into real social ownership, that is to say ownership under the direct democratic administration of the community of producers'.

Basically this was just what the Soviet trade unions asked of Lenin.

The expositions that precede Marxist criteria on some basic problem, such as the collectivization and the administration of sources of production, show how vague were the ideas of Marx and Engels and how vacillating were even those of Lenin. This is a confirmation of the view that the Marxist doctrine has set up theoretical objectives without finding out if they were or were not realizable in practice and above all whether they were attainable without extinguishing the freedom of the individual. The lack of a guide to reach such objectives was lamented by Lenin, as has been seen in his report to the XI Party Congress, but not even he has left a clear directive and it has therefore been doubted by some socialists if the form in which some Marxist postulates have been put into practice really corresponds to the ideals set up by Marx and Engels.

8

Now let us see how state capitalism began in Russia and how it works.

There was a moment, at the beginning of the Bolshevik revolution, when, strong in the promises of the Party, the workers took possession of the factories and administered them through their factory committees, and the peasants took possession of the land.

One of Lenin's first government actions was to inaugurate full equality of economic treatment among workers, technicians and directors in order to show in a tangible way the final condemnation of the régime of free bargaining which had kept alive 'the discipline of capitalist slavery', 'the discipline of the lash' and 'the discipline of hunger' upon which, as he was wont to say in those times, the capitalist organization of labour was based.

The VII Pan-Russian Soviet Congress in December 1919 established a universal food ration (*paiok*). Every worker received rations according to the size of his family. The principle of the dictatorship of the proletariat was still further applied by making the engineers dependent on, and therefore at the orders of, the workers. Since production began to show signs of slackening at once, many persons were tried for sabotage. Famous among these trials was that of the engineers of Shakhty in 1928, which ended with five shootings.

Put into practice, the system showed itself for what it was—a utopia. The results of the experiment were already evident four months after the decisions of the VII Pan-Russian Soviet Congress. Complaints began pouring in. 'He who works and he who doesn't, the idler and the lazybones, all draw on the same scale as the real workers. All get the prescribed ration.' A. I. Rykov said loud and clear that a system of this sort would 'sap the foundations of economic renewal and labour yield'.

Production collapsed. The workers abandoned the factories or wasted their time idling. And since one absurdity gives birth to other absurdities, there seemed no other cure than to make work compulsory by the introduction of a directed labour service. Thus, after the promises to emancipate the workers from capitalist slavery and after the Leninist preaching in favour of voluntary and unpaid labour 'independent of any coercive apparatus', we come to the institution of effective slavery or forced labour. That is what is now taking place in China. That is the proved and re-proved demonstration that the introduction of communism leads inevitably to forced labour. That is what happened in Russia. The IX Party Congress decreed mobilization and militarization of manpower, exactly as is now happening in China with the communes. Three labour armies were set up with units freed from active service. At the beginning of 1921 there were eight military labour units with 280,000 men.

Naturally the Soviet leaders did not lack ways of justifying the institution of directed labour by the sacred principles of Marxism. The first creator of the system, Trotsky, assumed the ungrateful task at the III Trade Union Congress (April 6 to 13, 1920). 'By directed labour,' he said, 'we mean labour in which every worker has his proper place allotted him by the economic organs of his region, province or district, a regulated labour which does not obey the blind game of the laws of supply and demand but is in accordance with an economic plan covering the whole country and which involves the working class. It is said,' Trotsky went on, 'that all forced labour is unproductive. If this be the case, all socialist economy would collapse because there is no other way that leads to socialism save the authoritarian direction by a central economic organism of the whole of the labour force of the country, according to the needs of a national economic plan.'

Trotsky had the sincerity to acknowledge that this labour was directed, 'forced' he called it. 'By admitting this,' he said, 'we acknowledge not in form but in essentials the right of the proletarian state to send any worker, male or female, wherever he be needed to carry out important economic tasks, and to punish the worker who refuses to obey a state order or who does not subordinate his own will and the will of the working class to the economic aims of the state. This is the basis of the militarization of labour.'

From these premises he reached the following incontestable conclusions. 'The militarization of labour, in the fundamental sense that I have indicated, is an essential way of organizing manpower by its forced grouping, in conformity to the exigencies of building socialism during the transitional phase from capitalism to the communist state. If this manpower, organized and grouped by coercive methods, is unproductive, then so much the worse for socialism. The entire organization of society may be regarded as the organization of labour in ever new forms in order to increase its yield. If the new form of organization involves reduction of yield, then we shall inevitably be doomed to disappear.'

Here, at last, is plain speaking. Trotsky has given us, with irrefutable logic, the true essence of communism.

The truths which he had the courage to proclaim are today still, more or less, at the base of the system. In actual fact every individual in Russia is tied to an obligatory task, because the state keeps a whiphand over everyone through hunger. Every worker, as Trotsky said, has 'a determined place allotted to him by the economic organs'. There is no place here for the liberty of the individual in a system planned in every detail. Individual liberty would be an anarchic factor which would upset the plan and make its fulfilment impossible. The fact that the owner of the sources of production and the employer of labour is the state and the state alone, means that every infraction of labour relations is a crime and the state has the right 'to punish the worker who refuses to obey its decrees'.

All this means that only coercion can assure the fulfilment of the plan. It is now clear why the communist state can only exist in a dictatorial form. Only in such a way, says Trotsky, is it possible to pass to communism; nor does he hesitate to declare that such a form of forced labour is the highest form of the evolution of society. If it fails 'then so much the worse for socialism'; if 'the new form of labour organization means reduction of yield, we shall inevitably be doomed to disappear . . .'

The result of this experiment was brusquely negative. The failure of the militarization of labour forced the disbandment of the military units whose productive capacity was shown to be nil. The experiment only lasted a few months. On March 3, 1922 a decree of the Central Committee abolished the directed labour service.

With the NEP (New Economic Policy) there was a return to the régime of free contracting, that free contracting which Lenin had defined as 'the discipline of capitalist slavery' and which, according to Trotsky, obeyed, to use the words of the Communist Manifesto, the blind game of supply and demand. It is a fact that whereas after the experiments described above real wages dropped 12.3% below the 1913 level, under the NEP they doubled and at the same time the working day was reduced by an hour.

The suppression of the NEP was a step backward. The five-year plan and armaments involved enormous expenses and to meet them it was necessary to keep wages low and give priority to heavy industry, with a consequent reduction of consumer goods and a rise in living costs. The result was a reduction in real wages.

But no one dared to go back to the past. Stalin introduced state capitalism, unashamedly adopting the greater part of the criteria of private capitalism for the administration of the enterprises. Whereas these, save for a few exceptions, were before 1929, that is to say before the beginning of the five-year plans, financed by common funds into which their takings were poured, Stalin imposed upon all of them the system of *khozraschet*, which consisted of 'the covering of money expenditure of enterprises by their own money revenues, ensuring the profitability of enterprises'.[3] Stalin realized that it was not possible to fulfil the five-year plans if the control of the factories was not restored to competent technicians with disciplinary powers comparable with those of the directors of Western enterprises. He also introduced the principle of differentiation of wages according to the qualifications and yield of the workers.

All this was the antithesis of the egalitarian criteria of Marx, Engels and Lenin. Therefore there was no lack of resistance and doubts which provoked and kept on provoking waverings. From time to time the principle of equality prevailed, then that of divergence of economic treatment. Thus in 1925 and 1926 the trade unions, at their Central Council, stood out for equating the wages of the skilled workers with those of the labourers. But Stalin, in a speech on June 23, 1931, harshly condemned the system of fixing wages without distinguishing 'between skilled and unskilled labour, between heavy and light labour'. 'Equality,' he said, 'has the effect of taking from the unskilled worker every incentive to pass into the category of skilled workers. . . . You know that we have need of thousands, even of millions, of skilled workers but in order to train them the unskilled worker must have the chance—and be stimulated thereby—of being able to get on and to better himself.' He therefore restored to the leaders of the enterprises the privileges, taken from them by the revolution, of organizing production and controlling factory discipline. The decree of May 28, 1940 laid down these functions and responsibilities in detail, taking as a norm that the

[3] Alec Nove, *Soviet Economy*, George Allen and Unwin Ltd., London, 1961.

heads of the enterprises be chosen from the engineers, the technicians and the more highly skilled workers, and that they must be given higher wages than the average for qualified workers.

These directives of Stalin, considered contrary to the fundamental principles of communism, provoked sharp reactions from the trade union leaders and Party officials, which were implacably suppressed. But today, with Stalin gone, the egalitarian tendency is once more coming to the fore and the way favoured by Khrushchev was to eliminate the maximum and the minimum wage and to take a middle course.

9

Wherein does state capitalism differ from private capitalism as far as the workers, for whose benefit the sources of production have been expropriated, are concerned?

Marx based his thinking on the idea that exploitation of the workers was possible because possession of the means of production was not available to them. The workers are dependent on, though in a position of shattering inferiority to, the capitalist. Marx described this servitude of the workers in searing terms: 'The Roman slave,' he wrote, 'was bound to his master by chains; the wage-earner is bound to his by invisible threads.'

The truth of this statement is disputable, but it is the basis upon which Marx built his whole theory. To end the inferiority of the worker, it is, according to Marx, only necessary to restore ownership of the sources of production to the workers. Until these two elements are united, confiscation of surplus-value by the capitalists will remain.

It must be recalled that, according to current Soviet doctrine every form of profit is, as Marx taught, a part of the worker's labour unpaid for by the capitalist, who wrongfully takes possession of it. An article by A. Bakumenko in the *Krasnaya Zvezda* of December 1959 enters into polemics with Cabot Lodge and describes as 'ingenuous' his statement that profit is the remuneration of those captains of industry who 'by their initiative and energy have achieved great results'. Bakumenko explains that such a justification is untenable because 'a century ago Karl Marx had already poured ridicule on those economists who sponsored such theories and showed convincingly that profits (the converted form of surplus-value) were the result of the unpaid labour of the workers and were pocketed free by the industrialists, the shopkeepers and the bankers. In a bourgeois society the capitalists own the sources of production and the workers have naught save their hands. In order not to die of hunger they are forced to sell their labour, that is to say to work for the capitalists who own the factories, the plants, the mines, the railways and the electric power stations. Even more, the owners of capital do not pay for the whole labour of the workers but only a part of it, in the best case the cost of his labour (that is to say the cost of supporting the workman).'

That is the theory. Let us see it in practice. The régime now existing in the countries of the socialist bloc has not restored to the workers the ownership, nor even the use, of the sources of production, nor has the state refrained from levying on every enterprise a proportion of its turnover and a part of its gains. In other words, the state forces the enterprises to include in their costs the 'turnover tax' which each one of them has to pay; furthermore, it takes a portion of the gains which the enterprise has made from the sale of its products thanks to the high prices fixed by the state.

It follows that these profits repaid to the state capital are incomparably higher than those made on the free market, where competition intervenes to reduce costs and profits. The extent of the profits paid by the Soviet enterprises to the state can be deduced from the statement made by Khrushchev to the XXII Party Congress in October 1961 that in the five-year period 1955-1960 profits from industry and transport were doubled.

We are therefore on the same plane as private capitalism. In the Soviet Union and the other communist countries, the workers 'have naught save their bare hands' as Bakumenko said, and 'are forced, lest they die of hunger, to sell their labour'.

It remains to be seen if the position of the worker be worse or better and if his rights be more guaranteed or less guaranteed in a régime of private capitalism or in one of state capitalism.

Marx put forward the theory that the lower the wages the greater the surplus-value confiscated by the capitalist. He says in Vol. I, Chapter 24 of *Das Kapital*: 'The capitalist gets rich, not like the miser, in proportion to his personal labour and his restricted consumption, at the same rate as he squeezes out the labour-power of others, and enforces on the labourer abstinence from all life's enjoyments.'

One might say that he is describing the system of state capitalism now in force in Russia. There wages are a quarter of those paid in America and about a half of those paid in Western countries. It must therefore be concluded that there is no capitalist state that squeezes the labour-power as dry as does the Soviet Union. There is no private capital that levies so high a quota of profits. Marx has taught that 'the rate of surplus-value depends, in the first place, on the degree of exploitation of the labour-power'. Applying Marx's criteria it must be acknowledged that in no country is the labour-force so exploited as in those countries where state capitalism exists.

Let us now compare the rights and guarantees of the workers in each régime.

In order to eliminate, or at least to reduce, the inferiority of the worker to the capitalist, the democratic states apply a social legislation which assures the workers the rights of assembly, union and strike action. The guarantors, and at the same time the executive organs, of such rights are the political parties and the trade unions. In Russia and the other communist states a single party is the only wielder of power; the trade unions are organs of the state under the control of the Party. Faced by the state the individual is powerless, since in a communist régime the state unites to its already formidable powers which it derives from its dictatorial position those still more formidable which it derives from being the sole owner of all sources of production. The individual, bound hand and foot, is dependent on the goodwill of the state since from it he derives his means of livelihood, the only possibility for him and his family to survive. Marx speaks of a tie between capitalist and worker similar to that between owner and slave; but can one imagine a more total form of dependence than that now existent in the communist lands?

The Russians are well aware of their situation. No one has defined it more clearly than Pasternak in *Dr Zhivago*. Speaking of the condition of the Russian peasant, he makes one of his characters say: 'When the revolution came and woke him up, he decided that this was the fulfilment of his dream, his ancient dream of living anarchically by the work of his hands, in complete independence and without owing anything to anyone. Instead of that, he found he had only exchanged the old oppression of the tsarist state for the new, much harsher yoke of the revolutionary super-state.'

All these doctrines which without any ethical principle wish to impose their own form of emancipation on man end by going to the opposite extreme of what they declare to be their intention. They proclaim that they will put an end to servitude of man by man and then reduce him to the most desperate servitude to the machine of the state, which denies him every political freedom and every economic initiative. A strange liberation this, that exchanges one servitude for another and more hopeless one.

The conclusion to be drawn is that the socialist world, involved as it is in economic conflict with the capitalist world, has been forced to apply capitalist norms and follow capitalist methods, but within the framework and with all the authority of a totalitarian régime. However paradoxical it may appear, it is a fact that the advances of Soviet economy, so vaunted by communist propaganda, are due, not as this propaganda claims, to the merit of Marxist systems and formulas, but to those principles and methods that the Soviet state had adopted from capitalism and introduced into its structure and into its industrial hierarchy, especially those concerning factory discipline and the encouragement of productivity by material incentives. Moreover, every time the ideological influence gains the upper hand and imposes its egalitarian principles, its dictatorial methods and its economic controls, then production falls.

None the less the correctives imitated from capitalism cannot erase the primary cause of the inferiority of the régime set up in the Soviet Union, that is to say state ownership of the sources of production. The Soviet state, and with it the countries of the socialist bloc, have renounced the greater number of the postulates set up by Marx and Engels, for example the withering away of the state, the suppression of money, the control of the factories by the workers, and free love. But the expropriation of the sources of production, even though put into force with some modifications as regards ownership of the land, remains the pivot of the system. Not for nothing did the Communist Manifesto declare that 'the theory of the communists may be summed up in the single sentence: abolition of private property'.

This is the essence of communism but at the same time its Achilles heel, since it is not easy to root out of men's hearts the instinct of personal interest which is at the base of private ownership. To abolish ownership without having first eradicated this natural instinct, which is the real motive force of human activity, means to mortify the individual, to mutilate his capacities and to crush his energies.

It can be said that in the Soviet Union productive effort strikes against the iron curtain of the ideology. Khrushchev's constant urgings, the more and more numerous and widespread controls of the Party, the watchfulness of the trade unions, the recriminations of the Central Committee and the Presidium, the sanctions against those guilty of 'social parasitism', are all proofs of the feeble commitments of the social body when it lacks the productive spur of individual interest. The day this pressure from above slackens, for example during a crisis of power in the Soviet Union, production immediately falls. A proof of this is the agricultural crisis, responsibility for which Khrushchev attributed to the diminished interest and less rigid control of the Party organs.

In the capitalist world the fulcrum of progress is that individual initiative which has been replaced in Russia by state initiative, which means bureaucratic initiative. It is easy to see what it means to bar the way to millions of human motors working at full power to produce ever greater wealth.

Despite propaganda vociferations, the communist worker is fully aware that he is being exploited; his low productivity is a proof of this. The peasant who aspires to the ownership of the land he works is even more aware of suffering an injustice. The aspirations of the workers are for an active participation in the profits of the enterprise and therefore of its administration. What has been granted, albeit in a limited form, to the kolkhoz workers is claimed, for the same reason, by the industrial workers. Soviet propaganda has insisted too much on the right of him who works to own the means of production. This right, which has been conceded in theory to the worker, has not, save for a few brief interludes at the beginning, yet found any means of application. The result is a sense of impatience, of justice denied, in fact of frustration.

It is what the original trade unionists put vainly before Lenin, who deprived the trade unions of any effective power to safeguard the interests of the workers. This injustice has never been redressed, nor can it ever be, for to do so would mean the bankruptcy of the régime.

11

In short, the abolition of private ownership is at the root of all the evils from which the régime suffers.

From the state control of the sources of production stems the necessity for planning which, despite some favourable features, sharpens certain defects of the régime and produces results markedly inferior to those of a free market economy.

Land collectivization means an endemic agricultural crisis in all the communist lands, which in turn influences the scarcity of consumer goods in the Soviet Union, the need for rationing in the satellite countries and famine in China.

It is impossible to see how the transition from the state-communism now in force can be made to integral communism. The reason officially given for the continual postponement of the intro-duction of communism is that it is necessary, before taking the next step, to assure a maximum availability of goods. Such an explana-tion not only fails to convince, but proves that only under the present régime, and not in the communist one, can an increase in production be reached sufficient to ensure such a maximum avail-ability of goods. In fact today production is increasing thanks to material incentives, making private interest its fulcrum. This is thanks to the catch-phrase now in force 'to each according to his yield', but when one passes to the communist catch-phrase 'to each according to his needs' the interest in producing more in order to gain more will have to be replaced by the interest of working for the common good. What is the economic value of so altruistic a for-mula? That is the unknown. Up to the present all such experiments mentioned in history have been, without exception, failures.

It has been shown that the principle of compulsory labour is basic to the Soviet régime. Men and women are equally affected. Article 12 of the Constitution sanctions the principle: 'He who does not work does not eat'. This principle has recently had a particularly rigorous application. Everyone must show the source of his gains. No one is allowed to dispose freely of his own time. Anyone may be haled before the judgment of his fellows in a People's Court on an accusa-tion of parasitism and exposed, for poor yield, to disciplinary measures which usually involve being sent to a re-education centre which is virtually a concentration camp where the culprit is sub-jected to forced labour.

The programme adopted by the XXII Party Congress insists on the principle of compulsory labour: 'Whosoever receives any form of advantage from society without taking part in social work is a parasite, living at the expense of others. In a communist society man is bound to work. Idleness is incompatible both with his own conscience and with public opinion.' This is not a matter of a simple social obligation; to work is obligatory and whosoever avoids it is subject to punishment.

In face of the power of the state, armed by the laws, the courts and the police, the worker is powerless. Whoever protests, whoever tries to react, condemns himself to virtual civic death and must re-sign himself to accept the most lowly and the worst paid work. On December 20, 1938 it was decided that from January 15, 1939 every worker must be provided with a labour-card in which, as well as his personal details, should be registered all information on the profes-sional activities of the holder, his transfers from one enterprise to another and the reasons therefor, the date of entering any under-taking and of leaving it and the reasons for his dismissal. No enterprise is allowed to hire any person who does not have such a labour-card. It is a sort of good-conduct certificate without which no one can be employed, since all enterprises belong to the state and its orders are mandatory. A note of censure on the labour-card is like the brand of shame in other times. What Western worker would agree to submit to so humiliating a discipline, without escape and without defence?

It is not surprising that in a régime of this sort productivity should be so low. That, in turn, is one of the causes of low wages and of the low level of consumer goods.

Nor does the worker enjoy any trade union safeguards to protect him from the threat of exploitation.

All the problems referred to here—planning, agricultural crisis, transition to communism, trade union safeguards, low wages, short-age of consumer goods—will be dealt with in full in the chapters which follow, and reasons will be given for the conclusions here reached.

12

What credit does the Marxist ideology still enjoy among the Soviet public? In private conversation one often comes across persons who make game of it as a doctrine that has been overtaken by reality. Setting aside the official homage and the efforts of the hierarchy to create a sort of Marxist myth and to encourage a popular cult of its prophets, whose pictures are carried in procession at all great meetings, individuals show only too clearly their disgust for this ponderous and hermetic doctrine, to the extent that students consider its teaching the least attractive part of their education and most of them find it frankly repulsive.

The same may be said of the Party propaganda. There are com-plaints about its exasperating boredom. It has reached a saturation point, common to all dictatorial régimes, where it only creates irrita-tion and insensitiveness to arguments which, by constant repetition, have become trite and stale. The Soviet hierarchy is clearly and in-cessantly worried about this indifference to, and impatience of, Party indoctrination. On several occasions the Central Committee has de-nounced the public's lack of response and coldness, which keeps it away from political meetings.

This fossilization of the doctrine is harmful. It lacks the charm of novelty, the interest of new problems, which hold the attention of its hearers, especially the young. We have already noted the reasons for this inertia and more especially the need to avoid discussion of dissensions that are splitting the communist world.

In their *Philosophical Writings* Marx and Engels warned that the need for solutions and final truths was over. 'It is always evident,' they go on, 'that every acquired knowledge is necessarily limited and is conditioned by the circumstances in which it has been acquired.' But though the circumstances in which Marxism was conceived are now more than a century old and in the meantime we have entered an atomic age, with space-flights and automation, it remains anchored to a political, economic and social conception which is a hundred years out-of-date. As has been seen, the current doctrine of the communist world has not budged, for fear of heresy, from the concepts or even from the very words of the much venerated sacred texts.

It should not be forgotten that when the Communist Manifesto was published and when Marx wrote *Das Kapital* the West was shaken by subversive movements caused, especially in England and France, by the intolerable conditions of the working class. The most convincing part of Marx's *Das Kapital* is not his theory of value and surplus-value but his detailed evidence of the state of the working classes. He showed the ruthlessness, the cynicism and the stupidity of the ruling classes of his times and came to the conclusion that they deserved to be swept away by the just exasperation of the oppressed classes. In doing this Marx committed an error of perspective which today, after so many years have passed, is easy to see. What was in fact the opening phase of capitalism was regarded by him as the ultimate and definitive phase, forerunner of the revolution. He did not understand that the crisis which he saw before his eyes had arisen out of the unexpected invasion of machines into an economy mainly made up of craftsmen and agricultural workers and that the working class, collected haphazardly and badly amalgamated, was forced to submit, because of its disorganization and lack of skill, to the most odious oppression by its masters. This was the picture of a very limited moment in history which Marx, Engels and Lenin regarded as a normal and stable condition incapable of change.

The manoeuvre of communist propaganda is to present capitalism today as it was a hundred years ago. It is a manoeuvre that shows how short of arguments this propaganda is and proves to what expedients it must go in order to keep the masses in a fictitious state of unrest. In fact the social reforms, introduced in the intervening years in the Western countries, indubitably because of agitation in which Marxism too played its part and by the initiative of the socialist parties, have assured the workers economic conditions, guarantees of rights and a trade union safeguard incomparably superior to those enjoyed in the communist countries including the

Soviet Union itself, despite the advantages given to the latter by its immense wealth.

Without doubt advances in production, advances in science and advances in military and political power have created a somewhat flattering image of the Soviet Union. The error is to attribute these advances to the ideology. For centuries Russia has been one of the world powers. After the Napoleonic wars it was second only to England, even as today it is second only to America. To attribute the position that it holds today to the communist régime would be the same as, at the beginning of the last century, to attribute Russian power to the autocratic régime of the tsars.

From the last century those who have studied conditions in Russia foresaw the exceptional increase of her power as soon as her immense natural resources were exploited. That is what is now taking place. Modern technique is such that industrialization, once set in motion, continues with accelerated rhythm. It should not, however, blind us to the defects and weaknesses of the régime or to the contradictions and limitations inherent in the application of its ideology.

The important thing is that these negative aspects should be recognized by the Western world. They will be evident, sooner or later, to the communist world also. Since, as Marx observed in one of his youthful writings, 'facts are stronger than theories'; and it is not possible to halt the march of ideas.

CHAPTER IX

Planning

I

THE economic rivalry between communism and capitalism is a rivalry between planned economy and free enterprise.

Planning in its authoritarian form is only possible on two conditions; that the state administers all sources of production and that it has sufficient powers to enable it to impose the integral application of its plans, that is to say that in cases of non-fulfilment it can have recourse to coercive action against defaulters.

Lacking private initiative, which is the pivot of a free economy, it becomes necessary to have recourse to force which can, as in Stalin's time, even amount to terror. All the internal propaganda of the communist world, as Khrushchev's speeches show, is concerned with the need for controls and the threat of sanctions. This creates an atmosphere of restriction which, it is easy to understand, makes life in Russia particularly unpleasant.

In the régime of free enterprise the communists see a permanent source of anarchy, of squandered resources, of insufficient employment of the labour force and, above all, of a lack of balance between production and consumption which gives rise to recurrent crises with the enormous losses that they involve.

Marx and Engels believed that they had avoided this instability of capitalist economy by introducing the principle of planning. Marx set out his ideas in the Constituent Manifesto of the International Labour Association of 1864, contrasting 'the blind dominion of the laws of supply and demand which represent bourgeois economic doctrine' with 'socialized production directed by forethought and understanding which represents the economic doctrine of the working classes'.

Engels in his turn stated that only a conscious organization of social production by means of planned production and planned distribution can elevate the human race above all the other animals in the social field, even as it is elevated by the general effect of production in the strictly biological field. Planning, in fact, is an advance in social organization in order to bring to an end the struggle in which the strongest eliminate the weakest, for a reason similar to that whereby the state has brought to an end the system of private justice.

It has already been said that planning is the logical corollary of the expropriation of the sources of production. Lenin, therefore, as soon as he took over power, proclaimed that 'the planning of the national economy is one of the main aims that the new Soviet state intends to achieve'.

The Soviet boasts of the results of planning. Khrushchev, speaking to the National Teachers' Conference in July 1960, expressed himself thus:

'The socialist economy of the Soviet Union is governed by the laws of planned and gradual development. In all our activities, both present and future, we have before us a clear perspective of a sound development of all sectors of the national economy, a perspective defined by our plans. We do not have, nor can we have, the crises and recessions which are inevitable under capitalism. When we lay down the lines of the development of our economy over a specified period, we establish the type and the quality of the goods and the raw materials to be produced and we indicate the economic areas where it is preferable to produce them.'

Basing their activities on such criteria, the communists make planning the fulcrum of their economic progress and stress the superiority of those who are organized rationally over those who trust in luck and cannot have a clear picture of what the future holds for them.

The main accusation made by the planners against free enterprise is the chaos of production, the bitter struggle between competitors and the unruly multiplicity of initiatives, often identical and exceeding the needs of the market, resulting in a waste of capital. In free enterprise, they say, no producer knows what another is doing, because everyone looks after his own affairs and surrounds his activities with the maximum of secrecy, whereas in planned economy there is a central direction which has before it the entire panorama of the economic activities of the nation and co-ordinates them in a common framework. The conception which is at the basis of planning is to administer the state as a single economic unit.

Planning is undoubtedly one of the most serious and efficient tenets of Marxism. Its positive advantages have induced many non-communist countries to welcome it, if only partially. The art of government is essentially in the order of priorities, since all problems are subordinated to one another, and political skill is to know how to solve basic problems rather than to become lost, as so frequently happens, in partial reforms which are fragmentary and of dubious effect. It must be granted that the Soviet statesmen have a very clear sense of the natural order of things; they have begun with the schools and have then organized heavy industry in order to create, with the cadres coming from the schools and with the armaments provided by industry, a military potential of the very first order. The great advantage of planning is precisely to be able to organize production according to an order of priorities, taking all needs into account according to their importance and urgency. Thus the development of the national economy proceeds progressively and in good order, with a sense of continuity and with the regular progress of a natural process. With planning it is possible, among other things, to make use of the most convenient deployment of labour, a rational specialization and a distribution of enterprises in conformity with the general interests of the nation.

Planning tries to achieve the maximum efficiency of productive organization by the maximum co-ordination of economic initiative; for its part, free enterprise aims at achieving results by favouring individual initiative and selective competition.

The principal advantage of free enterprise is to be able to find in private interest the most powerful spring of progress, through the vigilant watchfulness of the employer to increase his profits and diminish his costs. In free enterprise, observes Professor Campbell, comparing the two systems, 'producers, whose aim is to make as much profit as they can, adjust their plans in accordance with these price movements. If the price of a given commodity increases, that encourages the production and discourages the consumption of that commodity—and conversely, lower prices encourage use and discourage production.'[1]

Campbell observes that in order to obtain maximum profits the employer is driven to reduce his costs to a minimum, which is in accord with the general interests of society.

Profits, costs and prices are the basic elements that control the activities of producers. In an economy of full and free competition, the law of supply and demand operates with the automatism indicated by Campbell. But with the growth of technical progress, which urges enterprises to expand and to give predominance to monopolies and trusts, the automatic play of supply and demand is hampered by the strategy of the great industries, by the intervention of the banks and by coercive action by the public authorities. Free enterprise thereby tends to lose its flexibility and its automatic action.

[1] Robert W. Campbell, *Soviet Economic Power*; Atlantic Books, Houghton-Mifflin Co.; Boston, 1960, p. 84.

Though within these limits producers never proceed blindly, as their rivals' propaganda asserts, but on careful calculations of the state of the markets and above all bearing in mind possible price fluctuations, many of the Marxist criticisms of free enterprise, more and more dominated by the great industries, still hold good.

In planned economy, on the other hand, both production and consumption are dependent on decisions imposed equally upon producers and consumers. By manoeuvring prices independently of costs, the planner can modify artificially the volume of demand in any sector, even as he can, at will, modify the volume of supply. He is therefore freed from the demands of the market as well as from international price fluctuations and is independent of the force that tends to reduce costs, that is to say free competition.

From a purely economic standpoint it is difficult to strike a balance of advantages and disadvantages between the two systems because of the effect of those correctives which are constantly sought for by one or the other and which tend to bring them closer together. It is not so much on the economic plane that the positive and negative aspects of both may be assessed, as on the social and political plane, bearing in mind, as has already been said, that authoritarian planning is not possible without the collectivization of the sources of production and the drastic curtailment of individual freedom and initiative.

The ideal would be, as will be pointed out later, to combine the two systems in order to enjoy the advantages of both and to eliminate, or at least reduce to a minimum, their disadvantages.

However that may be, the Soviets hold jealously to planning. They may have doubts about many things but certainly not about the superiority of their system over that of free enterprise, as they are absolutely convinced that their indubitable industrial progress is due to planning. They agree therefore with Khrushchev's diagnosis that free enterprise 'is the sign of a society torn asunder by antagonistic contradictions which give rise to the changeable and irregular nature of the development of capitalist economy', as he said in his speech to the teachers quoted above.

However, notwithstanding these contradictions and its inferiority, the capitalist economy has gone on progressing and is today more full of vigour than ever. In Western countries poorer than Russia in natural resources the workers' way of life is far superior to that of the Soviet workers.

The reason for the Russians' jealous attachment to planning is that they have by now become familiar with the system; their great industrialization was born of it, as a result of the five-year plans, and they would find themselves bewildered at having to change.

From this viewpoint, Marxism is solidly anchored in the minds of the rulers. They would feel completely bewildered at living in a free economy, outside the ruts of the now traditional programme formulated in advance. Theirs is an industry to a great extent hot-house grown, that is to say developed in a régime of monopoly and autarchy. How would such an economy, characterized by very high costs and high prices and by a constant wastage of labour, react when their markets would be invaded by competitors from the more skilful, more modern, more expert and less expensive Western industries provided with great resources for financing themselves?

2

The father of Soviet planning was G. Krzhizhanovski, a friend of Lenin, to whom he suggested that the industrialization of the country be founded on a large power reserve provided by a network of power stations, either hydro-electric or thermal to be fed by peat or other low-cost fuel. On his advice the State Planning Commission, or Gosplan, was created on January 29, 1921. It received from Lenin the task of 'assuring unity of objectives and the harmonious economic development of the country, as well as the rational utilization of material and labour resources'. Krzhizhanovski was its president for many years. On January 9, 1948 it became the State Planning Committee attached to the Council of Ministers.

The change of title from Commission to Committee implied a reduction of functions. It followed a dispute between its president, Nikolai Voznesenski, and Stalin, who had him shot. The duties taken from the Gosplan were assigned to committees attached to the Council of Ministers. Thenceforward the Gosplan underwent a series of transformations; its tasks were increased or diminished according to the humour of the men in the government or the responsibility imputed to it for the lack of success of one plan or another. Furthermore it was considered indispensable to separate long-term planning, which demands active theoretical study and calculations of future developments and needs, from current planning, which requires practical directives, co-ordination and control. Therefore, in 1955, the Gosplan was split into the State Planning Commission, which retained the name Gosplan, entrusted with the task of long-term planning, and the State Economic Commission, or Gosekonomkommissia, entrusted with current planning. To these two organs was affiliated the Gostekhnika, entrusted with the study of new technical processes to be put into effect in various production sectors.

The Gosplan was originally assigned two objectives which at once were shown to be contradictory. It had to develop the productive forces of the country 'in the sense of industrialization and socialization'. But socialization was incompatible with rapid industrialization. Which of the two aims would have to be sacrificed? Stalin denied that there was any contradiction between them. His order was to 'reach and surpass' the capitalist countries. 'We are,' he said, 'fifty to a hundred years behind the advanced countries. We must catch them up in ten years. We shall either do it or bust.'

It seemed therefore that priority must be given to production. But it was not possible to sacrifice communist principles, in whose name the superiority of the Soviet Union over the capitalist countries must be ensured. Therefore the stress was clearly placed on socialization. It was at this time that the NEP, or New Economic Policy, which had restored private initiative, was finally abandoned. In the struggle between realism and ideology it was the latter which prevailed. In April 1929 Stalin denounced the 'Party right-wing' to the Central Committee. 'Is it correct,' he asked, 'that the central idea of the five-year plan in the Soviet lands should be the increase in the productivity of labour? No, it is not correct. We do not want an increase in our labour productivity at any cost. What we need is a closely defined increase of that productivity, an increase which systematically makes the socialized sector of the national economy prevail over the capitalist sector. That, comrades, is the crux of the matter. A five-year plan which pays no heed to this central idea will not be a five-year plan, but a five-year absurdity. . . . What distinguishes Soviet society from every other society is that it is interested, not in an increase of the productivity of labour by any and every means, but in an increase which ensures the predominance of socialist forms of economy over all other forms, and above all over that of capitalism.'

It was a clever declaration since, while it reaffirmed indisputable homage to principle and ensured its rigid application, it in fact concealed the violation of that very principle or at least concealed the modification of its rigidity in order not to compromise the basic aim of the five-year plans, that is to say increase in production. As has been said earlier, Soviet industrial organization has been closely modelled on the organization of capitalist countries. It has returned to the bourgeois system of entrusting wide powers of control and responsibility to the directors of its enterprises. It has restored money wages in place of the *paiok* or rations in kind desired by communist canons, which champion equal remuneration for all. It has introduced the system of piece-work which the Chinese have rejected, thereby recognizing an incentive which is purely capitalist. The

control and administration of the factories by the workers themselves, which took place in the early days of the revolution, has been
abandoned. It has furthermore jettisoned the principle of equality
by differentiation in payments according to position, ability and
yield. Still wider breaches have been broken in the fortress of
doctrine for the benefit of workers on the land.

3

Despite Khrushchev's statement quoted above that the Soviet
Union neither has nor can have crises and recessions, there has been
crisis even there and the Soviet press itself has reported it. In August
1963 *Pravda* was the first to mention it and to try to analyse its
causes. There was no crisis of over-production, like those which
harry so many capitalist countries, but of under-production, or better
to say production chaos, an evil endemic in all the communist states.

The crisis has affected agriculture as much as industry. In agriculture the gravity of the crisis has been shown by the need for Russia,
in 1963 and 1964, to make massive grain purchases from the
capitalist countries. It is estimated that the delivery of bulk cereals
in 1963 was about twelve million tons less than in the previous year.[2]
This great deficiency of cereals has taken place in a country which
before the Bolshevik revolution was one of the principal grain ex-
porters and despite the fact that in recent years the area of cultivation has been increased by more than fifty million hectares of virgin
soil. In industry the gravity of the crisis has been shown by the
failure of the seven-year plan, though official statements boasted of
its complete success and claimed that in many sectors it had, in its
first four years, surpassed the quantities foreseen. It later became
known that the seven-year plan had not attained such objectives in
those very sectors where the greatest progress was expected in
remedying certain fundamental shortcomings of the Soviet economy,
especially in the sectors of chemical industry, metallurgy, cellulose,
synthetic fibres and resins, and plastics, to say nothing of consumer
goods. This fact is the more serious inasmuch as even the previous
plan, that is to say the sixth five-year plan, was abandoned as unattainable almost as soon as it had been put into operation, that is
to say for the same reason as the seven-year plan has been abandoned
two years before its term. In place of the seven-year plan a two-

[2] In 1962, 56,600,000 tons of cereals were delivered. According to estimates
at the end of 1963, 44,700,000 tons were expected to be delivered. Up to
November, 1963, the Soviet Union bought abroad a further nine million tons
by exporting 325 tons of gold.

year plan has been drawn up, for the years 1964 and 1965, after which there is to be a return to the system of five-year plans.

Detailed analysis of the causes which have led to the failure both of the sixth five-year plan and of the seven-year plan has brought to light the gravity of the crisis which has affected the whole system. This was shown by a decision of the Central Committee of the Soviet communist party to change radically the structure of the planning organs. Is it a question of a crisis which can be solved or is it a crisis of the system? For a judgment, albeit approximate, of the nature and gravity of the crisis, one must examine in considerable detail the organization and operation of Soviet planning.

4

Planning is based upon two factors: the aims to be achieved and the means available to achieve them.

The aims to be achieved are set by the political organs.[3] These establish the sectors in which efforts must be made for an increase in production, not merely for economic reasons but for the aims of military potential and prestige.

The basic directives for the drawing up of the plans come from the Party. The Party is the inspiring spirit, the motive force and the watchful eye which controls all the activities, not only economic, but political, social and cultural, of the whole country. This is what Stalin repeats in his instructions:

'In the elaboration of the working plans of this or that department, whether it be for industry or agriculture, or even for trade or cultural organization, the Party lays down the main lines which decide the character and orientation of the departments for the duration of the plan. . . . The Party controls the activities of the executive organs of control and of those which exercise power, correcting errors or making good inevitable shortcomings; it aids these organs to apply government decisions and tries to assure them the support of the masses. No decisions are to be taken unless they are inspired by the appropriate directives of the Party.'

These are very clear and peremptory instructions. The Party is

[3] In 1952 Stalin stated in the pamphlet *Economic Problems of Socialism* that 'the problem of the rational organization of productive forces, the planning of the national economy, etc., are not the subject of the economy but of the political economy of the organs of direction'.

omnipresent and omnipotent; the task of the other organs, and in particular the participation of the people in the drawing up of the plans, is reduced to a very small matter.

The directives approved by the Party Congress are transmitted to the Council of Ministers, which hands them on to the technical departments whose task it is to elaborate them in a final plan.

This political strategy of the development of production is undoubtedly justified. Apart from the fact that policy is dependent on economics in every state, it is not possible to continue with planning a gradual and balanced production if the directives, based on a universal view of the country's requirements, do not come from the centre. But in fact this comprehensive view almost always is at fault, even with the most foreseeing and highly skilled planners, as is proved by the errors and deficiencies which have little by little become obvious. Only in theory is the state all-seeing and omniscient. In practice, authoritarian planning owes its efficiency to a firm unity of direction, lacking which it plunges into an anarchy of opposing initiatives. It will later be seen that with the development of planning the errors and the deficiencies from above tend to increase and to become worse, since it becomes impossible to keep control of the machine, to know everything and to decide everything, even with the aid of an ever greater experience and an ever more efficient technical staff. Therefore, once the planning organization has been given the go-ahead and certain basic directives have been stated, it must have a certain amount of autonomy. At what level this is to be put into practice is the great problem which has not yet been solved.

Once the political organs have decided in which sectors to concentrate their forces to increase production, it is up to the technical departments, the Gosplan and its like, to decide the levels to which production can be raised, taking into account the means available. Therefore the departure point of this technical design is made up of the so-called 'material balances', that is to say the calculation of production factors; capital to invest, labour available, raw materials and plant, either available or which can be made available. It is up to the technical organs to point out the best method of distributing them among the enterprises so that they may be in a position to carry out the task assigned them in the plan. The success of this depends above all on the rational use and prompt employment of such resources.

Investment capital is for the most part provided by the state budget. In 1964, out of a total budget of 91,385 million rubles, 38,700 million were earmarked for the national economy, together with a further 29,800 million provided by the self-financing of the enterprises. The total of investments for 1964 amount to 68,500 million. For 1965 it is known only that the total investments will rise to 74,400 million but it is not yet known what part of these will be provided by the state budget whose total expenditure has been provisionally fixed at 101,200 million rubles; nor has the quota of investment from the funds of the enterprises themselves yet been indicated.

It is estimated that about two-thirds of these assignments go to investment in the strict sense of the word, both fixed and fluid capital, and that the rest is spent in various ways not always clearly specified.[4]

Other than the budget funds there is available for investment, as has been seen, the capital raised from the funds of individual enterprises. This is made up either from profits or from amortization payments. Another source of investment is bankers' credits. It should be noted that the plans only take account of a part of such investments, that is to say of those approved by the central organs, so that those of lesser scope are decided by the enterprises without requiring authorization from the centre.

By and large, it is estimated that investments amount to a quarter of the national income. Once this total has been settled, it is split between expenditure, administrative and military expenses, and productive investments. The state budget is one of the basic elements of the plan.

The Soviet state determines how much of the national revenue is to be set aside for expenditure. This means that it establishes finally the level, and consequently the volume, of wages and pensions, even as it establishes the total funds destined for the so-called social services. It thus fixes the scale of the demand for consumer goods and adjusts their supply, that is to say their production. The more the part of the national revenue destined for expenditure is reduced, the greater is the part destined for productive investment.

Obviously, forecasts on the scale of consumption can only be approximate, since an unpredictable part of the income of the consumers is set aside for saving as, furthermore, a part of these savings is destined for consumption.

The main difficulty, however, is estimating the probable amount of consumer goods is due to the uncertainty of some fundamental data, such as the approximate number of wage-earners and the total of wages, including piece-work, bonuses and overtime. In the fourth five-year plan (1946-50) it happened that the labour force employed

---

[4] For 1961, 1962 and 1963 investment figures in the state budget were:
1961: 33,908 million out of a total of 77,590 million
1962: 32,469 million out of a total of 80,370 million
1963: 34,543 million out of a total of 86,203 million

in the factories exceeded by more than five million the number of wage-earners foreseen by the plan and, consequently, the wages costs exceeded the amount allowed for, thus creating a lack of balance between the supply and demand of consumer goods. The frequency with which this has been repeated, and the wages fund foreseen in the plan has been exceeded, shows that it is not easy to avoid this error. It is one of the unknowns in planning, even as is the total of the harvest because of varying weather conditions.

The uncertainty of the total number of wage-earners is due to the fact that the labour force is not equally distributed over the vast extent of the Soviet lands. There are centres in which there is an excess and therefore there is unemployment or more or less disguised under-employment, while there are others where there is a shortage. Since the Soviet government has renounced its powers of forcing the workers into enterprises which need labour, these enterprises are forced to compete with one another, as happens in all industrialized countries, for workers, especially the more skilled workers. They have no other means of attracting them and keeping them than increasing their wages. But since wage-levels are fixed at the centre for every category or grade of workers' skill, and since the directors of the enterprises are strictly forbidden to increase the prescribed wage-levels, all that remains to be done is to circumvent the law either by classifying workers in a grade superior to that for which they are qualified, or by arranging piece-rates, or by paying them overtime for work which has not been done. The consequence is a chronic inflation, because of the scarcity of consumer goods by comparison with the demand. The rise in prices which results is a serious and disturbing factor, because it reduces real wages, complicates calculations and creates general discontent. The queues outside the shops are the most visible sign of the chronic scarcity of goods.

It is more difficult to decide what is the role of capital assigned to productive enterprises, a part of which may end, due to speculation, in increasing expenditure. It is a notorious fact that there are in Russia a growing number of persons who have at their disposal financial means far superior to their wages or normal income. This phenomenon has been the butt of sharp criticism by the Soviet leaders, from Khrushchev downwards, who have pointed out the necessity of tracing these illicit sources of income.

To conclude; the success of planning is dependent on the limitation of consumption which is only possible if one begins by freezing wages.

5

The main obstacle to the successful working of Soviet planning is neither the scarcity of investment capital, which in Russia amounts to a percentage of the national income considerably in excess of what the capitalist countries destine for the increase of production, nor the insufficiency of the labour force, though that may not be, as we have pointed out, any too abundant; the real obstacle is the difficulty of efficiently providing the enterprises entrusted with the task of carrying out the plan with the necessary supplies, that is to say raw and semi-manufactured materials, tools and spare parts. In a régime of free economy every enterprise gets its supplies when and where it can, at its own convenience, choosing the materials most suitable to its needs and at the best available price. In Russia the materials are provided through the state organs, following a long routine which is not always sure of being successful, with the result that the enterprise lives in uncertainty of receiving in good time the supplies indispensable for its operation.

The prime condition, moreover, of a good planning system is perfect co-ordination between production plans and supply plans. Perhaps the fundamental difference between a state economy which is developing more or less on an autarchic basis and a free economy is that the former has not got at its disposal the unlimited resources that the international market puts at the disposal of the free economy countries. Everything in a directed economy is measured, controlled, co-ordinated. But this effort of forecasting, of calculation and of co-ordination becomes more and more difficult the more the economy is developed and becomes more and more complicated and diversified. It lacks, in short, reserves freely and immediately obtainable, an irreparable defect of all autarchic economies.

The Soviet Union has not so far succeeded in evolving a system which ensures supplies to its enterprises without uncertainties and without delays. A great part of the reforms in planning is concerned with the attribution to this or that department of the difficult task of ensuring supplies. Must they be forecast by the centre or by the peripheral departments nearest to the productive enterprises? If, as logic demands, only those who have drawn up the plan can take the decisions necessary to fulfil it exactly, then it is clear that it is up to the central powers to use their authority to overcome the resistance of the intermediate departments. This gives rise to another problem; must the formidable organization of supplies be focused in a single unit or distributed among a number of central organs, as were the ministries in Stalin's time? Then too there are some who ask if it is not a good thing to imitate the capitalist systems by giving the enterprises a broad autonomy in matters of supply. A clear directive has not yet been given, since every solution poses almost insoluble difficulties and therefore it oscillates from one solution to another without succeeding in escaping from the vicious circle in which it is imprisoned.

It is not in fact sufficient for the enterprises to send their requests to the planning authorities and that these give their approval, giving the enterprises which ask them certificates of allocation; after that there must be negotiations between the enterprise which has been granted the allocation and the supply enterprise, which is frequently overburdened with work and not always in a position to fulfil all its orders in good time. Thus begins, after a long procedure, that chain of delays which, increasing from one enterprise to the next, slows down and hampers the whole system of production.

Initially, the supplies intended for enterprises of the economic sectors of major importance were assured by the central ministries, each for the sector of its competence. They obtained the necessary quotas from the Gosplan which they handed on to the enterprises, controlling their effective fulfilment. After the administrative reform of 1957, of which we shall speak later, the channels between the Gosplan and the enterprises for such allocations were the planning departments of the federated republics or the republican gosplans. But recently there has been a tendency to return to a centralization of allocations, as will be seen in greater detail.

6

The first five-year plan was launched in 1928, to run from September 30th; in fact, it ended on December 31st, 1932. The second was carried out from 1934 to 1937; the third was interrupted by the war. The plans were resumed in 1946.

The failure of the sixth five-year plan towards the end of 1956 and even more the abandonment of the seven-year plan led the Soviet leaders to a serious reappraisal of the planning system. It clearly emerged from their discussions that the more developed a planning system is, the more difficult it is to control it and to remedy its defects. The Soviet Union has created an organization so complex because of its gigantic size, due above all to the vast extent of its territory, that, despite the aid of electronic computers and despite the technical skill of a personnel abounding in first-class men, it seems to exceed the possibility of an efficient and well-informed direction. An analogous criticism was levelled by Marx at capitalism, guilty, according to him, of having, like the sorcerer's apprentice, evoked powers it was no longer able to control. But this is just what seems to have happened in the Soviet Union. Once a planning organization has been created it continues to develop by its own momentum.

In the Soviet Union, haste to surpass America in productive competition has helped to accelerate this process; but it has also created a chaos which has paralysed many vital sectors. In a speech to the Party Central Committee on November 19, 1962 Khrushchev said that 'during the first four years of the seven-year plan more than three thousand seven hundred large plants have been begun'. How many of these have been finished? How many are working at full productive capacity? In the June 1963 session of the Central Committee, Khrushchev said: 'Perhaps it will not be advisable to open fresh factories in 1964 and it will perhaps be necessary to decide to postpone some construction in order to finish as quickly as possible those which have already begun.' It was therefore better to call a halt. On August 11, 1963 *Pravda* said that it was considered better to concentrate investment on 635 plants chosen from amongst those regarded as 'particularly urgent' but that, even so, it had not been possible to put even so reduced a programme into operation.

Khrushchev became aware that the planning machine had escaped from effective control because of its gigantic size. In May 1957 he therefore proposed a radical reform in order to decentralize the unitary organization created by Stalin. It was on his suggestion that the Supreme Soviet passed the law on 'the improvement of the organization for industry and building' by virtue of which a hundred and forty ministries, both central and federal, were abolished and their tasks transferred to a hundred and five economic councils, or sovnarkhozes, scattered over the whole Soviet territory and invested with broad powers of direction, initiative and control.

The regional economic councils are government organs of the federated republics which appoint their members. Usually the enterprises are controlled not from the centre but by the sovnarkhozes, with the exception of those of minor importance which depend on the local soviets. Supplies to these enterprises are decided upon by the republican gosplans and carried out through the sovnarkhozes which take over responsibility for the actual delivery of the materials. To co-ordinate and control the activity of the sovnarkhozes in the larger federated republics, that is to say in Great Russia, in the Ukraine and in Kazakstan, a republican Commission of National Economy was founded in each one of them in December 1960. But not even these measures were sufficient, so that from May 1961 the hundred and five sovnarkhozes were grouped into seventeen 'great economic regions', each with its own co-ordination and planning council. There are ten in Great Russia, three in the Ukraine and one in Kazakstan which forms a single region by itself; of the three remaining, one is for the group of Baltic states, one for the Transcaucasian republics and one for Central Asia.

These regroupings show the need to avoid the effects of excessive decentralization.[5] The most important problem was, therefore, not merely the co-ordination of the sovnarkhozes but the preservation of a single strong central control. Provision was made for this by restoring full powers to the Soviet Union Gosplan. The Gosekonomkommissia was therefore abolished and its responsibilities restored to the Gosplan.[6] But this concentration of power in a single organ rather than strengthening control paralysed it or at least made it less rapid and efficient. It was established that the Gosplan, absorbed by the needs of current planning, could not attend to its studies and the preparation of long-term planning. This led, in 1959, to the creation of a new organ, the Gosekonomsoviet or Council of Economic Science, entrusted with the study of questions relating to economic development and the progress of economic scientific culture. In fact this new organ has equal responsibilities and undertakes tasks in no way inferior to those of the Gosplan. The two bodies were called upon to make joint decisions, by agreement, on the proposals transmitted by the regional departments and by the enterprises, not only as regards planning but for everything relative to labour productivity, technical development and the most profitable exploitation of the natural resources and labour force of the country. This type of condominium lasted until 1960 when current planning was once again separated from long-term planning. By a decree of April 7, 1960, the Central Committee and the Council of Ministers reorganized and extended the Council of Economic Science (Gosekonomsoviet), entrusting to it the preparation of long-term plans and in particular the maintenance of a balance of materials,

[5] At the first session of the Central Committee held in November 1964 after the fall of Khrushchev, the Second Party Secretary, Podgorny, in his report on the organization of the regions, both industrial and agricultural, upheld the need for the Party to re-examine their territorial boundaries.

[6] In the law of May 10, 1957, referred to above, the functions of the Gosplan were thus stated: 'Global study of the needs of the national economy, formulation of long- and short-term plans for the national economy, bearing in mind the advances made in science and technology, the putting into practice of a strongly centralized policy for the development of key sectors, assuring on this basis the correct localization of production and the balanced development of all sectors of the economy, as well as the drawing up of plans for technical and material supplies and the assurance of the full observance of state discipline in the delivery of industrial products.'

the study of problems relating to the economy of the Soviet Union and the preparation of reports on the aims of the programmes. The Gosekonomsoviet took precedence over the Gosplan, whose functions were curtailed and its importance diminished.

Not even the new measures, however, could assure a steady guiding hand and an efficient control of the complex organization. The failure of the seven-year plan led to a re-examination of the causes which, in 1957 and in 1962, had prevented the fulfilment of the programmes. An enquiry on the structural defects and the in-sufficiency of controls was held by the Central Committee. The most severe criticisms were made by Khrushchev in his speech, already quoted, of November 19, 1962. It was, in fact, an indictment, in order to justify the radical structural changes for which he asked approval.

Very grave disadvantages were revealed in the allocation of im-portant tasks and in the control of the plans. Regional patriotism had been aroused, which drove the federated republics to even greater independence of the central organs and made them act on their own responsibilities, thus making the application of the global plan more difficult. In consequence, regional problems here and there took precedence over national problems. Central supervision was re-laxed, and everywhere there was a tendency towards waste and un-productive expenditure. Khrushchev declared that in this way 'the interests of the common policy of the country' were being forgotten and that less heed was being paid to 'collaboration in production'. It was necessary therefore 'to overcome local trends and avoid a vicious circle of production'. That was why they were forced to tighten the reins, to dismiss the directors responsible and to create fresh organs of control which were to keep watch on the periphery from the centre.

It was acknowledged that decentralization had weakened the unifying action of the control organs. The need of a unified control had been very clear in Stalin's mind when creating the system of planned economy. He had organized a centralized machine whose control levers had been entrusted to the central ministries. Direction and control were thus in the hands of a state bureaucracy which, by the importance of its tasks and by the powers with which it had been invested, became the real ruling class of the country. It had always remained a docile instrument at the dictator's nod. That was one of the reasons why the new régime had hastened to liquidate it as soon as it had prevailed over the anti-Party group.

But it was also true that the plurality of ministries had given rise to conflicts of competence, to the formation of closed cliques, which made the work of co-ordination and the free circulation of supplies rather difficult. At the time of the administrative reform it had been considered possible to replace the ministries at the centre by technical committees directly dependent on the Gosplan and competent for various more important problems, such as those concerning reserves of supplies, disposal of the labour force and so on. Amongst these should be mentioned the state committee for mineral reserves, the central office of statistics, the state committee for labour and wages, and the central organization for the distribution of consumer goods. But the activity of these bodies was far from being as efficient as that of the suppressed ministries.

There was, in fact, a continual wavering between centralization and decentralization, nor has a point of balance between these two tendencies yet been found. If decentralization was both possible and useful for certain production centres of local interest and lesser importance, a 'centralization and concentration of power', to use Khrushchev's phrase, was necessary for the vast industrial architecture of the nation, based on the great pillars of industry. Authoritarian planning is essentially a unified system which requires a universal vision of national interests and an organic programme which stimulates simultaneously the progress of all sectors. This is above all true for the Soviet Union which, notwithstanding its federal form, is a strongly centralized state; its economy is unitarian. All the federated republics are interdependent and the basic industries which have been created there must serve not local but national interests; that is to say, they form part of a unified system which can only operate at the direction of a common centre.

The difficulties which Russia has had to meet in solving the fundamental problem of centralization or decentralization, both of them indispensable for the better yield of the planning system, makes even more evident the value of free enterprise in which the decentralization of decisions is an everyday fact. Every interested person solves his own problems with full freedom and responsibility according to the criterion of maximum production and maximum profit, which as a rule harmonizes individual and collective interests.

7

The reforms adopted after the failure of the seven-year plan have strengthened the control of the centre, which, according to a decree of the Presidium of the Supreme Soviet dated November 24, 1962, is made up of the following organs:

1. The Gosplan of the Soviet Union, made up in part from the Gosekonomsoviet which has been suppressed.
2. The Sovnarkhoz of the Soviet Union, or the Council of the National Economy of the Soviet Union. V. E. Dimsciz has been appointed president with the rank of a vice-premier of the Soviet Union. His task is to direct the regional sovnark-hozes, that is to say the regional economic councils, and to control the execution of the plans, making such rectifications and variations as may be shown to be necessary during their application. He is therefore responsible for all current planning.
3. The State Committee of the council of Ministers for Con-struction, derived from the transformation of the Gosstroi. Its president is I. T. Novikov with the rank of a vice-premier of the Council of Ministers.

By joint decision of the Presidium, the Party Central Committee and the Council of Ministers, dated March 13, 1963, a Higher Council of the National Economy of the Soviet Union (VSNK) was created to direct and co-ordinate the activities of these three organs. It is 'a higher state organ for the direction of industry and con-struction' which has been given very wide powers of intervention in all matters concerning planning and with full responsibility for its actions. This has meant diminishing the powers of the Gosplan, or Central Planning Commission, which has been entrusted with long-term planning. The president of the Higher Council of National Economy is Dimitri Ustinov, a man of great energy, who has given good proof of his abilities as director of the armaments industry. To increase his authority Ustinov has been at the same time advanced to the post of First Vice-Premier of the Council of Ministers. A number of departments with duties similar to those of the central ministries suppressed by the administrative reforms of 1957 have been placed directly under the new council. At the same time the regional economic committees, or sovnarkhozes, set up by the same reform, have been reduced in number from a hundred and five to forty-seven. There has been a return in practice to a centralization of power very similar to that of Stalin's time, though the federated republics still retain the initiative for drawing up 'concrete plans of economic development'.

The main difference between Stalinist procedure and that now in force is the greater participation of the peripheral organs in plan-ning. This takes place, roughly speaking, in four phases. A first programme is drawn up by the Party which indicates the basic aims to be achieved. On this basis the Gosplan prepares long-term 'out-

line plans'. Within the limits of such outlines the federated republics present concrete plans relative to their needs. It is finally the
task of the Economic Council of the Union 'to examine', as Khrushchev has said, 'the plans proposed by the republics and, so to speak,
sew them together and create a general plan'. The first and last word
comes, as can be seen, from the centre.[7]

8

The decentralization carried out by the law of May 1957 has
radically altered the planning process. Whereas before this law the
directives were sent from the centre to the peripheral organs, to
whom no other task was left save to carry out the plans entrusted
to them, it is the peripheral organs, that is to say the republican
gosplans, which, on the basis of proposals sent them by the republican economic councils, transmit their planning projects to the
centre which, after having revised them in accordance with the
general line, decides the final plan.

The republican gosplans have, within the limits of their regions,
similar tasks to those of the Gosplan of the Soviet Union; they draw
up in advance long- and short-term plans and suggest initiatives,
but their proposals are transformed into definite plans only after
revision by the Gosplan of the Union.

This new system undoubtedly has great advantages insofar as it
permits a better knowledge of local problems and needs, and avoids
the issuing of directives by persons totally unacquainted with conditions in the regions in which they must be applied, as so often
happened in Stalin's time.

In this way the republican gosplans, upon which depend in their
turn the sovnarkhozes, that is to say the local economic councils,
are associated with the Union Gosplan, the supreme planning organ.
The sovnarkhoz has wide powers of direction, initiative and control
for all economic and technical problems in its district. It appoints
the executives of the enterprises or confirms their appointment,

[7] The Prime Minister, Kosygin, is said to have proposed that the work of
the Gosplan be reassessed and that it should once more become the controlling planning organization, with functions similar to those which it had
when Kosygin himself was its President. The First Party Secretary, Brezhnev,
re-echoed this, saying in his speech on November 6, 1964 that 'whenever the
science of the economists is replaced by subjectivism, failures become inevitable; the mania for constructing and then tearing down again is the greatest
of all possible misfortunes. Success comes, not from continual reorganiza-
tions, but from men and control over their activities.'

defines production programmes, introduces new types of goods and new procedures, stabilizes prices, redistributes investments, supplies the factories with machinery or raw materials of which there is a scarcity, and draws up long-term plans.

In particular, as far as planning is concerned, the economic councils have the following tasks:

—to improve the organization of production and planning, to assure a higher standard of development of the forces of production and to make rational use of the means and resources of their respective economic areas;
—to plan the system of supply to the independent enterprises;
—to draw up the local financial plans in advance;
—to stimulate the workers' initiative and improve their productivity;
—to study the economy of their respective zones and put forward proposals based thereon to the Gosplan.

To carry out these tasks the economic councils make use of data provided by the enterprises, whether industrial or agricultural, within their jurisdiction. The enterprises are in fact required to draw up in advance their particular production plan, to draw up in advance their technical plans for the utilization and supply of plant, their wages plans, their production costs plans, their building plans and their finance plans.

The total of these plans is called the *tekhpromfinplan*.

9

Planning proceeds, therefore, through the following phases.

The Party gives the general directives which will be approved by the Central Committee.

The Council of Ministers draws up, with these as a basis, the main lines of the programme. The Gosplan edits a sketch of the individual sections of the plan, stabilizing for each sector, industrial, agricultural, construction, etc., the amount of investment necessary, and fixes the wages scale.

This preliminary phase is completed in the first months of the year. In June the Gosplan sends to the republican gosplans and the sovnarkhozes the estimates for the programmes to be put into operation in their respective districts. These estimates indicate, broadly speaking, what a specific region will receive as investment, in raw materials and manpower and what it must provide.

The planning offices of the sovnarkhozes carry out a detailed study of these data. After which the sovnarkhozes send their chiefs to Moscow to discuss their projects with the central Gosplan. Having reached an understanding, each region finally revises its plan which must be ready by July 1st.

To draw up their proposals, the peripheral planning organs make use of the planning cells which exist in every undertaking, whether industrial, agricultural, commercial, transport, constructional, etc. In practice the directors and technicians of individual enterprises provide the detailed data, estimate the projected plans, ask for modifications, changes and additions. For form's sake, employees and workers take part in the initial phase and also the concluding phase of the drawing up of the plans. For that purpose the so-called sector conferences are summoned, that is to say the assembly of the factory personnel, in order to become acquainted with the projects, to put forward their opinions and to give their formal approval to what has in fact already been decided. Particular importance is, however, given to consultations between the directors and the shock-workers, that is to say those who have the greatest yield, usually those most closely linked with the Party.

Thus every undertaking draws up, within the framework of the directives it has received, its own production plan, specifying its requirements in raw materials, plant, labour and the like and preparing its relative financial plan. Every economic body, whether it be a factory, an agricultural unit, a shop, a restaurant, or a transport organization, must have its own programme and its norms of fulfilment which, once approved, become final.

From this mosaic of fragmentary programmes the procedure continues, after co-ordination with the district, regional and republican programmes, ending with the general plan drawn up by the Gosplan.

In practice the greater part of this work of co-ordination is done by the sovnarkhozes which examine the proposals of their planning departments and issue final instructions for the drafting of the regional plans. From August 10th onwards these must be submitted to the central Gosplan which, in September or October, sends them back in a finally approved form to the sovnarkhozes. By November at the latest every enterprise receives its production plans for the coming year.

As can be seen, the final decision belongs to the central Gosplan. It is its special task to determine which of the products that figure in the national plan are intended for export. On it therefore depends, in the final analysis, all commercial agreements and trading contracts.

10

Khrushchev introduced the principle of long-term planning. Other than the five-year and seven-year plans a twenty-year plan has been drawn up. Furthermore, though the plan for the coming year is drawn up in every detail, a plan for a five-year period is added. A system of this sort permits wider perspectives and more distant points of reference in directing the course of national production. In this way the producers know the objectives they must attain and the time of their disposal to attain them. They can therefore take all the necessary measures in good time. The aim is to eliminate the unforeseen, the uncertain and the improvised.

The Soviet planning system has been little by little extended to the other communist states (Bulgaria, Czechoslovakia, Eastern Germany, Hungary, Poland and Rumania) and that has permitted the co-ordination of the development of their economics through the formation, in 1949, of the Council of Mutual Economic Assistance (Comecon or EMAC).

The Council of Mutual Economic Assistance entered a phase of practical fulfilment in the two-year period 1955-1957 in which, for the first time, the long-term plans of the member countries were co-ordinated.

In 1956 the production of a number of basic products was co-ordinated, such as: oil, minerals, cast iron, steel, plastics, electric power, etc. In 1957 the co-ordination of the main economic sectors was finally perfected and later (May 1959) a seven-year plan, 1959-1965, was drawn up which envisaged a sub-division of labour among the communist countries and established various forms of specialization.

In 1956 the communist countries founded the Joint Institute for Nuclear Research for the study of nuclear physics and the peaceful uses of atomic energy. Within the scope of this institute the Soviet Union provides atomic reactors and cyclotrons to Poland, Czechoslovakia, Rumania and Eastern Germany and also gives aid for the installation of atomic electrical power stations in Eastern Germany and Czechoslovakia.

11

The plan interests all the citizens of the Soviet Union, as they are all mobilized to carry it out. It is split up into regional plans, district plans, urban plans and so forth, down to the detailed plans of individual enterprises. Within the framework of these last every worker has his own plan which he must carry out day after day in conformity with the established norms. Take, for example, a transport enterprise. This has a certain number of vehicles at its disposal. Each of these is entrusted to a pair of drivers, who take turns at the wheel. During his day's shift of seven working hours each driver must cover, in the service of his customers, more than a hundred kilometres. The pair of drivers is completely responsible for the upkeep of the vehicle. If at the end of every month the plan has been fully carried out the drivers receive a premium equal to a half of their wages. Since these amount to about sixty rubles, they receive on an average about ninety rubles, equivalent to about a hundred dollars. Other bonuses are granted if they save on the wear of tyres, on petrol consumption or on upkeep expenses. For example, if the pair of drivers manage to cover two hundred thousand kilometres without having to take their machine to a repair shop they qualify for a special bonus. There is, in fact, a mass of incentives to increase yield and diminish costs.

The same may be said of any other type of enterprise, whether it be a restaurant, a shop or a factory. Every worker has his norms, that is to say his well-defined task which he must carry out fully in order to pocket a bonus. There is therefore a dual system in force; low wages and piecework.

All these plans, whether collective or individual, are co-ordinated like the pieces of a mosaic in order to make up the general national plan. Everything is forecast, calculated, ordained, to the minutest detail like the activities of a beehive.

This capillary distribution of tasks allows the fulfilment of the plan to be anchored to the activity of individual sections, thus avoiding the risk that the plan may remain, so to speak, suspended in mid-air without any concrete guarantee that it will be fully applied. Only on this condition, namely by linking all its executants, is a plan a serious thing and the state is certain that the productive aims that it has fixed shall be attained. But that is not possible save when the state has the power to mobilize labour and to assign to each individual his little particle of activity. Thanks to this division of labour, which descends in depth to the individual, only a minimum is left for the imponderable and the unforeseen. It is, on a national scale, the system of the building contractor who translates in the work in progress the plan designed in the minutest particulars and in the most exact dimensions.

These are considerable advantages. But the disadvantages are far greater. Every individual becomes a cog in a gigantic machine. Bound to his allotted task, he does not see beyond it, does not aspire beyond it. When, day after day, he has completed his norm he is satisfied and has no further worries. Perhaps this is just the aim of the system, to dry up the roots of individual interest and ambition. Certainly we have reached the antithesis of what happens in a régime of free competition, where each man thinks unceasingly of bettering his own position and the goal which he has reached today is only the point of departure for more distant goals. All his faculties are thus sharpened and used to advantage. The essential is to be free in movement. In this atmosphere of harsh struggle the individual draws to its fullest extent the bowstring of his will in order to rise even higher. Society is perpetually on the boil and general progress is born of the maximum efforts of all and, contrary to the false statements of Marxist propaganda, the enrichment of the individual is turned to the advantage of all.

In the communist régime man ends by becoming fixed in his routine; he becomes an automaton. The annihilation of personality, which Marx reproved in the machine age, is the inevitable result of an economic order that regulates the actions of the individual down to the minutest detail without ever leaving him a minimum margin for his initiative. This leads to a sense of fatalism, of resignation, of the grey monotony of existence. The savour of life is lost. The feeling of being one of a herd ends by paralysing intelligence and will, because habit, which is the sister of instinct, replaces creative activity. Society becomes a phalanstery, a beehive, an anthill. It is a return to the forms of animal life.

What is more serious is that this pigeon-holing of individuals extinguishes in them the hope of a better future, that hope which is no less important for the life of the spirit than is food for the life of the body. The tourist is struck by the look of the Moscow crowds, so different from the crowds in Western cities. They have a subdued look, the look of people who have lost the habit of smiling; they are wrapped up in themselves and seem disinterested in everything which in the West gives zest to life.

The Soviet individual, and there are many of them, who does not adapt himself to this automatism, who cannot endure this pigeon-holing and who suffocates in this sort of regimentation in which everything is disciplined like the rule of a convent imposed by the will of the Superior, ends by being cast out of the ranks and devoted to virtual civic death. The instinct of the herd to expel the asocial element which disturbs the working of the group prevails. The expulsion takes place by order of the group. It must not be forgotten that on the rigorous application of individual norms depends the fulfilment of the collective plans of the factories, the kolkhozes, the sovkhozes, the shops, the restaurants and so on. So all the units of such enterprises are concerned in the fulfilment of the plans and, if possible, their over-fulfilment in order to get the consequent bonuses and, furthermore, to avoid the sanctions imposed in case of non-fulfilment. The poor yield of any one of the members of an enterprise means a loss to all, who react by casting him out. It is, as can be seen, a reversion to the system of the mediaeval guilds which bound their members for life and enmeshed them in a network of prohibitions.

12

The immense effort made by the Soviet leaders to eliminate the more serious defects of the system is undeniable. The decentralization set in motion by Khrushchev is the criterion followed today in order to allow planning at the periphery to reach, through various screens, the centre and thence return, via various intermediate organs, to the periphery. It is an unquestionable advance.

But certain defects, inherent in the nature of the system, persist. Khrushchev has made a merciless analysis of them, which allows one to understand more clearly than in the past how this gigantic organization works. In a report to the Party Central Committee on November 19, 1962 on 'The development of Soviet national economy and its direction by the Party' he denounced fundamental errors in the laying down of the plans, especially those concerned with the distribution of production factors (capital, labour force, raw materials) among the various production sectors. This has prevented the exploitation of material, financial and labour resources in the most rational and efficient manner. He added that the introduction and increase of new techniques already widely developed in the West is fundamental in importance, as well as the elimination of obstacles and losses, of which he painted a highly impressive picture.

The Soviet Prime Minister insisted at great length on the inability of the planning organs to correct certain grave shortcomings in the industrial set-up in order to enable it to compete with the constant advance of the Western countries. 'One of the most serious defects of our economic planning,' he said, 'is that it is not always based on accurate economic calculations and careful research; periods of development of individual sectors and economic regions have been determined from piecemeal and sometimes merely superficial forecasts. Such an attitude leads to errors of calculation in planning. What has taken place amongst us in the past with regard to the development of the chemical industry? This most important sector, which has a very great future, has not been sufficiently valued.' If it be true that the present phase of industry is notable for the triumph of chemistry, then the absence of a large-scale chemical industry, so lamented by Khrushchev, cannot but leave one unconvinced of the efficiency of a provident programming activity. The delay in the development of the chemical industry is shown by the very small investments assigned to it in the plans prior to the seven-year plan. Thus, while in the seven-year period 1952-1958 only two thousand million rubles were invested in this industry, the investments in the next plan were increased fivefold. But this sudden increase of programmes and means has choked the industry and created chaos.

Khrushchev attributed to this delay the very serious losses of the Soviet economy, such as those of the agricultural crisis due, in his words, to the shortage of fertilizers and also to the impossibility of replacing expensive materials, such as ferrous and non-ferrous metals, by synthetic materials. He mentioned the cable industry in which, instead of a cost of 108 million rubles to produce 67,000 tons of necessary lead, it would have been sufficient to spend 23 million rubles, that is to say five times less, for polyethylene which advantageously replaces lead.

'If the organs of planning and economics had paid closer heed to the basic needs of the economy, they would have established when and in what quantities it was necessary to replace ferrous and non-ferrous metals and other materials by synthetic products and, in consequence, to develop their production. Furthermore, the economic and planning organs do not pay sufficient heed to the advances of science and technics.'

13

Another consequence of the scanty technical know-how of the planning organs is, according to Khrushchev's accusations, the production of many 'outmoded machines and materials', though machines and instruments of high precision are available. The result is 'the declining quality of industrial products and goods of wide consumption'. Khrushchev gave the following example: 'In the clothing factory at Nikolaevsk it has reached a point where out of a hundred articles only five were found on inspection to be of good quality.'

Many of the deficiencies of the system affect the consumer because in the assignment of investments the lion's share is reserved for heavy industry. The housing crisis shows how little interest the planners have taken in the past to assure decent housing for the workers. In the fulfilment of the plan all the interest has been centred on the increase in industrial supplies, and priority given to raw materials, machinery and labour.

The interests of the consumers are also sacrificed because in a planned economy a sellers' market prevails, selecting the goods to be produced, whereas in a free economy it is the consumer who imposes his tastes. In a régime of free competition the natural urge is to increase the production of consumer goods and therefore to increase the general well-being, whereas in a planned economy the level of consumer goods production is decided by the planner who fixes, as has been seen, the volume of wages. The state establishes the limits to be set for the well-being of everyone, even as it establishes the measure of living-space for the individual and tomorrow perhaps will fix the menus in the canteens. Life tends more and more to take on the character of a coenobitic community.

The need to vary the quality of consumer goods and to try and meet the demands of the public has now become evident to the Gosplan which tries to satisfy them by leaving a remarkable margin of freedom to the factories. These are authorized, among other things, to take into consideration the quarterly orders sent them by the wholesalers who make it clear in such orders the types they wish to be produced.

Even in such a manner, however, the problem remains to a great extent unsolved because of the lack of a well-organized publicity system to draw the attention of the public to one product or another.

On several occasions Khrushchev did not fail to point out these deficiencies. In his speech to the XXII Party Congress he said: 'The variety of the goods in our shops is often insufficient, although the warehouses are frequently crammed with unsaleable goods. What kind of goods are these? They are goods of poor quality which the public refuses to buy. The demand for shoes, for example, is far from being satisfied, though shoes to the value of 1,500 million rubles are piled up in the warehouses.'

These are the disadvantages of production organized from above. When one stops to think that progress is stimulated by variety, by competition to increase the comfort, the pleasure and the variety of existence, one sees at once how far, in this matter, planning lags behind freedom of initiative.

'There is little joy in living in the Soviet Union,' remarks Herbert Stein in *The Saturday Review* of January 21, 1961. 'If I put myself in the shoes of a Soviet citizen, his life seems to me grey, sad, insipid, graceless, conformist and devoid of individuality, of creativeness and of independence.'

The production apparatus tends to become bogged down in routine since, as Khrushchev admitted 'the elaboration and above all the introduction of new techniques, of progressive technology and of advanced production experience, drags on for years'.

The cause of this habitual backwardness is above all to be found in the limited margin of initiative left to the enterprises. Modernization and innovation require capital, to obtain which a long and tiresome procedure must be set in motion with the risk of a final refusal, as is shown in Dudintsev's novel *Not by Bread Alone*. On the other hand it is necessary to suspend the fulfilment of the plan for every plant renewal and the plan has priority over every other need. To sum up, the obstacles and the risks discourage any initiative for improvement. The fundamental law of all bureaucracies is still the golden maxim: let sleeping dogs lie.

It should, however, be added that for some time past the planning authorities have taken into account the need to stimulate the inventive spirit of the directors, the technicians and the workers. Special prizes, to be drawn from special funds, will be given to those who introduce new technical procedures, and greater generosity is being shown in authorizing enterprises to spend money for introducing assembly-line techniques and modern tooling. But these are partial expedients which do not solve the serious shortcomings mentioned above.

14

Very serious errors in calculation have been made in establishing the size of the planned enterprises. At one time there was a mania for gigantic enterprises destined to serve vast areas and become the centre of their industrialization. But it was soon discovered that the transport costs of sending the products of such factories to the more distant centres dependent on them had been seriously under-estimated and that therefore it was not possible to exploit the full capacity of these gigantic plants.

Khrushchev denounced even more serious errors in establishing the priority of investments, namely that certain regions were overlooked which, because of their natural resources, were susceptible to even more rapid industrial development than others. It was, for example, an error to have given preference to certain districts of Siberia rather than to Central Asia. 'The planning departments,' he said, 'should have known that many regions of Central Asia have exceedingly rich potentialities for the development of cotton, fruit-farming and vines, but that these have not been exploited owing to lack of water. By building hydro-electric power stations we shall give water to the steppe regions and will bring fresh life to them. Furthermore, Central Asia is rich in mineral resources. With low-cost electrical energy it will be possible to develop a great industry. The planning departments should have taken account of all that when they decided where to build the great power plants, whether in Central Asia or, for example, in Siberia.'

15

Soviet economists, when criticizing along Marxist lines the free market economy, repeat that it leads to a dispersion of energies and a destruction of wealth by the chaotic multiplication of competitive initiatives, whereas in authoritarian planning everything is coordinated and rationally disposed, thus avoiding duplications by the full correspondence of means to ends. But this is how Khrushchev made the same accusations against planning that Marx made against capitalism:

'The dispersion of energies of the scientific and planning departments cannot but render more difficult the fulfilment of a unified technical policy in the various branches of the national economy; even more, this puts a brake on the fulfilment of large-scale specialized production. Let us take, for example, machine construction. There are four hundred independent technical offices working on this, of which only seven per cent are under the state committee for automation and machine construction. How then can the committee ensure the necessary technical level in this field and rapidly introduce modern techniques in place of old-fashioned ones? . . . This dispersion inevitably leads to duplication in the planning of machine construction and in the elaboration of technical processes since each organization makes its own designs and its own technology and, so to speak, invents bicycles.'

The same thing happens in tractor construction, one of the most discussed sectors, a sore point in the Soviet machine industry. Khrushchev said: 'We have thirty specialized design offices for tractors, motors, etc.; in these offices about three thousand draftsmen are employed.' The situation is no better in automobile production, where there are about forty technical offices; nor in the field of turbine and generator design. Each of these technical offices creates its own machine. The same is said to be true of radios, television sets and the like.

Khrushchev's criticisms have also stressed one of the major disadvantages of authoritarian planning, namely that it is a monolithic system, whose parts are closely interdependent like the gears of a machine all set in motion by a single motor. It is enough for this motor to slacken its drive for the rhythm of the whole mechanism to slow down; it is enough for one gear to jam for all the others dependent on it to come to a stop. An error of calculation, a detail overlooked in the long chain of co-ordinated production, is enough to paralyse whole sectors of production without any of them taking the trouble to find out what has happened in the sector upon which it depends. 'Many automobiles, for example,' Khrushchev pointed out, 'remain unused because they have no tyres . . . yet despite that, decisions are taken to increase the production of motor vehicles . . . with the consequence that many drivers, instead of sitting at the wheel, are forced to lounge around their motionless mechines. . . . In the Gosplan (Central Planning Commission) everyone looks after his own affairs. Whoever is interested in automobiles pays no attention to anything else. . . . This is a serious shortcoming of the planning organs . . .'

Sometimes the results are compromised by mere lack of foresight. On April 13, 1960 the *Komsomolskaya Pravda* pointed out, for example, that in the state school building plan for that year there was provision for schools for 620,000 pupils, but there were only 223,000 desks available.

Khrushchev quoted sarcastically more than one example of these failures of foresight, so easy to understand in the fulfilment of programmes drawn up by an innumerable crowd of bureaucrats. Cultivation began on the virgin lands before the plough and tractors were ready. When the harvest had been brought in, it was found that there were not enough silos in which to store it. The machines for one plant were ready but construction work on the factory itself had not yet begun. Cinema projectors were distributed to the schools but there were no lamps to make them work. Houses were built, but there was no furniture. It was enough for one of the cogs to be jammed for the whole machine to grind to a standstill. Provision was made for decentralization but it was then found necessary to increase control over the decentralized bodies. 'Circulars are sent and that is all,' Khrushchev told the Central Committee at its session between the 24th and 29th June 1959, which was discussing the deficiencies, the errors and the shortcomings both in industry and agriculture. 'What should happen,' he said, 'is not to write circulars but to take a good look at things from beginning to end and foresee the necessary organization. That is what nobody is doing in a realistic and practical manner.'

In another speech, delivered in winter 1961 Khrushchev mocked at the gosplan directors who failed to provide fittings for electrical milking machines.

'It would be a good thing to tell those gosplan officials to go and work in the stalls. Then they would know what hard work milking is. The sovnarkhoz (regional economic council) presidents should go too. We will choose two especially good cows for comrades Novikov and Zadatkov (the president and vice-president of the Esthonian gosplan).'

To plan the economy of a country of about twenty-two and a half million square kilometres is no small undertaking. Therefore the argument still remains valid: can a planning organization take millions of decisions, all those that are necessary during the production process, with the same sureness and efficiency as private industrialists who are personally interested in the results?'[8]

17

'There are cases,' Khrushchev continued in his criticisms of the planning system on November 17, 1962, 'in which the plans have not been sufficiently matured or considered. . . . The construction of factories and other enterprises is often included in the plans without taking account of the project and without any possibility of providing such establishments with raw materials, labour and necessary plant. It happens that establishments with machinery already supplied are built slowly or even not built at all, and many buildings already completed are not being made use of because of lack of machines'. Such cases as Khrushchev has quoted are considerably more frequent than is generally supposed. The newspapers are full of incredible cases of industrial construction which drag on for years, which change destination or end by being abandoned, of very expensive machinery which has been deteriorating for years while waiting to be used, without even being protected by improvised tarpaulins, of railway warehouses crammed with equipment which no one has even bothered to look at. Khrushchev scarcely lifted

[8] *Kommunist* No. 3, 1962, pp. 6-7, in an editorial entitled An *immutable law of economic construction* says: 'Unfortunately we still have serious shortcomings in planning, shortcomings in various production sectors, errors and mistaken calculations; many enterprises incur considerable losses.'

a fringe of the veil which conceals this immense chaos, the enormous wastage of energy and materials due to this mastodontic planning. The principal reason for these delays or the abandonment of buildings already begun is to be found in the shortage of materials at the disposal of the enterprises. The plans are almost always out of proportion to the existing resources. There are errors of calculation easily comprehensible in an organization of such immense dimensions as the Soviet, which has always made the mistake of an excessive fractioning of investments.

It is evident that the economic losses, the high cost, the wastage of materials and machinery would make it very difficult for Soviet industry, with the exception of certain very limited sectors, to maintain free competition with Western industry on the international market. 'The wastage,' Khrushchev said, 'takes the most varied forms, from the mistaken use of too expensive materials to the excessive use of labour and electrical energy.'

To these errors and shortcomings must be added the insufficiency of the infrastructure. Transport is continually breaking down and there are few roads and railways, the port installations are inadequate and the depreciation of the rolling stock is very great because of the excessive traffic that it has to carry. Every year part of the harvest is lost because of lack of transport or because of its very poor condition. Fruit, potatoes, tomatoes, cabbages, onions and other widely consumed vegetables do not reach the markets in the quantities produced because of the deficiency of transport. *Pravda*, on August 27, 1963, wrote of 'rivers of gold' flowing away down the couplings of the trains transporting the grain from the Volga region.

The backwardness of the enterprises is to a great extent due to the tendency of the planners, for prestige reasons, to concentrate the great mass of the investments in new plants, rather than in the maintenance, the amortization or the reconstruction of those already existing.

The consequence is the excessive deterioration of many plants for lack of the necessary funds to ensure their modernization. The often lamented fact that they go on producing outmoded machines is a fault of the bureaucratic routine which is inevitable in an industrial organization which operates in a monopoly régime, sheltered from the harsh struggle with international competition. The existing norms allow the directors of the enterprises to make use of their amortization fund for repairs, but not for replacements, which require an authorization from the centre. The result is that repairs are carried out even when it would be less costly and more productive to renew the plant.

To complete the picture of the defects of the planning system as a whole, it should be borne in mind that though it is possible to plan with a certain amount of approximation for the increase of industrial production, it is far more hazardous to establish norms for agricultural production which is subject, especially in Russia, to vast meteorological variations. It is a fact that the plans for agriculture have almost always proved deceptive, beginning with the first which foresaw for 1932, that is at the end of the five-year period, a cereal production of 106 million tons, whereas less than 70 million tons was obtained.

18

In Soviet planning especially a factor which tends to aggravate its difficulties is the bureaucratization not only of the direction but also of the productive enterprises themselves. The Russian system relies upon the activities of tens of millions of workers, each one of whom is paid according to a complicated system of wages and bonuses, which requires a no less complicated accountancy and a widespread system of controls. Therefore the clerks in the kolkhozes, the factories and the shops form a high percentage of the personnel, which means an enormous waste of human energy and consequently low productivity. An enormous mandarinate has been created which does not see beyond its dusty files and the mass of figures which are pigeonholed day after day. Mountains of scribbled paper accumulate because the accountancy files must register day by day to what extent each individual has fulfilled his plan. The system lays itself open to countless frauds. The master-state cannot supervise the administration of its goods with the strict wariness of a private employer. Therefore wastages are considerable. The evil is destined to become worse, since the sole remedy is to multiply the controls, that is to say to intensify this bureaucratic elephantiasis. Naturally, everyone tries to be the controller and not the controlled. Now the first symptom of the decadence of a society is its bureaucratization. The process, once set in motion, is hard to halt.

This is what happened after the administrative reforms of May 1957. Decentralization multiplied the bureaucracies of the federated republics. Now if it is difficult for a central administration to recruit well-trained and honest staff, the difficulties of the peripheral administrations are far greater. Therefore the so often lamented disadvantages of an inefficient and venal bureaucracy, its administrative delays, its traditional laissez-faire, have become greatly exaggerated. Khrushchev launched his most violent accusations against this bureaucratic elephantiasis and directed against it his principal reforms. There is, however, no doubt that the bureaucratic octopus is the real cancer of state planning and one of the principal reasons for the high costs of Soviet production.

19

In conclusion, the major defects of Soviet planning are its enormous size, the disproportion of its aims to the material available for carrying them out, the successive fractioning of capital investment, the difficulty of organizing a central control capable of impressing a uniform directive on the operation of so limitless and complex a mechanism, the plethora of bureaucrats and the errors of calculation in the drawing up of the plans. This last is, perhaps, the most serious defect. It is therefore on this that Khrushchev insisted most heavily and it is to this that above all imputed the failure of the seven-year plan. According to Khrushchev, the greatest fault of the planners is to have overlooked the need for the development of a great chemical industry destined to produce lower cost materials, an abundance of fertilizers needed for the increase of agricultural production and a large range of low-price consumer goods.

What is the main cause of these errors of calculation in the drawing up of the plans?

The most eminent Soviet economists have found it, in accord with those Western economists who have studied the problem, to be the lack of a sure canon both for establishing the best order of priorities and for a choice between alternative solutions. At the beginning of planning under Stalin the system proceeded by trial and error, but little by little, as the system developed, serious shortcomings became evident and it became necessary to base it on precise economic calculations. It was evident that certain investments such as the creation of armaments plants, the development of the infrastructure or the production of equipment of high scientific value such as that required for space flights could not be dictated by economic interests alone. But apart from exigencies of this kind, economic programme-making can only have as its aim the increase of the national yield and therefore can only be based on the yield of the capital invested. It is precisely that which Professor Libermann of the Institute of Economic Engineering at Kharkhov has stressed in a press campaign which began on September 9, 196 and has had immense repercussions throughout the Soviet Union.

How is one to measure the economic utility of a specific use of capital? How is one to compare the administrative results of individual enterprises? How is one to avoid such enterprises operating at a loss? How is one to decide if such losses be considered as due to administrative errors when, for example, the imposed price-levels do not even cover the basic costs? In short, how is one to judge if the economic progress of the country is or is not comparable with the energies and sacrifices made to encourage it, without taking account of the capital invested and the profit attained? But, according to Marxist doctrine, capital is not productive; it adds nothing to the value of the product. Only in this way could Marx justify the thesis of 'surplus-value' wrongfully subtracted by the capitalists from the workers. Consistent with this theory, Soviet enterprises in their balance-sheets pay no attention to the cost of capital investment, that is to say interest charges, because they consider capital as a free contribution from the state which does not merit any remuneration. The state recoups itself by levying on every enterprise a part of the value of the gross product (turnover tax) and a good part of the difference between income and expenditure (profits tax), but takes upon itself the losses sustained by the enterprise. These two sources of income, the turnover tax and the profits tax, are the principal resources of the Soviet budget.

It is superfluous to underline how rudimentary a system of this kind is, based as it is on arbitrary criteria instead of on a uniform measure, that is to say on a tax system which permits a comparison between the financial contribution of the enterprise and the capital received.

In a private economy it is only the attainment of maximum profit which decides the operator in planning his initiatives, which are always aimed at satisfying market demands as shown by the fluctuation of prices. It is the market which determines the laws of investment, whereas in a planned economy the will of the producer, that is to say of the state, predominates. But what motives guide the will of the producer if no heed is paid to maximum profit? Khrushchev, with his usual realism, was fully conscious of this, as was shown by his bitter admission, when talking in Moscow with John Harper, president of the Aluminium Company of America on November 17, 1963, that 'the capitalists know what produces a profit because they are not Soviet bureaucrats'. In actual fact, however, the Soviet planners try, by indirect means, to take account of the yield of invested capital. For example they opt for solutions less costly than others if these allow them to recover the maximum quota of invested capital in a specified number of annual repayments. This is an application of the criterion of the 'period of recovery'.[9] The planners thus behave

[9] R. Campbell (op. cit.) says: 'Thus the planners manage to bring the condemned rate of interest in through the back-door' (p. 103). See also Harry Schwartz *Russia's Soviet Economy* (p. 183, et seq.) on the application of 'the coefficient of relative yield'.

like the private capitalist who takes account of the interest on the capital invested. Such a procedure arouses objections from the pure Marxists who see in it a denial of Marxist doctrine. Notwithstanding these objections, the criterion of taking account of the 'period of recovery' has been authorized. From this precedent it would be logical to proceed, as has sometimes been suggested, to an obligation by the enterprises to remit to the state a contribution proportionate to the invested capital, that is to say an interest payment, instead of a percentage of the cost as is the case today.

There remains, however, in the planning proposals which come from the enterprises, pass through the sovnarkhozes and the republican gosplans and finally reach the centre, as well as in the final programmes themselves, an empirical criterion in giving preference to some sectors rather than to others in the distribution of productive factors between industry and agriculture, between heavy and light industry, between directly productive activities and services, as Khrushchev repeatedly complained. It naturally follows that the priority granted to certain sectors without a precise calculation of the economic advantages often implies, as has been seen in the case of the chemical industry, the retardation of others with the consequent result of slowing down the general advance as soon as the effect of slackening production of machinery, raw materials and semi-manufactured goods indispensable to a continually growing economy makes itself felt.

The most serious consequences of these decisions from above is not so much the frequency of errors as the difficulty of correcting them. Even private industrialists make errors. Marx's criticisms on the frequency, indeed the inevitability, of such errors are still valid today. But the advantage of free economy is that it puts into operation the mechanism of reaction to restore the balance, whereas in a planned economy one must wait until the bureaucracy realizes that it has made a mistake so that it may change its directives.

20

The defects mentioned up till now concern the drawing up of the programmes and the actions of the departments entrusted with their fulfilment. But in the crisis of planning are involved, in no lesser measure, the defects from below, which limit the productivity of labour. It has been shown in the first section how low is the yield of the Soviet worker. The Soviet leaders are worried about this. In his speech to the Belgrade workers, on August 12, 1963 during his visit to Tito, Khrushchev declared that if the communist countries wanted to catch up with the more advanced countries they must still make great efforts both in work and in better organization. 'In economy,' he said, 'there are no miracles. . . . If we want to increase consumer goods we must work harder and increase productivity. . . . If the worker maintains his productivity at the same level as at present then living standards can even decline, for society increases and fresh consumers are added whereas material goods remain the same.'

Khrushchev therefore recognized the dangers of a freeze in productivity and, in consequence, a lowering of living standards in the communist lands.

'It is intolerable,' he told the Central Committee, 'that in many enterprises, in many sovnarkhozes and last year (1961) even in certain republics, the tempo of labour productivity has been less than the tempo of average wage increases.' The truth is that the average wage is too little and the living standard of the workers is too low. It has already been said that to increase wages there must also be some increase in the production of consumer goods. Khrushchev was aware of this and arranged for larger investment quotas, in the coming years, for the development of light industry.

At the same time he stressed that the slackening of productive energies was equally to be blamed on the inadequate vigilance of the control organs. In his report to the Party Central Committee in November 1962 he stated that it was imperative to put a stop to 'boasting, falsification of statistics, the predominance of regional interests, corruption, wastage and the pilfering of state goods. These ills,' he added, 'have become widespread in the local sections and the central institutions of the Party and have affected high-ranking officials. By corruption,' he specified, 'I mean the squandering of state funds, the illegal allocation of apartments, distribution of land, assignment of pensions and the admission of students into institutions higher than those for which they are qualified and the granting of degrees.' In the first six months of 1962 alone, cases of embezzlement referred to the courts meant a loss to the state of 56 million rubles.

As has been seen, Khrushchev's mistrust was not limited to the state bureaucracy but extended to the Party apparatus itself which should have supported the administrative organs in controlling the fulfilment of the plans. Hence the necessity of changing the control system and organizing it not on a territorial basis but on a productive basis, that is to say in every production sector. 'What is necessary,' said Khrushchev, 'is the unification of the control of the state and the Party by the creation of a single state and Party centre with local departments under its control. In order that these local departments should in fact become a powerful lever in the hands of the Party they must have all the powers and directives that they need . . . it is of the extremest importance to establish a day-to-day control.' In short, the centre must be so capillary that, to use one of Khrushchev's expressions, not even the flight of a gnat should escape it.

Practically speaking, the Party was reorganized as a dichotomy by the creation of control committees, some over industrial production and others over agricultural production. This chain of committees stemmed from the Party Central Committee which had two dependent offices, one for the direction of industrial production and the other for the direction of agricultural production. These committees ramify down to the control of individual factories and individual agricultural enterprises. All Party members who were working in the factories, in the kolkhozes and in the sovnarkhozes were mobilized to take their part in these committees. In fact an army of informers was organized.

21

The great remedy for planning evils is, therefore, control. But when one says control one says sanctions. This is the only alternative to private initiative. There remains a system of coercion, though its results, such as the shortage of agricultural products and the low productivity of labour in the workshops, prove its inefficiency. But the ideological principles of the régime do not allow it to avoid the system and therefore nothing else remains than to make it more rigid and extend it.

The consequences of this aggravation of the system are many and various.

The intervention of the party in all sectors and in all phases of production ends by destroying the last vestiges of democratic usage in the régime. It is true that the Central Committee, in order to give a democratic façade to the reforms, has decided that the workers, the specialists and the employees of every enterprise elect a production committee which assists the directors of the plant in the preparation of plans, controls their execution and participates in the drawing up of labour norms and in the engagement of workers. But Khrushchev clearly stressed that the function of these committees was purely consultative, since the director, who is the absolute arbiter of the working of the enterprise, 'must take decisions on his own responsibility and must answer in full to the state for the conduct of his enterprise.' Furthermore these organs of workers' participation are all under the vigilant eye of the Party. In reality, from the time when the attempt of the opposition workers to wrest the control of the national economy from the trade unions was suppressed by the Party in 1922 and 1923, the working class, which had been the great revolutionary force under Lenin and Trotsky, has been losing all influence in the political and economic direction of the state. The structural reforms already referred to, together with the concentration in the Party organs of the duties formerly entrusted to the local soviets, have already deprived it of every remaining competence.

At the same time the autonomy of the federated republics of Central Asia, where Khrushchev aimed at quickening the rhythm of production, both industrial and agricultural, by assigning to them a high proportion of investments, has been practically suppressed. With this end in view a Central Asian economic council has been created, with powers of direction which reduce those of the governments of the federated republics to insignificance. The council is supported by inter-regional organs to encourage cotton cultivation, irrigation, building and the like throughout all Central Asia. In its turn this council receives the directives of the Party Central Committee through its Central Asian office—the Sredasburo.

Practically speaking the planning machine was handed over to the Party which, as an effect of its new structure, had been split into two autonomous bodies, one for industrial the other for agricultural production, and had been turned towards production missions rather than towards political tasks and ideological propaganda. Is the Party the most suitable body for this job? Khrushchev's criticisms of the Party organs, both high and low, which have let themselves become riddled by corruption and laxity, leave one perplexed, to say the least. On the other hand one can foresee an intensification of the latent conflict between the Party apparatus and the technical direction of the enterprises, because the question always remains open whether, in case of conflict, a political or an economic decision should prevail. In the field of production it is clear that political authority moves with difficulty when confronted by competent persons who are at the same time the directors of the enterprise. Stalin always supported the technocrats, to whom he reserved full powers, high salaries and privileges of various kinds. Khrushchev in practice followed a similar line, though trying to amalgamate politicians and technicians by calling upon the most highly qualified representatives of the great economic units to take their part in the political and executive organs of the state.[10]

22

It is in the interest of the régime to continue firmly along these lines. One cannot but be sceptical about the efficiency of a complicated harness, like that now devised, which makes universal, and therefore suffocating, the control of the Party through an immense network of committees. The real guarantee of a high level of productivity is not external control by a political organism but the independence of the enterprises. It must above all be borne in mind that a rational and practical decentralization is not so much on a regional level, which has already shown serious defects in the general line, as in the autonomy of the enterprises which will approximate to the efficiency of those in a free economy. Czechoslovakia has set out along this road by the structural reforms of 1958, by which the draft plans are drawn up by the enterprises, which gives them opportunity to conclude contracts among themselves for the sale and purchase of supplies.

The power of an economic régime, whether planned or not, is in its productive energy. The Soviet Union is so aware of this that, as has been seen, it has turned the whole procedural order of planning head over heels in order to find a way for the enterprises to formulate their proposals and to send them, through the sovnarkhozes and the republican governments, to the centre. This makes it possible to loosen the grip which restricts the enterprises within a rigid system of detailed ordinances from which they cannot escape without exposing themselves to the risk of serious punitive measures. In short, it is necessary to give them a chance to reduce their costs and sell at profitable prices, since only thus can they acquire the responsibility for their own initiatives and be in a position to organize the most profitable system of production. Anyone who has worked in private industry knows how keenly forecasts of expenditure and prices are watched. In the preparation of plans bureaucracy is not always influenced by the fears of those who know that they must pay out of their own pockets for their errors in forecasting. Full freedom in this field is not to be foreseen, however, because of the danger that the enterprises will be forced to increase prices in order to get higher profits. Therefore the state must reserve the right

[10] At the Central Committee meeting held in November 1964, Podgorny upheld the need to return to the Party organization as it was before Khrushchev's reforms, that is to return to the 'territorial' basis instead of the 'production' basis.

of fixing them by its authority. What is required is that they be fixed rationally, bringing them as close as possible to international prices which reflect the state of the market.

This is Professor Libermann's thesis. It has the full support of very many Soviet economists, among them Professor A. Birman, vice-rector of the Plekhanov Economic Institute of Moscow, who in the review *Soviet Economics* and in *Izvestia* has maintained the need to give a wide margin of freedom to the directors of industrial enterprises, since Soviet economy has now reached a new phase of development which calls for a 'radical improvement of planning methods'. The official organ of the Party, *Kommunist*, has declared itself of the same opinion. In January 1963 it accepted the thesis of Professor E. Libermann, namely to concede a greater autonomy to the industrial enterprises.

The aim that these enterprises must pursue is, in the view of all these economists, a real index of maximum productivity. As is the case in Czechoslovakia, a part of the profit must be left to the enterprises and used by them in the most suitable way to improve their own equipment and widen the sphere of their activities. In Czechoslovakia rises in wages are tied to productivity according to tables published in every factory.

In the article quoted above *Kommunist* upheld these views, suggesting that industrial enterprises should enjoy greater freedom to increase their gains and to dispose to a great extent of these gains in their own interest in order to quicken the rhythm of production. Naturally the first to enjoy the increased profits will be the directors and workers of the enterprise which has increased its productivity.

Such incentives will again put into operation that individual interest which Marxist philosophy wishes to replace by complete disinterestedness. Perhaps it is really an ideological preoccupation of this kind that has prevented the Vestals of communist orthodoxy from following the example of Czechoslovakia, of Poland and above all of the far more radical model of Yugoslav industrial organization. The whole ideological house of cards has been violently shaken by such innovations, since the more the autonomy of the enterprises grows the greater the discrepancy between the prosperity of one and another and, in consequence, the difference in bonus and wages levels between them is accentuated. This means that the formal equality, which is one of the dogmas of Marxism, is compromised. It is always the ideology that is opposed to the free play of economic forces.

None the less this is the highway which is opening to the countries of the Eastern bloc. It leads one to believe in the growing influence of the technocrats, that is to say the real General Staff made up of the directors of the enterprises. In the Soviet Union the power of the technocrats is derived from the application of the Leninist principle, confirmed by Khrushchev, of unity of direction in every economic enterprise. The rise of this new power is quickening as productive forces develop; and as it is being extended over the whole vast territory of the Soviet Union it seems destined to have an influence on the evolution of the régime, because these technicians, these economists and businessmen obey criteria, incentives and methods very different from those of the politicians bound to the rigid framework of their ideology. Reality always ends by prevailing over principle and therefore the practical exigencies of production and well-being cannot but clash in the end with the obstacles, the brakes and the limitations opposed to them by doctrinal demands.

It must not be forgotten that the power to which the Soviet Union aspires is economic power, to assure itself by this means both military power and political predominance. All other exigencies will end by being subordinated to this fundamental aim, despite all the disguises and adaptations that may be necessary. Russia is already on the way to this transformation. She will not renounce planning which has now become part of her mentality and a part of the habits not only of the ruling class but also of the working masses; but one cannot exclude the possibility of an evolution which will bring her closer to the systems of free economy, which will take account of profits in the balance-sheets of her enterprises, which will approximate internal prices to those of the international market and which will open possibilities for private interests, responsibilities and initiatives to come to the fore. Among its other effects, the crisis in planning has induced the Russian leaders, both economic and political, to compare the Russian system with the system of the West and to draw from this comparison judgments to correct their errors. This comparison cannot but quicken such an evolution.[11]

23

Notwithstanding the errors and shortcomings that contradict the superiority of the system of planning over the régime of free competition, it is undeniable that the Russians have set up a formidable machine which they are continually improving, thanks to an ex-

[11] Brezhnev seems to be referring to the criteria of those Soviet economists who stress the need to base planning on accurate economic calculation. In his speech on November 7 1964 he says: 'Objective criteria are needed for the correct application of economic laws.'

perience which stresses the parts which have to be modified and also thanks to the ability of men of exceptional worth and training who are at its head.

This machine is nourished by the resources of the immense reserve of raw materials of the Soviet lands and by a flow of investments which grows with regular rhythm from year to year. From the modest financing of its early stages it has now reached the spectacular concentration of means shown in the seven-year plan; from the partial results of the first plans it has now reached the present exploitation of the entire territory. The continental scale of this advance leaves even more grandiose developments to be foreseen which the West must follow with the closest attention in order to parry them and prevent being outdistanced in wealth and power.

The logical conclusion which springs from these premises is that the West must operate over an area not inferior to that of the Soviet Union, with no less a concentration of means and resources. The superiority of its system will allow it to retain its advantage. What is necessary is the co-ordination of the Western economies, which is only possible by means of common objectives and programmes of collaboration. The problem, in other terms, is not to match planning with planning, as is the view of those who see no other way of advancement save by imitating the Soviet system, but by agreeing on the main lines of a combined activity. It may be said that this too is a kind of planning. To this one may agree, but one must differentiate between guided planning which preserves the freedom of individual operators and directed planning which is imposed by authority. One will thus be able to match the development of Soviet economy by opposing to the organization of the communist world an organization, no less valid, of the democratic world.

CHAPTER X

The Agricultural Crisis

1

THE application of Marxist principles to the peasants has reduced labour productivity to exceptionally low levels when compared with those of the farming communities of the West. The Soviet state has poured out capital and been lavish with the supply of machinery and skilled technicians. It has adopted alternately the methods of the mailed fist and the velvet glove, but the agricultural crisis remains.

In all the countries of the world the peasants want the same thing—ownership of the land.

The Russian peasant has fought for land ownership for more than four centuries, ever since the Russian aristocracy, rallying about the princes of Moscow, forced the cultivators to become serfs. The beginnings of this process go back to the reign of Vladimir Monomach but it reached its conclusion under the Romanov dynasty which established as a canon of its policy the obligation of the nobility to give lifelong service in the army or the public administration, imposing as a counter-balance the obligation of the peasants to work the land of the nobles.

The country people rebelled against this slavery. The resistance of the peasants was one of the main causes for the exhaustion of the former régime, as it will be for the exhaustion of the present one. It must not be forgotten that for centuries the common people of the countryside have lived like beasts; hard-working serfs forced to labour without even a minimum of comfort in the dreariness of the Russian lands, living in ramshackle huts and isolated for more than six months of the year by snow and mud; a people old before its time because of hard labour, harsh weather conditions, disease and poverty, and therefore condemned in tsarist times to a short life despite its exceptional physical robustness. The revolts of this brutalized multitude, such as those of the Cossacks during the crisis that preceded the coming of the Romanov dynasty to the throne, of Stenka Razin and of Pugachev, were terrifying in their ferocious explosions of hatred and revenge.

In the twenty years of the reign of Nicholas I there were five hundred and fifty-six peasant revolts. Despite the cruelty of the repressions, the succession of massacres of landowners, of arson and of sabotage continued and even increased. Dostoyevsky's father was strangled by his serfs. Popular revolts, of which there were twenty-seven in 1846, rose to forty-five in 1848. In that year half the serfs of the Vitebsk district revolted and marched on Petersburg and only when half way there was the army able to stop them. The situation grew worse from year to year. In the two years 1858-1860 there were two hundred and eighty-four peasant risings in the countryside. The harvests were burnt, the landowners killed and sometimes tortured.

The emancipation of the serfs under Alexander II did not remedy the evil; in fact in some ways it made it worse because the peasants received a half of the land which they had worked, for which they had to pay and to cultivate in common. The allotments sanctioned by the reform were therefore insufficient and, furthermore, weighed down by a heavy burden of redemption. In such conditions it was in no one's interest to improve the land. This led to the fractioning of properties and to misery among the peasants. Their land-hunger remained unsatisfied. The peasants were still the most turbulent element in the country. Thus even after the emancipation of the serfs the unrest in the countryside continued. There were thousands of cases of crop-burnings and thefts of stock.

With the birth of industry, the ablest elements emigrated to the cities. Work in the fields was entrusted to women, with the result that conditions in the countryside became even worse. Even after the exodus of the men the human burden on the land remained excessive. The peasants took advantage of the crisis caused by the disastrous war against Japan in 1906 to start a ferocious agrarian revolt. As in the times of Stenka Razin and Pugachev the land was seized, the landowners killed and their houses burnt.

The tsarist prime minister Stolypin was one of those who understood what a conservative force a farming population of yeoman and smallholders would be. He put into effect an agrarian reform based on the dissolution of the *mir*, or agricultural commune, and on the distribution of its land to those who had been members of it. The law of November 2, 1907 sponsored by him gave the peasants the right to become the owners of the land they tilled. For the first time a wise reform countered the collectivization of the land and diffused private ownership among the peasants. The reform was everywhere well received and led to the best possible social, political and economic results.

By this radical measure Stolypin divorced the peasants from the revolutionary movement. A period of prosperity and social peace began for Russia. Production rose rapidly, thanks also to a succession of good harvests. By 1916 there were already six million two hundred thousand smallholders. Amongst these, those of special importance, because of their contribution to the national economy, were the larger homesteads of the *chernozem* which produced for sale and not, as in the majority of cases, only for the personal needs of the owner and his family. It was to these homesteads, which multiplied very rapidly, that the great agricultural progress of Russia was due. Cultivation of beet, forage crops and flax was widespread, as also was stockbreeding. From 1909 to 1913 Russia exported annually an average of fourteen million tons of foodstuffs, mainly cereals. Agriculture, which had been more or less static till then, as it has again become under the régime of land collectivization, showed of what development it was capable if the interest of the landowners was aroused.

It was necessary to persist along these lines, the only ones in accord with the expectations of the rural population. The general drive towards ownership of land encouraged a group of agitators to base their activities on an organization of the peasants, convinced that a party which could succeed in winning their support by getting its programme of 'the land for the peasants' recognized, would be able to seize power and establish a democratic state. This was the origin of the Narodni or People's Party, which aimed at coordinating and controlling the hitherto disorganized and impulsive movements of peasant unrest in order to promote a well organized and disciplined action obedient to well-planned methods and precise aims.

2

After the outbreak of the revolution in March 1917, the first aim of the government should have been the solution of the agricultural crisis in order to assure the support of the peasant masses which were the great majority of the population. But Kerensky did not dare to risk the opposition of the Cadet party, the party of the landowners, and referred the question to the Constituent Assembly. By doing this he lost his trump card to the Bolsheviks who were thus able to attract to their side the people of the countryside. The progress of a revolutionary party is always helped by the mistakes of those who govern. What Kerensky did not dare to do, Lenin did. Till then he had always maintained the most intransigent communist thesis on land collectivization. For example at the IV Congress at Stockholm in 1906 he had opposed not only the Mensheviks who supported the institution of smallholding but also the opinion of his own party which considered it indispensable to take the peasants' land hunger into account.

But at the time when he set the revolutionary machine in motion, on October 26, 1917, he realized that the movement would fail without peasant support and published a decree abolishing the large landed estates without compensation. At the same time he granted all the demands of the local soviets, even though they were in contradiction to the communist programme. Lenin justified the decree by his famous declaration: 'We, a democratic government, cannot ignore the will of the masses, even if we do not agree with it.' It was, in fact, a mere expedient to deceive the masses, whose support the Party needed, and he was ready to withdraw the concession as soon as he was strong enough to do so. This he himself cynically admitted later. 'Our government promulgated this law on October 26, 1917 on the morrow of the revolution,' he said. 'In that was our strength and for that reason it was easy for us to gain the support of the vast majority of the peasants. In an exceptional situation we succeeded in getting, for several months, the support of the whole peasant body. That is a historical fact. At least up until the summer of 1918, up to the time of the foundation of the Committees of poor peasants, we were able to remain in power because we were supported by all the peasants.' This expedient should not be forgotten, since it explains all communist tactics. They will revert to such expedients unscrupulously in any difficult contingency. It is the tactics of the end justifying the means. On many occasions the peasants have fallen victims of their own trustfulness.

Lenin's cynical attitude was sharply criticized by Rosa Luxemburg who said publicly that the most serious consequences for the future of communism would arise out of the difference of treatment of the workers and the peasants, to the first of whom was refused and to the second conceded ownership of the sources of production. Since the peasants made up the great majority of the population, it could be foreseen that the exception made in their favour would end by weakening the basic canon of Marxism, namely the abolition of private ownership. But Lenin objected that it was only by giving way to the peasants that he could induce them to make common cause with the workers, upon which the success of the revolution depended.

The decree of October 26, 1917 was immediately put into force. The peasants did not wait for the intervention of the expropriating authorities but without further ado took possession of the land of the wealthy landowners, whose houses they sacked and burnt.

3

It was a short-lived success. A few months later the communists rigorously began to apply their programme by the abolition of the private ownership of land without making any distinction between large, medium and small holdings. Such was the provision of the 'basic land law' of February 19, 1919.

This was the beginning of the struggle against the *kulaks*, the well-to-do cultivators who, under stress of expropriation, were forced to hand over the whole of their produce. It was in reality a struggle of poor against rich, since the poor peasants were not aiming at fulfilling the state plans but at realizing the eternal dream of themselves becoming landowners. If the state had ever believed that it could rely on the poor peasants to expropriate the *kulaks*, it must have very soon become aware that the poor peasants were expropriating the goods of the richer in the hope of themselves becoming landowners.

In practice, however, this mob of poor peasants found that there was an insufficient area of land to be divided, the more so as the number of those who wished to take part in the division of the spoils was increased daily by the return from the cities to the countryside of a good eight million persons anxious to appease their land-hunger. Once more expectations came to nothing and the lands of the *kulaks*, divided amongst millions of peasants, only increased the fractioning of the holdings.

The farms producing for the market disappeared, which meant the disappearance of the usual sources of supply. It was famine. The government thought to find a remedy by forced requisitions. But that only worsened the evil by creating absenteeism. Nobody, logically, wanted to work for the state which had stripped them of everything. That was the peasants' reply to Lenin's directive, by which the state had imposed forced labour on them and compulsory requisitioning of grain in order to give food to the workers in the cities. It thus obtained neither the one nor the other. It was a similar logic to that of Peter the Great who imposed obligatory service on the nobles and *corvées* on the peasants to the advantage of their lords.

4

The revolution showed its real face: famine, misery, epidemics. As always in such cases 'the real responsibility for the situation' was sought for in the same way as the quest for 'plague-spreaders' in times of pestilence. But the cause was the revolution which brought with it its dismal train of misfortunes. That is the price of every communist revolution.

The demobilization of the Red Army at the end of the civil war increased the misery in the countryside to the utmost limits. Hundreds of thousands of workers and peasants returned to their homes. What was waiting for them? Famine. Was it for this they had fought? They realized that they had been tricked, and broke out in revolt. Lenin thought he could resist them and in a speech on March 27, 1921 stigmatized the rebels as *petit bourgeois* and 'anarchic elements'. But the revolt of the Kronstadt sailors, who had at the beginning been the mainstay of the revolution, brought home to him the gravity of the situation. It was March 1921. In Lenin's words all these movements, which spread everywhere, constituted 'a danger much greater than all the Denikins, the Kolchaks and the Yudenichs put together'. No one, he admonished, must have the slightest doubt on that score. It would be fatal. It was no longer the wealthy classes who were revolting; it was the people themselves, in whose name and in whose interest the revolution had taken place, but who no longer wanted even to hear of it and revolted against their leaders in the name of a right higher than all revolutions, the right to exist. The peasant revolts at Saratov and at Tambov in Siberia were particularly serious. Was this the dawn of counter-revolution? Was a fresh, even more bloodthirsty and destructive, civil war about to break out? The whole card-castle of the communist régime, imposed and enforced by violence, threatened to collapse. Lenin lived through days of panic. The demobilized Red Guards had made common cause with the rebels. Then, unbeknown to friend and foe alike, Lenin decided to annul all the communist reforms and recognize private ownership, private interest, private profit and individual initiative. He therefore turned to the much scorned capitalism to reconstruct on its principles the economy destroyed by communism.

Lenin did not hesitate to acknowledge the failure of communist agricultural policy. In his speech on March 15, 1921 to the X Party Congress he announced that the requisitions were abolished and would be replaced by a tax in kind on foodstuffs, that is to say the handing over to the state of a part of the yield. The remainder was left at the free disposal of the producer. Thus a free grain market was restored. 'This free circulation,' he said, 'will be a stimulus to the peasant. We must organize our economic system in a way acceptable to the average peasant mentality which we have not been able to change in three years and which we will not change even in ten years.'

The truth is that nothing, not even communism, is able to change the mentality of the peasant who looks only to his personal interests. The error has been to go contrary to those interests, to ignore the basic dynamic of human actions and reactions. The man who had driven the country into an untenable situation, who had been the cause of terrible destruction, massacre, civil war, hunger and endless misery, acknowledged that he had been at fault. He acknowledged it openly, without equivocation. 'To continue with such a policy,' he said, 'would be madness and would amount to suicide for the party that tried to do so.' Madness because such a policy was economically impossible; suicide because any party that tried to enforce it would surely be going to its downfall. It was useless to conceal that some communists had committed, in spirit, in word and in deed, a mistake by adopting this policy. 'We will do our utmost to correct it. That is absolutely necessary: otherwise things will go from bad to worse.'

5

The new policy was the NEP (New Economic Policy). As the Commissariat for Agriculture acknowledged in 1921 it used as a fulcrum 'the personal interest of the peasant'. This interest must become 'the basic principle of our agrarian policy'.

It was a complete victory for the peasants. They had struggled for centuries for just such a victory. Their resistance had weakened tsarism. In the last years of the old régime it had seemed that the goal had been won after the wise reforms of Stolypin. Then the revolution had come, which had promised them the land. Lenin had granted it to them, only to take it away again a few months later. Now it was again conceded to them. But Stalin was to take it from them once more because communism does not betray its principles and every concession is provisional, a mere expedient to delude the masses.

There was a period of truce. The peasants were allowed to keep a good part of their produce, 'that bourgeois ownership with which they can do as they like' in the words of Rykov, president of the Superior Council of National Economy, in his speech to the Congress of Economic Councils. 'It is a question,' he said, 'of a property right in the bourgeois sense of the term which is bound to lead to the legal development of a bourgeoisie on the economic basis that is being created in the countryside.'

For Russia it was like shedding the shirt of Nessus. The country at once recovered. Economic forces could expand freely; even though they clashed with the prohibition of utopian principles, they were no longer hampered and constricted by the rules of an obstructive and pettifogging bureaucracy. The area under cultivation, which had been reduced from 105 million hectares in 1913 to 77.7 million in 1922, again increased to 104.3 million in 1925 and 113 million in 1928. Was there any need of further proof of the superiority of a free market régime over a Marxist one than that provided by the Russian experiment itself?

But the damage done by that first communist experiment had been very grave and was in a certain sense irreparable, since with the fractioning of holdings the farms producing for the market disappeared. Therefore although the smallholder could be sure of the bare necessities of life, the cities continued to be short of supplies. That is the inevitable result of every agrarian reform which aims imprudently at the creation of smallholdings. The production of cereals, which had been 801 million quintals in 1913, was able to rise from 422.2 million in 1921 to 746.8 million in 1925, only to fall again in the following years; but the part of the harvest destined for the cities was scarcely a seventh, amounting to about 103 million quintals instead of the former 213 million.

The result was that the countryside fared better, the cities worse. Therefore the problem of assuring food supplies for a rapidly growing industrial population remained grave and urgent. It was one of the causes that drove Stalin to land-collectivization. The worsening of the situation meant the return of more rigorous measures; confiscations, perquisitions, controls. An inspection committee undertook the search for hidden foodstuffs, leaving the peasants only twenty-five per cent of the grain found. Those guilty of concealment were threatened with forced labour, fines proportionate to the value of the grain concealed and ultimately confiscation of goods and deportation. Rationing had to be introduced in the cities.

6

To give fresh life to the production drive it was believed indispensable to resurrect the great agricultural units, passing, as Stalin declared on June 2, 1928, 'from the small peasant farm, backward and ill-stocked, to the great collective farm with modern equipment and scientifically trained staff'. This was the idea fathered by Stalin's adversaries Trotsky and Zinovev. Once rid of both of them, Stalin adopted their programme. In April 1928 the Politburo decided and in July the Central Committee approved the organization on the free lands of the Russian federal republic and the Ukraine of great state farms known as 'grain factories', controlled by a Cereals Trust set up in August of the same year. Similarly 'meat and milk factories' specializing in stockbreeding and poultry farming were organized. But the experiment failed, with the loss of hundreds of thousands of head of stock, for lack of fodder, water, stalls and above all of skilled men. In these 'factories' not only the sources of production but everything brought in by individual members was put into the common pool and regarded as collective property. Stalin condemned them at the XVII Party Congress as 'petit bourgeois institutions' because they discouraged the members from producing more. They did not, however, become widely diffused.

Nothing therefore remained save to proceed ruthlessly to land-collectivization. When taking this decision the XV Party Congress of 1927 declared: 'This transformation can only take place with the consent of the agricultural workers.' It ruled that the Party commence widespread propaganda to convince those concerned of the importance of the reform. It was the usual communist confidence trick. While declaring itself respectful of everyone's rights, it used the most ruthless coercion to obtain the consent of those concerned. Even today it is still repeated that the collectivization of the land was carried out with the free co-operation of the peasants. In reality, as with all the Stalinist reforms, this too was put into force with an iron hand. The resistance of the peasants was equal to the ferocity of the dictator. Whereas Lenin had arrived at the conclusion that 'the peasant could not be transformed by force' Stalin was of the opinion that only violence, carried inexorably to its extremest limits, could shatter every resistance. His motto was: 'There is no fortress that Bolshevik determination cannot overcome.'

7

Stalin's first offensive was against the well-to-do peasants, the *kulaks*. The lands to be socialized were predominantly theirs. Having abandoned the NEP it was decided to eliminate all the remaining large and medium properties. Once more appeal was made to the poor peasants with the mirage of placing the farms of the *kulaks* under their control. At the same time the state farms, or sovkhozes, were multiplied. Their example, according to Stalin, should facilitate the adherence of the peasant masses to the collective farms. In order to encourage the poor peasants to join the struggle against the *kulaks*, workers chosen from those most devoted to the Party were sent into the countryside from the cities. The lands taken from the *kulaks* were allotted to the co-operative farms in order to attract the poor peasants to join them.

The expropriated *kulaks* were sent to Siberia or the Far East. 'They were left with nothing,' writes Sergei N. Prokopovich, 'except a pair of trousers.'[1] For the most part they were shut up in concentration camps or sent to forced labour felling timber.

The man who took upon himself this shameful task was the slave-driver I. Larin, who had the effrontery to put forward the following incredible query to the conference of Marxist experts in December 1929: 'What is to be done with the families of the *kulaks*? . . . They amount to several million persons. We do not think we can shoot all the *kulaks* and their descendants at once.' This is communist morality in action. The *kulaks* were not shot at once, but left to die a slow death, as was insinuated by Larin's statement. In the winter of 1929-1930 half a million of them were deported.

This meant the liquidation of the most intelligent and therefore the most productive of the peasants, who had put Soviet agriculture on the road to progress with rising yields of cereals and stock. It was a selective operation in reverse.

The main aim of the kolkhozes, that is to say the collective farms, was to increase production in order to supply the cities. They were forced to hand over the whole of their harvest in bulk, over and above the needs of the kolkhoz members themselves, at arbitrarily fixed prices. The violence with which the peasants were forced to join and the systematic plundering of their produce aroused their desperate resistance. The peasants preferred to kill their beasts rather than hand them over, and reduced cultivation to a minimum. The 68,100,000 head of cattle in 1929 was reduced to 38,600,000 in 1933.

Stalin broke this resistance by the most brutal methods. It seemed that the times of Stenka Razin and Pugachev were come again. The villages had to be conquered one by one by armed force, using tanks and artillery. The houses were burnt or blown up. The ferocity of Stalin equalled that of Genghis Khan or Tamerlane. All the grain reserves were confiscated. The population was left to die of hunger and privation, or deported. The countryside between Rostov and Krasnodar for more than two hundred miles was reduced to a desert, as Walter Duranty who travelled through it was able to testify. His evidence is especially authoritative inasmuch as he was Stalin's apologist. The black year was 1932. From the time when their produce was confiscated, the peasants refused to work. Schiller, the agricultural expert of the German Embassy at Moscow, testified

[1] Op. cit., p. 157.

that a great part of the grain produced was left to rot in the fields.

How many were the victims of this tragic experiment? Stalin confessed to Churchill, who mentions it in the fourth volume of his memoirs, that it cost the lives of ten million peasants and that this war seemed to him worse than that fought against the Germans.

Faced with the resistance and sabotage of the peasants, it was necessary to have recourse to the harshest régime of repression. Draconian laws were passed to punish acts of reprisal by kolkhoz members, especially sabotage, theft and neglect of stock. The penalties threatened by the law of August 7, 1932 included forced labour and even death. In 1933 the law was extended to cover reduction of the cultivated area, sabotage of agricultural work and the like. The penal code put on an equal footing damage to the national economy and acts of counter-revolution. On June 8, 1931 it was decided that responsibility for the political misdeeds of any member of a family should be extended to the whole family. On November 15, 1934 the Extraordinary Commission was formed. Its purpose was to send 'socially dangerous' persons to forced residence or concentration camps. Finally, on December 1st of the same year, a special penal procedure came into force which invested the police with judiciary powers and authorized them to sentence on the spot without appeal all persons guilty of acts of terrorism, whether actually carried out or merely attempted.

The revolt of the peasants was in fact a form of legitimate defence against the violation by the state of their elementary rights, as the Party Central Committee practically acknowledged by stating on March 15, 1930 that the principle of voluntary adhesion to the kolkhozes had been violated and that the process of collectivization had been carried out 'by compulsion and under the threat of applying *dekulakization* measures and deprivation of civil rights'.

What conclusions may be drawn from this bloody and desperate struggle of the peasants against the state? It is only too evident that collectivization was carried out, not in the interest of the peasants who wanted the free and exclusive ownership of the land, but in the interest of the working people of the cities who wanted to assure their food supplies. But by the collectivization of the land and the compulsory purchase of grain and other produce at very low prices, Stalin wished to obtain, through the re-sale of such products at extortionate prices, the capital needed to finance the five-year plans. This meant that the cost of industrialization was to be paid by the consumers, especially by the peasants who were reduced to poverty. Stalin adopted the thesis of Preobrazhenski, the theoretician of industrialization, according to which the accumulation of capital must be obtained 'by exploiting the peasants'. At the XII Party Congress when Trotsky spoke of the urgent need to amass capital Krosin asked him if this meant the exploitation of the peasants. Trotsky denied it, but Bukharin described Preobrazhenski's conception as 'monstrous' and put forward the thesis that the primary condition for creating a flourishing industry which required large concentrations of manpower was to create a prosperous agriculture able to provide an abundance of low-priced products. Bukharin referred to the example of North America to show, with an audacity that cost him his life, that American economic power rested on the free ownership of land. This he maintained in his *Notes of an Economist.* But such an attitude, contrary to the ideological line, even if justified by indisputable facts, became in the communist world a heresy, exposing its holder to the gravest dangers. To touch the ideology was to touch a high voltage line.

It has already been noted that Stalin turned to Bukharin in his fight against Trotsky, whose ideas he adopted as soon as he had defeated him. Those ideas had seemed to Bukharin extremely dangerous. He warned: 'Trotsky's followers, when they maintain the need to pump the villages as dry as possible ('take everything it is possible to take'—'take even more than the tsarists took') want to put the Soviet Union on the same path as the old Russia, just when we want to follow the path taken by the United States of America.' The truth is that Stalin had dared to pursue his policy of bloodthirsty repression to a point to which none of the tsars, not even Ivan the Terrible, had had the audacity to go.

Another fact was that all the leaders of the Bolshevik movement, from Lenin to Trotsky and Stalin, had never concealed their lack of trust in the peasants, just because of the peasants' attachment to private ownership. The moving force of the struggle against the country people was the ideology. Communism instinctively looked on the peasant as an enemy and therefore, up to World War II, excluded him from service in the armed forces. The prop of the régime was the working class. With its help it had won power, with its help it had won the civil war. The peasant was kept at bay with false promises right up to the time when Stalin threw off the mask. This will be repeated wherever communism tries to assert itself. The promise of the land for the peasants is a lie because it is contrary to the basic canon of Marxism: to abolish private ownership of the sources of production. Should communism recognize land ownership it would no longer be communism. Given these premises, the interests of the peasants will always be sacrificed to those of the workers who have, in the communist régime, an absolute priority.

The struggle against the *kulaks* and then against the kolkhoz members proved that when confronted by the state no one was safe.

257

First the wealthy classes were threatened, because their wealth was a temptation to the state. But immediately afterwards the threat fell upon the defenceless throng. What has happened and what is happening in Russia is clear proof that there is no worse master than the state. Workers and peasants can react against the private capitalist but they can do nothing against state capitalism.

8

The inflexible resistance of the peasants at last forced Stalin to come to terms. A minimum of rights had to be granted to the members of the kolkhozes. At the end of 1932 the government replaced the obligation to hand over all production, over and above immediate family needs, by a tax in kind whose size would be assessed annually. Furthermore twenty per cent of the harvest would be allotted to the Machine Tractor Stations organized in individual kolkhozes for the ploughing, sowing, reaping and binding, with the over-riding mandate of strictly controlling the conduct of the kolkhoz members. Once such obligations had been fulfilled, the members were authorized to sell whatever remained at free market prices on specified markets. In 1935 a fresh statute reaffirmed the right of every family in a kolkhoz to cultivate a market garden and to possess a few head of cattle and their own poultry. There was thus admitted, even though in ridiculously small quantities, a right of ownership to the peasant. It was a dangerous breach that the peasant sought to enlarge by every means in his power, and the state to close.

Even thus reduced, private ownership of a holding and permission to dispose freely of surpluses stimulated production, so that sales on the kolkhoz market rose from seven and a half milliard rubles in 1932 to roughly eighteen milliard in 1937 and to about twenty-four and a half milliard in 1938. During the war, however, free market prices rose sky high.

This was a proof of how powerful is the incentive of ownership. But it was admitted within ridiculously small limits and could not remedy the situation. The grain harvest which in the three-year period 1926-1928, that is in the times of the NEP, had been on an average 627,500,000 quintals, was reduced in the period from 1935 to 1937 to 590,000,000 quintals. Once more the government resorted to harsh measures. The quota of bulk deliveries was raised from 18 to 42% of the net harvest. Furthermore the prices at which the state bought its share were very low. A kilo of corn was worth ten kopeks, a tenth of a ruble, to the peasant whereas it was sold to the consumer at thirteen rubles.[2]

The peasants evicted or driven by hunger or simply unwilling to take part in collectivization sought refuge in the cities where they took jobs in factories. From 1929 to 1938 twenty-two million eight hundred thousand peasants left the countryside. The rural population therefore fell by about thirty per cent. What feelings such peasants, persecuted by the revolution, could have for a régime which had deprived them of everything is easy to understand, even if they were skilfully concealed by that capacity for dissimulation that has become second nature to the Russians, thanks to the experience of many centuries.

After all this we can judge what value should be put on the statement of the Party programme of the XXII Congress, section two, which says: 'The power of the Soviets . . . has fulfilled the centuries-old dream of the peasants for the land.' The dream has remained a dream, though still tenaciously cherished. It is this unsatisfied lust for land which keeps the agrarian crisis always acute. It is necessary to bear in mind the events referred to above, especially the inflexible opposition of the peasants, to understand how deep are the roots of this crisis. It is a struggle that has lasted for four centuries and will go on until the peasant wins his point. He has stood up against the tsars, against Lenin, Stalin and Khrushchev. Agriculture slackens because the peasant has no interest in productive effort, since he does not benefit sufficiently from it and since in the depths of his being he feels himself cheated of his rightful due. This is shown clearly enough by the fact that whereas in 1913 the gross yield per hectare in money calculated at 1926-27 rates was 120.1 rubles, in 1937 which was an exceptionally good harvest the gross yield per hectare of the collective farms was 109.2 rubles.

9

To show even more clearly that the cause of the crisis is ideological, it is worth while going into greater detail about the organization and operation of the Soviet farms. There are two categories of these: the sovkhozes, or state farms, in which the peasants are wage-earners like factory workers, dependent on the state which

---

[2] 'In 1948,' says the economist Alec Nove, 'the wholesale price of one hundred kilograms of rye was 335 rubles yet the *kolkhozy* received for compulsory deliveries a price of around 7 or 8 rubles. . . .' (*Soviet Economy*, George Allen and Unwin Ltd., London, 1961. Part I, Ch. 4.)

takes the entire yield; and the kolkhozes or agricultural co-operatives, which must hand over specified quantities of their products
established by the plan assigned to them and at a price fixed by
contract, keeping whatever is over for their own benefit.

At present there are about eight thousand sovkhozes. In 1960
there were seven thousand four hundred, and two years earlier about
six thousand. They tend to multiply rapidly because the state prefers them to the kolkhozes and regards them as the advance guard
of agricultural progress. The six thousand sovkhozes of 1958 possessed 168 million hectares, of which fifty-eight million were ploughland and the rest mainly pasture. In 1962 the ploughland of the
sovkhozes increased to eighty million hectares. The sovkhozes prevail in the virgin lands. The state likewise founds them near the
cities, mainly for vegetables, dairy produce and poultry, in order to
supply green vegetables, milk, cheese, meat and eggs to the city
markets in competition with the kolkhozes over which they exercise
a steadying influence.

As can be seen from Khrushchev's statement to the XXII Party
Congress, the sovkhozes at present provide the state with 43% of
the cereals, 28% of the meat, 32% of the milk and 31% of the wool
sold on the state markets. Nine million four hundred thousand
workers, clerks and specialists are employed by them, and since they
are state farms their losses are covered by state grants. For many
sovkhozes such grants are their main source of income.[3]

The kolkhozes, however, remain the predominating factor. They
own most of the best land in the Soviet Union. In 1961 there were
forty-five thousand one hundred of them.

10

The organization of the kolkhozes is regulated by the Artel
Statute of 1935.

At first the area of a kolkhoz comprised the territory of a village
and coincided more or less with that of a former rural community.
Later, a number of kolkhozes were merged into one. The territory
was ceded to the kolkhoz in perpetuity.

As we have said, a minute portion of the kolkhoz is handed over
to each family which co-operates in the farm as a 'family holding'.
Its area varies according to the region and is usually between a

[3] Of the eight thousand sovkhozes, six thousand produce at a loss. This
was stated in *Izvestia* in November 1964, which said that the consequent
loss to the state revenues was three milliard rubles, equivalent to 3,300
million dollars.

quarter and a half of a hectare. A kolkhoz member is authorized to keep not more than one cow with calf, ten sheep, an ass or a sow and an unlimited number of poultry.[4]

A kolkhoz is run by a council elected by the assembly of the members. This council appoints the chairman. It organizes the work on the basis of the plan that it receives from the competent regional departments.

The land of the kolkhoz is divided into fields according to a system of rotation which is drawn up every year together with the production budget and estimates of cost and revenue calculated on the yield of the various crops and the stock.

The kolkhoz members are divided into labour brigades of between fifty and a hundred persons. Each of these brigades is entrusted with an area for which it is responsible for the whole of the rotation period. The personnel entrusted with technical and administrative duties (tractor-drivers, shepherds, milkmaids, etc.) do not belong to these brigades.

The admission of a new member to the kolkhoz is at the discretion of the assembly of members.

Fifty per cent of the value of the whole property of the undertaking (registered stock, equipment and buildings) is accredited to the 'indivisible fund' which is kept going by a percentage of the revenue and is solely intended for expenses of collective interest. The remainder is considered the proportionate property of the members. When one of these withdraws, his quota of participation, as well as his duties for the year, is annulled.

Every brigade, as well as every specialized squad, must carry out the functions assigned to it calculated in time-labour units (*trudodni*) or flat-rate days. If in practice the brigade or the squad carries out such duties in a lesser number of full days it can undertake supplementary duties which are also calculated in days, thus increasing the number of time-labour units for which it will have a right to be paid. A larger or smaller number of time-labour units

[4] In Stalin's time the 'family holdings' were subject to a double burden: the obligation to hand over to the state a part of their produce at the same ridiculous prices as those current for the compulsory deliveries of the kolkhoz, and an 'agricultural tax' proportionate to the yield of the holding, which sometimes rose to as much as 48%. In the obligation of delivery the nature of the produce to be provided was specified and if the holding did not produce it the kolkhoz member had to procure it on the open market at his own expense. It was another way of plundering the peasant to discourage production on privately owned land. After Stalin's death the obligation to hand over part of the produce of the holding was greatly lightened and in 1958 abolished. The agricultural tax was also much reduced after Stalin's death and instead of being levied on the yield it was based on the area of the holding and assessed differently according to the region and the valuation.

will be recognized according to the qualifications of the members (mechanics, specialized workers, etc.) on the basis of a schedule approved by the government.

Up to the time of the reform introduced by Khrushchev in 1958 the state levied at exceptionally low prices specified quantities of products (obligatory quotas) and also acquired a part of the remainder at considerably higher prices. What was left could be sold by the kolkhoz on the free market. From 1958 the delivery of the obligatory quota at minimal prices was abolished and the state acquired on a contract basis the amount of produce that it needed at prices approximating to those previously paid for the remainder of the yield after the obligatory quota had been delivered. In a word, confiscation of a part of the yield ceased. Later, as will be seen, the prices fixed in 1958 for state purchases were diminished, as a result of criticisms of the excessive rate of such prices at the session of the Central Committee of December 1959.

In the past the kolkhoz members were able to sell that part of their produce left at their disposal; but from 1961 they were forced to make use of special co-operatives for such sales which thus controlled the quantities and prevented prices from rising excessively.

The proceeds of the collective production is in part intended to cover expenses and form reserves and in part, in a proportion that varies between 20 and 40% of the net income, to create a fund to cover the expenses of social assistance, school, cultural and similar expenses and the balance, divided by the number of time-labour units, is distributed among members of the kolkhoz according to the number of such units accredited to each member.

The obligatory minimum of working days per year is fixed by the assembly of kolkhoz members. It varies between two hundred and fifty days for men between sixteen and fifty, two hundred for men between fifty and sixty and for women under forty-five, and one hundred and fifty for women between forty-five and fifty. The minimum number of working days that every member of a kolkhoz must work is, however, fixed by law and this minimum varies from region to region.

11

Perhaps no Soviet institution has been the subject of such detailed legislation and such frequent legal provisions, inspired alternately by criteria now liberal now restrictive, as has the kolkhoz. No institution has been made the target of so many internal polemics or been so harshly attacked by fanatical and orthodox Marxists. These contrasts are enough to show how deep-rooted is the agricultural crisis and how precarious and uncertain the solutions proposed to solve it.

The intolerant doctrinaires see in the kolkhozes an intolerable violation of Marxist principles. They categorically condemn private ownership of the sources of production and do not admit of the enjoyment of revenue derived from the private exploitation of goods. Even though collective, the kolkhoz represents a form of 'inferior private ownership' in full contradiction to state ownership of the sources of production. Inasmuch as the kolkhoz is a producers' co-operative, the interest of the members predominates. They wish to assure themselves a profit in every way analogous to the income of an independent farmer and therefore based on principles diametrically opposed to those inspired by the fixed wages paid by the state to all workers in its enterprises, whether agricultural or industrial.

There is thus a lack of equality of treatment between members of a kolkhoz and wage-earners, which creates a legitimate reaction by the latter. The gist of the matter is that in the state farms the profit is pocketed by the state which pays a fixed remuneration to its dependents, whereas in a kolkhoz the profit is pocketed by the members who distribute it amongst themselves. Even more obnoxious to the strict communists is the concession to members of a kolkhoz to have a 'family holding' which, although of minute size, reintroduces the principle of private ownership, wherein the holder has full and exclusive rights.

The contradiction foreseen by Rosa Luxemburg when she opposed Lenin's decision in the October days to recognize the right of the peasants to the land has been proved to be true. The peasants have obtained, albeit only partially, the fruit of their indefatigable resistance and have assured themselves a privileged position. The conflict between town and country became even more acute during the last war because of the excessively high prices at which members of the kolkhoz sold their produce on the free markets.

The current that approves the transformation of the collective farms into state farms is thus gathering momentum.

I. Larin, who had played a primary role in the campaign against the *kulaks*, speaking to a conference of agrarian experts, said that from 1929 the interests of the collective farm had run counter to those of the socialist state. He ended with the following significant declaration: 'We shall admit to having in our countryside a typically socialist agricultural enterprise, consistent with socialist principles, wherein the peasants, whatever their tasks, are public workers paid for their labours according to the norm (i.e. of the wage-earners) and do not devote themselves to cultivating a small-holding for their profit alone, when the collective farms become the property and patrimony of the whole nation and not merely of the peasants living in a specific region and possessing collectively well-defined sources of production; in other words when these great collective farms have been transformed into great state farms.'

That was the directive. It corresponded to Stalin's view. But it was not easy to apply it against the resistance and watchfulness of the peasants. Thenceforth began a skirmishing which has had various phases. The Soviet government obviously aimed at depriving the kolkhoz members of their family holdings and industrializing the collective farms in order to make them similar to all other industrial undertakings. The idea slips out in these words of Larin: 'When we are able to provide electric power to the countryside as we do to the factories the peasant economy will be linked by grids to the state electric power stations. Then the peasant economy must depend entirely upon them and it will be possible to foresee the transformation of the great agricultural associations into the vast specialist farms of the future.'

But to do this, one must run the risk of reopening the struggle with the peasants. Up till now the government has hesitated, though proceeding to some preliminary steps, as for example limiting, by the decree of May 27, 1939, the family holdings of the kolkhoz members and establishing a minimum of days which every kolkhoz member must work. It seemed that Stalin was determined to carry this through, as can be seen from his statement to the XIX Party Congress in 1952, embodied in his pamphlet *Economic Problems of Socialism*. This predicted the gradual transformation of the kolkhozes into state farms. He intended to use taxation of kolkhoz profits so as to bring the members into line with the wage-earners, pocketing the difference. But he evidently changed his mind and limited the right of entry into the kolkhozes, in order to again make possible the flow of manpower from the countryside into industry. But his death in 1953 did not give him time to put his ideas into practice.

12

On the agrarian question too Khrushchev took a diametrically opposite line to Stalin. He did not share the well-known suspicion of the former dictator towards the peasants as he had lived amongst them and knew intimately their interests and aspirations. To the session of the Central Committee held in September 1953 he revealed the hard life of the country people, the backwardness of methods of cultivation and the low yield, the mistakes in directives and the waste and misery in many kolkhozes. It was therefore necessary to blaze a different trail from that hitherto followed and instead of suspicion to awake the trust of the country people by showing them by concrete provisions that the government wished to favour their interests, without worrying too much about ideological questions. It was the voice of common sense interpreted for the first time in favour of the tillers of the soil. Khrushchev believed that the indifference of the peasants must be overcome by putting into force incentives to persuade them to make a great productive effort. There were objections that by so doing the better organized farms would gain more and become rich, thus increasing the gap between them and the poorer farms. Was a criterion of this kind, proper to capitalist economy, compatible with progress towards communism? Khrushchev replied yes, inasmuch as to progress towards communism the prime condition was to promote such an abundance of goods as to be able to satisfy everyone.

The reply was a clever one, but it was not difficult to object that if communism intended to introduce full economic equality the way to get there was not by stressing inequalities. The measures adopted by Khrushchev to better the lot of agriculture were at once put into force. Only a few months after Stalin's death the charges on the revenues of the family holdings were reduced by a half. It was a popular move which brought a direct relief to the kolkhoz members. In September 1953, again at Khrushchev's proposal, the Central Committee reduced the quota of obligatory deliveries and improved the purchase price considerably, especially of meat products, potatoes, vegetables, flax and hemp. The price for potatoes was quadrupled and for meat quintupled. This proves how mercilessly the state had exploited the peasant in Stalin's time. There was not merely an improvement in prices but a more rational assessment of them in accord with the productivity of the regions.

Before the Khrushchev reforms, the prices paid for the produce that was handed over compulsorily were the same for the whole of the country and scarcely covered the costs of production, especially in the poorer districts. According to the new norms the Gosplan only set the quantities to be handed over and responsibility for fixing the prices, which had to be 'based economically', was left to the regional authorities. The practice usually adopted was to fix prices on the average production cost in the sovkhozes of the region, increasing it for food products and decreasing it for forage crops. In 1958, as has been said, Khrushchev abolished compulsory deliveries at minimal prices.

The measure that aroused the bitterest altercation was the

abolition of the Machine Tractor Stations. Stalin had made use of them to control the kolkhozes and had sent there carefully selected Party workers who enjoyed a privileged moral and material position. Their presence aroused the resentment of the kolkhoz members and many persons, as for example the economists Sanina and Venger, proposed that the machinery he handed over to the kolkhozes. But Stalin stubbornly opposed this, claiming that the acquisition of the machines would be a flagrant violation of the Marxist principle that forbade private ownership, whether individual or collective, of the means of production. He also stressed that the tendency to create privileged groups of producers who were owners of capital goods would be highly blameworthy in a Marxist society.

But Khrushchev cut the Gordian knot with his usual common sense. He realized that there must be an end to this 'co-habitation of two masters', that is to say of the kolkhoz members as masters of the soil and the tractor drivers as masters of the machines. It was especially necessary to put an end to the hated control of the workers over the peasants. The measure was enthusiastically welcomed by the peasants and gave an immense popularity to the new star. There were eight thousand Machine Tractor Stations, employing three million workers and provided with 680,000 tractors, 104,000 self-propelled vehicles and 264,000 other machines of various kinds. In a few months this was for the most part acquired by the kolkhozes, many of which paid for it in cash.

To crown this daring reform programme came the decision of the Presidium in May 1957 to exempt the produce of the family holdings from participation in the bulk deliveries.

Khrushchev also did not overlook the sovkhozes. He increased the pay of the personnel and approved a building plan which gave them schools, houses and hospitals, to be completed during the two-year period 1954-1955.

There was a close connection between these measures. They were intended to persuade the kolkhoz members, especially by the improvement in the prices to be paid for bulk deliveries, that their best interests would be served by devoting the greater part of their labour not to the minute family holdings but to the common property of the kolkhoz, to which they would also have an interest in selling their livestock, thus transferring them from their own properties to the collective farm. Thus, without pressure and without creating mistrust, the private property of the family holdings would spontaneously and gradually disappear. Another regulation, with a similar end in view, was to attach the poorer kolkhozes to the more prosperous ones so that the less fortunate too might have a share in the profits and ease their burden of expenses as well as assuring themselves a more capable technical administration.

The results of these wise reforms were not slow in making themselves felt. From 1953 to 1955 production increased as follows:

	Percentage increase
Cereals	30
Beet	34
Flax	133
Meat	8
Milk	18
Cotton	3
Wool	9

Perhaps the most important result was the increase in wheat production between 1953 and 1958, so that the consumers were able to replace rye bread by good quality white bread. The increase was obtained by raising the yields, since the area sown increased from 106.7 million hectares to only 125.2 million.

An even more significant figure was that of the revenues of the collective farms which rose from 48 milliard rubles in 1952 to 95.2 milliard in 1957. They were thus doubled within five years.

13

The peasants had won a signal victory. To see this it is only necessary to compare the regulations put into operation by Khrushchev with the policy of Stalin as outlined in his thesis *Economic Problems of Socialism* put before the Party Congress in 1952, which tended to restrict the initiative of the kolkhozes and extend state control over them in order to make their administration similar to that of the sovkhozes and the factories.

But this time too the victory was not final. The ideology is hostile to the kolkhoz. The Stalinist current, opposed to the kolkhoz, is still strong and the richer the kolkhozes become, widening the gap between the economic situation of the kolkhoz members and the wage-earners, whether peasants or workers, the more violent is the criticism and the opposition. This hostile current was supported by Matskevich, the Minister of Agriculture himself, who was dismissed in January 1961. He rebuked the kolkhozes for pursuing their own interests instead of those of the nation and therefore not paying enough heed to increasing the potentialities of their farms.

Before him, similar ideas had been vigorously supported by Belyaev, one of the most influential members of the Presidium and

First Secretary of the Kazakstan communist party. In December 1959, using the poor harvest as a pretext, he attacked Khrushchev's policy and criticized, among other things, the privileged position of the kolkhoz members by comparison with that of the workers. Khrushchev countered these accusations by saying that the blame for the poor harvest of 1959 was not attributable to the kolkhozes as much as to the sovkhozes which had produced five million tons less than was estimated, and dismissed Belyaev for incompetence. The most serious criticism was directed, with illogical incomprehensibility, against the price increases decreed by Khrushchev in the previous year. Many persons demanded that these be reduced, to equate them with those paid to the sovkhozes, even though these were not weighed down by the burdens and risks which affect the kolkhozes.[5]

Khrushchev was thus in the epicentre of the conflict between the anti-kolkhoz tendency and that favourable to giving them greater freedom of action. He had, however, only partially allied himself with the latter, limiting himself to recognizing their right to greater technical autonomy and greater freedom in establishing their annual production programmes; he rejected the thesis put forward, amongst others, by Polyanski, president of the Presidium of the Russian federal republic, to grant full self-administration to the kolkhozes together with the right of making price contracts for their produce and of disposing of the entire revenues of the community. Furthermore, Khrushchev said that the system of family holdings should be discouraged because, in his view, they took up too much of the working time of the kolkhoz members, and also that their private ownership of stock should be discouraged.

The fact is that Khrushchev's liberal provisions were not enough to convince the kolkhoz members to devote themselves exclusively, or even mainly, to collective production. They still feel the suspended threat of a step backward, as has so often happened before, and especially they do not feel free to use the profits of their collective efforts for their own advantage. Lack of confidence still exists on both sides. Khrushchev knew the aspirations of the peasants only too well not to be aware of the danger that every fresh concession means a step forward on the slippery path towards the full recognition of the peasants' right to dispose of the land as if it were their

---

[5] The following burdens are laid upon the kolkhozes, although the sovkhozes are exempted (or at least are paid by the state):
  A. Many productive investments;
  B. Insurance of buildings, stock and harvests;
  C. Social assistance to sick or incapacitated members;
  D. Taxes.

exclusive property. He acknowledged this unequivocally before 1948. 'We must bear in mind,' he wrote, 'that the little worm of individual ownership is still gnawing at the brain of the kolkhoz member. Today, as in the past, the most important residue of capitalism in the consciousness of the collectivized peasant class is the yearning for private ownership.' It is a grub that nothing and no one can destroy and which will end by eating away the whole communist régime.

Instead of an open understanding there is a hidden skirmish in which each side aims at outwitting the other, dissimulating its own suspicions and its own intentions. The policy fathered by Khrushchev from 1950 onward was to merge the collective farms into huge organizations which he called *agrogorods* (farm towns) with the aim of putting an end to the isolation of the peasants in the countryside, removing them far from their family holdings and regrouping them in new towns where they would enjoy modern comforts but where at the same time they would be more easily controlled and where, in the winter months, they would be able to work in factories, so that they would merge with the workers. Such towns would have an average of five thousand inhabitants each. But Malenkov at the XIX Party Congress quashed this proposal. None the less it seemed to have remained Khrushchev's fundamental idea. The aim was to bring the kolkhozes under the régime of the state farms and to transform the kolkhoz members into wage-earners.

14

Khrushchev said openly to the XXI Party Congress in January 1959: 'With the development of electrification in agriculture, with mechanization and the automation of production, there will emerge a typical amalgam of collective farm production and state production, and agricultural labour will gradually become transformed into a form of industrial labour.'

It seemed that this was an aim to be put into operation slowly, as technical advances made the work of machines more important than that of men in agriculture. That is to say unless the rapid evolution of the situation did not demand more urgent provisions. In his speech to the Central Committee on Christmas Day 1959, Khrushchev took a definite stand. He began by listing the measures taken in favour of the collective farms. 'In 1953,' he said, 'when many collective farms were in difficulties, the Soviet state, in order to aid them and to put them back on the right lines, agreed to a substantial increase in the prices of their products despite the fact that even then some of their products cost more than those of many state farms. . . . Now that the collective farms are once more in good working order and are making progress, the profits of the peasants on these farms have increased. In some regions they are higher than the workers' wages. This is unjust. The working class, as we all know, is the driving force of our society. The workers and the peasants fought closely united against the landowners and the capitalists, established and confirmed Soviet power and defended against counter-revolution the achievements of the great October revolution. They fought together against the fascist invaders to defend the honour and independence of the mother country and are now marching together, closely united, towards communism.

'What does it mean, to march together towards communism? It means to work together, to create a common weal and to receive a reward for their labours which will not arouse the resentment either of the workers or the peasants. In my view, that is just.'

This means that the limit of the profits of the kolkhoz members should not exceed the average level of the workers' wages. But in this case what happens to the incentives granted them to stimulate their productivity?

The representatives of Uzbekistan, of Tadzhikistan, of Turkmenistan, of Kirgizia and of Georgia, that is to say the more amenable elements who wanted a revision of the purchase price of certain products, echoed Khrushchev's views.

The Central Committee accepted Khrushchev's proposals and passed the following decisions:

(a) the remuneration of the workers on the collective farms should not exceed the level of the workers' wages in any specific district or region. The workers and peasants on the collective farms who by their common labours create wealth must improve their living standards in a uniform manner;

(b) there must be a reduction in the purchase price of certain agricultural produce sold by the collective farms to the state, in order to bring them into line with the prices paid to the state farms for their deliveries. This will eventually make possible the reduction of state retail prices for consumer goods and thus still further increase the living standards of the Soviet people;

(c) there must be a development of collaboration between kolkhozes to form great industrial units. The plenary meeting takes note of the fact that recently relations between collective farms have developed widely and that many building enterprises have been founded, as well as factories for the production of building materials, for the construction of electrical plant, for roads,

schools, hospitals, kindergartens, as well as factories for the processing of agricultural produce and the fattening of stock.

The reforms of 1953 and the succeeding years were to all intents
and purposes annulled. Perhaps it is just in these decisions of the
Central Committee in December 1959, that the germs of the
agrarian crisis of 1960 and 1961 are to be found. They not only
paralysed the will of the peasants to produce more in order to gain
more, but they confirmed them in their conviction that nothing was
to be expected from a government which, like those which preceded
it, was tightly bound by rigid doctrinaire formulas.

What was it that Khrushchev meant by his pathetic appeal for
unity among all the productive forces of the country? Purely and
simply he had confirmed the principle held by Lenin and Stalin of
the superiority of the working class over the peasant class in communist society. The task of the peasants is to be 'the allies of the
proletarian workers, leaving to them the leadership', as was stated
at about that time by Academician E. S. Varga, commenting on the
principles of Lenin. It could not be allowed that the peasants should
have a better economic situation and a privileged position. That
would undoubtedly arouse the resentment of the working class
which was the solid foundation of the régime. The variance in price
between the bulk market and the kolkhoz market was bound to
arouse the discontent of the city consumers, that is to say the
workers. It was inevitable that the liberal policy followed until then,
so contrary to the rigorous intransigence of Stalin, should create
lively preoccupations, because it was capable of undermining the
very foundations of the system. The accusations of the anti-Party
group had stressed the dangers of the situation. The greater the
resources of the kolkhoz members and the wider the gap that
separated them from the modest and static situation of the wage-
earners, the more urgent was the necessity of reversing the machine
and stemming the enrichment of the peasants. These are the
absurdities of an ideology that places the impossible claim of maintaining an iron egalitarian level above the need to increase production. But once the expectation of greater profits fell, so too did
the enthusiasm of the peasants. They merely noted that the limiting
provisions struck at the profits to be obtained by working on the
collectives' lands. . . . In fact the revenue from collective production
was reduced by the fall in the bulk purchase price and at the same
time the portion of the profits to be shared among the kolkhoz
members was reduced because they were compelled to increase the
proportion to be paid into the indivisible fund of the enterprise. It
followed that the kolkhoz members held even more jealously to the

possession of their family holdings which assured them a safe income without controls and which had to be shared with no one else. Thus the government's hopes of reducing the importance of the family holdings and giving preference to the collective vanished into thin air.

15

What conclusions are to be drawn from this experience? The peasants, after resisting Stalin's repressive measures, have succeeded in obtaining a position favourable by comparison with that of the workers. Khrushchev's measures in 1953 and 1954 increased this advantage. But the fact that the position conceded to them has not, as would be logical, been extended to the workers also has made it precarious.

The workers, instead of making common cause with the peasants and demanding participation in the profits, opposed the privileges of the kolkhoz workers; ingenuously lending an ear to the urgings of the politicians, they have demanded the elimination of the gap caused by the concessions to the peasants. They have recognized an egalitarian criterion, whereas one of the reasons that has induced the government to withdraw from the kolkhoz members a great part of what was previously conceded to them was that if economic conditions were better in the country than in the factories no one would want to work in industry. This would imperil the increase in industrial production and would lead, because of a shortage of manpower, to an increase in wages. The country population has therefore become what Marx called the army reserve to keep down wages.

The government thus makes use of the workers to beat down the demand of the peasants and of the peasants to keep the workers' wages low. Only a union of the two classes could help them to surmount the one real obstacle to the improvement of the conditions of both one and the other. This would be the deciding factor.

The peasants' discontent is justified by the excessive lowness of their remuneration. It has been shown by calculations which would be too long to give here that two-thirds of all that the Soviet peasant produces is taken away from him. Whether or not this estimate be correct, it is certain that the peasant receives too little because the state speculates on the re-sale of all that he produces and purchases it at a very low price. It should be added that the losses due to bad weather conditions fall entirely on the peasant since the state fixes annually the amount to be handed over, whatever the total harvest may be. After Lenin and after Stalin, the logic of the system forced itself upon Khrushchev also, despite his undeniable efforts to improve the condition of the country people. It is the logic of the system that demands that the peasants must not become rich, in homage to a utopian principle of equality which serves to justify the limitation of the profits both of the peasants and of the workers. The kolkhoz member knows what he will get from his minute family holding and calculates what he should get if the rest of the land were also his and if he could work it with the same love and dedicate to it the same effort; as also if he could sell its produce not at the bulk price but at its real value. He sees in fact the injustice and absurdity of the system and feels that he has been defrauded of a part of his labour.

The attachment of the kolkhoz member to his holding proves incontestably how deeply rooted in him is the instinct for ownership. The government is aware of this and therefore does not put into effect the reform, demanded by many, of abolishing the ownership of the family holding because a measure of this nature would provoke a reaction on such a scale as to create chaos and serious disturbances in the countryside.

It is clear that the peasants are now aware of possessing a formidable weapon and that is their ability to increase or diminish the volume of the nation's food.

Logically enough, the authorities do not like to say much about this systematic sabotage by the peasants, because it would show up the weakness of the régime which is being tacitly opposed by so large a section of the population. But the facts speak for themselves. They are to be found in the Soviet Statistical Institute, where they were obtained. They show that, after Stolypin's reforms, the yield of grain per hectare rose between 1909 and 1913, that is to say in only four years, from 6.9 quintals to 8.2 quintals. From that time until 1960, that is to say in little less than half a century, the yield has risen to 10.9 quintals. This means that it has increased by scarcely 2.7 quintals, an increase really paltry when compared with that in Western countries and when one bears in mind the tremendous advances in agrarian techniques over the past fifty years. Yet, as Soviet writers frequently love to point out, the Russian peasant between 1909 and 1913 had only wooden ploughs at his disposal.[6] On the other hand Soviet industry has now supplied the peasants with an almost unlimited wealth of agricultural machinery, to the

[6] In 1913 there were:

         7,800,000 stick-ploughs
         2,200,000 wooden ploughs
         4,200,000 iron ploughs
        17,700,000 wooden harrows

scale of one tractor for every 83 hectares of ploughland. The seven-year plan made provision for another million tractors and all relative equipment. Agrarian technicians number several hundred thousand. What is lacking? The goodwill of the peasant.

More than machines, more than technicians, the Russian peasant wants land, that is ownership of the fruits of his labour. He does not want to work for the state which exploits him but for himself, and himself alone, as is just, as is moral, as is his sacrosanct right, as was acknowledged in the promises of 'the land for the peasants'. The peasant reacts against this fraud of which he has been the victim in the same way as every peasant in the world would react, with passive obstruction, and sometimes also with active obstruction, despite the threats of the government.

In order better to understand the situation, it is worth while to go deeper into certain aspects of this struggle between the peasants and the state, as well as to examine the more and more serious contradictions between the kolkhoz system and the wage-earning workers and to indicate the problems which have been made insoluble by the intransigent application of Marxist principles.

16

Despite the fact that the area of every kolkhoz is some thousands of hectares, a considerable proportion of agricultural production is made up of what the kolkhoz member obtains from his family holding, even though the present trend is progressively to decrease its size.[7] It is enough to point out that in 1938 half the stock in the Soviet Union was the private property of the 25,000,000 kolkhoz families and was raised on the family holdings. Later this percentage rose to two-thirds both for cattle and pigs.[8] How has this happened? Evidently by allowing privately owned stock to graze on the common land by the complacent tolerance of the kolkhoz directors.

This is documentary proof of the absurdity by which tens of millions of agricultural workers, instead of devoting their efforts to the greater expansion of the common lands, devote their closest attention to a minute fraction of those lands because of an economic ordinance contrary to their interests. This means a waste of effort on

[7] In 1960 the family holdings amounted in all to 5,300,000 hectares, that is to say 2.61% of the cultivated lands. The average size of a holding is 0.31 hectares. The largest holdings are in the Baltic lands: in Lithuania 0.53 hectares, in Esthonia 0.48 and in Latvia 0.46.

[8] At the beginning of 1959 more than half of the cows were privately owned.

minute fractionings and insufficient exploitation of immense possibilities. It follows that lands which are among the richest in the world, like those of the Ukraine, are cultivated extensively whereas in all the Western countries lands far less rich are cultivated intensively. On the other hand these minute pieces of land are looked after as if they were gardens. It is sufficient to look at the tiny family holdings in Georgia, laid out in vineyards, citrus fruits, tobacco and tea, which have a very considerable output. These revenues, be it noted, are obtained solely by manual labour, since the use of machinery is restricted to the common lands. It is enough to prove the manifest absurdity that the profit is greater where agricultural techniques, mechanization and organized labour are least.

To give an idea of the total revenues that the kolkhoz members draw from their family holdings, it is worth while pointing out that whereas the gross revenue per hectare in the collective farms declined in the period 1929-1937 from 117.1 rubles to 109 rubles, the revenue from the family holdings rose in the same period from 162.1 rubles per hectare to 860.

It may therefore be foreseen that certain of the plans of the Central Committee will find very scanty application, such as that adopted at its plenary session in December 1958, which read: 'The family holdings of the kolkhoz members will little by little diminish in importance as the economy of the collective farms develops. It will become more advantageous for the kolkhoz members to obtain their produce from the collective rather than waste their energy in cultivating their private plots.'

The government's irritation at the behaviour of the kolkhoz members continues to increase. From an enquiry carried out by Khrushchev on the agrarian crisis of 1960-1961 such an abundance of abuses, frauds and thefts by kolkhoz members was revealed that it seemed as if the kolkhozes were becoming private farms for the use of the members of the collective and that the members would end up by regarding the undivided lands as a sort of appendix to, or reserve for, their family holdings. It is a sullen struggle between the peasants who try to exploit these lands in their own interest and the state which makes every effort to maintain its rights. Throughout almost the whole of Soviet territory, but especially in Central Asia, pressure is growing among the kolkhoz members to expand their family holdings by usurping the undivided lands, with the connivance of the other members and of the directors. Sometimes these holdings are expanded to four, five and even six hectares, that is to say several times the permitted area. There is also a tendency to restrict labour effort to the family holdings and to avoid all collective work. The Uzbekistan press[9] says that in many zones of the Tashkent district little more than a quarter of the workers assigned to cotton picking actually went to the plantations. In the nearby district of Samarkand the percentage dropped to 12 or 13% of the workers assigned to the job. In the Pravda kolkhoz out of 1,500 workers assigned to cotton picking and clearing the fields not a single one turned up. *Izvestia* on March 3, 1963 reported that the members of the Mekhat-Rokhat kolkhoz in Tadzhikistan took all the stock, both privately and collectively owned, sold it and divided the monies amongst themselves.

In Georgia the work of the collective squads diminished by a third while private work increased by 157,000 units.

Khrushchev harshly scourged the kolkhoz members for this usurpation of the undivided lands and for their frequent appropriation of state property. 'We have proof,' he said at Tbilisi, the capital of Georgia, where such misdemeanours were rife, 'that mortality among the stock is only reported when an animal belongs to a kolkhoz or sovkhoz. In 1960 for every hundred sheep reported dead or strayed in the collective farms not a single one was privately owned.'

Such revelations sharpen criticism and add fresh fuel to the press campaign against the family holdings. Diridenko, one of the best agrarian technicians in the Soviet Union, who was entrusted with organizing the cultivation of the virgin lands of Kazakstan, proposed the total abolition of the family holdings which were, he maintained, 'a real conspiracy against communist society'. The whole press applauded his proposal.

At first the government restricted itself to maintaining the taxation on the family holdings. The tax was reduced by 60% in 1953 and it was believed that this reduction foreshadowed its abolition, seeing that the yield to the state was only about four milliard rubles. But Khrushchev explained at a meeting of the Supreme Soviet in May 1960 that 'the agricultural tax is paid for the use of the land for market gardening which serves as a source of a certain income for the members of the kolkhozes in addition to the income that they receive from the collective farm. . . . The income from these plots,' he specified, 'is partly derived from the sale of their produce at market prices. This tax must remain because it has a certain importance in maintaining labour discipline in the collective farms and in assessing the income which the kolkhozes get from their personal holdings. No tax is recovered from the income of the kolkhoz members for their work in the collectives.'

In this somewhat involved manner, like that usually adopted

[9] *Pravda Vostoka* of December 4 and 7, 1961, and February 14, 1963.

when dealing with questions which might provoke dangerous repercussions, Khrushchev let it be known that the Party, for ideological reasons, looks askance at this perpetuation of private ownership even of these very modest plots of land, and therefore continues to tax them even though this tax only brings in about four milliard rubles. But it is the first indication of more drastic measures to come.

17

The most serious measure, and one which has still further caused the kolkhoz member to lose interest in working the collective lands, is the order to increase the proportion of the profits to be paid into the indivisible fund. In practice these payments are deducted from the profit to be divided among the members. The former norm was twenty per cent for the indivisible fund, but this proportion has now been doubled.

Naturally the state tries to ensure that these funds, which now amount to considerable sums, be used for collective interests. It counts on them to hasten the industrialization of the collective farms and tries to burden them not only with the expenses of improvements but also with the cost of the infrastructure, for example road-building, electric power lines and the like. The indivisible fund was conceived as liquid capital to cover administration and maintenance expenses, for the acquisition of stock, machinery and fertilizers and as a reserve for expenses concerned with collective interests, such as schools, housing, cultural centres and the like. But with the increase of this liquid capital grew the tendency for the kolkhoz members to make use of it for speculations to increase their revenues. It is no secret that the farms go in for conveyancing and increase the scope of their activities by building slaughterhouses, meat-canning plants, food processing plants, brick kilns, electric power plants and so on. There are some kolkhozes which have widespread business interests and a wide sphere of activities and income. In consequence the economic situation of their members differs more and more from that of the workers who must be content with a fixed wage. Thus there emerge privileged groups which owe their fortune to their own initiative, to their own ability, to good administration, to the greater fertility of the lands they work, and so on. But this enrichment, this differentiation, does not tally with the dogma of egalitarianism, excites the jealousy of the majority and weakens the system of standard remuneration. Therefore the state, in the name of the ideology, must lop these trees that raise their crests too high and in one way or another impound this excess of wealth, with the result that it weakens productive effort and, by levelling the whole of society, drives the more able and energetic back to the level of the grey masses. Here one touches upon the paralysing influence of the ideology.

18

This incompatibility between farms with a large degree of economic autonomy like the kolkhozes and the state enterprises, which are in the majority, came into the limelight when the kolkhozes, after the liberal measures granted them by Khrushchev, were able to remunerate their members not as hitherto in kind, but in money.

The new system began to come to the fore in 1957. It was naturally the richer kolkhozes which began to hand out to all their members a monthly payment on account of what would be due to them. The example was at once imitated and by 1959 many thousands of kolkhozes had adopted the system. The peasants greatly preferred it to a distribution of produce and the Central Committee itself acknowledged the value of money payments as an important production incentive. But the problems which such a system provokes in a Marxist régime are so complicated that the Central Committee was unable to solve them.

The fundamental problem is how to assure equal wages for equal work throughout the whole of the Soviet Union. In a country where the state is the owner of all the means of production it is inadmissible that some workers should receive more pay than others for similar work. It does not matter in the least to the worker whether the enterprise to which he is attached makes a profit or a loss, that is whether its revenues are or are not sufficient to cover the wages it is compelled to pay. The responsibility is the state's which in a unitary framework of production must make up the deficit of those farms which are run at a loss by using the revenues of those which are run at a profit. This redistribution of income is one of the greatest difficulties that has to be overcome.

The special circumstances imposed by facts are so diverse that it is not possible to cover them all in a single regulation. From these differing circumstances is born the well-known phenomenon of Ricardian yield; more fertile, better situated or better set-out lands will give a larger return on an equal investment. In capitalist economy even poor lands find someone to cultivate them, since the lowness of the yield is compensated for by the smaller capital needed to acquire them. But in a Marxist régime no one is willing to work unfruitful land if he is not guaranteed the same economic treatment as one who works land of maximum fertility. If the system of sovkhozes, that is of state farms, were in force throughout all Russia, where the worker is paid by the day and all production belongs to the state, the problem would not arise because the lesser income of one farm would be balanced by the greater income of another. But the prevailing system is that of the kolkhozes or agricultural co-operatives. They possess the best land in Russia. It should also be noted that there is a constant process of selection inasmuch as the less favoured kolkhozes, that is to say the poorest, keep urging the state to transform them into sovkhozes and thereby transfer their burden of debt to the state. Thus, little by little, the poorer lands become the property of the state, the richer ones the property of the kolkhozes. But even after this process of selection differences remain between one kolkhoz and another. How can an equal wage be assured to all their members?

In principle the payment to the kolkhoz member cannot be less than that paid by the state to its wage-earners. But can it be more? The state would like to avoid this, but clearly cannot do so, because in such a case the kolkhozes would in fact be transformed into sovkhozes or state factories on a fixed wage scale and would lose every incentive to produce more in order to gain more. If, on the other hand, the wages in some of the richer collectives are higher than in others, who will want to work in a kolkhoz in which he earns even less?

The introduction of a wage system is none the less inevitable, since without money payments to the workers there can be no exact costing system on which to base the profit and loss account of the establishment.

But many collectives cannot, because of their backwardness, afford such a reform because their revenues do not allow them to establish a sufficient wages fund.

The problem is a serious one because the variation in wealth between one kolkhoz and another is really large. This can be seen from the statistics which show that in 1957 and 1958 the average wage for a working day in agriculture in the Astrakhan region was twenty-five per cent higher than the corresponding average in the Kuban, in the Stavropol area and in the Altai, and that the wages paid in these three regions were three times higher than in the Tatar and Bashkir federated republics, in White Russia and in Lithuania, as well as in the Pskov and Smolensk regions. In these republics and regions the average wage of a kolkhoz member was less than that paid in the state farms.

The variance in agricultural wages has been carefully studied by

Soviet economists. *Voprosy Ekonomiki* (No. 11, 1959) quotes the results of an investigation carried out by T. Zaslavskaya. She points out that the kolkhozes can be divided into three categories on the basis of their revenue and if 100 is taken as the average wage of the kolkhoz worker in the lowest category, that of the members in the next category will be 162 and in the highest category 232.

19

It has been thought possible to eliminate these differences by replacing the system of standard prices for each product by a price system based on the actual production costs, region by region. In fact the state has handed over to the local authorities the stabilization of purchase prices. But this price difference for the same product has also its disadvantages because it discourages, by lowering prices, cultivation in the most suitable districts and encourages it, by raising prices, in less suitable areas. Thus it hampers the division of labour that comes about naturally because of variation in profits. It is a fact that price variations have already been applied but on a totally inadequate scale. They do not go beyond an increase of 40 or 50% on the minimum price. Even with such price variations wheat production assures the cultivators of the northern Caucasus and of the *chernozem* of the Ukraine and Moldavia a profit equivalent to 118 and even 168% on the cost; whereas it results in a loss, varying between 34 and 57%, to the cultivators of northern and northeast Russia, of White Russia, of Lithuania and of Latvia. The same is true of other products. For example the purchase price of wool assures a profit of more than a hundred per cent to the farms of Central Asia and a loss of more than 40% to the farms of European Russia.

Furthermore, even within a single region conditions may vary from one zone to another. It would therefore be necessary to draw up a detailed schedule liable to the most arbitrary variations. This was made clear by an enquiry by the Economic Institute of the Soviet Academy of Sciences into the economic condition of the collective farms in the area between Smolensk, Moscow, Gorki and Belgorod. The period investigated was from 1954 to 1957. It showed that in the Moscow zone the average annual income of the richest farms was eleven times higher than that of the poor ones. At Smolensk the difference was five times, at Gorki nine and at Belgorod only three.

It is clear from all that has been said that the kolkhoz system does not lend itself to an equalization of incomes. To explain why the Soviet state keeps the purchase price of some products high and others low would mean to go into the motives of internal policy by which the population of certain areas is given preferential treatment over that of others, why certain forms of cultivation are given precedence over others, and so on. But it is a fact that whereas in Uzbekistan and Turkmenia cotton production assures the kolkhoz members an income roughly double the wages paid in the sovkhozes, in the Urals, where stock-breeding is predominant, the income received is insufficient to support the peasants' families.

It has been suggested that the government equalize these vastly different incomes by means of taxation, taking from some and giving to others. But a régime that pursues a programme of abolishing taxation finds it difficult to apply it to one category alone without the tax becoming a discrimination.

It has also been suggested that the kolkhozes spontaneously create reserves intended to equalize wages in the various enterprises. These reserve funds should be made up of the profits remaining after wages have been paid corresponding to the average payments made locally on state farms. In practice this would mean to reduce the economic conditions of the kolkhoz members to those of the sovkhoz workers. That would mean to transform the collective farms into state farms, which would imply a step backward since it would eliminate the incentives which have driven the richer kolkhozes to outdistance the others. It must not be forgotten that even if the greater wealth of some is due to the phenomenon of Ricardian yield, factors of specifically moral character have had even more to do with it, such as the industriousness of the members, their technical skill, their thrift which has enabled them to use their savings to improve their funds, the ability of the directors and, in fact, the efforts made by all to increase productivity. Such things deserve to be rewarded. To curtail by taxation these legitimate profits for the advantage of less able and willing workers would be to reward the less worthy.

From whatever viewpoint the problem is considered, the same conclusion is evident and that is that if one places a limitation on the rewards of the worker, the worker will also place a limitation on his productive effort. The communist theoreticians are trying to reconcile two irreconcilable principles. On the one hand they wish to encourage production by granting incentives to individuals to produce more, which implies that each be rewarded in the measure of his productive effort; on the other they would like to reward everyone to approximately the same degree regardless of the effort made. After forty-five years communism has not yet been able to extricate itself from this contradiction. There is, it is true, a scale of wages; but wages are not enough, as Marx has taught, to suppress surplus-value. Only the system of co-operation permits the integration of wages with a proportion of profits. But co-operation is a breach of the wages system imposed by the resistance of the peasants as a class. The necessity for the régime to give way in order to assure the supply of foodstuffs to the cities is the proof that economic laws cannot be violated with impunity. Reality and utopia cannot live together. The kolkhoz is an arrow in communism's flank. The contradiction between the wages system and the co-operative system becomes more and more flagrant. Either the co-operative system must be eliminated or it must be extended to the whole of the working class, admitting it to a share of the profits and the administration of the enterprises. That would mean the end of state capitalism and the bankruptcy of communism.

20

The agricultural crisis has been born of these contradictions. After Stalin's death, when Khrushchev revealed the tragic condition of agriculture, it was found that from 1929, the year when the NEP was abandoned and land collectivization introduced, to 1955 production had increased by 35%; but the population, taking into account the post-war annexations, had increased by 45%. Therefore the *pro capite* production had diminished. The livestock situation was even more disastrous; in 1953 it had not yet returned to the level of 1913.

It was the indisputable proof of the failure of a system which had been imposed with promises of increased consumer goods and yet had brought the people to the brink of famine. Thirty-six years after the revolution, and eight after the end of the war, rationing of foodstuffs was still in force.

It is only by taking note of this situation, which appears to be incurable, that one can understand the motives which induced Khrushchev to abandon the rigid restrictive policy of Stalin and to approve liberal measures in favour of the kolkhozes. But much more should have been done to reach the production levels of North America, which had been held up to the Soviet peasants as an example.

Not being able to rely on intensification of cultivation, since all attempts to do so in the past had failed, it was necessary to push ahead with expansion of the cultivated area. Khrushchev decided to create, on the farther side of the Urals, in the virgin steppe, an immense cereal cultivation area. To that end he proposed the clearance of thirty-six million hectares in Kazakstan and Western Siberia. We have already noted the opposition of the anti-Party group to this programme. Molotov especially stressed that the steppe was unsuited, because of the aridity of the soil and the uncertain rainfall, for so great an experiment. There was a risk of losing two harvests out of three.

Khrushchev's thesis won the day and he at once began to put it into practice with a vast mobilization of men and means. The young people responded to the appeal with enthusiasm. In three years 425 state farms were set up with an average area of 25,000-30,000 hectares each. 350,000 young people were mobilized for the ploughing. It was estimated that in three years a good 3,000,000 students and workers helped to bring in the harvest.

Khrushchev reported the results to a plenary session of the Central Committee on December 17, 1958. He intoned a paean of victory. The anti-Party group had held that the exploitation of the virgin lands not only would not repay the expenses incurred but would lead to disastrous losses. Then Khrushchev announced that with a total expense of 30,700 million rubles in the four years 1954-58 a profit of 48,900 million rubles had been made and had already been paid over to the state. Kazakstan, with its twenty million hectares of virgin land, had become the second cereal-producing area of the Soviet Union.

But Khrushchev was still not satisfied and set a target for cereal production double that already attained.

In 1960 he therefore set up 'the territory of the virgin lands' under the management of a famous expert, T. J. Sololev. This includes the five northern regions of the Kazakstan republic, with an area of 600,000 square kilometres and a population of 2,700,000. Its capital is Akmolinsk. The area is intended for cereal production and stock-breeding. 500 sovkhozes have been founded. The ploughland amounts to 18,000,000 hectares. The state farms are intended for sheep farming, with flocks of hundreds of thousands of valuable stock, both for meat and wool. Karakul sheep predominate. The territory is to produce 10,500,000 tons of cereals, 220,000 tons of meat, 550,000 tons of milk and 15,000 tons of wool.

It was the government's intention to give preference to the organization of sovkhozes in the virgin lands. What was needed were model farms, with high yield, directed by the best Soviet technicians and with machine pools especially equipped with machinery adapted to the virgin lands.

All these predictions were proved false by facts, which confirmed the forebodings of the anti-Party group which had discouraged the costly experiment of expanding large-scale cultivation in the Kazakstan steppe. After the first harvests, which seemed to justify the bold plans of Khrushchev, and confirm the possibility of surpassing American cereal production in a few years, the harvests from the virgin lands began to diminish year after year, revealing a progressive exhaustion of the fertility of the soil. A striking proof of this is given by the cereal production figures of the Kustanai district which is in central Kazakstan :

	Million puds (a pud is about 35 lb.)
1956	227
1957	103
1961	62
1962	40

In the 'territory of the virgin lands', which covers an area equal to that of France, Belgium and Denmark, the 15,000,000 hectares planted with wheat, which in 1956 produced more than a quarter of the wheat requirements of the Soviet Union, in 1962 did not manage to attain 15%. It is necessary to distinguish between the virgin lands put into cultivation in Kazakstan, which together with the Ukraine was to become the granary of the Soviet Union, from those of Western Siberia and those on the Middle and Lower Volga. The desiccation of the soil in the cultivated steppe of Kazakstan is accentuated by erosion. In Western Siberia, which has very fertile zones, and in the regions of the Middle and Lower Volga, the damage to the harvests is caused by drought and especially by the hot winds that dry up the crops. Excessive exploitation without rotation and fallow periods has also helped to exhaust the land. Once the pastureland has been broken up for cultivation the productive humus, no longer protected by the grasses, rapidly dissolves into dust in the Kazakstan steppe under the action of frost and sun, and the wind disperses it in gigantic clouds, leaving the bare skeleton of the land, calcinated and lifeless. Thus the famous 'dust bowl' is formed. It means a return to the desert, the death of the countryside, as has happened in the Anatolian basin and in certain parts of North America. The Grain Research Institute at Shardanti in the virgin lands is attentively following the worsening of the situation.

According to its report the quantity of humus taken from the ploughland in a single hour by the fierce winds of the steppe is five tons per hectare. 'If we do not stop mercilessly ploughing up all the virgin fields we shall not be able to save ourselves from aeolic erosion,' said Academician V. Kuzmin. 'We must put a stop to the desiccation of the steppe.' On September 26, 1963 Khrushchev announced at Krasnodar in the Caucasus that the campaign for the cultivation of the virgin lands was over and that it was necessary to obtain increases in production by intensifying, and not by extending, cultivation.

21

Apart from the fate of the production in the virgin lands, the whole situation in the countryside took a turn for the worse a few years after the liberal measures taken by Khrushchev. A contributory cause was the restrictive regulations of the Central Committee in December 1959 which, as we have already said, were a retrograde step.

In order to get an idea of the seriousness of the agricultural crisis which has given rise to lively discussions in the control departments and in the Soviet press, it is as well to compare the targets set by the last two plans, the sixth five-year plan and the seven-year plan, with the actual results achieved by the beginning of 1961, which have been considerably less.

The sixth five-year plan, approved in February 1956 by the XX Party Congress, but abandoned because of non-fulfilment, should have covered the period 1956 to 1960. It was then replaced by the seven-year plan for the period 1959-1965. Here are the quantity targets set for cereals, meat and milk in 1960 and the amounts actually obtained:

	Targets of the five-year plan Million tons	Targets of the seven-year plan Million tons	Actual results 1960 (1959) Million tons	
Cereals	180.0	150.0	133.0	(124.0)
Meat	16.6	9.5	8.6	(8.6)
Milk	86.0	67.4	61.5	(62.0)

It should be noted that to increase cereal production from the 124,000,000 tons obtained in 1959 to the 133,000,000 tons obtained in 1960, 7,000,000 more hectares had to be sown. The yield of wheat per hectare in the Russian federated republic was 10.4 quintals; in Kazakstan, where most of the area of the virgin lands has been exploited, it was 8.4 quintals. In Italy the yield was 18 quintals and in France 26.

For meat the production was seventeen quintals for every 100 hectares compared with forty-two in the United States.

It is to be noted that the Ukraine, which in 1948 handed over 10,000,000 tons of wheat in bulk, in 1960 delivered rather more than a half of this figure, namely 5,864,000 tons.

These results were discussed in January 1961 in a series of

dramatic sessions of the Central Committee, to which the heads of government of the fifteen federated republics were summoned to give an account of themselves. Once again the causes of the uncertainty of the harvest were reviewed, and why the results were so inferior to the targets set.

The situation was clarified by Khrushchev's closing speech on January 18, 1961, delivered with his usual brutal frankness.

According to him, it seems that from 1953, the year of Stalin's death, when the liberal measures in favour of the peasants were approved, agricultural production increased overall by 80%; but after this rapid advance there had been a slackening of effort during the past five years. It was also clear from his words that in many regions there had actually been a recession which threatened to compromise the consumption plan necessitated by increased requirements. Khrushchev explained that the levels of agricultural production set up by the seven-year plan had been calculated according to the needs of the population, which was rapidly increasing. In seven years it had increased by eighteen million, of which more than seventeen million were in the cities as the result of immigration from the countryside. Consumption had also increased because of higher wages, increased pensions and tax reductions. Agriculture was not keeping pace either with the demographic curve or with the economic and social progress of the nation. The general tendency was to justify the paucity of the harvests by the bad weather conditions of recent years. But this was tantamount to acknowledging the correctness of the view put forward by Khrushchev's adversaries that it was not possible to rely on the regularity of the harvests in the arid steppe zone. Khrushchev therefore counter-attacked. Before the debates opened he presented his theses to the Central Committee in which he showed that the cause of the crisis should not be sought in adverse weather conditions but in the bad organization of the farms, their defective technical direction, the negligence of the farmers and the inadequacy of their productive efforts, in the absence of regular control by the local Party organs and in the frauds, the speculations and the false reports of a large number of the agricultural enterprises. He drew up a detailed indictment based on stringent investigations made by himself, and suggested a number of disciplinary measures against those mainly responsible.

Khrushchev's theses have not been published in deference to the communist principle of not washing dirty linen in public. But the substance of them has leaked out. Moreover they were widely circulated among the Party cells. Furthermore, his illustrative declarations have been published.

The basic point made by Khrushchev, which was backed up by all who spoke in the Central Committee, was that not only had the cultivation of the virgin lands given the results asked for, but that it was thanks to this cultivation that they had been able to make up deficiencies in other regions. For example, the premier of the Russian federated republic, D. S. Polyanski, said that six-tenths of the wheat sold that year in the republic had come from the virgin lands. 'The virgin lands,' he said, 'have been of decisive importance in the increase of production and deliveries. They have provided the state with more than a hundred million *puds* of wheat (sixteen and a half million tons). Thus the correctness of the policy of the Party and the government in developing the cultivation of the virgin lands has again been demonstrated.'

The first decision in the debate was to continue the development of the virgin lands. Polyanski approved the decision in dithyrambic terms. 'The country,' he said, 'has already had an adequate return for the monies invested. But the possibilities of the virgin lands are inexhaustible; we are only at the beginning of their exploitation.' He therefore announced the clearance of further terrains which could provide another six to six and a half million tons of wheat. In Kazakstan too, that other granary of the Soviet Union, cultivation would be extended to twenty-five million hectares. In the Far East, near the Chinese frontier 'where the land is excellent, well-watered and with long sunny periods', a million hectares were to be cleared for sowing wheat, rice and soya.

The responsibility therefore was made to fall squarely on the kolkhozes and sovkhozes of the old grain-producing areas, on the poor functioning of the Gosplan and on the inadequacy of industry which had not provided the necessary machinery in time. Undoubtedly an area of more than two hundred million hectares under cultivation needs a very large number of tractors and agricultural machines of all kinds. There were also criticisms of the scanty productive and financial autonomy of the kolkhozes which would like full freedom of control or at least freedom to choose the most profitable crops and to dispose of their own revenues to their own advantage.

All these criticisms were undoubtedly well-founded, but they did not touch on the real cause of the crisis. It is clear that a part of the harvest was lost because of the bad organization of the kolkhozes and sovkhozes. But that did not happen only in the old wheat-producing areas but also in the virgin lands which had only recently been cultivated. On many farms measures had not been taken for rapid harvesting and for the immediate storage of wheat. In some areas there had been no arrangements for the harvesters to arrive in time before the crops had been damaged by rain. The roads were not kept up and therefore the movement of transport lorries and even agricultural machinery was hampered by the mud. In some zones the giant tractors and the powerful machines, built on the latest American models, were not even able to move. No account had been taken of the fact that in America, even in the agricultural areas, there are asphalt roads leading to the places where the work is to be done.

But despite all these things, it was clear from Khrushchev's bitter criticism that the peasants had not taken any real interest in production since they lacked any personal incentive to do so. The real cause was the inefficiency of the system. On some farms the peasants had demanded, at the height of the harvest season, a seven-hour working day to bring them into line with all the other wage-earners.

It is a fact that since 1953, when the first liberal measures were introduced, the kolkhoz member has seen attacks on and threats against private ownership of the family holding become more and more frequent. He has therefore reverted to his former suspicion and lack of interest which certainly do not help to intensify his productive efforts.

22

A true picture of life in a kolkhoz has been given me by a member. His family of four lives in a house for which he pays a rent of 1,200 old rubles, equivalent to 120 dollars a year. The house is built of wood and stone and has two rooms and a kitchen. It has no lavatory and no running water. The whole building measures eight metres by seven metres and two other people live there. The men earn twenty new rubles a month, equivalent to twenty-two dollars, and the women fifteen, equivalent to sixteen dollars fifty cents. They also receive a certain amount of wheat. This is how the kolkhoz member expressed himself:

'The yield of the kolkhoz is considerable, but the state seizes most of the produce. . . . According to the kolkhoz rules the greater part of the produce should be divided amongst the members. But this is not so. Everything is sold without the peasants being able to do anything about it. The state takes all the best produce, paying a ridiculously low price. There is a swarm of bureaucrats in the kolkhoz responsible to the director. They live well and are paid well. Only Party members hold executive posts. They give orders but do not work.

'The cheapest suit costs between four and five hundred old rubles (equal to forty to fifty dollars), and shoes cost about a hundred rubles (ten dollars). The peasants do not use sheets and most of them do not have a mattress. Instead they use sacks stuffed with straw.

'The peasants complain about their living conditions, but they do so warily taking care not to be overheard by Party members. The old people say that they used to live much better before communism. They received a larger share of the produce as payment for their work than they do now either in the kolkhozes or in the sovkhozes.

'Organized theft is practised on a large scale in every kolkhoz. Each family steals all that it can in order to live. The kolkhoz directors are well aware of this but do not always dare to intervene. Everything grown in the kolkhoz is stolen: vegetables, fruit, eggs, etc. The peasants make wine at home from stolen grapes. Their hens are fed on wheat, maize and the oats for the horses. The women collect grass to feed their cows. Those assigned to the dairy steal the milk. The foremen too are poor and keep quiet because they too steal, as do the directors and the control personnel.'

23

Khrushchev's statements reveal the extent of this lack of interest by the peasants. Speaking on February 11, 1961, at Voronezh in one of the most fertile areas of the famous black earth, Khrushchev reproved the peasants for the low state of their funds and explained that their farms incurred great losses because vast areas were left untilled. 'To leave the land fallow,' he said, 'is necessary only in arid zones.' He explained to them that they must grow peas, spacing out the plants 'to preserve the humidity and destroy the weeds'; he concluded by telling them that 'pulse vegetables enrich the soil with nitrogen'. It may well be asked: who would even dream of teaching such elementary ideas to peasants in the West? If they are not applied, the reason is that the peasant is not interested in applying them, since the land belongs to the state.

It is absurd when Khrushchev criticizes many collective and state farms for wasting vast areas in low yield cultivation. Does he really think that the peasants do not know that certain types of sunflower, specifically those of the Ukraine where he was speaking, have an oil-content far superior to the types cultivated by them? Why then do they go on cultivating old types with very low yield? Such examples could be cited *ad nauseam*.

An enquiry into goods left in railway warehouses showed that machinery and fertilizers intended for the kolkhozes and sovkhozes sometimes lie there for years because no one troubles to take them away.

The real interest of the kolkhoz member is in his little family holding, which is his own property and assures him his highest income. Khrushchev's revelations after a tour of inspection throughout all Russia in February and March 1961, which provided detailed examples of continual abuses, proved this up to the hilt. 'Not even a saint,' he exclaimed in exasperation, 'could resist stealing state property.'

What is the extent of these thefts? It may be inferred from the following dialogue between Khrushchev and the First Secretary of the Ukrainian Central Committee:

'I am sure, Comrade Podgorny, that the figures for the harvest per hectare that you have quoted are only half of the entire harvest; the other half of the maize has been stolen in the fields.'

'That is true, Nikita Sergeivich,' Podgorny replied.

'Then where does the weather come in? The harvest has been neglected and stolen and you tell us that the weather has prevented you from having a good harvest. Is that reasonable?'

'No, it isn't.'

Sallies of this sort and even sharper censures were very frequent during the debate. Amongst other accusations, Khrushchev denounced a number of kolkhozes which, in order to make their deliveries to the state under the seven-year plan, bought the produce in the open market or from the state warehouses. 'This is a scandal, a speculation, a real crime,' Khrushchev stormed, and threatened to have laws passed against similar frauds and to have the perpetrators brought to justice.

24

One of the most serious aspects of the crisis is the decline in the harvests of the traditionally agricultural districts of Russia. 'Your black earth,' said Khrushchev during his visit to Voronezh, 'used to be one of the richest areas in the country. Tell me, comrades, why has your meat production not merely not increased but has diminished? . . . Can a director really be satisfied with getting only seven or eight, or at the most eleven, quintals of wheat per hectare? Do you really think you can reach communism like this? Communism, comrades, is not doled out with coffee spoons . . .'

On February 23, 1961, Khrushchev spoke to the peasants of the Moscow area. This is the heart of old Russia, with the ancient cities of Vladimir, Bryansk, Kaluga, Kostroma, Ryazan, Smolensk, Tula and Yaroslav, and has a population of 32,000,000 people. Khrushchev recalled that there are in this area 6,000 kolkhozes and 800 sovkhozes in which work 40,000 technicians, 134,000 tractor-drivers, 34,000 mechanics and 74,000 lorry-drivers. Despite this swarm of specialists production is declining. Over the last six years cereal production was abandoned on 3,000,000 hectares because of the very low yield. The state has therefore had to renounce its bulk purchases of cereals, and the peasants have devoted themselves to poultry farming. Khrushchev said that the government could not tolerate this. He proposed to restore the 3,000,000 hectares by the use of special agricultural machinery and the aid of advanced techniques.

But these proposals could not be put into operation because of the resistance of the peasants who maintained that cereal cultivation, at the prices paid by the state, must necessarily result in a loss. The situation tended to worsen from year to year because while production in all these regions continued to decline consumption increased because of the rise in population, and the government was forced to draw on reserves.

At last the government was forced to accept the facts. In a letter to the Central Committee dated March 19, 1963, Khrushchev acknowledged that a ton of wheat in the Rostov region (southern Russia) cost seventeen rubles to produce whereas in White Russia it cost a hundred and forty rubles according to 1962 figures. He therefore proposed that cereals should be cultivated exclusively in the areas most suitable for them and that stock-breeding be developed in the areas most suitable for that, namely in White Russia, the Baltic lands and the regions around Leningrad and Moscow.

Thus the area of cereal cultivation tended to become more and more restricted as a result of the abandonment of these regions and the crisis in the virgin lands.

Nor does it seem that the incentives to increase stock-breeding instead of wheat cultivation will turn out more satisfactorily, for in the same letter Khrushchev criticized the small scale of cattle raising in the districts referred to, especially in the district of Ryazan where the proportion of beasts was five cows to every hundred hectares. The average should be from twenty-five to thirty cows to each hundred hectares. 'It is a scandal,' he said. 'The directors in this region have deceived the Central Committee.'

This example shows the results of the system of directed economy. Is it possible in a country that covers a sixth of the world to indicate officially, region by region, what must be produced and what must not be produced? Who knows this better than the peasant who lives in constant contact with the soil? If he does not act accordingly there can be only one reason; he has no interest in doing so.

Anyone travelling in European Russia and remembering the opulent countryside of the Western countries must find the sight of the Russian and Ukrainian fields most surprising. Vast areas are left fallow. The fields are mainly sown with wheat. Fruit trees are rare. There are few cattle to be seen. The signs of land improvement so characteristic of the West are entirely lacking. It is an indisputable fact that whereas in the Western countries, thanks to the institution of private ownership, productive effort grows year by year, in communist Russia it is decreasing.

25

Can there be any more convincing proof that the interest of the Russian peasant is centred on his personal holding and that all his efforts are concentrated on the produce which he is allowed to dispose of freely? Such proof is provided by *Pravda* which published an article in April, 1960, which gave statistical data for the period 1956-1959 of the sales made on the kolkhoz markets where the peasants of the collective farms can sell their produce freely. It showed that whereas in 1956 16% of all milk production was sold on the free market, in 1959 the proportion was 48%. For meat the percentages were 19% in 1956 and 48% in 1959; finally, for wool the two percentages were respectively 11% and 64%. These figures are confirmed by other statistics which show that in 1961 out of the 204.6 million hectares under cultivation 4.27 million hectares were classed as family holdings. But on these 4,000,000 hectares 32% of the pigs, 16% of the sheep, 42% of the oxen, 84% of the goats, 84% of the poultry and 26% of the cows were raised. Furthermore from that two per cent of the land under cultivation 82% of the eggs and 50% of the green vegetables were obtained. These figures make it clear that roughly half of the supplies, at least as far as milk, meat, eggs and green vegetables are concerned, come from the free activities of the kolkhoz members. Who can deny, after such evident proofs, the irresistible yearning of the country people to dispose freely of their produce, that is to say their claim to the full and undisputed private ownership of the soil? It is the opposition of the régime to the recognition of this elementary right that has created this drama of the soil. Life stagnates and limits itself to the tiny plots over which the right of ownership is recognized.

26

Soviet economists quite rightly maintain that agriculture still employs too great a proportion of manpower. According to data published in Moscow by the Central Statistical Office on the Soviet economy in 1960, the Soviet working population numbers 99,130,000 persons, of whom 39,736,000 are employed in agriculture. Of these 32,280,000 work in the kolkhozes, 7,190,000 in the sovkhozes and 226,000 are peasants who work independently. Compared with the 40,000,000 who work in the fields, 22,000,000 work in the factories.

On his trip to America, during a visit to a farm at Des Moines on September 22, 1959, Khrushchev himself admitted that the human burden on the Soviet countryside was excessive. 'In your country,' he said, 'the laws of competition inherent in capitalism work. In our country, however, agriculture develops on different principles, socialist principles. The collective undertakings are great co-operative units formed by the voluntary(!) amalgamation of peasant farms. Therefore in our country the number of persons employed on a farm is not the minimum required to cultivate the soil, bring in the harvest, raise the stock and poultry.' It was a recognition of the superiority, at least from the economic standpoint, of the capitalist system.

Even more serious is the bureaucratization of the countryside. The sharpest criticisms and the most cutting sarcasms about this scourge of the Soviet economy came, as usual, from Khrushchev himself. From his speeches the public, half amused and half shocked, learnt of the deeds and misdeeds of bureaucracy: there are instances of the most crass stupidity, plans for the cultivation of fields from which it is not even possible to harvest enough seed for the next season. The climax of hilarity was reached when he referred to a regional committee which spent 1,600 rubles on telegrams saying that too much money was being spent on telegrams.

Still quoting Khrushchev's revelations to the Central Committee in December 1959, it appears that out of an average personnel of a hundred and ten persons employed in the sovkhozes of Kazakstan, where the cultivation of the virgin lands is mainly concentrated, there are twenty-five to thirty accountants or administrative personnel. 'In a single mouth,' he said, '15,000 vouchers must be filed for accounting purposes; there are 1,800,000 schedules concerning expenses, hours of work, payments and wages. It is impossible to control such a huge mass of documents; therefore in practice there is no control over how wages are calculated and serious violations have been confirmed, such as cases of payment for work which has not been carried out.'

Such are the joys of state control: bureaucracy, fraud and the impossibility of effective control. The more the state machinery increases the more complicated it grows and the more rapidly these inevitable evils spread.

27

Conclusions on the gravity of the crisis, on the causes for it and on the remedies to be applied were put before the plenum of the Party Central Committee by Khrushchev on March 5, 1961.

He began with the statement that the enormous efforts made by the Soviet state over the past decade to strengthen agriculture had not achieved adequate results. Investments had amounted to more than forty-one milliard rubles.[10] More than 1,000,000 tractors had been delivered to the collective and state farms.[11] Agricultural technicians, including specialists of various kinds, numbered 350,000.

Bearing these figures in mind, the question was what results had the mechanization and technical control of agriculture had in terms of productive increase? Practically speaking, none. Nor had they greatly reduced the burden on the countryside of excessive manpower, because the great immigration to the cities had taken place before the machines had been delivered or the technicians had arrived on the farms.

Khrushchev pointed out the danger that the seven-year plan would not be fulfilled, because even for 1961 the figures for agricultural production were considerably less than the planned targets, as is clear from the following table:

	Targets for 1961 Million tons	Results in 1961 Million tons
Cereals	155.0	138.0
Meat	11.8	8.8
	Million litres	Million litres
Milk	78.4	62.5

'The whole economy,' he said, 'may be brought to a standstill if we do not heed the warning and overcome the deficiencies of our agriculture in time.'

If one re-reads his statements made in September 1953, and February 1954, one finds precisely similar criticisms to those made in March 1962. Just as then, Khrushchev attributed responsibility for the poor production to the incompetence of the directors, the lack

[10] 13,900 million rubles from 1951 to 1955; 27,200 million rubles from 1956 to 1960.

[11] 427,000 tractors had been delivered from 1951 to 1955; 747,000 from 1956 to 1960.

of interest of the technicians, the insufficient vigilance of the government organs and the slackening of Party control. Therefore, despite the countless facilities put at the disposal of agriculture, archaic methods of cultivation are still being used. The fault was primarily that of the Ministers of Agriculture, who had known no better than to send out mountains of circulars and had been incapable of facing up to practical problems.[12] It was, he said, necessary to revise the whole administrative apparatus of agriculture from scratch, beginning with the management of the individual farms.

Echoing Khrushchev's words, the Central Committee criticized the activities of the Gosplan, the State Economic Council and the State Committee for Chemical Products, responsible for the insufficient production of fertilizers, as well as the local economic councils for 'lack of interest and responsibility in dealing with problems concerning the technical and material needs of agriculture'. The Central Committee condemned all such incorrect procedure. Therefore the agricultural crisis involved the whole state hierarchy.

It is worth recalling that the Central Committee approved some drastic measures to remedy the bad technical direction of the farms at the beginning of 1961. The competence of the Ministry of Agriculture was changed radically. Instead of being an administrative department, it became a controlling centre for the research institutes and the experimental laboratories, with the task of making generally known the results of their scientific and technical activities and new production processes.

Even more radical were the measures taken in March 1962, when the Central Committee issued rules for the new administrative structure announced by Khrushchev. The relative norms of application were published on the twenty-second of the same month. The pivot of the new organization was the Party, which was called on to take over the direction and control of everything connected with agricultural production, from individual farms to government departments.

At the apex of the hierarchy a committee for the whole of the Soviet territory was formed, presided over by one of the vice-premiers, flanked by Party leaders experienced in agricultural problems and representatives of the economic departments. This committee had to prepare plans for short- and long-term agricultural development and to give directives to industries producing agricultural machines, fertilizers, fungicides, etc.

According to Khrushchev's statement, the committee had the task

[12] Four Ministers of Agriculture were dismissed between 1958 and 1963.

of organizing a day-to-day control over the execution of Party and government decisions.

On it are dependent committees for the reorganization of agriculture in each federated republic or autonomous territory. They are presided over by the vice-presidents of the councils of ministers. Their task is to put the plans into operation and encourage the development of agriculture in their respective territories.

In each province and region similar committees have been formed, presided over by the First Party Secretaries of the respective provinces or regions. Upon them depend the administrative departments for the direction of agriculture, in which Party and Komsomol (Communist Youth Organization) members take part. These administrative departments are each responsible for a certain number of agricultural enterprises, both collective and state, especially as regards the fulfilment of the plans, sales to the state, the increase in productivity, improvement of methods of cultivation, preservation of farm machinery, the use of chemical fertilizers and the satisfactory completion of contracts. They work through 'inspectors', that is to say specialists who constantly visit the farms, control operations and give instructions.

These measures for the strengthening of control, both central and regional, are integrated by the formation of Agricultural Control Committees, made up of Party members, intended to supervise the activities of individual state and collective farms, as has been set out in the chapter on planning.

It is, as can be seen, a cumbersome machine which must multiply offices and office personnel in order to work. Wherever economic activities are administered by the state, bureaucracy finds fertile ground. The more the difficulties increase, the farther the bureaucratic octopus extends its tentacles.

To make this machine work an appeal has been launched to the Party, as the secular arm of the new organization. Khrushchev said that he is convinced that one of the principal causes of the crisis has been 'the slackening of Party vigilance over the past two or three years'. Therefore in his speech on March 5, 1962 he declared that it was essential that the whole Party organization should devote itself to agriculture. 'What is essential,' he specified, 'is systematic supervision and strict control. . . . The Party organs must control each collective and state farm and help it make the best use of its potential.'

It was a return to Stalinist methods. The old dictator, who had never trusted the peasants, had created the Machine Tractor Stations entrusted to Party men, whose supervision nothing could escape and who kept a record of everything down to the last grain of wheat threshed by their machines. The result had been a continuous struggle between these espionage centres and the farm workers. Sometimes it happened that even these Machine Tractor Stations let themselves be won over by the general atmosphere of slackness. Their political activity weakened, their work was carried out without enthusiasm, slowly and with serious deficiencies and losses. It had therefore been thought necessary, in September 1935, to reinforce them with trusted men sent from the cities. By the end of that year their personnel had increased by 1,400,000 men over the previous year. 10,813 engineers, 10,601 technicians and 104,644 agricultural specialists were employed by them. This General Staff was to provide technical guidance to the farms, to supervise them and also to direct them. Under Khrushchev the idea prevailed that these stations should be abolished. It was a gesture of trust in the kolkhozes, intended, as Khrushchev said, 'to develop the initiative of the collective farms and to increase their responsibility for the best use of their land and equipment'. Party control thus ceased to exist. It was an attempt to comply with the desire, so insistently repeated by the kolkhozes, to have their autonomy recognized and their freedom affirmed to make decisions, to act, to make use of their own funds, their own lands and their own energies. The experiment failed and everything went back to where it was before. Naturally difficulties again arose, as well as the resistance and misunderstandings which it had been hoped to avoid.

The remedy was sought in the intensification of those controls which had aroused the opposition of the peasants. It was a vicious circle from which there was no escape.[13] In March 1962 Khrushchev curtly refused the requests of the kolkhozes for autonomy. His ill will towards them is shown by the harshness of his criticisms. Today there is a great deal of confusion about what are the functions of a kolkhoz. According to statute, they are autonomous organizations but at the same time the central organs intervene to establish what the kolkhoz must sell to the state, and often it is those same central organs that decide how the kolkhoz should be organized and who must preside over it. This gives rise to a number of contradictions and problems, since many kolkhoz members claim that once the state has established its requirements it should no longer interfere in the internal affairs of the kolkhoz. That is inadmissible, the more so as many kolkhozes carry out badly the tasks assigned to

[13] A high scientific authority, A. I. Lebed, referring to the decisions of the Central Committee in March 1962 which had entrusted control to hundreds of thousands of inspectors, propagandists and the like, declared that the future would show if this control 'would succeed in breaking the passive resistance of the peasants'.

them and achieve less than they could. The same may be said about the sovkhozes which also enjoy wide autonomy. There must therefore be a control over all the activities of individual enterprises from the time the plans are drawn up and the contracts approved to the time of the harvest and its delivery. Thus the idea has been restored of having organs to direct and at the same time supervise every farm, taking an active part in the organization of production. On them falls the responsibility of adjusting production to the needs of the country.

This sense of suspicion and ill-will towards the kolkhozes can also be sensed in the manifest preference shown for the sovkhozes, or state farms. In the years 1955 to 1960 more than 3,000 large state farms were founded, especially in the virgin lands, for cereal production and stock-breeding. They were to serve as models for the diffusion of more rational methods of cultivation suggested by advances in agrarian technique. But in fact their production is very low. In the past the state has suffered great losses because these farms have proved to be very expensive to run. Therefore, a little before the war, their number was reduced and their area of cultivation limited. For political reasons there was a return to this type of organization in the lands annexed during World War II. In 1953 Khrushchev sharply criticized the cost of wheat, meat and milk produced by the sovkhozes and blamed them for neglecting their machinery. The low living standards on these farms led, after the war, to a great exodus of land workers, who preferred to try to find work in industry.

It is probable that many of these defects still exist, since Khrushchev, speaking to the Central Committee on March 5, 1962, complained that on some state farms fifty per cent of their land was untilled, and no one reproved the directors of the less productive farms. There was, he said, a complete *laissez-faire*. Therefore, in this oscillation of government policy, now in favour of the kolkhozes now in favour of the sovkhozes, everything remains within a closed circle and meets with the same insuperable difficulties.

In his efforts to extend cereal production to the maximum, Khrushchev pointed out to the new organization the aim of changing from extensive to intensive cultivation, beginning with the abolition of the old and complicated rotation system which left too large a part of the land unproductive. The fault for introducing such irrational measures was attributed by Khrushchev to Stalin, who imposed the system of cultivation known as *travopolye*, which left areas for pasture. It was proposed by Academician Vilyams (Williams), despite the fact that other academicians and many experts showed it to be a fallacy and pointed out the damage it could cause to the country's economy. But these opponents were punished, because there exists in communist countries an official and orthodox scientific doctrine which cannot be questioned without running the risk of political sanctions. Thus Academician Pryanishnikov was dismissed and in February 1947 the Central Committee recommended to the party that the *travopolye* system be universally applied. Now the Party had received contrary orders: to condemn the *travopolye* system and to encourage on lands now being used for pasture the cultivation of maize, beet, leguminous vegetables and forage crops.

The targets of the twenty-year plan, set by Khrushchev and intended to equate production to requirements, demand no small effort. By 1980 the enterprises, whether collective or state, must produce:

	Million tons
Cereals	300
Cotton	10
Beet sugar	100
Meat	30
Milk	180

Production of the main agricultural products must be increased to two-and-a-half or three times their present volume in a little less than twenty years. In the first decade production must increase 150%. The possibility of reaching such targets in so short a time is more than doubtful.

How does the Central Committee expect to be able to reach such high levels? Firstly, by assuring a sound technical management for all farms. This must be guided and inspired by the agricultural academies, the research institutes and the experimental stations. The Central Committee proposes to mobilize a General Staff of experts and scientists to solve the most serious and urgent problems of Soviet agriculture, namely selection of higher yield types, the breeding of high production thoroughbred stock, new types of pesticides, the designing of new forms of machinery, the development of irrigation, and so on. For more than a decade Khrushchev insisted on the need for a better scientific and technological basis for agriculture. He stressed this in September 1953 when he complained that out of 350,000 specialists only 18,500, that is to say five per cent, worked on the collective farms, while the percentage on the state farms was only fourteen per cent. The rest of them were in offices and scientific institutions. He repeated this in 1962, criticizing the experts who concerned themselves with the flight of black and white storks, the galloping times of horses or the aeration of stalls, while neglecting the essential thing, the increase of productivity.

Over and above these sarcasms, he criticized the fragmentary and badly co-ordinated work of the scientific research institutes and the experimental stations which lacked an overall picture of the problems to be solved and had no common approach to them. The Moscow Academy of Agricultural Science and the Ministry of Agriculture will now be responsible for this co-ordination.

It appears from the Central Committee debate that there are about half a million agronomists, veterinarians, tractor-drivers and other specialists and that 279,000 of them are working in factories or transport pools repairing machinery. The Committee was not sparing in its criticisms of the low yield of many of these specialists.

This was partly the result of poor technical training of the younger ones and partly the tendency, common to the majority of them, to keep as far away as possible from the actual production centres and take refuge in institutes, schools, etc., becoming 'gentlemen' (sic) who avoid manual labour. The Ministry of Agriculture was responsible for this state of affairs, because it had not paid enough heed to the training of the specialists.

The communique of the Central Committee then observed, in partial justification of the specialists, that the directors of the agricultural enterprises often behaved haughtily towards them and rejected their requests.

In some cases the wages of the specialists had been arbitrarily reduced, suitable housing had not been found for them and they had not been provided with the means of transport needed for their jobs.

The communique then listed the measures that would be taken to improve the yield of the specialists and their conditions of employment with the aim of eventually improving agricultural production.

It did not seem, however, that discipline in the kolkhozes and sovkhozes was such as to induce their personnel to pay much attention to the suggestions of young and inexperienced agricultural specialists. It seemed indeed that, especially in the virgin lands, almost all of them were members of the Komsomol and that they had done more harm than good by the application of their theoretical principles. However, the effort was undeniable. In the whole area of the virgin lands more than a hundred and eighty-three schools were set up for the training of a hundred thousand mechanics, tractor- and lorry-drivers.

The Central Committee also relies on a rapid mechanization of the countryside to help increase production. This too was especially stressed by Khrushchev when he outlined a programme of agricultural reform in 1953. And in fact, at the time of his report to the Central Committee, the delivery of tractors and other agricultural machinery from the factories was proceeding rapidly. However, from 1958 there had been a slowing down of deliveries because the factories had turned to other work that seemed more urgent. For example, Khrushchev reported, in 1957 the farms received 208,000 tractors and in 1960 only 79,000; equally, in 1957 they received 55,000 maize-husking machines and in 1960 only 13,000 despite the development in the meantime of maize cultivation for fodder.

According to Khrushchev's estimates, production of agricultural machinery will have to be doubled to meet requirements. In particular he recommended the use of heavy tractors, especially on well-watered land, because they were more economical and more productive and because they saved time.

A special organization, the *Selkhoztekhnika*, has the task of supervising the proper use of machinery by the farms. It carries this out through local agencies dependent on it, which seems to re-echo the activities of the abolished Machine Tractor Stations.

Liaison units have been formed between the factories and the farms to study and agree upon the types of machinery best suited to local needs, as also to provide spare parts and to ensure a rapid repair service.

Especial importance will be given to electrification from the hydro- and thermo-electric power stations; agriculture will be able to make use of growing quantities of power, not only to intensify its mechanization but also to intensify irrigation work and industrial processing.

Especially severe criticism was levelled at the chemical industry because of the slow production of fertilizers. It was recalled that in 1953 six million tons were distributed to the farms. The seven-year plan estimated that in the first three years of its application the amount produced should have been 23,000,000 tons, whereas the increase had been only 2,900 tons. There was also a shortage of weedkillers. The problem was again raised as a matter of urgency, as will be seen, in 1963.

Finally, Khrushchev reverted to the importance of widening economic incentives in the form of special awards to any person, agricultural worker or specialist, who contributed to increased production or reduced costs. On the other hand new measures provide for prison sentences for agricultural workers guilty of non-fulfilment of the plans.

28

These are the remedies which the Central Committee in 1962 expected to solve the agricultural crisis and inaugurate an increase in production sufficient to attain the high levels set by Khrushchev.

What is perplexing in this programme is the reversion to solutions which have already been tried and which have always failed. Everything is still within a closed circle and the root of the evil has not been touched. The crisis is in the system: the Soviet state bases its economy on low wages for the workers and peasants. It can control the workers, who depend entirely on the state for their means of existence; but it cannot control the peasants who dispose of the fruits of the earth which they themselves produce and therefore are immune from sanctions, threats or controls. No one was more merciless to them than Stalin and yet even he had to give way. No supervision was stricter than that he instituted over the kolkhozes through the Machine Tractor Stations in the very heart of the kolkhozes themselves; none the less, the system had to be changed. Agriculture has been mechanized, research and experimental stations have been multiplied and investments increased. But if the peasant does not co-operate, all this vast effort is in vain. Only by making his personal interest the fulcrum can his co-operation be obtained.

Khrushchev was on the right road in 1953 when he made himself the interpreter of the aspirations of the kolkhoz members and passed a number of measures in their favour. The results of his reforms were immediate and showed that all that was needed was to continue along the same path. But the ideology was against him. The system won and sent him once more back to his point of departure, namely threats: Party control, suppression of the autonomy of the kolkhozes, direction from above and bureaucratization. The strength of the influence of an anti-economic doctrine like Marxism is shown by the tragic contradiction of an energetic and volatile man like Khrushchev who, after introducing a liberal policy, was compelled to fall back on laws just as harsh as Stalin's. The coercive method, even if it achieves some short-lived results, will worsen the situation because it embitters feelings, accentuates injustice and provokes reaction.

Khrushchev pointed out many examples of the ill-will of the peasants. He said, among other things, that whereas in tsarist times when the peasants had not enough food to raise their pigs they killed them and either ate or sold them; at present the kolkhoz members—not being able to kill their piglets because this is forbidden by their rules—simply let them die of hunger and then enter the deaths in the registers. That, he added. is a crime, a real crime even if it is not punishable by law.[14]

---

[14] In 1960 11,500,000 sheep died, that is to say 8.4% of the flocks, from hunger and neglect. In eleven months of 1962 in the Pavlodar district of Kazakstan alone 18,000 cattle, 132,000 sheep and more than 19,000 pigs died.

This is the reason why the advances of Soviet agriculture are so slow, despite the vast material and technical resources placed at its disposal by the state. Khrushchev, in a report to the Central Committee on December 15, 1958, acknowledged the inferiority of Soviet agricultural productivity to American. It is estimated that American productivity is five times greater than Soviet.[15] There is no doubt that if the Russian peasant worked like the peasant of Western Europe in a régime of private ownership the level of his productivity would not differ greatly, as was shown before the revolution by the effect of Stolypin's reforms. If the enthusiasm of that time had continued, Russia would have today one of the richest peasant classes in the world. There was proof of this at the time of the inauguration of the NEP, when the confidence of the peasants revived. But land-collectivization led to catastrophe. It destroyed the more progressive and productive farms, caused the death of millions of peasants and paralysed the will to work. The total agricultural yield which in the years 1927-1928 had risen to a value of 9,200 million rubles declined in 1939 to 4,890 million, that is to say by almost half.

Khrushchev has praised land-collectivization because great farms make technical advances easier. That is certainly true in a régime of freedom and respect for private ownership.

29

Despite these grave deficiencies in the system, which slow down and sometimes paralyse productive effort, we must guard against the error of thinking that Soviet economy does not progress or, even worse, of thinking that it is sliding back to ever lower production levels. In the period from 1953 to 1961 total agricultural production increased by 60% according to Soviet statistics.

	1953 Million tons	1961 Million tons
Cereals	80.00	136.00
of which: Wheat	40.00	64.00
Maize	3.65	24.00
Meat (deadweight)	5.80	8.80
Milk	36.50	62.50
Sugar beet	3.43	6.00
	Milliards	Milliards
Eggs	16.00	29.00

[15] In the United States there are 5,900,000 farmworkers; in the Soviet Union the kolkhoz and sovkhoz workers number 32,000,000.

	Million head	Million head
Cattle	55.80	82.10
Pigs	33.30	66.60
Sheep	115.50	144.40

Great progress has been made since the colonization of the territories to the east of the Urals, especially with the cultivation of industrial plants. Thus the cultivation of cotton has been extended from an area of 636,000 hectares in 1913 to more than 2,000,000 in 1950 and from a crop of 7,500,000 quintals to one of almost 40,000,000 over the same period.

Beet cultivation has increased from an area of 770,000 hectares in 1913 to 1,319,000 in 1950 and the crop from 101,000,000 quintals to 240,000,000 quintals. Sugar production has risen from 4,881,000 tons in 1957 to 5,281,000 tons in 1958.

The production of sunflower seed has increased from 7,800,000 quintals in 1913 to 30,600,000 in 1950. Tea produced 1,300,000 quintals in 1913 and 120,000,000 quintals in 1945. Citrus fruit, cultivated on 200 hectares in 1913, was cultivated on more than 13,000 hectares in 1945.

It is, however, indisputable that if one considers the whole period from the outbreak of the Bolshevik revolution to the present day, the advances of agriculture in those countries under a communist régime are incomparably less than in those with a régime of private ownership. To compare only Soviet and American production, here are some production figures for 1960:

	Soviet Union Million tons	United States Million tons
Cereals	134.4	194.2
Meat	8.7	17.9
Milk	61.5	56.9

The most disturbing factor is that agricultural production, although increasing, is not increasing fast enough to provide even a gradual increase of consumption. Indeed, as far as cereals are concerned, the index of production increase is less than the rate of demographic increase.

Here are the figures of the cereal harvests in millions of tons:

Year	Tons
1958	141.2
1959	125.9
1960	134.4
1961	137.3
1962	147.5
1963	121.0 (According to Tass, the harvest has been 18% lower than in 1962. According to other sources it has been about 117 million tons.)

Without taking into consideration the 1963 harvest which has undoubtedly been a disaster, the increase from 1958 to 1962 has been 4.7%, whereas the population has increased by at least 6%. But if one considers that 1958 and 1962 were both exceptionally good years, the rate of increase in cereal production seems even lower. It is very far from the production targets, as can be seen from a comparison between the targets of the seven-year plan for 1962 and the actual results in that year:

	Target Million tons	Actual production Million tons
Cereals	163.8	147.5
Meat	12.9	9.2
Milk	85.0	64.0

The very serious agricultural crisis of 1963, whose causes we have just been analysing, is undoubtedly a symptom of the difficulties that still exist. But it must not be forgotten that it has followed an exceptionally good year, when Russian production reached its peak. Therefore the wheat shortage of 1963 cannot be considered as an inevitable first step backward in a decline that cannot be stopped. Even if a good part of the virgin lands put under cultivation in the Kazakstan steppe no longer give the hoped-for harvests and even if it has been necessary to renounce wheat cultivation in the northern regions of Great Russia, there is still plenty of fertile land in the vast spaces of the Soviet Union, even as there are plenty of peasants and a vast amount of technical equipment. The problem lies in the rational use of these resources, beginning with manpower. How long will it take to heal the crisis? Will Russia be faced by further years of loss? No prophecy is possible in a field like that of agriculture, subject to so many unforeseen influences. It will above all depend on the ability of the Soviet leaders to loosen the bonds of ideological restrictions. It has been seen that as soon as common sense prevailed, as at the time of the first liberal measures proposed by Khrushchev after his rise to power, agriculture responded with enthusiasm to the wise reforms. The same leap forward took place after the abolition of wartime communism with the introduction of the NEP.

30

None of the measures approved by the Central Committee in 1962 recognized the interests of the peasants. This has impaired their efficiency. The situation after these measures has increased their suspicion, their hardships and their opposition.

The dramatic debates on the agricultural crisis and Khrushchev's polemical fervour during his nation-wide theatrical propaganda campaign have rekindled criticisms of the kolkhozes. The leaders have taken advantage of this to give another turn to the screw of repression. The aim pursued is twofold : gradually to transform the kolkhozes into sovkhozes, that is to say co-operatives organized by the state, and to abolish the family holdings. In both they advanced warily, because the reaction of more than thirty-two million kolkhoz members and their families is a thing to be treated with respect. Despite this the measures adopted have been drastic, certainly the most severe of any adopted since Stalin's death. A whole series of decrees was published in the second half of February 1961. We have already mentioned several of them, for example the transformation of the Ministry of Agriculture, the formation of liaison bodies between industry and agriculture, and those concerned with the electrification, the mechanization and the technical management of the farms. Two more remain to be mentioned, one concerning the system for the sale of agricultural products in bulk and the other with changes in the system of sales on the free market.

The first of these was intended to prevent the non-fulfilment by the farms of the compulsory deliveries laid down in the plans. A system of advance sales contracts was established. The farms were committed by these advance contracts to carry out the orders given them by the state which cover a period of from two to five years. Production must therefore be organized not on a year-to-year basis but over multi-annual cycles which allow the farms to make adequate reserves for lean years. The fulfilment of these undertakings will be controlled by inspectors and by a special 'Council'. Production discipline will thus be tightened.

The second decree forbade the kolkhoz members to sell their produce on the free markets. Henceforth, all surplus produce, once the obligation of the bulk deliveries has been fulfilled, as well as all the produce from the family holdings must be handed over to consumers' co-operatives at agreed prices. The pretext used to limit the free bargaining of the kolkhoz members was to prevent their frequent absence from the work of the farm.

As can be seen, instead of taking a step forward in the direction hoped for by the peasants who loudly demanded greater opportunities for initiative and the free disposal of their products, many steps backward were taken. It is easy to forecast that the secular struggle between the peasants and the state will be accentuated.

The obligation to sell all the surpluses and the produce of the family holdings to consumers' co-operatives was exceptionally burdensome. It tended to make the free market disappear and to wipe out the income that the kolkhoz members got from it. The measure had a double aim: on the one hand to end the dualism of prices between state produce and kolkhoz produce, and on the other to reduce the income from the family holdings in order to induce the peasants to devote themselves wholly, or at least mainly, to work in the collective.

The publication of these measures had a very bad effect both among producers and consumers. The consequences were not slow in making themselves felt.

In the cities, beginning with Moscow, there was a meat shortage. The queues grew longer and longer. This is a sight typical of the communist lands and would in itself be enough to give the lie to their propaganda about the abundance of consumer goods. Even for the May 1st celebrations Moscow was without meat.

This time too the peasants' resistance defeated the government. The decree that forced them to sell their produce through the consumers' co-operatives remained a dead letter; a contributory cause was that the handling of easily perishable produce had proved disastrous to the co-operatives. The losses that they suffered forced them to increase their prices with the result of worsening the situation for the consumers instead of improving it which was one of the objects of the decree.

However, the real reason for this shortage of meat, milk and fats was the insufficiency of the purchase price which did not cover the costs. The Soviet government was therefore compelled to seek a remedy in the only possible way, namely by increasing the purchase prices. This is what it did by the decree of June 1, 1962 which increased the purchase price of produce obtained from the kolkhozes and the family holdings as follows:

	Average increase
Animal fats	10%
Meat	35%
Cream	5%

The purchase price from the sovkhozes was 10% less than that fixed for the kolkhozes.

Retail sale prices were increased as follows:

	Average increase
Beef	31%
Mutton	34%
Pork	19%
Sausages	31%
Animal fats	25%

The price of sugar was reduced by 5% and of rayon textiles by 20%.

To justify these price increases for meat and milk, the Party and the Soviet government published an open letter to *Kommunist* on June 8, 1962. This said that the production cost of a quintal of beef (on the hoof) in 1960 was 91.6 rubles and in 1961 88 rubles, but that the bulk purchase price was 59.1 rubles; that the cost of a quintal of pork was 122.6 rubles in 1960 and 118 rubles in 1961, but that the bulk purchase price was 82.3 rubles; that the cost of poultry was 140.5 rubles in 1960 and 135.5 rubles in 1961, but that the bulk purchase price was 82.2 rubles.

This series of examples could be extended. A ton of potatoes purchased in bulk at forty rubles was resold by the state at 100-140 rubles. A ton of milk bought previous to the price increases of June 1, 1962 cost 115 rubles and was resold at 280.

The open letter published in *Kommunist* provides official evidence of the policy of plunder carried on by the Soviet state against the peasants. This is possible only in a régime of state capitalism.

31

It is not surprising that with a system like this production declines.

The exceptionally poor cereal harvest of 1963 has shown the worsening of the crisis. The Soviet Union had to ration bread. According to reliable estimates, 26,000,000 more tons of cereals, of which 14,000,000 are wheat, are needed to cover requirements. The queues at the bakers have grown longer and the government has been forced to buy wheat on the capitalist markets and pay for it in gold and at a price which it has always refused to give to its home producers.

The principal cause of the paucity of the harvest has undoubtedly been the bad weather. For forty years there has not been so disastrous a season. Prolonged frosts with the formation of thick ice have, as Khrushchev said, 'destroyed millions of hectares of seed'. The rapid thaw led to no less extensive flooding, followed by a torrid summer which burnt up all the crops. Everywhere has been affected by these disasters which usually afflict either one or another region of this vast territory. But this time they struck at all the main producing centres, causing the loss of about 40% of the Kazakstan harvest and 20% of those of the Ukraine, Western Siberia and the Volga region.

But though we must bear in mind these bad weather conditions, a closer analysis of the situation also shows other causes for the shortages of 1963.

There is, for example, the lack of reserves despite the fact that 1962 was an exceptional harvest which exceeded by more than 6,000,000 tons of cereals the record year of 1958; but in that year there were 76,600,000 tons of wheat whereas the 1962 harvest was 7,000,000 tons less.

Furthermore the virgin lands made a contribution to the 1962 harvest of more than 56,000,000 tons of cereals, amounting to 38% of the total, whereas in 1963 the gradual exhaustion of the Kazakstan steppe led to a slowing-down of production which had ceased to be remunerative because of the smaller and smaller yields. It must be borne in mind that in the virgin lands state farms predominate, which hand over compulsorily the greater part of their harvest, so that in 1962 almost a half of the compulsory bulk purchases came from the virgin lands.

Though in such serious difficulties, the peasants still lack that unsparing effort which in countries where they have a direct interest in production multiplies their energy to save all that can be saved. Khrushchev did not conceal the truth even though it be unpalatable. Speaking on August 15, 1963, at an agricultural centre near Volograd (the former Stalingrad), he expressed himself, according to *Izvestia*, as follows:

'If we have to return to bread rationing, it is to a great extent the fault of our peasants. Everything possible has been done by the authorities to avoid reaching such a point. Yes, there have been mistakes, even in the highest quarters, and we will punish them, .but the real difficulty is from below, I repeat from the peasants. . . . Our peasants not only lack technical skill but they won't listen to advice, almost as if they wanted voluntarily to sabotage production.'

These are serious words which on the one hand show the resistance of the peasants to authority and on the other the government viewpoint about them. The atmosphere of sullen conflict is plain for all to see.[16]

In earlier pages we have analysed the causes of this struggle, which can be regarded as the continuation of that which the Russian

---

[16] In his report to the plenum of the Party Central Committee on December 9, 1963, Khrushchev modified his harsh judgment and praised 'the men and women of the kolkhozes and sovkhozes, the directors and the officials who have shown great organizing ability in overcoming the serious consequences of the hard winter and the drought'.

peasant began centuries ago to win for himself a minimum of rights and decent conditions of life. The agricultural crisis has led economists and technicians to make fresh studies and investigations of the situation in the countryside. The results of an enquiry carried out by the periodical *Ekonomika Selskogo Khozaistva* are particularly interesting. They are published in No. 4 of 1963. The investigation covered kolkhozes in the Ukraine, that is to say the most fertile area of Russia. It was found that the kolkhoz members received from 12 to 50 kopeks as a daily wage, that is to say from 13 to 55 United States cents. In many kolkhozes the system of money wages had not yet been introduced; in some of them there was no regular payment and the members had to wait a year, or even two, to get what was due to them. On the other hand the variations in the harvest from year to year meant that the peasant never knew what his remuneration for his work on the collective lands would be. He only knew that it would be insufficient, uncertain and variable, and that therefore he must above all rely on the income from his holding.

It is necessary to remember this in order to estimate the possibilities of success of the new programme that the Soviet leaders have launched to solve a problem which is already several centuries old. The new course turns the whole thing upside down; no longer extensive but intensive cultivation concentrated in the districts most suited for high yield, for fertility and good climatic conditions. It is a return to the thesis unsuccessfully maintained by the anti-Party group. Everything depends on increasing the average yield from the ten quintals which it is today to at least fifteen. This would be easy enough if the kolkhoz members were to devote as much energy to the collective lands as they now do to their tiny plots. But to obtain this it is necessary to make it possible for a kolkhoz member to be able to live from the results of his collective labour by giving him prices for his produce which will allow him a remunerative return. The solution of the problem lies there. If America has over-production and Russia under-production, it is because the Americans pay their farmworkers well and the Soviet Union badly. The Soviet Union must be convinced that economic laws were not invented by capitalists and that the results shown by these two economies, American and Soviet, show that the exploitation of man is greater in a communist than in a capitalist régime.

But the Soviet leaders refuse to recognize such elementary truths because the ideology does not admit them. For them the fundamental element in production is not the man, but the machine, the technique, the fertilizer. They pass from one myth to another, from mechanization, from technicalization and now to the chemicalization of agriculture. The factor that will create the miracle of abundant production will be the mineral fertilizer; they forget the old biblical maxim that the soil is made fertile by the sweat of man.

All efforts are therefore concentrated on the production of fertilizers, that is on the creation of an immense chemical industry. The programme is colossal. Production must be increased from the present 20,000,000 tons to the 70-80,000,000 tons planned for 1970. The capacity of the existing plants must be doubled and another fifty-five plants built, of which twenty-eight will produce nitrogenous fertilizers, nineteen phosphate fertilizers, six potash fertilizers and two phosphorates. The cost is estimated at 10.5 milliard new rubles, equivalent to 11.6 milliard dollars. In the second decade the production of fertilizers must reach the very high target of 150-170,000,000 tons. Even if one disregards this second phase, the programme of the first means quadrupling the present output. There are many justifiable doubts. It seems that this cannot possibly be done without obtaining plant from abroad on a very large scale. Will the Soviet Union have the means to pay for imports of the wheat itself and of industrial plants? The purchase of 14,000,000 tons of wheat has involved payment of a milliard dollars, that is to say roughly the value of the Soviet imports from the European Economic Community for a whole year; such imports comprise for the most part plant and machinery for the industrialization of the Soviet Union. Will the Soviet Union be able to continue its industrial plans with the same rhythm and at the same time provide for the deficiencies of its agriculture? It is true that payment for the imported wheat is twenty-five per cent on delivery and the balance payable in instalments over eighteen months. But who can tell if the Soviet Union will not be forced to buy wheat from abroad for several years to come?

This is clear proof of the close connection, only too often overlooked by Soviet leaders, between agriculture and industry. The agricultural crisis threatens to slow down imports of machinery. In a word, the slackening of agriculture means the slackening of industry also. Bukharin was the only man to see this connection as he was the only one to understand that the prime factor of agricultural progress is the tiller of the soil.

Everyone is now agreed that the salvation of Russian agriculture lies in the intensification of cultivation. To obtain this result Stolypin encouraged peasant land-ownership. That is the secret of success. When this elementary truth finds its way into the brains of the Soviet leaders the agricultural crisis will be solved. The conflict between ideology and prosperity has never been so clear, so dramatic, as in agriculture. For the moment the truth, the essential truth, is that the peasant is not co-operating. The whole meaning of the crisis lies in this: the peasant is against the régime.

CHAPTER XI

Transition from Socialism
to Communism

1

THE XXI Congress of the Soviet Communist Party held in January 1959 was known as 'the congress of the builders of communism', because it discussed conditions for the transition from socialism to communism.

The subject was taken up again and discussed more fully at the XXII Congress in October 1961.

The problem is therefore on the agenda; indeed the transition from one régime to the other is already going on, as the XXI Congress not only decided to intensify its studies but to make plans in advance for this decisive turning point. It also laid down the principle of marking out the stages of the process of evolution begun in practice by the triumph of the October revolution.

The very fact of bringing the problem of the construction of a communist society to the attention of the masses is a formidable incentive to propaganda because the masses are always impressed by the boldness of novelty and nothing appeals to them more than a programme of radical reversal of ideas, values and systems consecrated by millennia of human existence.

This great event was at once vaunted in dithyrambic terms by Khrushchev himself. Speaking of the resolutions of the XXII Congress, in his report to the Party Central Committee at its session in March 1962, he described this event as of the deepest significance for the human race. The programme of the XXII Congress was 'an event that lights the way for the oppressed and the disinherited in their struggle to abolish the régime of exploitation and to bring peace and happiness to the peoples'.

In fact, communism expects much from these new hopes, to begin again 'the triumphal march' of its ideas. 'The force of the example of socialism and communism,' Khrushchev said, 'acquires especial importance because hundreds of millions of people in the countries of Asia, Africa and Latin America who have been freed, or are being freed, from the yoke of colonialism . . . have to decide

313

what road to follow . . . that of capitalist or of non-capitalist development.'

The propaganda describes the aim to be reached as certain: communism is presented as the fulfilment of man's millenary dream of absolute equality and an abundance of goods for all.

But in fact how much of this programme is attainable and how much a utopia? The transition from socialism to communism means the transition from the present formula of 'to each according to his work', which implies a remuneration commensurate with every man's production, to the formula of 'to each according to his needs', which implies an equal remuneration for all regardless of the work which they have done.

The communists claim that they have opened a new road for humanity, that no one in so many millennia has been able to find, and translated the dream into reality. But this idea is not new. In the course of the centuries there have been many such attempts, all of which have failed, even though they developed within small groups of persons animated by some higher ethical ideal, often religious, which in some cases has risen to the height of an ascetic ideal. But never has such an experiment been tried in a society of more than 200,000,000 individuals as in Soviet society, or more than 600,000,000 as in China. The exceptional scale of the experiment makes it possible to speak of it as something new. But it is just this scale that makes it extremely difficult, even admitting, which is not the case, that the principles upon which it is based are capable of fulfilment.

Khrushchev asserted that even the realization of socialism, that is to say what Marx called the first step in the building of communism, was considered a utopia and is now in fact a reality. The second phase is only the perfecting of the first. 'The classics of Marxism-Leninism,' he told the XXII Party Congress on October 18, 1961, 'have stressed that socialism is not divided from communism by a great wall, that socialism and communism are two phases of the same economic and social system, distinct one from the other by the stage of economic development and the maturity of their social relations. Socialism does not develop on its own foundations. Despite the immense importance of its achievements socialism still bears, in many ways, both economic and moral, the brand of the old system whence it emerged. Communism is a higher and more perfect stage of human life and can only be developed after socialism has been fully consolidated. Under communism all that remains of the capitalist system will be finally annulled.'

It is easy to make two objections to these theses. Firstly, that Western critics, though acknowledging the utopian character of communism because it pays no heed to individual interest, affirm that state capitalism, which goes under the name of socialism, is less productive than private capitalism because even though it does not totally eliminate private interest it limits it in such a way as to reduce the effort and the yield of the individual. This has been abundantly shown in earlier chapters. If this lower productivity is compensated for in the Soviet Union by immense natural wealth, it appears in all its tragic gravity in all the other communist countries in which, just because of their lesser resources, Marxism should have been able to show its wonder-working capacity for raising the level of production and for creating the great abundance of goods promised by Marx and Engels. Therefore, if the present socialist régime still retains a certain level of productivity, it owes it to those 'blemishes' which are still a part of capitalist economy and which, as Khrushchev says, must disappear with the transition to integral communism.

No less contestable is the other thesis, that socialism and communism are phases of the same economic-social organization, whereas they are two systems which, though starting from a common base, are inspired by antithetical principles. It is not merely a wall that divides one from the other, but an impassable moat. It is easy for the doctrinaire Marxist to affirm that economic laws were invented by the capitalists to shore up their régime; it is more difficult to demonstrate it in practice. But communism wants to prove in practice that it can create and lead to maximum productivity an economic world based on laws antithetic to those which have always regulated the production of wealth and which still do so today.[1]

[1] It has long been held by Soviet writers, following the principles of Marx and Engels, that in an economy where all the sources of production belong to the state the notions of 'price, value and profit' would cease to have any meaning. This was the thesis maintained by Bukharin in his book *The Political Economy of the Transition Period*. He writes: 'The end of capitalism and mercantile society means the end of political economy.' From this springs the logical conclusion that, in a régime of controlled economy, laws that discipline economic facts do not exist, but only the will of the state which creates a rational order in the relation between the production and distribution of goods. Therefore a science of economics is lacking and between 1928 and 1954 not a single treatise was written, nor was economics taught.

However it was soon realized that economic laws cannot be violated with impunity and that these laws are no more than a demonstration of the reactions of economic behaviour between individuals and society. Whereupon the official thesis ran: 'The denial of the existence of economic laws in socialism means to decline into a vulgar voluntarism which substitutes arbitrary action, chance and chaos for the regular process of the development of production.' But wherein do these so-called economic laws of socialism differ from those which control all economic facts without exception?

Therefore the transition to communism still remains an enigma and no one can see how it is to take place without causing, as in all previous attempts, a complete economic collapse. This explains why, after the lack of success of wartime communism, Lenin fell back upon the NEP and Stalin anchored himself to state capitalism.

Moreover, after forty-five years from the triumph of the revolution, it is no longer possible to delude the masses. One cannot live on promises for ever. In fact the very existence of this world which calls itself communist and which contrasts the blessings of communist principles with those by which democratic society is ruled, and yet does not know how to put those so vaunted principles into practice, is a strange phenomenon. This absurdity would be quite enough, despite the propaganda fireworks, to show how far the credulity of the masses is abused, since until words are replaced by deeds they remain in a world of promises, that is to say of propaganda.

Various circumstances forced Khrushchev to post the problem without further delay; he was especially driven by the policy of Mao-Tse-Tung's China which, disregarding the orders of the guiding state, set itself to find a short-cut to communism, displaying a revolutionary ardour that seems an implicit condemnation of Moscow's lack of initiative. In order to maintain his own prestige, and not to incur the accusation of pandering to Western systems and of betraying, by a bourgeois laxity, the principles of the revolution, Khrushchev had to resume the march towards the Promised Land and gird up his loins to cross the Red Sea. Communism stakes its future on the success of this experiment.

2

How, in theory, is it possible to effect this transition from socialism to communism? The most subtle intelligences of the Soviet world have devoted themselves to a solution of this insoluble problem. One must admit that their efforts are ingenious in their attempts to find the way across this uncharted land of utopia. But perhaps it is in the interest of the ruling classes, seconded by the doctrinaires, to give the impression that society is on the march. When the goal, which no one can see, is to be reached is not important and therefore the end of the journey will always be postponed.

The chart of this risky pilgrimage is based on vague and generic hints thrown out by Marx, Engels and Lenin. In his speech to the Party Central Committee on March 5, 1962, Khrushchev quoted them, beginning with the 'classic' formula of 'the greatest theoretician of communism, Karl Marx' who said: '. . . together with the comprehensive development of individuals, productive forces also grow and will release all the sources of collective wealth. . . . Only then will it be possible to put into operation the principle "from each according to his abilities and to each according to his needs".'[2]

'In his *Principles of Communism*,' Khrushchev went on, 'Engels has said that the new society will produce sufficient goods to organize a distribution capable of satisfying the needs of all its members.

'Vladimir Ilich Lenin stressed that capitalist society will be replaced by a socialist one with the aim of assuring the full well-being and the free and conscious development of all its members.'[3]

The indications, as can be seen, are almost non-existent and it is necessary to search for original solutions to the innumerable and formidable problems that arise.

Marx and Engels have left only guiding lines, from which it is not possible to depart; they have pointed out the goals to be reached, but have not traced out the ways by which to reach them. It is these guiding lines and these goals that make the problem insoluble, because in fact Marx and Engels have merely appropriated the ideas launched by a swarm of romantic visionaries, often in contradiction among themselves. These are the ideas of Saint-Simon, of Fourier, of Louis Blanc, of Proudhon. These ideas had nourished the anarchist movement which was much in vogue in Russia and which exercised a decisive influence on Lenin.

All these doctrinaires, French, German or Russian, started out from a moralist viewpoint. According to them the ills that afflict society have their roots in individual egotism, justified by the moral code and supported by the laws, since both the moral code and the laws reflect the interests of the ruling class. Egotism has its citadel

---

[2] This quotation is taken from a letter written by Marx in 1875 to a German socialist, commenting on the draft programme of the Workers' Party. The full quotation is as follows.

'In a higher phase of communist society after subordination, servile and manual, has disappeared and after labour has become not merely a means of livelihood but also the prime need of existence, together with the comprehensive development of individuals, productive forces will also grow and release all the sources of collective wealth. Only then will society be able to go beyond the narrow bourgeois political outlook and inscribe on its banners: Each according to his abilities; to each according to his needs.'

Karl Marx, *Criticism of the Gotha Programme.*

[3] *Collected Works of Lenin*, Vol. 6, 5th Edition.

in the institution of private property, which must be abolished in order to root out egotism and replace it by altruism as the mainspring of all human activity. Only thus will it be possible to set up a régime of full equality which will permit a distribution of wealth without distinction between man and man. With the abolition of property it is also necessary to abolish the powers that defend it; the state, its laws and its currency, the army, the church, since these are all institutions proper to a régime based on class distinctions, and, in particular, the family.

Starting from such premises the Marxists have confused economy with morality, deceiving themselves by substituting altruism, which is basically an ethical quality, for individual interest which is the driving force of *homo oeconomicus*. It is a confusion of ideas, in contrast with the fundamentals of Western doctrine according to which ethics and practical activities, though obeying certain common general principles, belong to quite different sectors and are responsive to quite different aims.

Since a communist society must be able to assure a minimum of essential goods to all its members and must produce such goods in ever greater quantities, irrespective of the individual remuneration of each member, Marxist theoreticians state that the possibility of installing communism depends on two primary conditions: an increase of productivity that assures a high turnover of consumer goods and a radical change in human nature by which every individual must be moved by pure altruism, that is to contribute without any selfish intent to the well-being of the society of which he forms part.

Let us see how the Soviet doctrinaires expect to be able to fulfil these two indispensable premises.

The XXI Congress laid down the following itinerary. As a first stage production must be increased. One cannot, it said, think of dividing the cake if the cake is not there to divide. But how to reach maximum production in the shortest space of time? By appealing to private initiative, that is by rewarding him who works most and produces most. Were it not that by fulfilling in this way the first condition, thereby attaining the maximum of goods, the second premise is contravened, that is to educate the people to work, no longer with individual benefit in view, but for the good of the whole community. By relying on incentives it is not altruism but egotism that is stimulated, and egotism thus becomes openly recognized and rewarded. In preparing for this radical transformation of individual psychology, which must allow the most absolute disinterestedness, it must be recognized that socialism is paying very little heed to consistency. However that may be, and even admitting that by relying upon individual initiative one attains this abundance of goods which recalls Moses' prophecy of a land flowing with milk and honey, it remains to be explained how this production may be maintained at the necessary level to satisfy the demands of the consumers, when that individual incentive which has made possible the indispensable maximum level will no longer exist and there will no longer even be payment in cash wages.

The contradiction between the ideal aim, absolute disinterestedness, and the practical means, individual incentive, is so great that even the Soviet public, accustomed to accept everything that the official propaganda cooks up for it, has raised doubts and criticisms. This has necessitated a dialectical effort to reply to these logical objections. If one looks at these objections it will be recognized that they are dictated by the legitimate fear of the worker of being cheated of his just due in the name of a misty doctrine of equality. They are the first signs of popular resentment at the very idea of the abolition of wages.

The justifications of the official apologists are no less interesting than the objections to which they are trying to reply, since it is clear that, rather than have to prove the soundness of the principles they wish to apply, they want to reassure the workers that the principle of payment in wages and of material incentives will be retained and even reinforced. Thus the contradictions are accentuated and communism becomes involved in the mazes of a utopia from which it will not be easy for it to escape.

To allay these fears, one of the Holy Fathers of the communist church, L. Leontiev, published a ponderous article in *Pravda* on March 11, 1960 supporting the principle of material incentives. His first argument is that material incentives are not a prerogative of the bourgeois system of production nor are they inherent in a régime of private ownership. In the capitalist world material incentives only act to the advantage of the possessing classes, since the proletarians, because they own nothing, are forced to hire their labour to the capitalists and therefore do not draw any material benefit from the expansion of capitalist production and have no interest in it.

This is really a masterpiece of logic. When the Soviet raises wages it is an incentive; when the capitalists raise them it is not. That is the measure of all communist arguments. What communism says and does is true and just; the same thing said and done by capitalists is false and unjust.

Thus while on the one hand they speak of a transition to communism, the abolition of wages and the elimination of every private interest, on the other they exalt the principle of material incentive as a conquest of socialism and justify the need for it. 'Socialist society,' writes Leontiev, 'has written on its standard: "Who does not work does not eat". This formula,' the Soviet writer continues, 'is ancient in origin. It embodies the hopes and aspirations of many generations of workers and of the exploited, their efforts towards a just and rational social system. But only under socialism is this very simple and obvious truth being translated, to use Lenin's expression, into a living reality.' And he goes on: 'Lenin declared prophetically that this is the first and fundamental principle of socialism, the inexhaustible source of its strength, the guarantee of its final victory.'

It remains to be explained why, if the advantages of the socialist formula of remuneration according to the yield of each are so many and so great, it is necessary to pass to the communist one that rejects the whole idea of individual remuneration. It might be thought that Soviet writers are not greatly convinced of the possibility of passing from one to the other formula, especially since Leontiev does not hesitate to declare that the socialist formula inspires honest workers because they consider it a guarantee that not even a particle of their toil shall go to the lazy and the parasitic. This sounds like open criticism of the communist formula: 'to each according to his needs'.

It is a fact that Soviet writers, especially after the failure of wartime communism, while they exalt the need for material incentives, limit themselves to expressing a purely formal homage to the principle of absolute disinterestedness. First among them Lenin, in an article on the fourth anniversary of the October revolution, gave a warning that the highroad to socialism and communism is not found by enthusiasm alone, other than the enthusiasm caused by the great revolution, but also personal interest, a personal incentive of economic origin, 'otherwise you will never have communism nor lead tens of millions of others to communism'.

The least that can be said is that there is a real contradiction between the necessity to attain and maintain production at the highest level and the abolition of wages as well as of every material incentive. In order to show the way to communism one must first begin by denying its essence, that is to say complete altruism, because only by relying upon material interest can that increase of production be achieved which will permit that each be given according to his needs. It is an inconsistency that does no honour to the good sense or even the good faith of those who maintain it. It is equivalent to saying that in order to build communism one must begin by building anti-communism. Is it not more logical and more sincere to say that it is not possible to put the communist formula into operation because it is contrary to facts and to human nature? In other words, it is a utopia.

At the XXI Party Congress Khrushchev, who is a realist, drew up three directives: that the transition from socialism to communism must be gradual, that it must be very slow and that it must not lessen the principle that everyone is rewarded for what he produces.

One can only conclude that the so-called communist countries will never dare to suppress individual remuneration proportionate to the work done. And since such remuneration will continue, that is to say individual interest will prevail, albeit within narrow limits, it will not be communism. It will remain more or less the present system, called socialism but which is in fact no different from state capitalism.

3

The XXII Party Congress has sought to escape from the generalities about principles stated by the Congress of two years before and has drawn up directives, seemingly more precise, either concerning the production targets to be reached or for an equalization of economic treatment that foreshadows a distribution on egalitarian principles. It has even indicated the phases of the transition, and the dates when they will take place, up to the finishing line.

But the contradictions mentioned above still remain in all their gravity.

The XXII Congress has established the goal. 'The historic and world-wide scope of the Soviet communist party,' the Party programme says, 'is to ensure that in the Soviet Union the living standard is higher than that of any capitalist country.'

How is this still far distant goal to be reached? By material incentives, that is by relying on the self-interest of the individual encouraged to the maximum. 'The Party,' the programme says, 'starts from the Leninist conception, by which the building of communism must rest on the principle of material interest. For the next two decades payment in proportion to work must remain the main source for the material and cultural needs of the workers.' At the end of twenty years, however, payment according to work will be suppressed and be replaced by equal remuneration for all. It is essential to reach, during this twenty-year period, an equalization of economic treatment in order to create that 'perfect social equality of all members of society which is the essence of communism', according to the definition given it by the Party programme.

The terms of the problem are many: to increase production, to raise real wages, to eliminate inequalities of economic treatment among the various classes of citizens and to increase the social assistance funds, which must gradually replace individual remuneration according to work.

The Party programme deals with each of these points.

For the increase of production it specifies that the quantity of goods and public services must permit the living standards of the Soviet people to be 'higher than that of the most developed capitalist countries even as regards statistical equality with the average income of the population'. This is a very ambitious target. To achieve it, the Soviet Party and people set themselves the task of 'creating, in the course of two decades, the technical-material basis of communism'. This means, the programme goes on, 'the complete electrification of the country and the perfecting on this foundation of the technique, technology and organization of production both in industry and agriculture'. There followed detailed plans for the creation of this 'technical-material basis of communism'.

The Party aims at increasing the present volume of industrial production 'in the course of the next ten years by about two-and-a-half times and thus to exceed the present volume of industrial production of the United States; in the course of twenty years the present volume of industrial production will be increased sixfold and will thus exceed by far the present total volume of industrial production of the United States'.

To be able to attain this objective, the programme says, it will be necessary to double the productivity of industrial labour in the course of the next ten years and to raise it four or four-and-a-half times in the course of twenty years. Within twenty years the labour productivity of the Soviet Union will be about twice the present level in the United States. Here we begin to break away from reality. For anyone who knows the present levels of Soviet productivity such goals are purely theoretical. The Party points out that, to attain them, there will be some important changes in the structure of Soviet industry. Undoubtedly better tooling, electrification, mechanization and automation will increase production levels, but the most important thing is to pay heed to the productive effort of the entire personnel: executives, technicians, workers and clerks. Is it to be presumed that such effort will be stretched to the maximum tension if, as has been hinted, they reduce the higher wages, that is those of the most productive workers, to the level of the lower paid workers, that is to say the less skilled? Is it also to be presumed that such efforts will be maintained when payment according to work will be suppressed at the end of the twenty-year period?

Let us now consider the provisions for agriculture. The Party proposes 'to solve two fundamental tasks, closely linked with one another: (a) to obtain an abundance of foodstuffs of high quality for the population and of raw materials for industry and (b) to guarantee a gradual transition from the conditions in the Soviet countryside to social relations of a communist character and to eliminate the main differences between the peoples of the cities and the countryside'.

In fact these two tasks are not linked with one another but are contradictory, since the programme insists on speeding up the transformation of the kolkhozes, against which the country people have put up the most desperate resistance. The fulfilment of such a programme can only end by worsening the agricultural crisis and creating an eventual decline in productivity.

The programme forecasts that to satisfy in full the needs of the whole population and the national economy it will be necessary to increase the total volume of agricultural production about two-and-a-half times in ten years and three-and-a-half times in twenty years. 'In the first decade,' the programme states, 'the Soviet Union will surpass the United States of America in *pro capite* production of the principal products.'

Special attention is paid to cereal production, which must increase 'more than twice in the course of two decades and the unit of yield be doubled', and to stock-breeding, for which the following increases are forecast: 'For meat about three times in the first decade and about four times in the twenty-year period.'

Judging from the experience of the past forty years these goals do not seem attainable, especially when it is taken into account that 'agricultural labour productivity will increase at least two-and-a-half times in ten years and from five to six times in twenty years. The rapid increase in agricultural labour productivity—which will be faster than in industrial productivity—will make it possible to eliminate the lag in agriculture as compared with industry and will make it a highly developed sector of the economy of communist society.'

In the agricultural sector also it is expected that this increase in productivity will be attained by improved equipment, with especial attention to mechanization and electrification which must be the prelude to a general industrialization of the countryside. But it is evident that the results will depend primarily on the productive efforts of the cultivators. But what does the Party have in store for the kolkhoz members who form the backbone of the agricultural population? The programme vaguely states that it wishes to abide by the principle of 'higher remuneration for good work and good yield', but immediately specifies that it is especially necessary to increase the indivisible funds since 'the kolkhozes cannot be developed without continually expanding their own social assistance funds'. It recommends 'the introduction of forms of supplementary remuneration for work and other forms of material incentive for better productive results', but insists on the necessity of 'bringing them closer, in the elaboration and definition of labour norms, of organization and work bonuses, to the level and to the typical forms of state enterprise'. In fact, it wants to transform the kolkhozes into sovkhozes, that is to replace the co-operative enterprises by state enterprises. It especially wants to abolish the family holding for whose preservation the peasants have struggled with such indefatigable energy, because it represents the last vestige of private ownership. The programme states that 'the individual auxiliary holdings of the kolkhoz member will become economically outmoded' and that therefore 'he will renounce it voluntarily'. Everyone knows what that voluntary renunciation really means.

It is not easy to understand on what criteria these very high levels to be reached, both in agricultural and industrial production, have been based. It is not the first time that the goals set have proved to be unattainable. The failure of the seven-year plan and the agricultural crisis of 1963 have shown how far these forecasts are mistaken. It seems moreover that the material incentives to increase the productivity of the workers and peasants are totally inadequate, the more so as the Party insists that such incentives are temporary, since during the twenty-year period 'in the measure in which advances will be made towards communism, the importance of moral incentives for labour will become greater and greater'. Once again there is a confusion between moral and economic criteria. Yet experience, after forty-five years of the régime, must have revealed the inefficacy of moral incentives. How can it be thought to obtain today, when enthusiasm has cooled down and reality appears for what it is, what the enthusiasm of the revolution was not able to obtain? Reality today is not to be found in the chattering of the propaganda but in the low living standards of the people. It seems scarcely credible that today, after the agricultural crisis which has revealed the real feelings of the peasants, and despite the low level of industrial productivity, anyone can still believe that in twenty years the workers and peasants will be inspired by the sacred fire of communism to work for the abolition of wages and every material incentive.

It must not be forgotten that the congenital weakness of communism is low productivity which above all is due to low wages. But the whole programme of the transition to communism in twenty years is based on a vertiginous increase in productivity which must double in ten years and quadruple in twenty. Khrushchev stated clearly that only on these conditions can the programme be fulfilled because, he warned, the labour force can only increase by forty per cent in twenty years and 'a great part of this increase is earmarked for non-productive sectors, especially education and health, and the reduction in working hours must also be taken into account'. How weak are the pillars that support this imposing edifice was revealed to the XXII Congress by Khrushchev himself when he confessed that 'the planning departments estimate that more than nine-tenths of the national income in the period 1961-1980 must come from the increase in labour productivity'.

How much has labour productivity increased in the first two years of the anticipated twenty-year period set by the XXII Party Congress for the transition to communism? From Khrushchev's statements it may be deduced that productivity is more or less stagnant. 'It is intolerable', he said in 1962, 'that in many enterprises, in many sovnarkhozes (regional economic councils) and last year also in certain republics the rate of increase in labour productivity was as a whole less than the rate of increase of average wages.' And in Belgrade on August 21, 1963, when visiting a Yugoslav factory, he confessed: 'If we tell the workers that they must quicken their labour rhythm the workers protest.' He added: 'If one wants to increase production of consumer goods one must work harder and increase productivity. . . . If the worker maintains his productivity at his present level then living standards will certainly decline, because society increases, fresh customers are added, but material goods remain where they were.' He concluded that in such a way it would be hard to build communism which requires 'a continual and rapid increase in labour productivity'.

4

What are the incentives to reach so high a degree of labour productivity?

The Party programme specifies that 'in the course of the next ten years the real income of the workers and clerks (taking account of the social assistance funds) will increase on an average about twice, and about three or three-and-a-half times in twenty years. In the next decade there will be an increase in the real income of the workers and clerks who receive a relatively low wage, sufficient to relieve the low income of certain categories. In this period the real income of those with minimum wages will be raised, taking the social assistance funds into consideration, about three times.'

It is noteworthy that there is no word about tripling wages, either nominal or real, but only of real income of which a growing part will be made up of services and payments in kind from the social assistance funds. In other words the twenty-year period, which began with the XXII Congress, represents a transition phase from socialism to communism, during which there will be, as indeed there is now, two forms of remuneration, of which one is proportionate to the work of the individual, while the other is equal for all and is made up of charges on the social assistance funds. This latter form of remuneration is destined to grow in importance until it replaces, at some unspecified time, the payment of wages and salaries. The programme states: 'The closer one gets to communism, the more individual needs will be satisfied from the social funds, whose rhythm of increase will exceed that of individual payments proportionate to work done.' It adds: 'At the end of two decades the social funds will provide a sum equivalent to half of the total amount of the real income of the population. This will make possible the assurance at public expense of:

—the free maintenance of children in infants' institutions and boarding schools (at the desire of the parents);
—full assistance for those incapable of work;
—free education at all levels;
—free medical aid to all citizens, including the provision of medicines, and convalescence in nursing homes;
—free housing and subsequently free communal services;
—free urban transport;
—certain free public services;
—the gradual lowering of costs in holiday homes, *pensions*, tourist camping sites, and in some instances holidays without charge;
—more and greater subsidies, facilities and grants (e.g. grants to unmarried mothers, subsidies for students, etc.);
—a gradual transition to free meals at public expense in factories, in offices and for kolkhoz members engaged in production.'

5

That is the alluring programme, a great part of which is already in full operation in the capitalist countries under the aegis of public assistance.

There is no doubt that it will be put into operation: indeed to a great extent it has already been applied. But from it to the integral application of communism the step is enormous.

Not only from the theoretical but also from the practical point of view, it is quite conceivable that the state will reach a point where it will supply all its citizens with free lodging, food and clothing, and thus provide for all their elementary needs. The problem is not in the free distribution of all these benefits. Already today rents in the Soviet Union are so low that it would not be a serious burden on the state to abolish them altogether. The same may be said of urban transport. As regards food, there is a tendency to multiply collective *mensae*, as the Spartans used to do. The factories, the schools and many enterprises provide a hot meal more or less free. It is quite possible that one day free canteens will be installed in all the housing blocks for the families living there. It is not difficult to conceive a system of ration-cards for the free distribution, limited by specific numbers of points, of a minimum of underclothes, suits and shoes.

The problem is not distribution, it is production. It is not enough to ensure a minimum of consumer goods to all; it is necessary to provide them in such quantities as to be able to surpass the living standards which the lower classes enjoy in the capitalist countries. Only if it is successful can communism prove its alleged superiority over capitalism; only this can justify the necessity of social upheaval which opens the way to a more productive order, able to bring greater prosperity to all. But if the housing that it assures to the great majority is a sort of dormitory, or a cell of six square metres inferior to that of a convict, and if the meals resemble the soup distributed by the Capuchins to the poor, then one cannot say that communism has been achieved. But the egalitarianism of the communist régimes is always operational only at the lowest level. To attain a distribution of abundant and good quality consumer goods, production must be raised to a very high level. That is the gist of the problem. Communism, after abolishing individual remuneration and even after abolishing money itself, must prove how it can increase production to the point where it exceeds that of the capitalist states. The problem appears the more insoluble in that, as has been shown, in the state-capitalist régime today, that is in a régime based on wages and incentives, productivity especially in agriculture, which is the most important of all sectors, is much lower than in the Western world. This productivity is lower because wages are lower. Every worker produces what he is paid for; that and not the law cited by Marx is the iron rule of wages.

Soviet economists do their best to justify the lowness of wages by pointing out that, over and above payments in money, the state provides rewards in kind that supplement money wages by at least a quarter of their value. But the Soviet leaders are bad psychologists if they do not take heed of the fact that what interests the worker is how much he gets in money, because that is the basis on which he estimates whether his work has been adequately remunerated and how much he has freely at his disposal. For the worker the social assistance funds, even though they are an enormous burden on the costs of production, have much less importance than the actual cash wage that he receives.

Therefore the decision of the XXII Congress gradually to replace wages by free distributions seems difficult to apply, as the experience of the Soviet state itself shows, since, to increase productivity, it was forced little by little to increase wages, first maximum wages and recently minimum wages also. In view of these precedents, how can it be held that on the day wages are abolished productivity will be stimulated? That is the essence of the problem. Until this enigma has been solved it is reasonable to consider that communism, that is to say the free distribution of consumer goods to an extent greater than the consumption of the lower classes in the capitalist countries, is an unattainable goal.

Many other points still remain to be explained. Communism states, and the Party programme asserts, that it is 'a classless social order . . . where a perfect social equality exists among all members of society'. But not only does differentiation in wages remain, but there is a growing difference between wages and salaries, that is to say between the way of life of the working classes and that way of life which might fairly be called bourgeois. The Party programme also states: 'The reward for the work of many Soviet intellectual groups, such as engineers and technicians, agricultural specialists and veterinarians, teachers and doctors, will be considerably raised.' How then can one lessen the gap between the various living standards? How can the incomes of the various categories gradually approach one another? The reply is that the evolution of socialist society tends to suppress every distinction between intellectual and manual labour. The fact is that such an evolution will come about through the advances of culture and technology throughout the world, in capitalist as well as communist countries, at the same rhythm, which is a very slow one. For the moment the distinction remains, since it is founded on a difference of attitude and therefore of productive capacity. The inventor cannot be treated in the same way as the manual worker if one does not wish to drive productivity backward and humiliate the most gifted citizens.

6

The proposed abolition of currency and money exchanges raises even more perplexities. The programme says: 'With the transition to a unitary communist form of ownership by the whole community and to the communist system of distribution, mercantile and monetary relations will cease to have any reason for existence from the economic viewpoint and will disappear.' It is true that this prospect is so distant in time that it remains swathed in the mists of the future. Moreover, there will be 'a final consolidation of the Soviet monetary and credit system and a strengthening of Soviet currency'. How the consolidation of the monetary system and the increase of mercantile relations can lead to the elimination of both one and the other is not made clear by any Soviet source. The argument was treated by the economist D. Allakhverdyan in *Voprosy Ekonomiki* (No. 9, 1960). He expresses himself thus: 'In the higher phase, in communism, when instead of two forms of socialist ownership (private and collective) there will be only one (ownership by the community), when the production of goods within the framework of a monetary economy will disappear and the law of value will cease to operate, there will no longer be any need to use value and its forms in the process of social production. In such conditions there will no longer be any objective necessity to maintain the financial system. When the labour expended in the production of a product is measured not indirectly through the medium of value but directly on the basis of the amount of time-labour expended, then money, credit and finance will disappear. . . .' 'The people,' Engels wrote in *Anti-Dühring*, 'will be able to behave very simply without the intervention of the much boasted conception of "value".'

As can be seen, the abolition of money and of all dealings based on it, is linked with the abolition of wages, that is of remuneration for individual work. We have already pointed out the reasons why one cannot believe in the possibility of abolishing wages without risking the collapse of the whole economic scaffolding through the consequent decline in production. Even more utopian seems the suppression of money which, other than its function as a medium of exchange, serves as a unit for the measure of value. Soviet economists, following Marx and Engels, believe that money can be replaced as a unit for the measure of value by the time-labour unit. But up to the present all experiments of this sort have ended in chaos. It is sufficient to recall the policy of the Soviet government, inspired by the theories of Marx, put into force immediately after the October revolution. The Commissar of Finance, N. Krestinski, as early as 1919 fostered a programme of progressive devaluation of money to the point where it would disappear. 'The Communist Party,' it was said in the programme for that year, 'will make every effort to apply a series of measures which will extend the field of commercial operations without settlement in cash and will prepare for the suppression of money.' Consistent with such a course, the Council of People's Commissars on January 26, 1921 authorized the Commissariat of Finances to prepare decrees that would abolish money as a standard unit in state economy and replace it by the new time-labour unit. In the calculation of such a unit a working day of normal intensity was taken, an extremely vague measure. The date on which the new unit was to have come into force was April 15, 1921. But the NEP put an end to all these ridiculous essays.

7

Even more utopian is the liquidation of the state. The Communist Manifesto of 1848 condemned the state as the executive committee of the bourgeoisie. Logic would have demanded that, once the bourgeois class had been destroyed with revolutionary violence and the dictatorship of the proletariat established, the state should disappear. That is what Engels says in his *Anti-Dühring*. Starting from the viewpoint that the state is not a natural institution but a consequence of the class struggle, he predicted: 'When a classless society has been formed, the state will no longer be necessary and will disappear'.

The same Engels in his introduction to Marx's *Civil War in France* defined the state as 'nothing more than an instrument of oppression by one class over another'. This instrument of oppression has remained in Russia even after the bourgeois class has been exterminated and the *kulak* class destroyed.

When, wrote Engels, the proletariat shall have seized power, the institution of the state 'will be thrown on the scrapheap as a useless tool'. That was what Lenin proposed to do when he reached Leningrad from Switzerland in the famous sealed carriage. Addressing for the first time the Congress of Soviets in April 1917 he upheld in the famous 'April thesis' the necessity to proceed to the demolition of the state by suppressing the police, the army and the bureaucracy. There was general stupefaction. Excited cries rose from the audience calling the thesis 'the ravings of a madman'. It was therefore indignantly rejected by all those present. Many of his faithful supporters, like Kamenev, turned against him.

The episode is symptomatic since it shows to how great an extent the utopias of Marx and Engels had influenced an intelligence as realist as Lenin's. Later, taught by experience, he became more cautious.

In his *The State and the Revolution*, written subsequently, Lenin maintained that the state, insofar as it was an organ created for repression was necessary as long as an opposition existed, that is for the transition period from capitalism to socialism. Once the proletariat had seized power the state would inevitably disappear.

But reality soon made *tabula rasa* of the utopian predictions of Marx, Engels and Lenin. Once installed as head of government, Lenin declared that the bourgeois state must be replaced by a strong revolutionary state, firmly controlled by a minority, the Party, which would impose communism from above. Thus the trajectory was completed, from the affirmation of the disappearance of the state to the creation of the most centralized, most tyrannical and most powerful state machine that history has ever known.

Despite this evolution, diametrically opposed to that indicated by Marx, Engels and the pre-revolutionary writings of Lenin, discussions continued imperturbably among the Soviet authorities, press and doctrinaires about the imminent disappearance of the state, which would slowly 'wither away'. What is certain is that the state will not wither away because in the communist countries the state is everything. The initiative of the individual is nothing in comparison with the overwhelming power of the state. The very existence of every citizen will be imperilled on the day when the functions of the state become less, since the state provides for all. Therefore one must not pay heed to press and propaganda statements, nor even to official announcements, but to the facts that show incontestably the concentration of powers and functions in the dictatorial state. How this strengthening of the state can be reconciled with its imminent 'withering away' is hard to fathom.

The doubt also arises whether a multi-national aggregate like the Soviet Union would not find itself exposed to the centrifugal tendencies of regional particularism, shown with great virulence in certain decisive moments of recent history, should the formidable pressure of the central power slacken.

The Soviet leaders are well aware of this. They know that every measure granting an increase in the autonomy of the federated republics creates a strengthening of local patriotism. This forces them to organize new controls to restore the dependence on the centre of all sectors of vital importance.

The most recent manifestation of this centralism was the unification of the Central Asian federated republics, where the Soviet government proposed to intensify development projects, both industrial and agricultural, and to make heavy investments.[4]

The directive which, despite these facts, the Soviet state says that it is following to ensure its 'withering away' is formally inspired by Marx and Engels, according to whom the 'community' and not the state must have all the sources of production at its disposal. But how can it dispose of them without a sound organization? And in what way is a 'community' differently organized from a state? These are problems on which the theoreticians of communism are still unable to throw light. As was said in the chapter on Marxist ideology, it is just on this difficulty of distinguishing between the community and the state that the fiercest controversy has arisen between the orthodox and the revisionists. These last accuse the Soviet Union of transferring to the state rather than to the workers' community the sources of production and of extracting from them that surplus-value which it was the main aim of Marx to eliminate.

The Soviet government says that in order to prepare for the transition to communism it is now beginning to dismantle the state machine piece by piece. This dismantling of the state was discussed at the XXI Party Congress when the government took account of the provisions to effect it. But rather than dismantling, these provisions were only concerned with minor experiments in decentralization in two forms: the handing over of certain functions of the state central organs to the governments of the federated republics and the increase of powers granted to various public bodies, such as the trade unions, the local soviets and the Komsomol, or youth organizations.[5]

The declared aim of these decentralizing reforms is to instruct the masses in the management of affairs and to give them a knowledge of problems of general interest in order to train them for self-government when the state shall have 'withered away'. They are also intended to show that after the arbitrary dictatorship of Stalin there has been a return to the tradition established by Lenin of consulting, at least in theory, the masses. There is no doubt that such steps have been taken but, considered as a whole, they have done no

---

[4] A Central Asian Economic Council has been created with directive powers which reduce those of the governments of the federated republics to a mere nothing. The Council is supported by inter-regional departments whose aim is to encourage cotton cultivation, irrigation, building, etc., throughout Central Asia. The Council in its turn gets its orders from the Party Central Committee through its Central Asian bureau, the Sredasburo.
[5] How slight are these essays in decentralization has been shown by the loss of the autonomy of the federated republics of Central Asia mentioned above and the strengthening of central control over the economic development of the country, and subsequently the reform of the planning structure, described in the chapter on planning.

more than lengthen the chain, which indeed permits a wider range of movement but not beyond a certain limit. The chain is strong and the public cannot in any way decide problems of real and fundamental importance, because these are reserved to him in whom all power is centred. The façade is more attractive than in the past, but the substance is unchanged. One cannot, therefore, speak of a policy leading towards self-government.

Nor should the liquidation of the state be confused with decentralization. The transfer of functions from the centre to the federated republics is indispensable because of the immensity of the territory over which has been extended the process of economic betterment and especially of industrialization. The Moscow bureaucracy cannot from the centre supervise efficiently such gigantic plans. Nor should it be forgotten that the colonization of the virgin lands and the creation of new industries have resulted in the transference of considerable numbers of Russians and Ukrainians into the regions beyond the Urals. It is they who hold the commanding posts. They make up a connective tissue strong enough to bind together the alien elements there. This lessens the danger of autonomist movements which might be encouraged by decentralization.

The work of the trade unions might be expected to be of particular importance were it effectively exercised but, as will be seen later, they develop their activities under the orders and control of the Party and therefore their influence is nil.

Much was made of the suppression in January 1960 of the Soviet Ministry of Internal Affairs, whose functions were transferred to the ministries of the fifteen federated republics. The decision was presented as a first stage on the way back to socialist legality, decided upon as a result of the suppression of Beria in 1953, as well as the application of the policy of extending the powers of individual republics and thus bringing the government organs into closer touch with the people in the distant prospect of 'the total disappearance of the functions of the central state'.

As in all Soviet pronouncements the difficulty is to distinguish what is pure propaganda from what is a real step towards the goal.

The illusion to the disappearance of the state is pure propaganda. The Soviet state is not divesting itself of any of its functions nor is it ceding any of its basic powers. The Ministry of the Interior in fact exercised no control over the police which, on the morrow of Beria's elimination, were regrouped in dependence on the Committee of State Security, subject in its turn to the Council of Ministers. The Soviet state has always been, like the Hapsburg Empire, a police state. That is to say it is based on a strict supervision of all its citizens, exactly as in tsarist times. That is the fate of all totalitarian and anti-democratic states. The police force created by Lenin under the ill-fated name of Cheka was transformed into the OGPU and finally into the NKVD; ever since the revolution it has been a blind instrument of the régime and the support of tyranny. It is responsible for the suppression of millions of citizens.

Khrushchev deserves credit for having put an end to police terror and for having guided the régime towards a greater liberalism guaranteed by the wider powers granted to the civil magistrates. Thus the decree of May 24, 1955 assured the correctness of judicial enquiries and the legality of criminal procedure. In March 1956 the Ministry of Justice was suppressed and this therefore gave greater autonomy to the courts. In 1957 the Supreme Court was reorganized and the restoration of its authority has increased the prestige of the whole magistrature.

On the other hand much perplexity has been aroused by the formation early in 1959 of the Workers' Militia and the Comrades' Courts, with supervisory duties for the first and judicial functions for the second of these, even though limited to minor misdemeanours. They are Party organs, looked on askance by public opinion which regards them as centres of social espionage.[6]

[6] The Comrades' Courts are essentially political organs directed by the Party to control, in the guise of moral supervision, the political discipline of individuals.

Art. 1 of the law that founded them defines them as chosen social organs called upon to contribute actively in the education of citizens in the communist spirit as regards labour and state property, as also in the observance of the rules of socialist society.

Art. 5 exemplifies cases of competence. They will take note of infractions of labour discipline such as unjustified absence from work, late arrival or early departure, drunkenness at the factory or neglect and carelessness during working hours. They also deal with the illegal use of materials and tools, damage to state property, refusal to carry out socially useful work (that is obligation to perform unpleasant services), parasitism, failure to educate children or assist aged parents, the diffusion of false reports, speculations in, or theft of, state property, hooliganism, alcoholism, obscene acts, etc. As can be seen every action of private life is supervised. The Comrades' Courts are competent in cases of illegal distilling of alcohol, damage to houses, disputes between tenants or between citizens, as well as 'anti-social' actions.

The Comrades' Courts must forestall socially harmful actions and infractions, educate citizens by persuasion and social influence and create an attitude of intolerance against every anti-social action. They enjoy the trust of the collective and express its will. Everyone knows who is behind the collective and who suggests the decisions. In short, in order to forestall all anti-social actions and infractions, these organs must keep an eye on all suspicious persons. What then is left of individual liberty? It is a return to quakerism, the spying of all against all, to the systems stigmatized by Hawthorne in his *Scarlet Letter*.

The punishments include making the guilty one express public contrition,

Thus there is a gradual decentralization process going on, but it is accompanied, step by step, by a reinforcement of the organs of the Party, which are given the most urgent, severe and drastic instructions to be omnipresent, maintain the ideological atmosphere at boiling point and extend its functions to every facet of life.

Bearing this situation in mind, one can estimate the importance of the following statements contained in the Party programme approved by the XXII Congress: 'In the final process of development of socialist democracy there will be a gradual transformation of the organs of state control into organs of self-government.' By socialist democracy is meant the one-party régime, which is anything but democracy. How the transformation of the state organs into organs of public self-government is to be made is not made clear. But what is easy to understand is that these organs of public self-government will still be either Party organs or under Party control.

The programme also says: 'The Leninist principle of democratic centralism, which guarantees a just balance between the centralized direction and the maximum development of the initiative of the organs of authority, will be more greatly developed by expanding the rights of the federated republics and raising the creative activities of the masses.' It may be said that at every step towards the decentralization of state functions there is a corresponding step towards the strengthening of Party control. The programme in fact adds: 'It is necessary to consolidate discipline, to exercise a day-to-day control over the functioning of all the cogs of the administrative apparatus and to control the execution of the decisions and laws of Soviet power.'

The programme also insists on the necessity 'to create positive attitudes among the workers towards the direction of public affairs'. But surely the best way to cultivate such attitudes is to guarantee respect for public liberties?

No less vague is that part of the programme which outlines the evolution which will bring the present socialist state to an end. 'The evolution of the socialist state organization,' it says, 'will lead gradually to its transformation into a communist public self-government into which will be merged the soviets, the trade unions, the co-operatives and the workers' mass associations.' How this is to take place is not stated. It declares that the 'social tasks' now being

or a warning, a public censure, a public reproof and a fine of up to ten rubles.

The Comrades' Courts can propose the transfer of the guilty man to less remunerative work for a period of up to three months, or the downgrading of his job, or his dismissal, or his expulsion from his house, all punishments which, as can be seen, are particularly severe.

carried out by the state will be preserved in communism in a changed form and that 'the planning organs, those of economic direction and of cultural development, which today form part of the framework of the state, will lose their political character by becoming organs of social self-government'. Finally, the programme repeats the Marxist expression that communist society will be 'a community organized from above by the workers'. But how, one asks, does this community organized from above differ from the state?

What the programme takes care not to specify is when the 'withering away of the state' is to take place. It says that the 'historical process will inevitably lead there'. But when? The programme replies: 'For the state to be finally extinguished it is necessary that there be created in internal affairs an evolved communist society and in external affairs a final solution in the international arena of the contradictions between capitalism and communism to the favour of the latter.' This involved phraseology simply means that the extinction of the state will never happen. What in fact does the first condition—the building of an evolved communist society—mean? The programme replies: 'When universal rules of collective communist life are recognized by all and respect for them has become an internal compulsion.'

8

Khrushchev put the matter much more clearly when he said that communism cannot be built until communist man has been formed. Too many people are inclined to think that when the formula 'to each according to his needs' is applied all they need do is 'snatch for a soup-ladle'. 'Clearly,' he declared to the Central Committee on March 5, 1962, 'nothing could be falser than the tendency to attribute to the Marxist-Leninists the idea that communism means the land of cockayne and a time to rest when one is full. The programme of the Soviet communist party and the debates of the XXII Congress state clearly and persistently that communism and work are inseparable and that the communist edifice rests firmly on the altruistic and conscientious work of all members of society and that their noble labour is inspired by the great ideals of communism. The process of forming a new type of man is being carried on and will continue to be carried on during the construction of a communist society, endowed with an acute awareness and a communist morality.' Khrushchev referred to the doctrine of economic determinism in maintaining that little by little as men develop their productive activities their way of thought changes 'because it is not the mind that determines life, but life that determines the mind'.

But how long will be needed to create this new man, who is the indispensable premise of a communist society? Will the twenty years anticipated by the XXII Congress be enough to pass to the phase of integral communism? Certainly not. 'The formation of the new man,' Khrushchev warned in the speech referred to above, 'is a long and complicated process. It will require time and effort to eliminate the survivals of capitalism in the minds of men, to change in millions of men the habits and tendencies formed in the course of centuries. . . . The survivals of the past are a terrible force that fetters the minds of men. They keep a firm grip on the lives and minds of millions of persons long after the conditions that created them have disappeared. In the present phase of the building of communism one must wage an even more vigorous struggle against the survivals of capitalism, such as indolence, parasitism, drunkenness, theft, against the resurgence of chauvinism which still dominates the nations and against local nationalisms, bureaucratic methods, unjust treatment of women, etc.'

Khrushchev put his finger on the weak spot. The risk that one runs with the fulfilment of communism is to create a society of pensioners, ready to slow down productive effort from the moment when the state does their thinking for them. But when, we repeat when, will this new society of ascetics arise?

9

Let us now consider the second condition, that is when the international contradictions between capitalism and communism will be resolved in favour of the latter. Is it possible to see when such a condition will be fulfilled? Has it not been repeated that the contradictions between the two régimes are insoluble and that they will not disappear until the day when capitalism shall vanish from the face of the earth? Isn't that what the phrase 'in favour of communism' means? The condition therefore means that the state will disappear when communism will have triumphed over capitalism; which, one must admit, does not seem to be likely within the next twenty years. If, therefore, these are the indispensable conditions, it must be admitted that there is no possibility of achieving communism, either now or ever.

10

At the XXI Congress Khrushchev raised a preliminary question of primary importance: should the transition to communism take place in a specific country as soon as it has fulfilled the indispensable conditions to put it into operation or should it take place at the same time in all the socialist countries, that is when these indispensable conditions shall have been fulfilled in each one of them? Khrushchev replied that the advent of communism must take place simultaneously in all the socialist countries since it cannot be allowed that one should take his seat at the table while his friends have still not got enough to eat.

Khrushchev's reply was logical, but it poses an unrealizable condition. It amounts to saying that Russia, in order to pass into communism, must first help all the socialist countries to raise themselves to the same economic standard since, Russia being the richest country, it will be in advance of all the others which will not be able to reach such a standard without Russia's assistance. On the other hand, if in the meantime communism is propagated in yet other countries, it will be necessary, for the same reasons, to wait for these last also and to aid them, thus postponing indefinitely the date for the transition to communism.

For these reasons the thesis of simultaneity was abandoned and the programme of the XXII Congress recognized that 'the timing of social revolutions and the different levels of cultural-economic development of individual countries makes it clear that the final phase of socialist construction and the commencement on a vast scale of communist society must take place at different times'. None the less, the possibility of a 'more or less contemporaneous transition to communism within the limits of a single historical epoch' is to be expected. It is stressed, to justify this change of course, that 'the country which precedes the others in the advance towards communism aids and hastens the advance towards communism of the whole socialist world'. The Soviet Union, therefore, claims the role of guide in the building of communism.

Logic is, however, on the side of Khrushchev's first thesis, on the contemporaneity of transition. Not only was it logical, but it was the only one corresponding to the spirit of communism. It has already been said that the fundamental condition for the transition to communism is an increase of production sufficient to ensure a free distribution of consumer goods to all citizens, larger and of better quality than that available to the lower classes in the capitalist world. Now if there is a doubt whether the Soviet Union itself can make such a productive effort, it is totally impossible for countries which do not possess its immense wealth to do so. What will happen then? What will happen is what Khrushchev foresaw, that is the rich will sit at table and the others, like Lazarus, will watch the crumbs that fall from it. Is that the spirit of communism? Surely its mission is to ensure fraternity among all men in homage to the principle of absolute equality? If class differences are not admissible within the framework of a communist state, how can differences between rich and poor nations exist within the framework of a communist world? Can it be that political frontiers, which communism does not recognize, will form a barrier to the unity of the proletarians of the whole world, who follow the same ideal and who therefore aim at adopting the same rules and conditions of life? What then remains of the prophetic phrase of the Communist Manifesto of 1848: 'Workers of the world unite'?

The decision of the Soviet communist party to precede others in the building of communism cannot but deepen the fissures, already serious, of the communist world. If one examines the nature of these contrasts, it will be seen that they are above all due to the diversity of economic situations and the lack of solidarity among the countries of the socialist bloc. For China the Soviet Union is a bourgeois country, which does not feel the need of communist solidarity, as is shown by the paucity of aid that it provides. Whereas in China 650,000,000 people, who are increasing by 15,000,000 annually, live on the brink of hunger because of shortage of living space, nearby Russia has immense uninhabited areas to which she jealously forbids entrance to immigrants from neighbouring countries. Despite the loud cries of fraternity and equality, these are incontestable facts that give them the lie.

Therefore abandonment of the thesis of the simultaneity of communism is equivalent to reaffirming the egotism of each for himself and to admitting a scale of economic lack of equality among the countries of the communist world.

11

These are the facts that inspire doubt of the practical possibility not merely of attaining a free distribution of certain essential consumer goods but also of the possibility of abolishing wages, money and the state, to say nothing of raising the living standards of the Soviet people above the average of the lower classes in the capitalist states. The impossibility of building a régime of this nature is especially evident in the poorer countries of the Soviet bloc, unless the Russian people agrees to pool its resources with the poorer countries, that is to work and to produce not only for itself but for all communist humanity. There are the incontestable facts of the situation. This is how *Pravda* on October 17, 1961 put it in an editorial:

'History has entrusted a grandiose mission to the Soviet people and Party—to be the pioneers of a communist society. The Party has been given the task of building communist society, mainly within the Soviet Union, in the term of twenty years so that the present generation may live under communism. This task can be fulfilled. It is scientifically possible and has been tested in practice, and it will be solved by the creative effort of millions of men.'

Pravda recalls that at the time of the VIII Congress, held on the morrow of the October days that marked the triumph of the revolution, Lenin, in drawing up the second Party programme, proposed the construction of a communist society. What *Pravda* omits to recall is that Lenin made every effort to proceed at once to the building of a communist state. This attempt, known as 'wartime communism', ended in complete failure. None the less, it was a serious and binding effort. Lenin upheld exactly the same programme as that laid down by the Party today and the attempt failed for the same reason as one is permitted to forecast that the present attempt will fail, that is because of a catastrophic fall in production, inevitable as soon as payment on the basis of individual work is abolished.

Lenin never tired of repeating that 'communism, in the strict sense of the word, means unpaid labour for the benefit of the community'. And he added: 'We call communism a social order in which individuals get used to fulfilling their social obligations independently of any sort of coercion and in which unpaid labour for the good of all is universal.' In conformity to this principle complete equality of payment was established regardless of the work accomplished. Then came the decision of the VII Pan-Russian Congress of Soviets in December 1919 which established the *paiok*, payment in kind. This had to be proportionate to the number of members of a worker's family. Finally there had to be recourse to forced labour in order to increase productivity which, however, continued to decline until, with the NEP, Lenin reverted to private ownership, to private initiative, to freedom of trade, in a word to capitalism.

It is worth recalling the official comments of that time on this unfortunate attempt. In May 1918, that is only a few months after the October revolution, the president of the Central Trades Union Council, M. Tomski, said: 'The producer is being transformed into a state pensioner, a parasite living at the expense of others. Naturally such a situation cannot last for ever.' Today there is a return to the abolition of wages, to a free distribution of consumer goods 'to each according to his need', and the producer will again become 'a state pensioner and a parasite living at the expense of others'.

Another communist, A. Gostiev, told the First Conference of the Council of National Economy: 'We have to deal with a campaign of national sabotage, popular and proletarian. We shall meet with enormous resistance from the working masses when we want to impose production norms.'

The same situation was repeated in China as soon as the 'people's communes' were formed. The severest criticism of this new experiment came from Soviet writers, amongst whom the memory of the tragic mistakes made in their own country was still fresh. Khrushchev's criticisms are well-known. A. Sobolev, in the November 1960 number of the review *Problems of Peace and Socialism*, recalled that a similar experiment had been tried in Russia but had failed. 'In the villages,' he wrote, 'agricultural communes are being formed and a similar process is going on in the cities. Every member of these communes, be he a skilled worker or an apprentice, hands over all his wages to the commune kitchens which serve all in equal measure. Such a practice shows a grudging attitude to the increase of consumer goods, even though the development of productive forces is inadequate and there are only limited quantities of consumer goods available. This practice tends to minimize the function of material incentives for the increase of productivity and the training of manpower.' Reality shows only too clearly the drawbacks which it was easy to foresee with simple logic, even as it is easy to foresee them in this fresh attempt to make the transition from socialism to communism which Russia is preparing to carry out.

Sobolev observes:

'The application of such a distributive principle is an attempt to overcome at a single bound the still incomplete development of production, and this has always produced negative and painful results. . . . Such forms of distribution cannot survive for long and will, in fact, disappear. None the less, these levelling tendencies, in this or any other form, reappear even now from time to time among some Soviet people.'

A remarkable confession!

The Chinese reply that for forty-four years the Soviet leaders have been making the same promises and justify their delay in making the transition from socialism to communism with the same excuses. Perhaps the real reason for the Soviet criticisms is to be found in the fact that the Asiatic systems of Mao-Tse-Tung are repugnant to the Western mentality of the Russians. Mao has mobilized the whole population and imposed upon all, men and women alike, a very strenuous working day, splitting families and introducing virtual slavery. The Russians are afraid of the discredit that such methods must cast upon communism. After Lenin's disastrous experiment, the Chinese attempt shows to what excesses dictatorial power can go, in the name of building communism, in scorning not only the most elementary freedoms but also the most elementary needs of human life.

After such irrefutable proofs, is there any other country willing to volunteer for the role of guinea-pig?

CHAPTER XII

Wages

WHOEVER wants to prove that the application of Marxist principles leads to low wages has only to consider what has happened in Russia from the outbreak of the revolution to the present day. The putting into force of the so-called 'wartime communism' led to a fall of 12.3% in real wages compared with 1913 levels. As soon as there was a return to free economy with the NEP real wages doubled, exceeding the pre-war levels; at the same time there was, over and above the wage increases, a reduction of working hours which from an average of eight and a half hours in 1921 fell to seven hours and twenty-eight minutes in 1927-28.[1]

The suppression of the NEP was a step backward. The five-year plans required huge investments which were obtained by reducing wages to a minimum and raising selling prices, with the result of reducing real wages still further. Other curtailments were due to the compulsory loans deducted from the workers' wages.

The reduction of wages was accentuated little by little so that when Russia entered the war in 1941 wages had lost 58% of their purchasing power compared with 1913. Workers' unrest, due to very bad food conditions, induced many factories to grant wage increases. This resulted in the 'passivity' of many factories and the government had to put an end to such practices. The decree of December 15, 1931 threatened penal sanctions for those directors who paid wages higher than those established by the collective contracts or in the official tariffs. A decree of December 3, 1932 entrusted the Council of People's Commissars with the pegging of wage rates. Even today wages policy is the jealously guarded prerogative of the Presidium.

Stalin concerned himself with increasing the remuneration of directors and technicians, but he did not, or perhaps could not, find it possible to increase workers' wages. But that did not prevent him from saying that the living standard of the Soviet worker was far higher than in the West. Even today there is no clear idea among

[1] Sergei N. Prokopovich, op. cit., p. 406, et seq.

343

the Soviet workers of the scale of the difference between their wages and those current in the Western countries. The official propaganda continues to insist on the better economic treatment that the régime affords its workers. It was this argument that Khrushchev employed during his visit to America in order to maintain the superiority of communism over capitalism. There is no doubt that in the final analysis to judge of the superiority of one régime over another there should be a comparison of the benefits that each of them assures to its working class. Basing himself on such criteria the mayor of Los Angeles, Norris Poulson, in a message of welcome to Khrushchev stressed that American workers receive wages that are among the highest in the world. 'The average pay of a factory worker in Los Angeles,' he said, 'is $102.82 a week, about 1,028 rubles according to your tourist rate of exchange. Today the inhabitants of Los Angeles have more than 4,500 million dollars in their bank accounts.'

2

Actually, the average wage of an American worker in 1961 was about $98.00 a week, that is to say equivalent to what a Soviet worker at the top of the wage scale gets in a month.

If one goes on to compare the 'average' wage of an American worker and a Soviet worker, one finds that the Soviet worker gets less than a sixth of the wages of the American. If one takes account of real wages one comes to the conclusion that the Soviet worker receives, for equivalent work, a wage with a purchasing power equal to roughly a quarter of the American.[2]

3

The norms for the fixing of wages were established in 1947. Payment to the worker is in two parts: the basic scale and the premium. The basic wage is payment for the minimum service that the worker must do in order to fulfil his work-plan (norm). The premium is a supplementary payment if the worker exceeds his norm; it is proportionate to the extent by which he exceeds his norm. Up to the reform of 1960 the premium was frequently equal to the basic wage.

[2] *Institute for the Study of the USSR Bulletin*, Vol. IX, March 1962, No. 3, *The Problem of Raising the Living Standard in the USSR.* In calculating the wage of the Soviet worker the free, or almost free, services that he gets from the social funds were included.

Thus two systems of payment are in force: fixed wages and piece-work. The main consequence of this system is that the enterprises try to assure, in planning, very low production limits which can easily be reached in order to avoid the danger of non-fulfilment of their plan, which involves heavy penalties, and to win the premiums laid down in case the plan is exceeded.

In July 1955 the Central Committee discussed the drawbacks of this system and acknowledged the need of modifying the norms by raising the level of services which gave a right to the basic wage, but increasing the basic wage and diminishing the amount of the premium. The workers realized that the increase of the norm, paid for by the basic wage, would in fact mean a reduction of their total wages and showed their discontent. The reform, therefore, was postponed. The Central Trades Union Council returned to it a few months later and upheld the necessity of eliminating the great inequalities between workers in different enterprises and localities, and also the need to raise the basic wage which represented from 40 to 55% of the total remuneration of the workers. At the same time it proposed to limit the system of payment for piece-work and variable premiums, which lent itself to all sorts of abuses and helped to keep down the levels of basic production indicated by the so-called norms.

It must be remembered that it is not possible to have a general wage increase without at the same time having an increase in the production of consumer goods. This mechanism was explained by Khrushchev with great clarity in an interview granted by him to the American journalists Ridder and Ludicke. 'There cannot be inflation in our country,' he said, 'because when we agree the budget and the production plans we take into account the amount of money which will be paid out in the form of wages and the quantity of goods which is to be manufactured, in such a way as to stabilize the equilibrium between the amount of money available and the quantity of goods produced. This means to maintain the balance between demand—that is the income available for spending—and supply, in other words consumer goods.' Moreover in its planning the government decides, independently of the wishes and needs of the population, what part of the national income is destined for investments and public spending and what part for consumption. Wages therefore in practice depend on the total of which they form a part and, in the final analysis, on productivity. Since this is low, wages also are low and can only be raised very slowly because every increase in wages multiplied by the enormous mass of wage-earners creates an expansion of the income quota destined for consumer goods, to meet which other assignments, which have absolute priority in the Soviet budget, such as productive investments and military expenses, must be correspondingly reduced. It would therefore be necessary, in view of the reasons given above, to increase the production of consumer goods by developing the so-called light industries, which would require a slowing-down of the development of heavy industry, a slowing-down contrary to the basic canons of Soviet political economy.

4

Not only are wages low and their rate of increase very slow, but their purchasing power is very slight, since the Soviet state which holds the monopoly for the sale of all goods asks enormous prices for them with the exception of a very few types: medicines, infants' articles, books and the like.

Furthermore, the paternal policy of the state, in contrast to Stalin's directives, is gradually to reduce the gap between maximum and minimum wage rates, reducing the former and increasing the latter, in order to bring them both as close as possible to the average. How this will help to increase productivity is still to be seen, especially if one bears in mind that Stalin approved such diversity of wage-rates expressly to stimulate productive effort to the maximum. It is a fact that this differentiation was looked on askance by public opinion in general, always jealous of those who rise in the world. An article in No. 3 of the Party organ *Kommunist* in 1960 by B. Sukhorevsky entitled *Wages and the Working day in the USSR* defends the decision to introduce a levelling policy. In fact, there have been many hesitations on this point, as is easy to deduce from Khrushchev's statement to the Supreme Soviet in the session that began on May 5, 1960. 'We are strongly opposed,' he said, 'to every attempt to wipe out wage differentiations; we are openly opposed to any levelling of wages. . . . This is the teaching of Lenin, as it was also his teaching that one must always take heed of material incentives in a socialist society.' But Khrushchev at once added that the present wage differentiations between different categories were too great and must be reduced by an improvement in the economic treatment of the lower and middle categories.

5

The reform of the wages system, foreshadowed by the Party Central Committee and the Central Trades Union Council from 1955, was carried out in 1960, contemporaneously with the reduction of the working day to seven hours. Such a reduction should not, however, lead to a diminution but rather an increase of production. This increase should be, according to circumstances, between two and even ten per cent. In compensation the basic wage was increased; but because of the shorter working day and the greater production required as a minimum it resulted in a smaller payment of premiums. Therefore there was, on the whole, a reduction of overall pay. The top wage levels for qualified artisans were also abolished.

According to the seven-year plan minimum wages should rise first to 45 new rubles a month and then to 60, equal respectively to $50 and $66. It must be borne in mind, when estimating the value of these wages, that a pair of shoes costs from thirty to forty rubles.

As has been said, the seven-year plan has been withdrawn and a plan for the two-year period 1964-65 has been approved. This fixes the minimum wage at from forty to forty-five rubles. We are still a long way from the sixty rubles forecast for 1965. Furthermore, on the same occasion the Soviet Premier announced that for the moment it was not possible to improve wages.

The facts stated above prove the lowness of Soviet wages in comparison with those in Western lands. Therefore, being unable to justify after forty-five years of the régime the low levels of remuneration and the fact that, instead of increasing them, Soviet leaders have sought by various expedients to reduce them, communist propaganda makes every effort to create the conviction that the working classes in the Western lands are still, as in Marx's time, victims of the most merciless exploitation, from which, however, the Soviet worker has been freed, thanks to the communist revolution.

Here, for example, is Khrushchev's way of putting it. 'In the capitalist countries,' he told the Supreme Soviet at its session in May 1960, 'the capitalist class appropriates more than a half of the national income and the share of the working class is less than half. Because of this private appropriation the national wealth of the capitalist countries is not the wealth of the people but of the bourgeoisie. In the Soviet Union three-quarters of the national income goes to satisfy the personal, material and cultural exigencies of the population while the rest is devoted to the expansion of socialist production and other social needs.'

Khrushchev's statement is valuable since it confirms that even though three-quarters of the national income is destined to satisfy the needs of the population, the Soviet Union cannot assure a living standard for its people equal to that enjoyed by the lower classes in the Western countries, even though these receive less than a half of the national income. This is yet another proof of the superiority of the bourgeois countries.

The truth is that calculations of this kind are purely hypothetical and serve only as propaganda expedients. What Khrushchev was trying to prove is that the bourgeoisie grow fat at the expense of the proletariat by keeping for itself more than a half of the national income. Naturally, he insinuates that the bourgeoisie makes use of this for personal consumption, whereas Marx himself stressed that the greater part of this income is destined for investment, which brings into operation the law of progressive accumulation and concentration of capital. According to Marx this accumulation takes place because the worker is defrauded of the surplus-value. But is not this the same system as is followed in Russia? It is said that the high profit quota taken by the Soviet state is intended for investment, but doesn't the private capitalist do exactly the same? Only that the private capitalist, as has been proved, pays better wages to the working class. That happens because in the capitalist states the working classes are able to stand up for their interests, whereas in the Soviet Union that possibility is denied them.

6

The Soviet press, like the official propaganda, often refers to the economic treatment given in Russia to the working class and insists on the free, or almost free, services that the whole population receives irrespective of work done and which form an important feature of real wages. These services are provided by the 'public consumer funds' which in 1960 amounted to 247,800,000,000 old rubles, equal to about 25,000,000,000 dollars. The seven-year plan lays down that these shall increase in 1965 to 360,000,000,000 rubles, equivalent to about 40,000,000,000 dollars. The Soviet leaders announce that a third of the state revenue is earmarked for these funds, to be used as follows :

(a) Payment of pensions. The state maintains twenty million pensioners, that is to say about a tenth of the population, including old people, invalids, unmarried mothers and widows with many children;
(b) Maintenance of infants in children's homes, infants' schools, institutes, etc. Five million children are brought up there. The parents contribute a quarter of the costs when the children are in homes and a half when they go to infants' schools;
(c) School education, which is free. In the higher-grade schools

and universities students receive a grant. It is estimated that the training of a specialist in Russia costs about 30,000 old rubles, that is to say 3,300 dollars;

(d) Medical assistance, which is free for all; physical culture and sport. For these alone the social funds, according to the seven-year plan, will pay twenty-five milliard rubles, equivalent to two and a half milliard dollars. In 1965 the Soviet Union will have about half a million doctors, that is one for every 460 inhabitants, a very high percentage when one reckons that in the United States there is one for every 985, in France one for every 957 and in Great Britain one for every 1,140 inhabitants;

(e) Building construction. The seven-year plan destines 375 milliard rubles, equivalent to more than forty milliard dollars, to housing, which will cover an area of 650 million square metres. Houses are let at very low rents;

(f) Paid holidays. Every worker has the right to an annual holiday of from twelve to forty-eight days. Women workers during pregnancy enjoy 112 days paid holiday.

Every year about nine million persons spend a rest period in one of the so-called 'sanatoria' or holiday camps, paying a third of the costs; about a fifth of the visitors are exempt from all payment.

It is estimated that at the end of the seven-year plan the Soviet state will have to bear an annual average expense per inhabitant of 460 new rubles, that is about 500 dollars, for these services. It is undeniable that the Soviet budget has a very heavy burden to carry in order to cover these enormous social services. Some of them, like pensions, paid holidays and medical care are also borne by Western governments. Particularly valuable and worthy of every credit to the Soviet régime are the school organization and the health service; both are completely free and satisfy in the most efficient manner the needs of the population.

7

Khrushchev stressed another reform for the benefit of the workers and that is the gradual suppression of taxes. It is, according to him, a really revolutionary measure. 'It is the fulfilment of an old dream of the working people,' he told the Supreme Soviet which opened on May 5, 1960, 'but could it be realized under a capitalist régime? No, certainly not, because taxation is in fact the economic foundation of the capitalist state, the indispensable financial basis for the fulfilment of all its functions.' But perhaps the Soviet state lives on air? Shrewdly, Khrushchev omitted to say what will be the principal financial basis of the Soviet state and from what source it will draw its budgetary assets. These assets the communist state procures by the most anti-democratic and anachronistic system, that is its monopoly of the sale of the entire national production, weighed down by excessive profit. To give an idea of the scale of these profits it is enough to mention that a metre of woollen cloth, imported at a price of fifteen old rubles, is re-sold by the Soviet state on the internal market at four hundred rubles; that lemons imported at little more than fifty Italian lire (about 8 US cents) a kilo are sold at thirty kopeks each, about four times the price of the whole kilo; that a watch which costs thirty-seven rubles at the factory is sold to the public at 300 rubles. These are the democratic systems of the monopolist state, which on the one hand abolishes taxes and on the other sucks the meagre earnings of the workers, selling them at usurious prices articles of prime necessity, such as clothing.

The truth is that the imposition of taxes in a country where private property productive of income does not exist, nor do profits of private activity, is an absurdity. Taxation in the Soviet Union is no more than a reduction of the payments made by the state. The state takes away with one hand what it has given with the other. The elimination of taxes is no more than the suppression of a useless book-keeping transfer. What is surprising is that it has not been done before. These are the facts. Now for the propaganda. 'The bourgeois state,' thundered Khrushchev, 'which is at the service of the capitalists and their monopolistic alliances, places the burden of taxation primarily upon the toiling masses. . . . The complex tax machinery of the capitalist countries, like a gigantic pump, sucks the money from the pockets of the workers and pours it into the yawning purses of the monopolies, which make enormous profits from military supplies paid for at high prices mainly by the taxes. . . . The enormous sums taken from the taxes are used by the capitalist powers primarily for military purposes.' But are not the military expenses of Russia paid for by money 'pumped' from the pockets of the workers? How much of this money must be absorbed by armaments, since the Soviet Union boasts of being the most powerfully armed nation in the world? 'Even more,' Khrushchev continued, 'a considerable part of the budget funds is spent by the capitalist states in maintaining the police.' It would be interesting to make a comparison between the police apparatus in the capitalist countries and that existing in Russia where, as everyone who has been there knows, one cannot walk a step without running into a militiaman.

Khrushchev told the Supreme Soviet that those categories with salaries of more than two hundred new rubles a month will gain no advantage from the abolition of taxation, because their wages will be reduced proportionately. This proves that this reform is no more than a simplification of the administration. At the announcement of the said reduction there was a murmur of protest from the meeting.

'What does that mean?' asked Khrushchev, 'I think it is a good sign!'

Naturally the Assembly assented with obsequious applause.

The law of May 7, 1960, which provided for the gradual abolition of taxes on the wages of workers and clerks, was suspended by a decree of the Supreme Soviet on September 25, 1962, that is to say five days before the taxes were to be abolished on wages between sixty and seventy rubles a month, which would affect the majority of the workers and clerks. The suspension was necessary in order not to reduce the assets of the state budget by from one to two milliard rubles. Naturally justification was found 'in the intensification of the aggressive intrigues of imperialism and the consequent necessity to strengthen the defensive capacities of the Soviet Union', as *Izvestia* commented on the same date, September 25th. The costs of militarism in the Soviet Union always fall upon the workers.

CHAPTER XIII

Consumer Goods

1

SINCE wages, especially real wages, are low, consumer goods are bound to be in short supply. The outstanding fact that strikes every observer of the Soviet scene is the universal drive for an increase in consumer goods. This people, told daily that its production exceeds that of every country in the world except America and that it will soon exceed that also, cannot understand why its living standard should not be higher than, or at least equal to, that of most of the European peoples. This desire for a better existence is encouraged by communism itself, which at every moment renews its promise to the people of an abundance of goods such as capitalism will never be in a position to provide. Little by little as the building of the socialist state advances, it is stressed that the Marxist principles upon which it is based, and especially the abolition of private property, of profit and of social inequalities, allow it to pour out for the benefit of all, and in the same degree for all, the integral fruits of their labour without the deductions of wealth made by the privileged classes in the capitalist system. Yet despite that, the sufferings and sacrifices imposed on the people are far from light and its efforts are maintained by keeping alive the expectation of a better future, renewing promises to be fulfilled in shorter and shorter periods of time which are, however, continually being postponed.

This technique of 'promising much within a short time' began with Marx and Engels more than a hundred years ago. Lenin followed it forty-five years ago and Stalin continued it. It is being continued today with the grandiose promises contained in the Party programme approved by the XXII Congress. The mirage, however, constantly recedes farther and farther into the distance.

In order to save the régime which was to have given happiness to the people, Lenin was forced to abandon wartime communism. Stalin, who promised that the Soviet Union would soon surpass all the capitalist countries, provoked by his land-collectivization a terrifying scarcity of foodstuffs. Malenkov, who promised great abundance within two or three years, was removed from the premiership for having given preference to light rather than heavy industry. Now it is promised, as Khrushchev assured the Central Committee on December 9, 1963, that the industries producing consumer goods will be developed with an accelerated rhythm. But the hopes raised by these seductive promises have always been dashed by a stern recall to reality, as happened with the decree of June 1, 1962 which, as we have said, raised to such heights the price of meat and milk.

Therefore these promises have little credit. The general wish is that, from now on, a scaled plan of increase of consumer goods should be put into effect.

The need to raise as soon as possible the living standard of the people, to affirm which Marxism entered the lists, has always taken second place to needs considered more vital and urgent, especially the need to accumulate productive capital, as can be seen from the debates, which took place in the first years of the régime, on the productive course to follow and on the criteria for the distribution of the national income.

2

Probably the only Russian statesman who publicly maintained the need for the Soviet Union to increase the production of consumer goods if it wanted to keep the prestige of communism high was Bukharin. For him communism must be, in the eyes of all, an abundance of goods, a liberality of life, to show the superiority of the Soviet over the capitalist world. Should the régime not move along this path, he foresaw prophetically that famine would become a recurrent phenomenon in the Soviet Union. 'When we draw up our programme for the creation of capital', he wrote in his *Notes of an Economist*, 'we must bear in mind the directives of the Party on reserves (of currency, gold, wheat, goods, etc.) . . . Not only do we not have any reserves but, having to confront at once the problems of the supply of foodstuffs, "waiting in turn" and "queuing" have become a part of our way of life.' He concluded: 'The acute scarcity of goods must be tackled resolutely, not in some distant future but within the next few years.'

Bukharin's prophecy has been fulfilled to the letter. The Soviet Union, as at the present moment China, has passed through many very severe shortages, since this is inevitable under Marxism. In Russia the famine of 1921-1922 cost five million lives. The American organization ARA organized aid and sent to Russia 250,000 tons of cereals in 1921 and 787,000 tons in 1922.

The second famine, following the collectivization of the land,

353

lasted from 1932 to 1934 and caused the loss of eight million lives. Stalin refused every outside aid; despite the famine that ravaged the country he even exported the following quantities of cereals:

	Tons
1932	1,760,000
1933	1,717,500
1934	827,800

It was taking food from the people who were dying of hunger in order to make money.

It should be added that he blocked every purchase of consumer goods from abroad, though under the tsars there had been imports of considerable size, amounting in 1913 to the value of 412,500,000 rubles.

Food supplies were also very scarce during the war period. Ration cards were only abolished in December 1947. From that time the production of consumer goods began to increase, but certainly not to the extent required to satisfy the growing needs of the population. In 1963 there was an exceptionally poor harvest which forced the government to re-introduce bread rationing.

Whoever lives in Russia still feels today that the reserves recommended by Bukharin are lacking and that people live from day to day. In Moscow queues for milk, meat and green vegetables are an everyday sight. If this happens in the capital, it is not hard to guess what the situation is in other cities. Under-consumption is chronic. What Bukharin prophesied has proved true; the system of 'wait your turn' and 'get into the queue' has become the Soviet way of life. They can make all the propaganda speeches they like, but the truth can be seen every day in the streets of Moscow.

Therefore it would not be far from the truth to say that family reserves, so abundant in the Western countries, are as lacking as state reserves. Furthermore, as long as the housing crisis continues and the living space allotted to each person does not exceed the present measure of six square metres, there is no space to keep even small quantities either of clothes or foodstuffs.

It is not an easy matter to find out whether the Soviet Union has got any state reserves, and if so of what products and to what extent. It is evident that deficiencies of this sort could have the most serious consequences in the event of war. It is known that the Soviet Union has huge gold reserves. But it would not be very easy to transform these gold reserves into supplies, because the whole West, that is practically the whole of the highly industrialized world, would be ranged against it.

3

The propagandists for the régime repeat continually that the Russian is better off now than in tsarist times. That is indisputable. But it must not be forgotten that in the last forty-five years of tsarism the country had made very rapid progress in agriculture and had laid the foundations of its industrialization. A country potentially the richest in the world, as the Soviet people itself admits, and with a very low population density, should be able to assure its people the highest living standard in the world. Yet this standard is very low, as all who visit Russia can testify.

The increase in consumer goods has been far lower than the increase in production. Official statistics inform us that from the Bolshevik revolution onward the production of capital goods has increased about seven times more than that of consumer goods: this means that consumption has not kept pace with the economic progress of the country. It will be admitted that a situation of this sort could never happen in a free economy régime, where the interest of the consumer dominates and controls production, nor would it be tolerated in a democratic régime, since the trade unions would immediately claim, and with good reason, a greater share of the fruits of their labour for the working classes. But these trade union Vestals, who always see through dark glasses whatever happens in the democratic lands, can only admire unconditionally in the countries of the socialist world what would arouse their indignant protests were it to happen in Western countries.

4

It must always be remembered that, wages being fixed by the Presidium, the level of consumer goods production is established correspondingly by the central Gosplan, that is to say the supreme planning organ, which specifies the investment quotas destined for the development both of heavy and light industry. It thus determines the production volume both of capital and consumer goods. Everything is decided by a closed oligarchy, though, as we have seen, the fiction of wide popular consultation is maintained. Now it is clear that until the people is able to make its will felt through really democratic organs, it will have no part in deciding how the national income will be allotted. Therefore its interests will go on being sacrificed to the aims of power and its consumption will continue to be restricted to a very low level.

Mikoyan has denied that the rate of production increase in the Soviet Union is due to the restriction on consumer goods. Speaking at Havana on February 8, 1960, during the opening ceremony of the Soviet Exhibition of Science, Technology and Culture, he said: 'Do not believe those who say that the Soviet Union advances full steam ahead in heavy industry, but that this has been done at the expense of the production of consumer goods. That is the latest calumny against the Soviet Union circulated by those who wish to do us harm.' Such rumours are set in motion, according to Mikoyan, by the capitalists who wish to justify their lower production rhythm, which is due to an archaic system that perpetuates the anarchy of production. 'Hence the crises and booms,' he said, 'the depressions and recessions. They are not mere words; they reveal the tears and miseries of thousands who suffer from these recessions.'

The truth is that there are crises both in the capitalist and communist worlds; in the first of over-production and in the last of under-production, as in the case of the agricultural crises with the consequent chronic under-consumption. Everyone can freely judge whether the drawbacks of under-production may be or may not be more lamentable than those of a super-abundance of goods.

5

A vast literature exists on these contradictory aspects of the two systems, capitalist over-production and communist under-production. This would make it unnecessary to return to this question had it not once more become immediate in very recent times, after Khrushchev's attacks on the Stalinist directives about consumer goods. Speaking at the XXII Party Congress on October 17, 1961, Khrushchev inveighed against 'the stagnation of thought and the adoration of formulas which are not in accord with the present state of affairs'. As an example of attitudes which should be reproved because of their insistence on theses whose lack of foundation has been proved in day-to-day life, Khrushchev cited the criterion prevailing in Soviet economic literature, according to which 'under socialism the purchasing power of the population must always exceed production and this is the specific advantage of communism over capitalism and constitutes one of the motive forces of our development'. Khrushchev went on thus: 'This statement, which is obviously false and which contradicts the Marxist-Leninist theory of the relations between production and consumption, is derived from the dogmatic and uncritical acceptance of the erroneous theses of Stalin, who considered that in the Soviet Union the increase of consumption by the masses (purchasing power) continually exceeds the increase of production. The champions of this point of view do not worry about the fact that in this way they justify the scarcity of goods of prime necessity and the perpetuation of the system of rationing and the psychology that goes with it.'

Khrushchev's testimonies were always revealing. This attack on Stalin and his supporters confirms that the official policy of under-consumption had been in force until then. He claimed that such a policy was contradictory to Marxist-Leninist doctrine; which does not seem to be true. It is comprehensible that when one wishes to change a policy, as Khrushchev wanted to do, it is indispensable to cover oneself by the authority of the sacred texts, but in the case in question the texts justify the thesis of Stalin rather than that of Khrushchev. Both Marx and Lenin held that one of the principal contradictions of the capitalist system was to be found in this excess of production over consumption and that this was the main cause of the recurrent crises that disturb the economic development of society. This was what Marx wrote in *Das Kapital* and Lenin repeated in his *Note on the Problem of the Theory of Trade* and stressed in his book *The Development of Capitalism in Russia*.

It is a well-known fact that free economy régimes have always considered production in excess of consumption, naturally within reasonable limits, as an incentive to the consumers. This view had the authoritative support of Khrushchev. On January 28, 1961, speaking to the plenum of the Ukrainian Party Central Committee, he said openly: 'The condition for the satisfaction of the rising demand for foodstuffs and consumer goods is that production shall always exceed demand. That is the socialist law to increase the people's well-being.' Khrushchev's common sense recognized that communism justifies its reason for existence only if it succeeds in assuring an abundance of goods. Naturally, Khrushchev added that in a system of planned economy it is easy to keep account of the demands of the population. In reality, in a market the size of the Soviet one, it would not seem at all easy to maintain a balance between the demand and the supply of consumer goods even when the planning organs are able to control the greater part of the expendable income.

The Soviet leaders, until yesterday concerned to avoid over-production, so censured in the capitalist system, were ready to stick to under-consumption, but today they condemn this tendency and acknowledge, as capitalism has always done, that abundance can only be assured by an excess of production over the purchasing power of the people.

This dispute is rich in significance. It brings to light the influence which theses of a purely doctrinaire character have exercised, and continue to exercise, both over production and over consumer goods. These are paper obstacles, it is true, that do not resist the evidence of fact, but they none the less hinder the free expansion of economic forces and cause useless suffering to the population which pays for the expense of these experiments inspired by uncertain and doctrinaire cerebrations.

6

What strikes the foreign visitor is the constant pressure exerted in a myriad ways by the whole Soviet people for an increase in the supply of consumer goods. The increase in tourism and the growing frequency of contacts with Western people make comparisons possible and make clear to all a reality quite different from that described by the official propaganda. Everyone is being forced to recognize that people live better in the West. That is one of the most frequently discussed subjects, especially among young people. There is no tourist who is not asked how much he earns in his country, what his house is like and how he lives. One often hears Soviet acquaintances complain about the poverty of their homes, their clothes and their food.

When Khrushchev, after his trip to America, lauded the superiority of communism over capitalism at a meeting at Novosibirsk, a voice from the crowd asked: 'When are you going to lower prices?'

One asks students, technicians, members of the new bourgeoisie, if they intend to spend their holidays in the rest-homes. They laugh at the very idea that anyone can find pleasure in living in community with people such as are found there, in sleeping in dormitories and in taking meals in communal messes. Stoicism is not the ideal of this new class, which inevitably will end by imposing its tastes, its needs and its aspirations, which are those of all the bourgeois of the whole world.

They all revolt against the restrictions of Spartan life, the workers who complain of low wages and reduce their productive effort to a minimum, the kolkhoz members who want to share the profits of their labours rather than pour them into a common fund, the new bourgeoisie that wants fine houses, elegant clothes, motor-cars and trips abroad. The more this yearning to live well is accentuated among the Russian people, that is to live like all other peoples of similar mentality, similar race and similar culture, the more such contacts, not merely touristic, but economic and cultural, will bring them closer to the Western world.

7

The American Exhibition in Moscow opened by Nixon in July 1959, was a demonstration to the Soviet people of the living standards of the Western worker. The evident, almost defiant, affirmation of American wealth, the evidence of the indisputable superiority of the Western way of life, struck the crowd and irritated the Soviet leaders, beginning with Khrushchev. When he visited the kitchen of the model house of the average American worker in the centre of the exhibition, he could not repress a start and contested that such a kitchen could belong to a worker, as if this were some trick of American propaganda.

Nixon was clever and most convincing. In his speeches he described the American way of life, giving the reply that millions of Soviet people expected of him. He took the chance of pointing out that the average weekly wage in the United States was 90.54 dollars, that is to say as much as a skilled Soviet worker at the top of the wage scale earns in a month. With this salary, Nixon went on, a worker can acquire on deferred terms a house, a television set and a motor-car similar to those exhibited. Every American family buys, on an average, nine suits and fourteen pairs of shoes annually. The unemployed receive social assistance of 131.49 dollars a month, more than a Soviet worker receives when employed. In America, Nixon specified, everyone has the right to express his ideas freely. No one is so criticized as the President of the United States. Everyone is free to listen to the Soviet radio and to get the Soviet newspapers. That year eleven million Americans had gone abroad, since in America everyone is free to go where he likes. Finally Nixon recalled that at the end of the war the United States had not asked or received a hectare of land from any other people.

This is the kind of propaganda that is needed, made up of facts and figures that speak for themselves. The terms of comparison are thus displayed before the eyes of all. 'Perhaps they want to put a mine under the social foundations of the Soviet state and arouse among its people a desire to slip back into a capitalist system,' said Khrushchev. 'Is it possible,' he asked, 'that there are still some who hope to shake the faith of our people in socialism? It seems almost incredible.' But when a people is mute no one can know what its thoughts may be.

How did Soviet propaganda react to the American offensive? 'You are showing here,' said Khrushchev to the Americans, 'your house and your kitchen and hope to make the Soviet people marvel. To buy such a house an American must have very many dollars. . . .

You speak much of your freedom, which includes freedom to spend the night under a bridge.' The Soviet press rubbed it in. 'In America the worker is under the iron heel of the monopolists who are the masters of all,' thundered *Pravda*, and went on : 'It is only the full purse that controls everything in America. Only he who has possessions enjoys every freedom. How can you call the millions of unemployed free, who are openly called "superfluous people"?' Thus they countered Nixon's facts with words, words and yet more words.

The truth is that the American exhibition opened the eyes of the public to the gap that separates America from Russia. The initiative came at the moment of maximum receptivity, prepared for by the Soviet propaganda itself which had continually been insisting on the need to reach the American level. Everyone was anxious to see how far he had to go.

No less effective was the speech of Harold Macmillan on Soviet television on March 2, 1959. He too proved the extent of social and economic progress of which the democratic world was capable. 'England,' he declared, 'produces *pro capite* twice as much as Russia. Since the war we have built more than three million homes, the greater number of which are for a single family and have a garden. . . .' To a people afflicted with the chronic plague of overcrowding it was like describing Paradise.

8

An idea of the amount of Soviet consumer goods may be gained from the annual publications of the Central Statistical Office in Moscow :

	1958	1959	1960
		Million metres	
Cotton textiles	5,790.0	6,150.0	6,387.0
Woollen textiles	302.9	326.0	342.3
Linen textiles	480.8	527.1	559.1
Silk textiles	844.5	799.7	810.0
		Million pairs	
Shoes	887.7	926.1	963.8
		Millions	
Watches	24.8	26.2	26.0
		Thousands	
Radio sets	3,902.0	4,035.0	4,164.0
Television sets	979.0	1,277.0	1,726.0
Refrigerators	359.6	426.1	529.5
Washing machines	538.7	724.0	953.0
Vacuum cleaners	245.2	367.5	453.8
Sewing machines	2,686.0	2,941.0	3,096.0

	1958	1959	1960
		Thousands	
Cameras	1,472.0	1,615.0	1,763.0
Motor-cycles and scooters	400.1	499.7	552.7
Motor-cars	122.2	124.5	138.8
		Thousand tons	
Paper	2,236.0	2,327.0	2,420.0
		Million tons	
Window glass	133.1	139.8	147.3

The same Soviet statistics give a comparative picture of United States and Soviet production in 1961. They give the following data:

	U.S.A.	Soviet Union
	Milliard square metres	
Cotton textiles	8.4	5.3
	Million metres	
Woollen textiles	270.0	355.0
	Million pairs	
Leather shoes	610.0	442.0
	Million tons	
Granulated sugar	3.7	6.1

As regards 1961 production it appears from these publications that the increase in the production of consumer goods in 1961 was only 6.6% more than in 1960, whereas the seven-year plan had budgeted for an increase of 6.9%. It is, however, worthy of note that the production of capital goods had exceeded the quota laid down by the plan, with an increase of 10% over 1960 whereas the plan had budgeted for an increase of 9.5%.

Therefore, despite the protestations of the Soviet leaders that they wanted to favour an improvement in the living standards of the population, the plan was not fully carried out in 1961 as far as consumer goods were concerned.

The national income was to be increased in 1961 by 7% over the previous year.

Retail sales to the population should have registered the following increases and decreases in 1961: refrigerators and washing machines +30%, eggs +15%, milk +10%, footwear +6%, fish +5%, meat −4%, textiles −6%, motor-cars −11%.

The same Statistical Office report shows that the growing demands of the population remain unsatisfied for many products and that these, for example clothes and footwear, leave much to be desired in quality.

If one compares American with Soviet food production for 1961 we have the following data, based on the reports of the Moscow Central Statistical Office:

		Soviet production	United States production
		Million tons	
Cereals		133.2	194.2
(of which :	Wheat	(63.7)	(37.1)
	Maize	(18.5)	(110.6)
Potatoes		84.0	11.6
Meat		8.7	17.9
		Million litres	
Milk		61.5	56.9
		Thousand tons	
Butter		848.0	665.0
		Milliards	
Eggs		26.4	62.4

Finally the data concerning the most important consumer goods in the first three months of 1962 are:

	Soviet Production	Increase over first three months of 1961
	Thousand tons	
Artificial and synthetic fibres	68.0	10%
Paper	685.0	9%
Fats	101.0	8%
Soap	430.0	13%
	Milliard sq. m.	
Cotton textiles	1.2	2%
	Million sq. m.	
Woollen textiles	118.0	3%
	Million rubles	
Ready-made clothes	2.5	6%
	Million pairs	
Footwear	116.0	4%

In May 1960 Khrushchev, speaking to the Supreme Soviet, said that in 1959 the Soviet Union had produced 6,000,000 tons of sugar, that is more than the total production of England, France, Federal Germany, Italy, Belgium, Holland and Denmark. Butter production had exceeded that of the United States and milk production would shortly do so also. However, in October 1961, Khrushchev was forced to admit that milk production was insufficient for the needs of the population. This shows how much importance may be attributed to comparisons of this kind. It is a fact that milk, whether or not production has increased, is still impossible to find. The queues at the milk shops are endless; in 1961 it was impossible to get any in hotels and restaurants. The little that could be found was an unappetizing mixture of sheep and cow milk.[1] This did not prevent

[1] Moscow receives 522,000 tons of milk annually, whereas it needs 1,180,000 tons.

Khrushchev from concluding his statement with the words: 'The Soviet people will show once more what a people freed from capitalist exploitation is capable of.'

9

Generally speaking, forecasts are preferred to actual consumption figures. The Soviet government is aware that a greater effort than in the past is needed to increase consumer goods. Speaking to the Central Committee on January 18, 1961, Khrushchev solemnly pledged his intention to do so. He said:

'The well-being of a state is judged not only on the amount of metal that it produces but on many other things, for example the diet of individuals, the production of clothes and shoes, in a word the degree in which the needs of everyday life are satisfied. We must not, therefore, be like the flounder which can only look in one direction. If we leaders permit the normal proportions of the development of various sectors of the national economy to be distorted, we shall betray the people's trust, because it asks us to look into the future and guide the development of our economy in the right direction.'

At long last! No one before has had the courage to proclaim self-evident truths like this. What does it mean that the well-being of a state is not judged by the amount of metal produced but by the production of consumer goods save that it is necessary to guard against sacrificing light industry to the needs of heavy industry, as has been the case up till now? It is a truth that was a heresy as long as it was on Malenkov's lips, but which became orthodox when it was said by Khrushchev.

It is therefore certain that Khrushchev intended to take firm measures to increase the production of consumer goods. He announced this to the Supreme Soviet at its session in May 1960. After recalling that the seven-year plan had earmarked from eighty to eighty-five milliard rubles, that is from eight to eight-and-a-half milliard dollars, for the development of light industry and foodstuffs, he pointed out that in its first two years of operation the levels of production budgeted for had been greatly exceeded. Such a result made it possible for him to give free rein to the decision of the XXI Party Congress to devote to the production of consumer goods the greater part of the cash takings derived from this over-fulfilment of the plan. Investments intended for the increase of production of sugar, meat and textiles were therefore increased by a milliard rubles.

Khrushchev said that in the seven years of the plan's operation another twenty-five or thirty milliard rubles would be earmarked for the production of textiles and shoes.

No less binding promises were made by him to the XXII Party Congress of October 17, 1961. He said that by 1980, at the end of the twenty-year plan, the number of plants for the production of consumer goods would be increased thirteen times, whereas those for heavy industry only about six times. Meanwhile the national income would increase from a hundred and fifty milliard rubles in 1960 to seven hundred and fifty in 1980. This would make it possible to assure a separate apartment for every family, to provide hot meals in all schools and school books and uniforms for all pupils.

Unfortunately these seductive promises benefit only future generations whereas the public wants to begin to enjoy these benefits now, convinced that an egg today is worth a chicken tomorrow. While waiting for these promises to be carried out, there is still a considerable shortage of consumer goods. Khrushchev was himself forced to admit this when speaking to the XXII Party Congress on October 17, 1961. 'Comrades,' he said, 'our advances in agriculture are remarkable and indisputable. But another question arises: why are we still short of certain products, especially meat? This is primarily due to the fact that the rate of increase in agricultural production is still much lower than that of industrial production and does not answer to the growing needs of the population. . . . Moreover many government and Party organs slackened their supervision over agriculture in 1959 and 1960 with the result that the rate of production, especially of meat and milk, has fallen far below the quota of the seven-year plan.'

In fact, plans and promises do not always correspond to reality. It remains to be seen how well-based are some of the comparative data used and abused for propaganda purposes. Khrushchev, for example, declared: 'Our country has surpassed Italy in *pro capite* consumption of textiles; we are equal to France and in the next three or four years will surpass Federal Germany and England.' Khrushchev did not specify which textiles are in question; but from the statistics it appears that they are mostly cotton. The confession that the Soviet Union has just equalled France and that it is still behind Federal Germany, England and the United States is of particular interest. It must be remembered that the Soviet Union is not merely a cotton-producing country but also a cotton-exporting one. It is therefore not surprising that it should have surpassed Italy, above all if one considers that the Russian people, four times more numerous than the Italian people, has at its disposal a country seventy-five times larger than Italy and rich in every gift of God.

Khrushchev's statement, therefore, is anything but a proof of abundance.

According to Soviet statements, fulfilment of the seven-year plan should have made possible full satisfaction of the needs of the people for food, clothes and shoes. By the end of the plan the Soviet Union should have exceeded the *pro capite* consumption of the more important consumer goods in the most advanced European capitalist countries, and in another five years should have reached the level of the United States and even exceeded it in *pro capite* consumption of shoes and textiles.

But these declarations, however attractive they may appear, are a confession of inferiority. From all that has been said in this and in earlier chapters, it is quite evident that consumption in the Soviet Union today is still below that not only of the United States but also of the countries of Western Europe.

To these incontestable facts the Soviet leaders can only answer with promises. But the democratic countries too advance, some of them at a faster rate than the Soviet Union. What matters to Soviet propaganda is that the people should not look at the present day, at the scarcity of essential goods and the lowness of wages, but towards the future. Here, for example, is how the First Secretary of the City of Moscow Committee, Pyotr Demischeff, expressed himself at the Bolshoi theatre when commemorating the 91st anniversary of Lenin's birth. 'Before long the Soviet Union will have the highest standard of living in the world. Then we shall be able to tell the world: Look, this is communism which has penetrated into the hearts of men.'

There is, however, another tactic, even more efficient, to distract public attention from the low level of Soviet life, and that is to dramatize certain aspects of Western life in order to show by contrast the inestimable benefit of living in a communist régime. Khrushchev was a master of this art. After enlarging on the magnificent prospects opening before the Soviet people, he closed his speech to the Supreme Soviet in May 1960 with this exalted description of the democratic lands: 'Compared with these prospects, comrades, let us cast a glance at what is happening in the capitalist lands. Taxes increase rapidly, unemployment reigns and prices rise to the skies; the workers' lack of trust in their morrow places a great burden upon the mass of the people.'

10

But perhaps the comrades, instead of looking at what is happening in the capitalist countries, should take a look at the everyday reality in which they have been struggling for the past forty-six years.

The difficulties of the public in obtaining goods of prime necessity are much increased by the very limited organization of retail trade. Shops are few, especially when compared with the number in the cities of the free world. This lack of shops helps to give the Soviet cities that drab and monotonous atmosphere characteristic of centres with little traffic, without luminous signs and without the elegant shop-window displays which in the cities of the West expose to the admiration of the public all that the most refined and artistic crafts-manship is able to create. The reasons for this serious lack must on the one hand be sought in the government neglect of the needs of the consumers in Stalin's time and on the other in the scarcity of workers who are for the most part swept away to work in the factories.

When, therefore, Khrushchev posed the question of increasing the supply of consumer goods he had also to provide, with the increase in light industry, for an expansion of the network of retail shops. The government decided to open a hundred thousand of them within five years. The press praised this as a measure of great liberality, whereas it is both insufficient and tardy. What are a hundred thousand shops for a population of two hundred and twenty millions? Nobody in Moscow seems to realize how little it adds to the prestige of the capital to see perambulating barrows, wooden kiosks and handcarts surrounded by sad and patient queues of people waiting their turn to buy a cabbage or a litre of milk.

Another serious lack is the disappearance of the craftsmanship which had ancient and glorious traditions in Russia and was greatly prized even abroad for its artistic talent and skill in execution. The quality of the goods, therefore, is declining. This is how the editor of *The Christian Science Monitor* of Boston, Nate White, writes about Soviet goods in an article dated July 1960: 'The choice is very limited. The goods are of inferior quality, in atrocious taste and ex-tremely expensive.' Khrushchev himself had to acknowledge, when speaking to the XXII Party Congress, that 'the lack of certain goods in the shops is a serious reflection on our work' and that 'the moment has come to raise without delay the question of a great im-provement in the quality of our goods'.

The Soviet people suffers from the poor quality of their home products and searches with increased interest for foreign goods. Often tourists, when leaving their hotels, are approached by specu-lators, for the most part young men, who ask to buy their clothes, shoes, raincoats, ties and even wrist-watches.

11

If one turns from the Soviet Union for a moment to cast a glance at the satellite countries, once happy and now reduced to the poverty of communism, the picture is even blacker. The example of East Germany will serve for all. No one can have a moment's doubt that if it should again become a part of the Reich, it would participate in the same enviable prosperity as Federal Germany enjoys. By opposing reunification the Soviet Union has condemned it to hunger, despite its predominantly agricultural economy. It too has been given the most seductive promises. Ulbricht boasts of surpassing, within a few years, the productive levels of Western Germany. But in the meantime there is famine. East Berlin is without butter, meat and vegetables. The government was forced to impose rationing in 1961. The consumption *pro capite* of cheese has been reduced, as well as of coffee, fish and citrus fruit, while in West Berlin the people wallow in plenty. The Minister of Internal Trade and Supplies, Kurt Lemke, has exhorted his countrymen to eat less butter 'firstly because it is harmful to health and secondly because there is not enough to go round'. Any comment would be superfluous. Whoever has been able to flee from this inferno has hastened to do so and the communist government has found no better expedient to halt the general exodus than to put up the shameful wall, displaying to the whole world the spectacle of a government holding an entire population prisoner.

It is superfluous to speak of the People's Republic of China where, in the midst of the twentieth century, people are literally dying of hunger while in the capitalist countries production exceeds consumption and enormous stocks of cereals, fats and sugar are piling up.

Despite all the propaganda efforts, consumer levels in the communist countries are low. Communism, which ought to stimulate production, slows it down as is proved by the endemic agricultural crises caused by land-collectivization. In its practical application, the Marxist ideology has not been able to keep its promise of assuring a greater abundance of consumer goods for the people.

CHAPTER XIV

Overcrowding

1

THE most evident proof of the low living standard of the Soviet people is the persistence of overcrowding. The housing crisis has lasted from the beginning of the régime. It is a scourge that any Western people would consider intolerable.

It is fair to say that the great effort now being made to solve this painful problem began with Khrushchev who boasted quite rightly that the development of house building had assumed a 'really unprecedented rhythm'. In his speech to the XXII Party Congress on October 17, 1961 he said: 'The building programme for the period 1951-1960 has been carried out. More houses have been built in the past five years than in the preceding fifteen. In other words, comrades, about fifty million persons, or about a quarter of the whole population, are now in new houses.'

Despite these efforts and these undeniable results, the crisis persists. It is acknowledged in the Party programme for the XXII Congress. This admits that there still remains to be solved 'the most burning problem of the well-being of the Soviet people, that of housing'. As usual there are plenty of promises, but it has been carefully pointed out that overcrowding will continue for another twenty years. 'At the end of the second decade,' the programme states, 'every family, including young couples, will have a hygienic apartment to itself, with all conveniences. The old style peasant houses will be replaced, in the majority of cases by new modern houses, or—wherever possible—rebuilt with the aim of installing the necessary services.' A revealing confession this, that the peasant houses lack the most elementary hygienic services.

The seven-year plan earmarked three hundred and eighty milliard rubles, equivalent to about thirty-eight milliard dollars, for housing, intended to assure homes for about twenty-two million families, a little more than a third of the population. The programme provided for the building of houses with a total roofed area of 650,000,000 square metres.

Khrushchev has boasted of this programme, saying that for size

368

and speed of construction the Soviet housing programme is first in the world. 'In recent years our country has built, per thousand inhabitants, double the apartments built in the United States and in France and more than double the number built in Great Britain and Italy.' In order to prove Soviet superiority over the capitalist world, he based his figures on the data supplied by the United Nations Economic Commission for Europe for 1958. This shows that the percentage of apartments built in that year for every thousand inhabitants was as follows: England 5.5%, Italy 5.7%, France 7.2%, United States 7.2%, Sweden 8.5%, Federal Germany 9.4%, the Soviet Union 13% which rose in 1959 to 14.5%.

The head of the United States Housing and Home Finance Agency, Norman P. Mason, rejected such comparisons on August 15, 1960, when he declared that the Soviet boast of building houses at a faster rate than the United States was unfounded and created a false impression. 'Housing in the United States,' he said, 'is so much more advanced than in the Soviet Union that no comparison is possible.'

In fact, Khrushchev omitted to specify that the Soviet apartments do not measure more than forty-five square metres; often they are only thirty-six square metres, compared with a minimum of seventy-one square metres in the Western countries. A newly-built Soviet apartment is usually made up of two little rooms of four metres by four with fittings; in this space four persons must live. It is thus that the Soviet Union solves its housing crisis.

2

Even reduced to these minimal terms, it has not been possible, nor will it be possible for a long time to come, to assure housing for the whole population of the cities. As to the country people the situation, as will be seen, is far worse.

Khrushchev was forced to acknowledge, in his speech of October 17, 1961, that there was still 'a scarcity of accommodation' and that 'the housing problem remains acute'. The justification that he gave is typical of the Soviet system; after abounding in promises, he was later forced to admit that circumstances amounting to *force majeure* had postponed its being put into effect. These circumstances of *force majeure* are always the same: the calculations, the forecasts, the plans, have in actual performance proved less than the demand. 'The increase in the urban population of the Soviet Union,' declared Khrushchev, 'has in recent years considerably exceeded that estimated. By the end of the seven-year plan the urban population will have increased by about 15,000,000 more persons than was forecast; this means that more accommodation will be necessary. The Central Committee and the Soviet government are doing all that they can to speed up house construction.'

It seems incredible that the planning departments could have committed so glaring an error. It is, however, noteworthy that the planning system can be involved in errors of this scale.

The position is as follows. At the beginning of 1959 the housing area in the cities was, according to Soviet estimates, 789,000,000 square metres for an urban population of about 100,000,000 inhabitants. There was therefore an average of eight square metres of living space per person, whereas according to American standards, in normal conditions, the average is eighteen square metres. If this eighteen square metres be taken as the mean, the Soviet Union, in order to solve its crisis, would need to plan for more than 1,000,000,000 square metres of living space instead of the 650,000,000 laid down in the seven-year plan. Taking into account the increase forecast by Khrushchev of a further 15,000,000 new city dwellers, it would be necessary to add another 270,000,000 square metres, that is to say double the seven-year plan's programme of new housing. Perhaps this mean of eighteen square metres is too high, but undoubtedly the present one of eight square metres is too low, especially if one recalls communism's claim to be the régime of plenty and its promise to give its workers a living standard higher than that of the workers in capitalist countries. Therefore the effort to be made to equal the average living space of the Western worker is far more than that now being made. Nor will the problem be settled then. It will also be necessary to rebuild all the village houses, the famous wooden *izbas*, all, or nearly all, of which are very old, ramshackle and falling down, as is easy to see in the countryside near the capital.

In practice it also means to rebuild a great part of the old cities, beginning by abolishing all the damp, dark unhealthy basements that get their light from street level.

The two-year plan for 1964-1965 budgets for housing for 15,000,000 persons.

3

The new apartment blocks each contain hundreds of apartments. Two or three families camp out in each apartment, since no one, by law, can have a living area of more than nine square metres. But in the great cities, and especially in Moscow, it is very rare for any

Soviet citizen to have this maximum space. In Moscow the average up till now has been six square metres per person. Einaudi referred to these habitations as *loculi* (reserved graves). The area reserved for each person is roughly equal to a convict's cell. In fact, the cells in the Peter and Paul prison at Petersburg were six metres by three and a half, that is about twenty-one square metres, three times the area that the Soviet government allots to each of its citizens.

In the old buildings every large room serves several families, divided from one another by curtains. Countless anecdotes about overcrowding are current in Moscow. One of the best is as follows. A schoolmistress distributed pictures of Khrushchev to her pupils to hang in their homes. Next day one of them gave the picture back to her with a message from his mother to say that she couldn't hang it up.

'I will come myself to show your mother how to do it,' said the schoolmistress severely.

The boy answered that it was not ill-will, but that the family really had not got a wall to hang it on.

'Why? Haven't you a home?' asked the mistress. 'Don't you sleep in a room?'

'Yes,' replied the boy, 'but we have the middle of the room.'

4

The Soviet government tries to conceal the real reason for the housing shortage, because it is a reason that reflects no credit on the régime. Moscow was not bombed, so the crisis cannot be attributed to war damage. The reason is that the very rapid development of industry, at the very moment when land-collectivization was being carried out, drove millions of peasants into the cities to find work in the factories. The Soviet government concerned itself with building the factories and getting machinery for them; but did not trouble to provide housing for this immense mass of workers. From the first five-year plan to the beginning of World War II the urban population rose by 21,300,000 inhabitants to 58,000,000, that is to say it nearly tripled; but the housing area was increased by less than a third, from 127,800,000 square metres to only 164,700,000 square metres. In consequence the average living space per person was reduced from six square metres to less than three, scarcely 'twice as large as the grave in which a body is buried' as the Russian economist Prokopovich put it.

This is not a situation limited to Moscow. It is the same throughout all Russia and all the communist world. Whoever travels on the

Trans-Siberian is struck by the contrast between the impressive industrial plants in the new cities and the wretchedness of the houses. In the Western lands the flourishing of an industrial area, even as the fertility of an agricultural area, is shown by the comfort of the population on whom the wealth produced is poured out. But in Russia everything is forfeit to the state. *Vos non vobis mellificatis apes.* The workers have only the absolute minimum, the dregs, whatever the enterprise for which they work. Factory chimneys and cranes stand out against the skyline like giants crushing down the miserable hovels of man. This is state capitalism, which erects monumental factories, grandiose government offices and Party seats, as the Egypt of the Pharoahs raised temples and the tombs of its kings while its people rotted in the slime of the Nile.

The ramshackle *izbas* flank the railway line; in the stations old railway wagons are used as shelters; wherever you look there is a resigned multitude cramming the benches or sleeping on the ground as in the time of Tolstoy or Dostoyevsky.

It must be admitted that the Soviet people have started almost from scratch. When I visited Moscow in 1933 the people were living in the former shops or displaying their misery on the pavements. Today this sight is no longer seen, but almost a half of Moscow is made up of tumble-down hovels or old buildings ready for demolition. Even today the most frequent notice to be seen is 'Corner of room to let'.

5

Soviet builders are extending the use of prefabricated materials; light panels are lifted by a forest of cranes and fitted into frameworks of reinforced concrete. Work goes on day and night; in winter, even on the coldest days, and in summer. Whole districts spring up like mushrooms. Khrushchev boasted of the originality of the new technique. Instead of brick which has the measure of a man's hand, huge panels are used whose measure is that of the gigantic arms of the cranes.

But frankly these buildings, so praised by Soviet propaganda, have all the ugliness and all the drawbacks of every over-hasty operation. The new quarters are immense agglomerations of buildings all similar, mass-produced, of an exasperating banality, without originality of architectural form or pretence at elegance. The materials are sub-standard; the plaster peels off, the fixtures are flimsy, the doors and windows fit badly. These new homes, already peeling and badly finished, are old and worn out before they are inhabited; in a short time they are covered with a coarse filth like the hovels of the poor. One is struck on entering one of these dwellings by the stench of overcrowded humanity; a stink of boiled cabbage pervades everything.

Khrushchev himself has had to admit that 'sometimes, because of too great haste, the new buildings have many defects. The people, naturally, are angry and rightly so'.

6

Lack of an adequate maintenance system contributes to the rapid delapidation of these buildings. Communism boasts of the superiority of a régime of state ownership over one of private ownership; but reality shows that state property is no one's property, because no one looks after it.

Therefore everything goes to ruin. This spectacle of universal neglect would be enough to prove the utopia of a system that persists in denying the virtues of private property. On April 8, 1960 *Izvestia* describes the condition of a large building built scarcely five years earlier at 68 Mira Prospekt (Peace Avenue). The building comprises hundreds of apartments, as do all these Soviet ant-heaps. Several families live in each apartment. Naturally every family takes care of its own room only. A journalist made an investigation for *Izvestia*. Here is his description of the corridors: 'Walls peeling, ceilings and floors filthy, doors in a deplorable condition. The kitchen looks like a warehouse.' 'Why,' the journalist asked the tenants, 'don't you have the kitchen whitewashed? Why don't you clean the corridors?' 'The kitchen is not mine; it is communal,' he was told by everyone he asked. It was communal and therefore belonged to no one. The corridor too was nobody's business. Not to speak of the stairs, the lifts, the waste-chutes. They belonged to no one.

7

This overcrowding is an intolerable martyrdom for the Russians, as it would be for any other people. Sanitary services are communal. One must queue up to use them; one must wait one's turn to use the kitchen ranges. Friction between co-tenants because of gossip, suspicions and rancours is continual and there is always a tense atmosphere of distrust and hostility.

In the tiny rooms there is scarcely room for a bed and a table. There is no possibility of storing what makes up the household equipment of even the poorest Western family: linen, clothes, domestic utensils. No one knows where to put them. Many young people must postpone their marriages for lack of housing. Parents live in the same room as children and since marriages take place at an early age it often happens that still young parents live with children who have already passed the age of puberty, to their very great mutual embarrassment.

Cases of promiscuity and adultery are, naturally, common in such circumstances. The court records abound in tragi-comic episodes caused by overcrowding and anyone who has the chance of attending the hearings can tell of some very funny ones. Here is one that happened a few days after my arrival in Moscow. A young couple had to take accommodation in a room inhabited by an old woman. Shortly afterwards, the wife tired of her husband and remarried. Not being able to find anything better, she brought her second husband to the room, now divided by curtains into three parts, one for the old woman, one for the abandoned husband and the third for the newly-weds. Then the abandoned husband also remarried and brought his new companion to the hospitable room. What happened is easy to guess; the two brides soon began to tear one another's hair out. The dispute was brought before the magistrate who delivered a judgment of Solomon; both the husbands and wives had to go and live in the factory where they worked. At this point the old woman, who had till then been a silent witness of the proceedings, asked leave to speak. The judge in surprise asked what she had to say in a dispute that was none of her business.

'I want to say,' said the old woman, 'that the sentence is just. Now I shall have the whole room to myself. Long live Soviet justice!'

8

The most obvious consequence of this overcrowding is reciprocal control. Everyone knows everyone else's business and is a witness of the most intimate behaviour of his neighbours. The tenants' collective supervises everybody's way of life and in many cases gives information to the police. Often a girl may be censured for having relations with a foreigner or because she dresses in a way considered unbecoming for a worker. There is suspicion of anyone who spends more than his legitimate wage. On the slightest suspicion, the culprit is subjected to interrogation by the collective and forced to self-criticism.

There is an atmosphere of puritanism, which fails to hide

jealousies and which lends itself to the most repugnant forms of hypocrisy, reprisals and corruption.

It may therefore be easily understood what a torment it is for someone who has been working all day not to have a place in which to withdraw, in which to live his family life away from the prying eyes of his neighbours. Never can the Soviet citizen have a moment's freedom; never has he the right to be alone. It is like condemning a whole people to supervised imprisonment. Perhaps it is this lack of a domestic hearth that is the reason for the deep melancholy that one sees in so many Soviet people, and especially the people of Moscow.

9

All this is brought out, not only because the alleged Soviet lead in house construction is one of the most abused propaganda subjects, but because, despite the seriousness of the situation, the Soviet press is constantly reviling the Western countries for their workers' housing policy, and comparing the slums of London and New York with the newly-built quarters of the Soviet cities. Not a day passes without *Pravda* or *Izvestia* printing reports from Italy with descriptions and pictures of the slums of Naples, the *sassi* of Matera or the Quarticello of Rome. But what are we to say about the Moscow quarters of bad repute, where the foreigner is not encouraged to go, or the damp, crumbling Armenian quarter of Tbilisi or the mud hovels of Tashkent, Samarkand and Bukhara, or the miserable shacks of so many of the Siberian cities?

The truth of the matter is that the process of industrialization in Russia has resulted, despite communism, in the same sacrifices and the same sufferings that marked the rise of modern industry in the capitalist world. The same conditions, so criticized by Marx in the England of last century, are now being repeated, in an even worse degree, in Soviet Russia. Marx then wrote: 'The more rapid the accumulation of capital in an industrial or commercial city, the more rapid the inflow of exploitable human material and the more miserable the improvised shacks of the workers.' The situation is the same, whether the capital be state owned or privately owned. The creation of a modern industry in People's China is now going on at the price of even greater sufferings and sacrifices.

There is no need to go far from Moscow to get a clear idea of how the country people who make up half the Soviet population live. One of the favourite spots for a Sunday outing for the people of Moscow is Voskresenskoe, because of the natural beauty of the site.

It is about twenty kilometres from Moscow. In the centre of the village are the administrative offices of a kolkhoz and around them are grouped the houses, built for the most part of wood, wretched, ramshackle, and badly kept like almost all the Russian *izbas*. When I visited Voskresenskoe in April 1960 the houses were wallowing in a sea of mud after the thaw. The women, in waders, had to fetch their water from the well in buckets balanced at the two ends of a long pole, as they do in China. The village is linked to the capital by a bus route; but the road is almost impassable although at one time it was asphalted. That is the situation in the countryside only a few kilometres from the capital.

10

Though the houses are so poor and insufficient, it would be wrong to think that the Soviet cities are without a monumental magnificence. They have impressive vistas, and are notable for the frequency of public buildings, parks, avenues, open squares, especially in the town centres. Soviet urbanism deserves the most unstinted praise for its broad conception of a modern city; wide streets, good placing of markets, educational centres, institutes of culture and sportsgrounds. All the cities throughout the Soviet Union have architectural vistas of vast blocks, somewhat on the heavy side because modern functional architecture made from light materials is still little known, and therefore somewhat solemn and severe in general effect. The old houses, the churches and the palaces of the aristocracy have been restored with the greatest care. No churches have been built in the new cities.

It is fair to speak of Soviet urbanism. The cities have been multiplied by the stimulus of the régime and the creation of all these new centres is an undoubted sign of youthful vigour. The once deserted open spaces of Russia in Asia are spangled with farms, factories, power stations and cities. It is a flood of humanity expanding into a virgin world and showing all the signs of its natural exuberance. For the first time in history the heart of Asia is no longer the home of nomad peoples but of a settled population. A grandiose plan for the founding of new cities is being put into operation. The most picturesque sites in the heart of the Siberian forests on the shores of natural or artificial lakes are being chosen with the greatest care by the urbanists. Their plans provide, for each of these new cities, residential quarters for from five to ten thousand inhabitants, with parks around the schools, children's playgrounds and sportsgrounds. In this way the necklace of cities along the river Chulym is being created: Nazarovo, Kritovo, Achinsk, Itat, Bolshoi, Uliu, Bogotol. The same may be said of the garden-cities of the Taishet.

There is a state institute for the planning of these centres. It is headed by an engineer, Y. A. Babanyan, who is assisted by a band of young and enthusiastic designers, real poets of nature. Their ambition is to adapt the new cities to the natural scenery, retaining its original beauty. I have visited one of these centres in course of construction, Bratsk on the Angarà, in a landscape of woods, lakes and pine forests like a Japanese print. There live the experts who work on the dam and the electric power station on the river. It gives the general impression of a little Swiss city transported into the heart of Siberia.

But perhaps the most magnificent metropolis in this emergent world is Khabarovsk, the Russian gateway to China, from which it is separated by the impressive stream of the Amur. The city stretches along the bank of the Amur and its affluent the Ussuri, with a frontage of a good forty-five kilometres. It bristles with factory chimneys, pulses with life, with hotels, museums, institutes, wide tree-lined avenues that link its seven hills. It is these cities that are the real centres of civilized life amid the flood of the Asiatic peoples.

CHAPTER XV

The New Bourgeoisie

1

REDUCED to its simplest terms, communism means the organization of a classless society. Marx began with the idea that only in full economic and social equality was it possible to eliminate the exploitation of man by man.

When Marx, during his stay in France, began to shift the basis of his studies from philosophical to social and economic problems he was unable to avoid falling under the influence of the socialist thinkers then in vogue, who proposed to take up once more the process of social renewal which had begun with the French revolution and bring it to the final development which had been checked by the events of Thermidor. Having suppressed privileges of birth, it still remained to abolish those of wealth. Babeuf, who had tried to encourage the people along this path, was condemned, not without logical reason, for betraying the ideals of the Revolution. The men in the government who condemned Babeuf considered that an economic and social levelling such as that preached by him might involve the loss of the greatest conquest of the Revolution—liberty —and might imperil that measure of equality that the new laws had been successful in obtaining. In a word, there would have been a risk of compromising by fresh social conquests the political conquests of the Revolution.

What has happened in the communist world confirms the accuracy of this forecast. Soviet propaganda flatters itself by representing the Bolshevik revolution as the complement of the French; but nothing is more false historically than such a claim. To complete the French revolutionary movement, the Russians would have had to follow up the democratic reforms born of that movement, but instead they have followed quite a different path which has taken them far not only from those reforms but from the systems in force in the Western countries. These have been proved resistant to communist propaganda just because they do not want to lose the advantages assured them by the French revolution, which communism, with its egalitarian measures, would destroy.

2

On the other hand communism, while it has meant the loss of liberty, has not been able to install an egalitarian order. Furthermore, it is getting farther and farther away from such a mirage. The reason is simple enough; the more a society progresses, the more it splits up, as do all higher organisms, into a multiplicity of organs corresponding to a wide variety of functions. Therefore the social hierarchy becomes indispensable. For that reason the classes that the Bolshevik revolution claimed to have suppressed have been restored in the Soviet Union. It is noteworthy that neither Marx nor Engels ever defined a 'social class'. They considered that the difference between the bourgeoisie and the proletariat lay in the ownership by the former of the sources of production which made possible the exploitation of man by man. From this viewpoint the Soviet revolution, by its expropriation of all sources of production, has eliminated one of the causes of disparity between the classes. But is what the Marxists call the exploitation of man by man limited by the ownership of the sources of production or does it extend to every individual or collective superiority of economic and political power? In other words, if one understands by class differences disparities in economic, social and cultural position and especially functions, influence and power, then no one can deny in face of the evidence that classes have again been formed in Russia. This means that the supposed egalitarianism, to achieve which Marx entered the lists, does not exist in the country that is the cradle of communism.

3

The Soviet experiment could not be more completely bankrupt. After imposing the principle of equal remuneration for workers and executives, that is for manual and intellectual work alike, the Soviet Union under Stalin had to recreate the hierarchy when the dictator saw the factories deserted by the engineers and specialists and even by the skilled craftsmen. China, which is at the beginning of the itinerary followed by its ally, accuses Russia of becoming bourgeois, that is of re-creating the social hierarchy. That hierarchy has not only been re-created but was strengthened by Stalin who granted its members the fullest powers and an economic treatment quite different from that of their subordinates. Only at such a price was Russia industrialized.

Can a state live without such a hierarchy? That question had been debated by the socialist writers and especially by Saint-Simon, Fourier and Proudhon who had reached the conclusion that to install equality it was necessary to suppress the state since, as long as it existed, there would always be rulers and ruled, privileged and oppressed. Thus from one absurdity one reaches another absurdity. The Chinese have a well-known proverb: Who rides on a tiger cannot dismount. Paraphrasing this proverb, one may say that every utopia is tenable on paper; the difficulty is to apply it. Marx and Engels inherited from the socialists the conception that the state is the instrument of oppression by one class over another and that therefore communism, in order to create a classless society, must begin by abolishing the state. But the Soviet leaders, departing radically from the masters' teaching, have reinforced the state instead of abolishing it. By doing this they have formed a new hierarchy; in a word, they have created a new and very powerful ruling class. The withering away of the state has been postponed until the moment of transition from socialism to communism.

4

This is the thesis reaffirmed in the programme of the Soviet communist party at its XXII Congress and this is what Khrushchev repeated in his speeches to that Congress. It follows that only at the moment when communism is installed will the present order based on class differences be transformed into a classless social system. Khrushchev has been very explicit on this point. By reaffirming, in his speech on October 17, 1961, that 'the material and technical basis of communism will be built in the Soviet Union in the course of two decades' he has made it clear that such a pledge involves tasks of special importance, one of which will be to create a classless social system. 'The elimination of class differences,' he said, 'towards which we are tending will make possible an even greater homogeneity of society. . . . It is evident,' he underlined, 'that this will be a long and gradual process. Class differences will not be totally eliminated until a communist society has been wholly set up. . . . The classless communist society will be the highest form of human organization.'

The admission is clear that, as things are today, class differences still exist in the Soviet Union and their elimination has been postponed to the moment when it will be possible to put into practice the utopian dream of the transition to communism. We are still in the world of promises and propaganda. The reality is quite different. It is not true that the Soviet Union is tending towards the elimination of class differences; the truth is quite the contrary. These differences are becoming greater and everything is conspiring to increase them. That is the point.

5

The truth, which every visitor to Russia can see with his own eyes, is that inequalities of payment, of housing and of clothing exist. In Moscow, as in all other cities, there are hovels and palaces. Some have flats in marble skyscrapers whence one enjoys a superb view over the city, while others must content themselves with wooden shacks swarming with bugs. There are high, airy quarters that look down over Moscow and there are human ant-heaps of the workers' quarters. There are high salaries and minimum wages. Some go about in cars and others on foot. There are, in fact, rich and poor. And it always will be this way, because only a few privileged persons will have a car, a flat with a view, a private *dacha* (country house), and even if communism is installed these luxury dwellings will certainly not be demolished, nor the splendid *dachas* pulled down.

The tourist who visits Moscow must not fail to wander in the surroundings of the capital, which are perhaps the most picturesque districts of all Russia; huge watercourses meander through a rolling countryside of dense forests of fir, pine and birch. These woods are mostly enclosed and reserved for the enjoyment of the privileged few. Often a metalled road leads off the highway; these are private roads to which the public is forbidden access and which lead to the villas of the leaders. The whole countryside around Moscow is dotted with these *dachas*, always built in the loveliest spots, on little lakes or watercourses with private beaches. The palisades which surround them are high, so that no furtive glances may penetrate their inviolable recesses. There is little difference between the villas of the former aristocracy and those of the new aristocracy. The buildings have several storeys, with wide verandas, terraces and galleries. Nothing is so true as the French adage: *Plus ça change, plus c'est la même chose*. The eternal principle of all revolutions is monotonously repeated: Get up that I may take your seat.

This economic inequality and the formation of new classes in the heart of Soviet society not only impresses the foreign visitor but is looked on with grave disapproval by the Soviet people themselves who still believe in the validity of Marxist principles. Here is the confession of one of them, the poet Yevtushenko, who expresses himself thus in his autobiography: 'With revolutionary vigilance I looked uneasily at the skyscrapers rising in Moscow for the bureaucratic élite, whereas the mass of Muscovites live in noisome over-crowded dens. . . . I compared the privileges of many state officials who enjoy, other than their salaries, fringe benefits, the so-called "blue envelopes", which often exceed by two or three times their actual salary, with the misery of some badly-paid professions.'

Such a variance of social situation has now been reached after the frantic efforts of the first years of the revolution to level society. But evolution has forced the restoration and accentuation of inequalities between class and class. Every bourgeois family tries, with all its force, to hand on to its children the superior social position which it has attained. The transmission of inheritance, which in the Soviet Union is almost exempt from death duties, makes it easy to hand on what has been acquired from father to son. Khrushchev tried to swim against the tide, and the scholastic reform, among other things, aimed at checking this tendency towards bourgeois ideals, by preventing entry to the higher educational establishments from becoming a privilege of the bourgeois families.

6

But beyond this unrestrained tendency of the upper classes to consolidate their positions and make them permanent, there are many other forces that converge to accentuate social inequalities. Predominant among them is the drive for an increase in consumer goods. The government, if it wants to keep even a semblance of democracy, cannot escape this tremendous pressure towards higher living standards. Nor will it be able to satisfy so universal an aspiration without stimulating the interests of the individual to produce more by remunerating him, not according to a universal norm common to all which would make his productivity decline to the lowest common denominator but according to his individual yield. Therefore the disparities become more acute.

It is this that hampers the transition from the socialist to the communist formula. The socialist formula 'to each according to his abilities' is merely the capitalist formula of material incentive, as the communists themselves admit, to the point of saying that it is necessary to pass on to the communist formula of a purely moral incentive just in order to eliminate this relic of capitalist influence. The fact is that these relics of capitalism are the only ferments of progress. The socialist—or capitalist—formula relies upon self-interest, upon the urge to become rich. It is not possible to dissociate it from this basis without provoking a collapse in production. But the maintenance of the socialist formula not only prevents the elimination of inequalities, but it accentuates them, since it relies on differing physical and intellectual abilities in the interest of maximum productivity. Therefore the present so-called socialist régime, while it affirms the principle of equality, in reality admits and encourages inequalities. It is one of the fundamental contradictions of the régime which is compelled to put into operation principles that it continually violates in everyday life.

How did Khrushchev envisage the creation of a classless communist society? He explained this in his speech on October 17, 1961, to the XXII Congress. He outlined three phases: suppression of the exploiting capitalist classes based on private ownership of the sources of production, the organization of a collective economy of wide scope, and the elimination of class distinctions between workers and peasants, between the cities and the countryside, between physical and intellectual labour. 'It is evident,' Khrushchev insisted, 'that our further progress towards a classless society is bound up, above all, with the rapid increase of productive forces.' This confirms the necessity of keeping in force for the meantime the socialist formula, that is to say strengthening and developing class differences.

CHAPTER XVI

The Party Dictatorship

1

TO the Soviet claim that true freedom exists only in the communist world, it is easy to reply that there can be no freedom where only one party exists and that party is identified with the state. Wherever a one-party system is in force, voting can only be a plebiscite since the elector is allowed no choice. Voting therefore becomes merely a formality.

During Khrushchev's visit to America, Senator Green asked him to explain Soviet electoral mechanics. 'It is true,' Khrushchev replied, 'that there is only one party in the Soviet Union. At first, when we too had antagonistic classes, there were other parties in our parliament. But later the structure of our society was changed. Now we no longer have antagonistic classes and the interests of the whole of the working people are represented by the communist party, that is the party of the working people.' Khrushchev returned to his argument in greater detail in a television appearance during his visit to France. 'We are often reproached,' he said 'for having only one party in our country. But this can only be argued by someone who does not know Soviet reality and has a poor understanding of those communal ideas of what a class, a party and a people are. Let us suppose for a moment that various parties spring up in the Soviet Union. Then the question would arise who would they represent and of what interests would they become the mouthpiece. No party, large or small, exists in a void, but represents a particular class or social state and expresses its interests. But in the Soviet Union there are no antagonistic classes and in consequence there is no basis for a multi-party system.'

The reply repeats an old Stalinist thesis that sins against logic and is not in accord with historical truth. Parties contend for the votes of the electors independently of the class to which they belong. According to Soviet logic, there must be dozens of classes in those countries which have dozens of parties, and in those countries where the electoral struggle is restricted to two parties only that party which represents the interests of the most numerous class, the proletariat, must always win. Now it is a fact that in England and the United States where a two-party system prevails, the two parties alternate in power for the simple reason that each of them obtains the votes of electoral supporters who are not necessarily members of any particular class.

Nor is the Soviet thesis in accord with historical truth, because for some years after the October revolution which suppressed class differences the soviets, that is to say the assemblies of workers, peasants and soldiers, the sole remaining class, were composed not only of Bolsheviks, but also of Mensheviks, revolutionary socialists and anarchists. These parties were a formidable competition to the communists. And it was just in order to rid themselves of this opposition that the communists suppressed the rival parties.

In the light of these precedents one cannot but feel surprised at the outbursts of indignation in the Soviet press against Federal Germany for having outlawed communist organizations. Was it acting any differently from Soviet Russia in defence of its régime?

A confession that the single party serves to hinder the free expression of the people's will was unconsciously made by Kadar, the head of the Hungarian government, during Khrushchev's visit to Budapest towards the end of 1959. Speaking to the Hungarian Communist Party Congress, while the memory of the tragic events of three years before was still fresh, Kadar announced that the Soviet troops would remain in Hungary and rejected the idea of a return to a multi-party régime because, he said, such a system would inevitably lead to a new 'counter-revolution', that is to say the expression of the contrary will of the majority. 'The government,' he said, is developing democracy within the framework of the National People's Front which united all the best elements in the country.' This is democracy in a communist country; one party imposed by a dictatorial government which rules by the aid of foreign bayonets under the nightmare of imminent counter-revolution. That did not prevent Khrushchev in his reply from reaffirming imperturbably that freedom existed only in the communist world.

No example shows better than the one cited above that the single party means the denial of liberty. A régime based on a single party betrays its lack of confidence in the maturity and the sense of responsibility of the electorate and reveals its fears of not being able to rely on the firm support of the majority.

2

In fact the communist party was not conceived by Lenin as a

democratic organization destined to compete with other democratic organizations, but as a revolutionary force representing the will of the proletariat and designed to ensure its predominance according to Marxist dogmas. In this conception there is no room for dialectics and even less for collaboration with other parties, save to use them as stepping stones to power and to kick them down again afterwards.

The anti-democratic tradition, therefore, began with Lenin. To ensure the predominance of his ideas he provoked the split in the Russian social-democrats in 1903 between Bolsheviks and Mensheviks at the second Congress held in Brussels and London in that year under the chairmanship of Trotsky. A large number of the delegates opposed him because, respectful of democratic principles, they wanted the party to be the real interpreter of the wishes of the people and to be at its service. Basically the conflict was between the democratic and revolutionary viewpoints, between the rights of the majority and those of a minority resolved to impose its views by force.

The conflict which had already divided Western socialism between the reformers and the extremists thus emerged during the congress debates. The majority of the Russian socialists stood for the democratic principles prevailing in Western lands. The responsibility for causing a fresh split between Russia and the West rests squarely on Lenin.

His genius was in conceiving and organizing a party that was to become the most reliable, manoeuvreable and deadly revolutionary weapon. This weapon had to serve not only to overthrow the established order but to keep the people under its control, were it or were it not in agreement with the postulates of his policy. When the Party is defined as an anti-democratic organization, it means that it pays no heed to the will of the people. Lenin never made any secret of his distrust of the judgment of the proletariat. This is the salient feature of his writings. From the first numbers of *Iskra* (*The Spark*) he supported the idea that the working class could not by itself acquire a knowledge either of its interests or of the method of making them prevail. At the Social-Democratic Congress of 1903, where the schism took place, he declared that it was untrue to say that 'the development of class-consciousness is spontaneous. . . . There is no conscious activity among the workers'. This meant that it was a result of propaganda. That, in a nutshell, was the doctrine set out in Lenin's book entitled *What's to be done?*

Once one refuses to admit 'any conscious activity' among the people, little importance can be attached to its will, since this is not inspired and directed by any clear awareness of its interests. These are to be watched over by the Party, the depository and interpreter of the Marxist doctrine.

Here one comes across one of those 'dialectical contradictions' so frequent in the socialist doctrine, because of the difficulty of putting into practice certain ideological postulates without becoming involved in the most obvious inconsistencies. By a process whose nature no one has been able to explain, Lenin derived from historical materialism the theory that the protagonist of history is the anonymous mass of the people, in which the consciousness of fresh historical exigencies will mature. He rejects with polemical intransigence the humanist conception of Plekhanov of the function of the individual in history. But at the same time he denies the people any ability to express its will and, in actual fact, concentrates all power in his own person. The mass reveres him as the real artificer of the revolution. Thus he affirms a theory which he is the first, by his own behaviour, to belie.

All Lenin's thinking and activities revolve around this inherent contradiction. Since it is the historical protagonist the proletariat must confirm his dictatorship; but it must be kept, as indeed it is today, under a constant guardianship as though it were still in its minority. The organ of control is the Party, which perfected its organization once its task as the advance guard of the revolution became less after the proclamation of the dictatorship of the proletariat. From that time onward it concentrated on its task of controlling the proletarian masses.

3

It was not easy to get the people to accept so anti-democratic an idea: that the Party was not the organ by which the will of the people is expressed and put into action, but the central power that issued and imposed its orders. The conflict which had arisen between Bolsheviks and Mensheviks in 1903 flared up again, even more dangerously, between Party and people when, after the revolutionary cycle had been closed at the end of the civil war between Reds and Whites, there was a demand for the setting up of really democratic ordinances. It has already been noted that many of his most faithful supporters, who had stood by Lenin during the revolution, turned against him when they became aware of the irremediable conflict between their wishes, their interests and their demands and the will imposed on them by the higher Party organs.

What else, in fact, did the Kronstadt sailors demand in their revolt against the dictatorship of the communist party than to return to the origins of the revolution when the power was in the hands of the soviets of soldiers, workers and peasants, that is in the hands of the freely elected representatives of the people? Already the parties hostile to the Bolsheviks had been suppressed and no opposition was being tolerated in the Party itself or in the government.

The crisis came during the debate at the X Party Congress when the leaders of the workers' opposition, Shlyapnikov and Aleksandra Kollontai, insisted that, consistent with the promises of the revolution, the trade unions should be granted autonomy and control over the economic life of the country. Only in such a way would the dictatorship of the proletariat and the transference to the workers and peasants of the sources of production be a concrete reality and not an empty formula. In fact, the soldiers and workers wanted a real democracy which would be able to enforce the people's rights. But the dictatorship of the proletariat was opposed by the dictatorship of the Party.

The reaction was harshly crushed and with it disappeared the last supporters of the democratic revolution. Once again violence won the day. 'We have wasted enough time in talk,' Lenin declared to the X Congress on March 9, 1921. 'I must tell you that it is better to argue with rifles than with the theses put forward by the workers' opposition. . . . We have no need now, comrades, of an opposition. This is not the time for it; either here or there, either with a rifle or with the opposition. . . . What are we to do with an opposition, comrades?'

The crisis ended with the decision of the Congress to forbid the formation of any opposition group within the Party. It was the gravestone of any attempt to make the Party a democratic organization. Its dictatorial character was finally approved and, consequently, its separation from the people, which no longer had any power to influence its decisions.

Trotsky was the most energetic supporter of Party omnipotence in the struggle against the 'workers' opposition'. He declared that the Party was the only force 'capable of safeguarding the October conquests', 'the only instrument of historical progress' and that 'nothing can be right which is against it'. He thus signed his own death-warrant; the omnipotence that he wanted for the Party smashed him to pieces.

One who had a clear vision of the evils in store was Bukharin. He did not hesitate to say: 'The root of the evil is in the complete fusion of Party and state.' It was the logical consequence of the single Party thesis. Trotsky, when he became aware of the danger, demanded that Party leaders be elected by all members by secret vote, rather than be selected from a restricted group. But by then the oligarchic structure had become firmly established.

4

It is hard to understand Lenin's ideas and actions if one does not start from the conception that the aim to which he subordinated all else was the triumph of the proletarian revolution. This explains the novelty of the political organization created by him, radically different from all other political parties. He needed shock troops which would break open the way for the disorganized violence of the proletarian masses. He therefore conceived a very closely knit association of selected working class elements, unquestioningly and unhesitatingly obedient to the orders and the will of the supreme leadership. He thus had at his disposal a force devoted to his will, ready to broadcast his ideas and to overwhelm by its force and resolution the ignorant and the waverers who are always in the majority.

In this lay the genius of Lenin and the secret of his success.

It is possible to see in the dictatorial character impressed by him on the Party organization a reflection of his own temperament, little inclined to discussion or to compromise. That is incontestable. He assigned to it the duties of a commando group, a reliable, disciplined and fanatic advance guard, always ready to hurl itself into the mêlée. When Lenin first began his revolutionary activities, he found himself having to deal with the amorphous mass of the Russian proletariat, which in the early years of this century was mainly illiterate and totally inexpert in any form of organization. It is true that a class consciousness had been awakened among the workers and that after the triumph of the October days it would have been comprehensible for him to have agreed that the people should express its will freely and that the Party should interpret its desires.

The real reason for his intransigence and for the dictatorial structure given to the Party is not only, nor even mainly, to be sought in the causes mentioned above, but essentially in the dogmatic nature of the doctrine that inspired his actions. The people, that is to say the electorate, whatever its will and its interests, could not impose the aims to be achieved nor even express its preference, because these aims had already been rigidly established by the official Party doctrine, which had even laid down the means by which they were to be achieved. The people must advance along the narrow path indicated by Marxism. Any other way was out of the question. Therefore it was impossible for anyone to opt for any other party, since all formulas must be heretical if they were contrary to the truth laid down by the doctrine, nor could he dissociate himself from that one party which alone held the true doctrine, whose interpretation was the privilege and monopoly of a few initiates.

The anti-democratic nature of the régime conceived and constructed by Lenin with iron logic derived from its ideological basis. The programmes and formulas of the Party cannot be disputed because they represent scientific and absolute truth. This is the absurd conception, more mediaeval than modern, on the basis of which the world is to be revolutionized. Elections are a pure formality without importance, because the will of the electors carries no weight before the dogmatic impositions of the truth from above. We are, obviously, at the very antithesis of liberty.

There are two consequences of this Marxist dogmatism; an undisputed authority, the interpreter of the doctrine, and an organization able to impose this truth upon all. In other words, dictatorship of the leader and dictatorship of the Party. From one consequence to the other, we reach the cult of the personality from whom, in the final analysis, all orders come. In the Party structure as demanded by Lenin after his break with his colleagues on *Iskra* there is no place for 'collegial direction'. This was a convenient thesis to mask the unpalatable reality. From then on it was not difficult to foresee the inevitable development of Lenin's premises. Leon Trotsky, who presided over the debates at which Lenin put forward his ideas, prophesied: 'The Party apparatus will take the place of the Party itself; the Central Committee will take the place of the apparatus and finally the dictator will take the place of the Central Committee.' Thus the façade is saved, because the Party speaks in the name of the people, the Central Committee in the name of the Party and the dictator in the name of the Central Committee.

The system is devised in such a way that whoever dominates the Party rules Russia on the sole condition that the unity of the Party itself is maintained. This must be, to use one of Khrushchev's favourite expressions, monolithic. 'Our Party is now more monolithic than ever,' he said after the elimination of the anti-Party group which had tried to overthrow him. But sometimes that unity is like the Axum monolith—in several pieces.

5

Unity depends on the cohesion of the apparatus. Without this there is no Party, even as there is no church without clergy. The

Marxist doctrine is so hermetic that it is hard to reveal it to the people without the aid of official interpreters. Carew Hunt in his *Theory and Practice of Communism* justly observes that Marx 'for a writer who claimed that his work was scientific, took altogether insufficient pains to make himself understood, and was often obscure and careless in expression'.[1]

Perhaps just because of this hermeticism which makes the doctrine incomprehensible to the masses, the Soviet leaders have succeeded, even if not completely, in avoiding the impassioned controversies that rend so many other parties. The controversies about dogmatism and revisionism which agitate the communist world find a weak echo among the masses who can only with difficulty understand the agreed terminology, the more so as these controversies barely conceal, under an ideological veil, clashes of political and economic interests. The abstruse nature of the conceptions makes an exegesis necessary, alien to the population which, in the final analysis, is called on to suffer the application. Therefore an intelligentsia is called for, a virtual General Staff, whose cadres are formed in the Party schools.

Into the higher Party school at Moscow come persons from all parts of the world to receive a sort of official consecration that will serve them as an ordination.

In this way the apparatus is formed that helps to maintain on the same model hierarchic structure of the communist parties of the various countries. So too are diffused the instructions that Moscow circulates to the masses of the communist obedience throughout the world. Therefore the hierarchs continually come to the Mecca of the Red world, nor do they omit to celebrate the ritual at the tomb of the prophet.

The conception of this apparatus is also, by its peculiarity, an innovation of communist genius. Even before Lenin, his master Yuri Valentinovich Plekhanov had realized the necessity for a corps of propagandists specially trained in the study of Marxism to indoctrinate and organize the masses. But Plekhanov always began with the idea of a democratic party and not a revolutionary force.

Today the apparatus is still the essential force of every communist party, the advance guard of the revolution, the hard core of the movement. *Pravda* was quite right when it said in its editorial of July 6, 1956: 'The Party has been, is and will be the sole master of the will, the sole exponent of the thoughts and hopes, the sole guide and the sole organizer of the people.'

It may well be said that the successes of the communist parties

[1] R. N. Carew Hunt, *Theory and Practice of Communism*, Chapter 4, Section 5. Geoffrey Bles, London, 1950.

are due more to their iron organization than to the value of the ideas which they represent. Their rapid diffusion throughout the world recalls the amazing expansion of Islam, more by force of arms than for the substance of its ideas.

Against this rigid structure the democratic parties fight in a situation of marked inferiority, all of them more or less hampered by the rules of the electoral and parliamentary game, their scrupulousness in observing legality and their respect for the ideas of others.

6

The reforming genius of Lenin was not shown only in the conception of a party exactly corresponding to the tasks assigned to it, but also in the elaboration of the tactics which should follow the triumph of the revolution that was his prime objective. These tactics, which he drew up on the inspiration of the military science of Klausewitz, were designed, as they still are today, to confuse his adversaries and to take by surprise those who hold power.

From this was born the idea of a militarily disciplined party entirely dependent upon him personally. From the first moment when he collaborated on *Iskra* Lenin claimed a monopoly of the orthodox interpretation of Marxism. The bond between him and his followers had to be unconditional and fanatical adhesion to his ideas.

He formed these first communists according to a model that has become a mould. By the sole fact of belonging to the Party they must renounce every belief, every personal desire, so that they no longer had any will or any belief save that of the Party as impersonated in himself. He appropriated the reckless doctrine of the nihilists and modelled the communist type on their followers. But what was new was that these followers instead of acting in isolation, as was the nihilist tactic, were trained to act in groups. Thus were formed the cells, linked to one another through a hierarchy that moulded them into an organization with responsible cadres, General Staffs, plans and a rational apportionment of duties.

From the chaos of nihilism, which had never succeeded in forming a disciplined movement, Lenin forged the iron rule of an organized party. His central idea was always the necessity for a revolution which should make *tabula rasa* of the social order, so as to build on virgin soil, freed from the relics of the past, the society dreamed of by Marx and Engels in its entirety and without modifications of any kind.

The extremist nature of his propaganda attracted to him the most combative elements, ready for anything. He himself chose his close collaborators. For that reason he instituted the principle of co-option, that is of appointment from above. He rejected on principle and by inclination the democratic system of election. There was no congress in which he did not manoeuvre, often by irregular methods, for the adoption of his own ideas and the appointment of his nominees, without troubling himself about majorities. For a revolutionary, legality, order and good faith are merely prejudices devoid of meaning. It was in fact a personal dictatorship, which created the tradition that still exists.

7

This should be remembered; because the doctrine and the practice of Lenin remain the doctrine and practice of all communist parties. Absolute automatism, *perinde ac cadaver*, is demanded from every member. Every tie of family, country or religion, every duty towards him or his, every bond of blood, every interest is cancelled by the tie of obedience to the Party chiefs. The real obstacle to the diffusion of the movement is the Christian conscience of the Western peoples. The more enlightened the consciousness, the stronger the sense of personal dignity, the more repugnant is the annihilation of personality and the idea of becoming a mere instrument of another's will for the execution of schemes whose value one is unable to assess. Such a conception can thrive in the Orient but can never take root in the Western world.

The existence of communist parties outside Russia raises serious problems, especially as their leaders receive secret orders from a foreign power. Such orders are secret, precisely because they come from a foreign power. It follows that the disciples of these organizations are required to carry out orders whose origins they cannot know, nor can they know in whose interest these orders are given nor what power they benefit. There is no cultivated, active and intelligent body of youth that will countenance so slavish and irresponsible an adhesion to the occult intrigues of a tyrannical, distant and hostile power. 'This association of communism with Russia,' observes Isaac Deutscher, 'has been a basic cause of the failure of communism throughout the West during the greater part of this century.'[2]

Once accepted by the Party, the applicant becomes its prisoner, forced to obey unconditionally the orders of its leaders. The well-known principles apply: 'The Party is always right', 'The only truth is to be found in the Party', 'Only the Party's interests matter'.

[2] Isaac Deutscher, *The Great Contest*, p. 58, Oxford University Press, London, 1960.

Criticism is not tolerated, still less opposition, the recognized sign of an independent attitude, incompatible with discipline.

Control over the conduct and opinions of every member is rigorous and continual; informing is universal. The ways of exerting pressure in order to keep members in the ranks are many and varied, the punishments exceedingly severe. Special dossiers are kept on every individual in order to exert pressure or retaliation. Individuals under suspicion are subjected to self-criticism, the most humiliating method of destroying personality. Weighed down by the accusations, unable to stand up for himself, the suspected man, to avoid the worst, humbles himself. There is no escape for the individual from the monstrous Party machine that crushes him. From self-criticism the communist emerges morally prostrate; every sense of dignity is stripped from him. Not even the Chinese have invented so refined an instrument of torture to destroy the soul. Herbert Preuss, who was a communist leader in Pankow, Germany, says that it is remarkable that under the pressure of the Party atmosphere so many comrades allow themselves to be forced into the most degrading self-criticism. There are some who have admitted things and confessed to weaknesses (and even the deepest causes of those weaknesses) which they themselves did not believe. Some make a pitiful impression, because they admit everything that is put into their mouths, with a doleful voice, swearing servilely that they will do better. How is it possible, he says, that grown men, some of them even respected savants, can degrade themselves in so shameful a manner, often against their own inner convictions.[3]

The author mentions the reprisals put into effect by the Party to shatter even the proudest temperaments. He says that recalcitrant comrades are publicly inscribed on the roll of shame, their names posted on the factory news-sheet and quoted in the radio transmissions as reactionary and backward elements. What is worse, they and their families are reduced to hunger.

In the countries where communism is in power it is not possible to resign from the Party. The Party can, however, as a final punishment, expel the member who no longer adheres to the communist faith, branding him as 'an enemy of the Party', which amounts to a sentence of civic death.

[3] Pasternak in *Dr Zhivago* says: 'People slandered and accused themselves, not only out of terror but of their own will, from a morbidly destructive impulse, in a state of metaphysical trance, carried away by that passion for self-condemnation which cannot be checked once it has been given free rein.' Boris Pasternak, *Dr Zhivago*, p. 409, Collins, London, 1958.

To maintain such an iron discipline, which ensures an unbreak-able cohesion, carefully selected cadres are trained in the Party schools. There are schools of every grade with courses of every duration for training officials, from local schools with short courses to the higher schools which are virtually Party universities. Pupils that show proof of greater ability are sent to finish their training in Moscow. The teaching at these schools is both theoretical and practical. The student is trained in public debate, in giving lectures, editing reports and problems of organization.

These cadres form the skeleton of the Party. The network of cells, like the tentacles of an octopus, extend from the major to the minor centres, supervising all the details of individual and collective life. In the Soviet Union the Party organizations extend to the sections and cells which are the nerve-ends of the system. They are dependent on the *raikom*, or district committee, on the *gorkom*, or city com-mittee, or on the *obkom*, or provincial committee. In the villages the secretary of the *raikom* is a sort of universal arbiter.

To give an idea of the capillary ramifications of the Party in all sectors of economic and social life, it is enough to say that, according to Khrushchev's reports to the XXII Party Congress, the Party has:

41,830 organizations in industrial enterprises;
10,427 organizations in building centres;
18,938 organizations in the railway and transport services;
44,387 organizations in the kolkhozes;
9,206 organizations in the sovkhozes.

'These organizations,' commented Khrushchev, 'are the backbone of the Party and daily develop their activities among the mass of the people. The success of our cause depends on the quality of the organization and political work of these lower units of the Party.'

After the November 1963 reforms the Party organs at city and *oblast* (regional) level are no longer based on territorial but on pro-ductive criteria. In every *oblast* or *krai* there is a Party industrial committee and a Party agricultural committee. On them are de-pendent the production committees in the collective and state farms and in the factories.

The Central Committee, which is the directive organ of the Party, controls the activities of all these committees through two offices directly dependent on it; one for agriculture and one for industry. There is also a commission on ideological questions and another on Party organization, both dependent on the Central Committee.

Through this network of organs the orders of the Central Committee, which is the directive organ of the Party, reach the periphery. All the sections are thus kept in touch with the questions of the day and are instructed in the manner of thinking about them. One of the elements of Party strength is this indoctrination at all times which enables its members to set the tone of public opinion.[4]

In the communist countries the competence of the Party extends to all state affairs, because it issues directives on all of them, carries out the preparatory studies, sets the tone for the press and leads public opinion. Because of this very wide competence the Secretariat of the Central Committee is a sort of state within the state. Its countless departments or sections not only concern themselves with organization and propaganda but are virtually duplicates of the state administrative departments and deal with matters of internal and external policy, finances, economy, education and the like, always in the greatest secrecy. Since often, as was until recently the case in the Soviet Union, the Party Secretary is also Head of State he relies on the co-operation of the Secretariat in competition with, often unbeknown to and sometimes even in opposition to, the competent state authorities.

In this way the Party is well informed about everything and is well able to control, to support and to urge on the departments which must carry out the application of the orders. In the factories, in the kolkhozes, in all enterprises, the watchfulness of the Party is incessant and its activities multiform.

9

The secret of its success is mainly to be ascribed to the detailed preparation of every undertaking. Before taking part in meetings of any importance, there are preparatory meetings in which the subjects to be discussed and the aims to be achieved are explained; the duties are apportioned and the names of the comrades to be elected are made known. The tactics to be followed are described in detail. Everyone receives clear orders so as not to be taken by surprise and to have an answer for everything. Thus even small minorities, compact and well managed, are able to prevail in the disorder of the discussions and the uncertainties of the many.

Another secret of its success is the unscrupulousness of its methods. The only thing that counts is success. What is useful is true. Thus a principle may be temporarily renounced in order to

[4] The Plenum of the Central Committee at its session in November 1964 announced that 'it is necessary to return to the territorial principle in the structure of the Party and its control organs', in conformity with the Party programme approved by the XXII Party Congress.

save the day. Lenin's famous decree of October 26, 1917 which granted the land to the peasants renounced the principle of expropriation of the means of production.

For the communists contradictions and violations of principle are only transitory phases, through which it is sometimes necessary to pass to reacquire popularity and strength. 'It may be objected,' Stalin observed in such a case in his report to the XVI Party Congress, 'that it is a contradiction to put the question in this way. But do we not find the same contradiction in our conception of the state? We stand for the abolition of the state. None the less we are for the strengthening of the dictatorship of the proletariat which means the strongest and most powerful of all forms of state hitherto existent. . . . Is this contradictory? Yes, it is contradictory. But it is a vital contradiction that Marxist dialectics perfectly reflect.'

10

These unscrupulous methods, in which what is promised today is taken away again tomorrow, make it extremely difficult to find an answer to communist propaganda. Its tactics are to take every advantage of the good faith of the masses, twisting the sense of words to make them mean the opposite of what they say. This is especially true for those much-abused words: liberty, justice, democracy and peace. In Russia public opinion is so experienced in these tactics that there is a story about a man who called in the doctor to treat him for a nervous disturbance.

'You have nothing the matter with you,' the doctor told him.

'Yet, doctor, I always seem to be hearing one thing and seeing another.'

Thanks to iron discipline, its solid organization and the elasticity of its methods the Party, despite the number and variety of its organs, is a machine docile and obedient to him who commands it. There is no personage, no matter how popular and powerful, who can save himself if he sets himself up against the Party. Trotsky, who had led the Red armies to victory and saved the revolution, did not succeed; nor did Marshal Zhukov, the hero of the last war. Almost all of Lenin's original companions have been liquidated under the shameful accusation of treason. Nor did the power of the terrible police save Beria and his predecessors from execution.

The power of the Party is concentrated in the hands of the First Secretary. The means at his disposal to put pressure on all the leaders and members of the elective organs allow him to overcome every resistance. Stalin succeeded in suppressing seventy per cent of the members of the Central Committee; which shows how weak is

397

the power of that supreme organ which was not even able to save the lives of its own members.

11

The existence of a single party which controls everything and decides everything and which has such formidable powers at its disposal reduces the freedom of the individual to nothing. The reforms which the Party proposed to the XXII Congress and which Khrushchev boasted of in his speeches must be evaluated in the light of this situation. In fact, these reforms were of very little importance. 'It is opportune,' the Party programme says, 'to renew at each election at least a third of the representatives in the soviets.' This is intended to give the largest possible number of persons the chance to rise to positions of control and gain experience of public affairs. Therefore the principle was accepted that 'the executive leaders of the organs of authority of the Union, of the republics and of the local soviets cannot be elected for more than three successive terms'. Exceptions are made in cases where the candidate is re-elected with not less than three-quarters of the votes.

But it is difficult to see in such a system 'a great step forward in the development of democracy' as Khrushchev has defined it. He tried to prove that the workers take an active part in the direction of public affairs. The Party has proposed, for example, that the most important law projects be subject to a referendum. A reason for pride, frequently repeated in official speeches and in the press, is the existence of real democracy in the Soviet Union, that is to say the direct participation of the masses in the control of the economy through the medium of collective decisions. But this is a mere fiction, as workers in the factories have told us so many times, because the decisions are taken without the most elementary guarantees for the respect for freedom of opinion.

Formally, there are consultations on matters of importance with the factory workers, the members of the collective farms, the workers on commercial, construction and transport enterprises, who are summoned to full assemblies. But it is the Party which takes the initiative through its members and which keeps control of the deliberations; for example it decides the agenda beforehand and chooses those who are to speak. The speech which the man chosen will make is drawn up earlier and he must stick to his text. There is nothing left for the public save to act as chorus. If it is a question of internal elections, the lists are prepared beforehand.

There is, therefore, a democratic façade based on Khrushchev's liberalizing reforms; but behind that façade the threads remain firmly in the hands of the Party even when it is a question of hundreds and thousands of assemblies, which give the impression of a popular referendum. In a word, it is not the masses that control the Party but the Party that controls the masses. Because the Party is unified it is able to impose its will.

In his speech on October 18, 1961, at the XXII Party Congress, Khrushchev quoted, as a proof of the democratic system in the Soviet Union, the debates on the Party programme which had taken place 'on an unprecedented scale' at meetings in all sections, at local and regional conferences, as well as in the Party congresses of the communist parties of the federated republics. There were in all more than half a million meetings at which 4,600,000 persons spoke in the presence of 73,000,000 participants. 'The Congress has every right to claim,' Khrushchev declared, 'that this programme has been unanimously approved by all communists and by the whole Soviet people.' This is the sort of democracy existent in Russia. But can it be called democracy? And what Western people would be content with it?

The Soviet press and propaganda, speaking of the transition from socialism to communism, insist on the importance of a series of reforms destined to promote 'popular self-government' in anticipation of the disappearance of the state apparatus. The review *Sovetskaya Gosudarstvo i Pravo* (No. 4, 1960) published a detailed study of these reforms, stressing the 'transfer to society, to social organizations and to the people itself of the functions now entrusted to the state administration'.

The point is to specify what functions are to be transferred and, primarily, whether a democratic organization exists that makes possible an effective transfer of state functions to organs neither belonging to nor controlled by the state. As long as the single-party system exists, where the Party is the secular arm of the government which orders and controls everything, the transfer of these functions is a mere pretence since there is no guarantee that the bodies to which such functions are transferred will act autonomously and will not be mere appendages of the Party, acting under its orders and supervision.

It is possible to speak of liberalism insofar as Khrushchev's régime was incomparably more moderate and humane than Stalin's; but what effective guarantees exist based on the will of the majority that there will not be again a dramatic turn at the first sign of setbacks?

12

Soviet writers stress that the communist doctrine rejects the

399

Western theory of the division of power and is based on the unity of power. But that means the autocratic state. Thus it was in tsarist times; thus it is now. The tradition persists. It cannot be said, as socialist doctrinaires claim, that the 'universal priority of the people's will' is affirmed when there is unity of power. In Russia there are no signs of this people's will that influences public affairs. If there were, then its first logical manifestation would be against this preponderance of the executive power in order to support the principle of a power balance.

'The abolition of any form of judicial procedure not covered by the constitution' is often cited as a guarantee of freedom, but the very fact that such special judiciary powers contrary to the constitution could ever have existed is a proof of how ephemeral are constitutional guarantees when a principle of balance of power is lacking and when there is only a single party.

In substance, what does this popular self-government amount to? To the creation of 'people's voluntary squads' to safeguard public order. This means squads of workers with modified police powers, a sort of popular militia. This system is all the more suspect because of the abuses to which it gives rise; informing, arrogance, settling of private grudges. Who controls these voluntary squads? Who promotes them, who supervises them? The Party, always the Party, which extends its control over all the individual and collective activities of the country.

They cite 'the permanent workers' representatives' in all the enterprises, that is to say the permanent production assemblies; but what guarantees have they and what is their scope? Guarantees do not exist, for no worker dares to set himself up against the Party lest he become a target for its reprisals; and as for scope what is wanted from these assemblies is an increase in production to be obtained by the supervision of the individual worker. It always comes back to the fact that where there is no freedom there is control, that is secret denunciation.

The most recent innovation is the creation of the Comrades' Courts, competent to pass judgment on misdemeanours, breaches of discipline and minor offences. In place of penal sanctions there is social censure and admonitions under the supervision of the collective. It is a system of schoolboy justice which degrades the dignity of the individual.

Finally, there is talk of the transfer of sporting activities, social insurance and medical assistance from state bodies to bodies more or less under state control, certainly not private bodies since in the Soviet Union private initiative does not exist.

That is all there is to this much-vaunted popular self-government.

CHAPTER XVII

Trade Union Safeguards

1

After all that has been said about the overwhelming power of the Party and its detailed control over all public and private activities, it might seem superfluous to speak of trade union safeguards for the Soviet worker. But it is absolutely necessary to explain the effective duties of the Soviet trade unions because it is mainly through them that the workers participate in the settlement of great problems, especially economic ones. According to Khrushchev this is really democracy by contrast with that false and only apparent democracy which exists in the Western world.

In the free countries the essential task of the trade unions is to safeguard the interests of the workers against the high-handedness and abuses of power of those upon whom they depend. To carry out such a task efficiently it is essential that they enjoy the maximum autonomy, which means that they must be recognized by law and their powers guaranteed. That is the trade union régime in the so-called capitalist countries.

In the Soviet Union, where state capitalism is in force, they should be autonomous and free of state control. That is what they demanded at the X Party Congress in 1921. It was through the trade unions that the workers demanded to retain control of the factories and to have handed over to them the direction, which the Party claimed for itself, of the whole economic policy of the state and, in particular, planning.

Shlyapnikov and Kollontai, who made themselves the mouthpieces of the workers' claims, stressed that the real significance of the Bolshevik revolution was the transfer from the capitalists to the workers of the ownership of the sources of production. In drawing up the Party programme in March 1910 Lenin had admitted this in Article 8, which read thus: 'The trade unions must finally concentrate in their hands the entire control of the whole of the national economy as a unified economic entity.' In order to see this right recognized, Shlyapnikov became one of the most indefatigable organizers of the Leninist party, mobilized the workers' masses in the October days and continued to throw the support of the workers on Lenin's side to suppress the Kronstadt revolt.

But after the triumph of bolshevism in the October days, Lenin's ideas were no longer those of seven years before, when he had drawn up the statute. In 1910 he had remained loyal to the Marxist precept which, as soon as the proletariat had seized power, should have proceeded at once to the liquidation of the state whose functions should pass to autonomous organizations such as the trade unions. But now that the tsarist state had been replaced by a dictatorial state, which admitted no power above it or alongside it, the claim of the trade unions appeared, as set out, to be inadmissible. That was Trotsky's thesis in maintaining the obligation of the trade unions to subordinate themselves to the state and to the Party.

Yet the demands of Shlyapnikov and Kollontai had an indisputable foundation in Marxist doctrine. Lenin was well aware of it and did not conceal his embarrassment. It seemed, at first, that he would oppose the theses of Trotsky and Bukharin which recommended the absorption of the trade unions by the state. He pointed out that if it was the workers' duty to defend the state they logically had the right to defend themselves from the state through the trade unions, that is to be independent of the government.

But it was not the moment for a calm appraisal; the communist state was threatened with collapse before the revolts of the sailors, the workers and the peasants. The conquests of the revolution could only be saved by a dictatorial régime. The day when the democratic norm of respecting the will of the majority was applied in the factories and the farms would mean the end of communism. There was an absolute incompatibility between democracy and communism, since communism paid no heed to private interests and all that remained for it to do was to impose its system by force.

The trade unions never managed to free themselves from the subordination imposed upon them. Stalin kept them under strict control. Tomski, the old revolutionary, who wanted to go on fighting, was forced to commit suicide. These precedents must be recalled in order not to fall into the false belief that the Soviet workers are satisfied with the present trade union régime, or that they have not fought for their rights. Not only did the workers fight, but the sailors and the peasants fought with no less tenacity.

The Soviet trade unions are state organs and carry out their duties in the interests of the state. They are, in fact, the master's eye. The Soviet workers have towards them the same lack of trust and interest as the Italian workers had towards the similar corporative organs in fascist times. Nor do they show any greater enthusiasm for the summonses to oceanic gatherings or depressing propaganda lectures.

2

This is how Khrushchev described the Soviet trade unions and praised their tasks in a speech to French trade unionists on March 31, 1960.

'In our country,' he said, 'we are now living through a period in which many functions of the state are gradually being transferred to semi-public departments. For this reason the importance of the trade unions is increasing in all walks of political, economic and public life.

'Lenin called the trade unions a school of administration, a school of management, a school of communism. What does that mean? In the trade unions the factory and office workers are being directly trained for the management of the factories. It is there that they receive a full scientific training in economic management and state administration. A trade union is an academy in which every worker learns this art. Therefore our people can always say: "We, the workers, are the state."

'Here is an example. There are permanent production committees in our factories and on our building sites. Who takes part in them? Mainly the workers themselves. The best and most skilled and most intelligent workers are elected to them. There are also engineers, inventors and factory managers at these conferences. . . . They give their considered recommendations on the main questions concerning the organization of productive processes. The Soviet workers take part in the management of production as masters in their own right.

'The production conferences have become very important in our country and are very popular. Able organizers, managers of shops and directors of enterprises, both men and women, have risen from the ranks of the workers and have shown themselves to be capable. More than seven million workers have been chosen for the production committees.

'Here you can see an example of socialist democracy.

'Our trade unions are rich. Last year (1959), for example, their funds exceeded 7,300,000,000 rubles. They have clubs, palaces of culture, sports grounds, stadia, etc.

'Social insurance is exclusively the prerogative of the trade unions. They control the social insurance funds, which this year amount to seven thousand million rubles. Let me add that in the Soviet Union this amount is provided from government funds and not from contributions paid by the workers, as in other countries.

'I could quote many other examples to illustrate the position of our trade unions in Soviet society: their participation in the preparation of the national development plans, their control of work safeguards, their part in the maintenance of public order and the development of public initiative.

'I have quoted a number of facts which show that our trade unions stand at the helm of our economic, cultural and public life and do all in their power to make the life of the workers easier, richer and more cultured. No one hinders them. On the contrary, the communist party and the government favour such activities.

'The government, the workers and the trade unions in the Soviet Union work together, shoulder to shoulder, to fulfil as well as possible and as quickly as possible the task of permanently raising the living standard of the people. Only in a socialist régime can one think of reducing working hours and raising wages as a pre-eminent function of the state. Could a capitalist country plan for an increase of forty per cent in the workers' wages in seven years as we are doing? No, it could not; and what capitalist government could assure a reduction in working hours to thirty or thirty-five while at the same time increasing wages? There is no capitalist government of that sort. That is the reason why the Soviet trade unions are the loyal allies of their government and active fighters for the fulfilment of the state plans.'

That was Khrushchev's harangue; an able presentation of the manifold activities of the trade unions, to which one can only raise the criticism that it did not touch on the one point that everyone wanted to know and that is how the trade unions carry out the task, which is their proper function, of defending the rights of the workers against those in power. Whether those in power means the state, as sole owner of all sources of production, or the private capitalist is not important. What matters is that the trade unions should be independent, that is free from all pressure or threats in the exercise of their functions. Khrushchev talks of permanent production conferences, of sports activities, of sanatoria and such things; all arguments that are, so to speak, subsidiary. The essential is not there.

Giuseppe Boffa, who was correspondent of *L'Unità* in Moscow, admite this in his well documented volume *La Grande Svolta* (*Inside the Khrushchev Era*)[1] when he says that in the trade unions the task of stimulating production takes pride of place over that of simply safeguarding immediate interests. This is exactly what the president of the Central Trades Union Committee, V. V. Grishin, said in his report to the XXII Party Congress. 'The main task,' he said, 'on which the trade unions are now concentrating their energies is the

[1] *Inside the Khrushchev Era*, George Allen and Unwin Ltd., London, 1960.

struggle for the further development of the productive forces of the country and the construction of the material and technical foundation for communism.'

3

The functions of the trade unions have been laid down, on the proposals of the Party, by various decisions of the Central Committee and especially by a resolution of the plenum in December 1957. These norms replaced the code of labour laws of the Russian federated republic ratified in 1922, which were in force in the other federated republics also. It was known by the initials KZOT, but soon fell into desuence because the guarantees it assured to the workers were felt to be excessive. It is a fact, however, that the new code, even if not as liberal as the KZOT and even though it has not accepted all the workers' demands, has increased the powers of the factory committees, both as regards the control of production and as regards the improvement of the working conditions and life of the workers.

It must honestly be admitted that Khrushchev's efforts to liberalize the internal situation have been sincere. What is to be contested is not his good will but the results of his liberal policy, because in order to get good results it would be necessary to change the régime. One does not pour new wine into old bottles with impunity. The partial reforms have been of little effect and have even increased the discontent since they have stimulated the desire always to have a little more.

The aims of the new code are explained in an article in the review *Sovetskie Profsoyuzy* (No. 8, 1960).

This very detailed study says: 'The trade union committee of the factory, the enterprise or the office acts as the authorized representative of the workers of the enterprise or institution in all matters concerning their work, their living conditions and their cultural activities.'

Because of the rights granted them the trade union committees have the opportunity to make suggestions to increase and improve production (which they do evidently in the interests of the state whose organs they are), to raise labour productivity and get the seven-year plan fulfilled in advance. These are all control functions in the interests of the factory owner, that is to say the state. They also have powers 'to satisfy, as completely as possible, the growing demands of the workers concerning their living conditions and cultural activities, and to protect their legal rights'.

But when one begins to examine one by one the tasks of these trade union committees, one sees that their first and paramount duty is to develop the socialist emulation of the workers, that is to get them to compete in obtaining the maximum yield. Would such a trade union task, which reminds one of the competition to be top of the class, be conceivable under Western régimes?

Khrushchev attributed great importance to the educative functions of the trade union committees, which introduce the workers into the secrets of the enterprise and make them participate in the decisions on production programmes and labour systems. The trade union committees are called upon, by law, to take part in the drafting of projects, of production plans, of building and house repairs, as well as in matters concerning cultural institutions and services. All these projects, in virtue of the Central Committee decision of December 1957, must be submitted to the planning organs, which must take account of the opinions of the trade union committees.

In particular, the economic councils and the regional and local executive committees must examine the draft annual plans of the enterprises, together with the representatives of the respective trade union committees and council, but not before such drafts have been discussed in the general meetings of the factory workers. In this way every technician, engineer or employee is able to express individually or through his squad or section his opinion of the draft as well as to put forward suggestions.

4

A decision of the Council of Ministers on July 9, 1958 transformed the production conferences from bodies meeting occasionally into 'permanent production assemblies' and established their duties. Apart from the workers, engineers, technicians, clerks and representatives of the management take part in them, as well as representatives of the Party and the Komsomol and scientific and technical institutes. The workers called upon to take part in them are elected at general meetings of the staff.

By this means it is hoped to make an advance towards co-administration, by combining the principle of single direction at the top with control from below.

These are reforms of undoubted value. But the assemblies have still only a consultative character and the matters of greatest interest to the workers, primarily wages and prices, are excluded from their competence. Therefore the spirit in which the workers participate makes them of little value. Only if they had a real interest in the progress of the enterprise in the one efficacious manner, namely participation in the profits, would their attendance become a willing contribution to the progress of the undertaking instead of being, as it is now, a mere formality.

5

The trade union committee, representing the workers, concludes the 'collective agreement' with the management. But the substance of these agreements is meagre, since wages, working hours and conditions of work—holidays, compensation and such matters—are fixed by law. A commission of the trade union committee draws up the draft of the agreement with the aid of trade union activists and management representatives. The commission has already sounded the workers' proposals in order to include them in the collective agreement. The draft is first discussed by the squads, sections and shifts and then submitted to the general assembly of the factory personnel, to which the president of the trade union committee and the factory manager present a report. Only after all the proposals and comments of the personnel have been considered is the draft signed by the manager and the president of the trade union committee. In a similar manner and at the same time the agreements for the protection of the workers and the plans for the introduction of technical methods and organization are also approved. The trade union committee supervises the application of the collective agreement and makes its report, together with the manager, to the general meeting of the personnel.

6

Every industrial undertaking which has an autonomous budget, that is one which is not directly financed by the state, is authorized to form a fund for the enterprise, always on condition that it has fulfilled the state production plans.

Half of this enterprise fund is expended on the introduction of new techniques and equipment intended to increase production and to build or repair workers' dwellings, over and above whatever has already been allotted in the investment plans. The other half is intended for the distribution of premiums to the staff, to improve or increase the rest homes and sanatoria where the workers spend their holidays, and, finally, to develop cultural services. The decision of July 1958 granted the trade union committees the right of expressing their opinion on the use of the enterprise fund.

7

The factory director must tell the trade union committee about the progress of the production plan. This confirms that the main function of the trade unions is to safeguard state interests. The director also consults the trade unions about the completion of the obligations which the enterprise has undertaken in the collective agreement and on the general progress of the enterprise itself. The trade union committee then takes measures to eliminate any short-comings that have been pointed out to it. It refers infractions of the social insurance norms by the management to the competent regional authorities; it presents its proposals and awaits their approval.

The management establishes conditions for piece-work and levels of payment by agreement with the trade union committee after these have been discussed with the factory wages commission. In other words the management does not set production quotas and wage scales without the approval of the trade union committee.

The trade unions control the Society of Inventors, which has branches in all factories. The trade union committee promotes initiatives and encourages inventive effort.

The committee also controls the observance of the workers' protection laws. 'Special technical inspectors have the right to give necessary instruction and also have the right to close temporarily any section of a factory or warehouse or even an entire enterprise if it reports that working conditions there endanger the workers' health.' Khrushchev stated this to the association of Austrian trade unionists in Vienna on July 2, 1960. 'And I must say,' he added, 'that a manager who disregards the inspectors' recommendations pays dearly.'

In every factory there are commissions for labour disputes, made up of equal numbers of representatives of the management and the workers. The worker has the right to appeal to the trade union committee if he is not satisfied with the commission's decision. The committee has the last word. 'No factory or office worker,' stated Khrushchev in Vienna, 'can be dismissed without the approval of the trade union committee. If there is any question of promoting a worker to a position of responsibility, the management must pay attention to the advice of the trade unions.'

The trade unions have full competence in matters of social insurance. The trade union committee administers the state workers' insurance funds of the respective factories, administers the sanatoria, pays compensations and participates in the granting of pensions.

The same committees, through their activists, control the execution of plans for workers' housing and cultural institutes and take part in the commissions for the allocation of housing according to the rules of priority in force.

The trade unions exercise public control over the activities of commercial and retail institutions, both state and co-operative, as well as public restaurants. Their committees control food and wine shops and canteens. Elected inspectors supervise the type of goods sold in the shops and canteens, the quality and variety of the food, the observance of hygiene and prices.

The trade unions collaborate with the Party in promoting ideological propaganda to combat survivals of the past. To that end they encourage the creation of cultural centres, clubs and libraries through the trade union committees.

The lead in this field is taken in every factory by the activists appointed by the trade union committees. They participate in all the various factory commissions: piece-work, production, labour protection, housing, insurance, cultural activities. They are, in fact, the key men of the trade unions and of the Party, trusted elements who control the workers as sheep-dogs control their flocks. They are protected by trade union rules 'against every arbitrary action and every open or covert persecution resulting from their public activities'. These words of the *Sovetskie Profsoyuzy* are clear enough to make it easily understood how much these activists are loved by their comrades and how they are regarded by them.

Particular importance is attributed to the powers of the trade union committee to dismiss the factory director. In theory this power exists; in reality the director is the arbiter of the enterprise upon whom the state confers plenipotentiary powers and responsibility. The trade unions collaborate with him to supervise the personnel and squeeze the maximum productivity out of them. The Soviet workers are well aware of this collusion and are suspicious of the directors, the trade union committees and that special type of *agents provocateurs* who, under the name of *stakhanovists*, or shock-workers, are the activists of the Party.

8

In the article in the *Sovetskie Profsoyuzy* already quoted, one of the trade union committee presidents, Nazarov, tells how these committees work in practice. Writing of the collective agreement which 'represents an important factor in the lives of the workers' and which 'is concluded every year between the trade union committee and the management' he gives an idea of the important questions dealt with and settled by the agreement. Here are his words: 'On the basis of the proposals made by the workers and the commissions appointed by the trade union committees, we succeed in obtaining the inclusion in the collective agreement of a number of measures that we consider of vital importance. For example, we asked that this year a laundry should be built to wash the working clothes of the workers, that a kindergarten for a hundred and fifty children be built and that a new kitchen and dining-room be constructed at the young pioneers' sportsground and that six arbours be planted in the country house where the children under school age spend the summer.' The trade union committee also insisted that 'the collective agreement should include an obligation by the management to improve the ventilation system, should build a new canteen, etc.'. 'The management,' Nazarov goes on, 'did not agree with us and therefore these matters were submitted to the assembly of the whole staff; it supported the trade union views and all our requests were included in the collective agreement.'

Such are trade union victories in the Soviet Union, to which the press gives such great prominence—kitchens and arbours!

9

What is the aim of these trade union activities?

Grishin, speaking to the Central Trades Union Council in July 1960, insists on the growing importance of the trade unions 'in promoting the progress of industry and transport, in encouraging the most modern technical achievements and in increasing productivity to the maximum'. After reviewing the organizing and educational tasks of these bodies, he recommended that the propaganda be improved. 'In some places the ideological and political level of the educational activities entrusted to the cultural organs of the trade unions are very low.'

There is especial stress on the principle of the closest dependence of the trade unions on the Party. 'The power of the trade unions,' comments the trade union daily, Trud, 'should be guided by our Party. Therefore they must carry out their duties under the guidance and by the direct aid of the Party organizations. They should consult them more often and lay before the Party organizations important questions concerning labour in industry and transport.'

One of the themes to which Grishin often returns, most recently in his speech to the XXII Party Congress, is that 'there are still many shortcomings in the work of the trade unions. Many of them do not make enough use of their rights, do not show enough initiative in raising and solving questions concerning the improvement of productive and cultural organization, to say nothing of services for the factory workers and employees. They do not always stand up for their principles against violations of the labour laws. There are also many shortcomings in the workers' education.'

10

The criticisms of the workers themselves are many and various. They are well aware that the much vaunted innovation of the permanent production assemblies is a fiction, since the workers take part on a purely consultative basis, and the really important decisions are taken by the control organs, economic and political.

Here is how one workman described to me the consultation of the personnel which took place in his factory on the draft wages law. One day the director called all the workers together and proposed the appointment of a commission to discuss the project. He added that the oldest of the workers, a Party member, should make the nominations, naturally of Party members only. The workers unanimously approved. The commission examined the draft law and approved it without comment.

It may be asked why no one protested, why no one opposed this. In fact, all knew that it would mean setting oneself up against the Party which had already apportioned all the tasks.

Therefore a complete disinterest in the affairs of the enterprise is the usual reaction. The workers know of the extortionate prices asked for the products of their labours, of the waste in production, of the neglect of machinery and state property in general, of the disorganization of productive processes, of the couldn't-care-less attitude of the directors who are reluctant to try anything new and are suspicious of every initiative that is not imposed from above.

The slackness of trade union supervision of physical safeguards for the workers is also a cause of astonishment to those who have had the chance of seeing work going on in the workshops and factories. Luigi Barzini, Jnr., wrote in the *Corriere della Sera* on April 19, 1960: 'A highly-placed socialist member of the CGIL (Federation of Italian Trade Unions) recently saw women employed as bricklayers working in mid-winter on the sixth floor of buildings under construction without any of the safety measures which are in general use in the civilized world.

'If that had happened in Italy he himself, with the collaboration of the communists, would quite rightly have called a strike which would have had the approval of all honest citizens and would have led to the arrest of the employers.'

Similar statements have been made by Italian industrialists after visiting Soviet factories and even by left-wing politicians, one of whom was unable to conceal his indignation at seeing welders carrying out their dangerous work without even the most elementary safeguards for the protection of their sight.

The Soviet workers feel that their rights are not being safeguarded and that they have no way of having their claims considered, since they are denied their most efficient weapon, the strike. This is what the workers yearn for most of all. Strikes do break out here and there, but in a disorganized manner and without a common plan and with great danger for the organizers who expose themselves to the harshest reprisals.

11

In practice, the strike is forbidden throughout the communist world. The police, who do not hesitate to use firearms, almost always intervene against the strikers. This was the case in East Berlin in 1953, in Poznan, and in Budapest in 1957. In all three cases the workers' demonstrations were crushed by the police and, when this was not successful, by the Soviet armoured divisions. After these examples Gomulka in April 1958 declared himself against the right to strike, which the Polish government had been compelled to recognize. In 1960 Ulbricht decreed the prohibition of strikes.

The opinion of the Soviet leaders about strikes is illustrated by the following episode related by the American ambassador, Bedell Smith. The American delegate Hopkins had to discuss the lend-lease law with Stalin. On one occasion he excused the delay in the delivery of a consignment of war material caused by a strike. Stalin raised his eyebrows: 'A strike? Haven't you got a police force?'

How the Soviet authorities justify the lack of strikes in their country was made clear by Khrushchev in a speech to the Austrian trade unionists at Vienna on July 2, 1960. He upheld the thesis that strikes were conceivable in bourgeois régimes, where antagonism between capitalists and workers still existed; but this was not so in socialist society where there are no class antagonisms and 'where the workers are masters in their own lands and where they govern the state'. It is always the same legal fiction; in theory they are the masters, in fact all they can do is obey.

'That is why,' Khrushchev went on, 'the workers will certainly not strike against themselves. In your own country a peasant who works for himself does not strike against himself. In the same way in our country the workers do not strike against themselves, since all the factories, the plants, the land and all that is on it belong to the workers. Our government expresses the will of the workers.'

In fact the situation is somewhat different, insofar as it is true that workers strike even in Russia, with difficulty and with a thousand risks, but they do strike to defend their rights, to demand special payments due to them, to protest against the way of running the factory, in other words to make their claims known against those in command, that is to say the state which is the owner of everything and controls everything. It is also true that in theory the right to strike exists even in Russia. Khrushchev has admitted this explicitly, in these words: 'Perhaps you will understand more clearly why the Soviet workers do not think of resorting to strikes and do not organize them, even though they have the right to do so.'

The question then arises: why does the law recognize the right of workers to strike against themselves? If it is absurd to strike against oneself, a law that authorizes such strikes is surely equally absurd?

The reason why strikes are impossible in Russia is not that generally stated. It is not a theoretical but a practical reason. The Soviet state cannot renounce its right to fix wages by decree without compromising its planning. The reason why the freezing of wages is the primary condition for the success of the plans has already been explained. It prevents the increase in consumer goods to the detriment of productive investments.

For the same reason the state cannot tolerate any form of pressure, least of all a strike, intended to further wage demands which it would not be in a position to grant without compromising the fulfilment of its plans. But without the right to strike the Soviet workers cannot look forward to an increase in consumer goods which would mean an improvement in their living standards which, as everyone who lives in Russia knows, are remarkably low.

The result is that while communists in Western lands are continually pressing for wage increases, in the communist countries they curb by every possible means any attempt to increase wages. The first result that the workers may expect from a communist revolution is a massive reduction in wages.

12

Khrushchev explained his theory of the right to strike to the representatives of the American trade unions, Walter Reuther, president of the Automobile Workers' Union, and James Carey, chief of the Electrical Workers' Union, on the evening of September 20, 1959, after a supper given for the Soviet Premier by the trade union leaders. It began when Reuther asked if the Soviet workers had the right to strike. Khrushchev replied that they had this right and that there had been strikes 'since the revolution'. 'But,' he added, 'there have been no strikes recently because the workers know that the government is on their side.'

Joseph Carran, president of the Seamen's Union, put the question in this way: 'Let us come to the point. Is it or is it not possible for the workers to obtain redress for wrongs done to them by withdrawing their labour *en masse*, the only way consistent with industrial democracy? On what occasions can the Russian workers hope to reach negotiations which include the right to strike?'

Khrushchev replied: 'I understand you perfectly, but you understand nothing about labour under a socialist system. I don't mean to be offensive but you know nothing about it, you have never been there. You measure everything by the yardstick of the United States. What I like about you is that you have a sense of class-consciousness. Very well; amongst us the workers have this right. I understand your question. The working class has the theoretical right to strike. But can the worker exercise this right in practice? Yes. Have there been strikes since the October revolution? Yes. I myself have been on several strike committees. Are there strikes now? No. Because the workers, the trade unions and the government all think the same way; in what other country could the government announce, without any pressure exerted on it, a rise in wages and a reduction of working hours? In capitalist countries there would have to have been a struggle to achieve this.'

'Our workers,' Khrushchev went on, 'are all organized in trade unions and have learnt to know economic conditions and the economic possibilities of our country.'

Carran insisted: 'Despite all that, even knowing the economic conditions and possibilities, have they the right to strike?'

Khrushchev: 'By law, yes.'

Reuther: 'I was born in a working-class district in West Virginia . . .'

Khrushchev interrupted him, waving his hands.

Reuther: 'Are you afraid of my questions?'

Khrushchev: 'I am not afraid of the devil himself, and you are a man.'

Reuther: 'I took part in the underground struggle in Germany against Hitler before going to Russia. What disturbs me in your social system is not that you do not make economic advances to the advantage of the workers and peasants. You have made remarkable technical advances and I know your way of thinking very well, namely that the workers do not strike against themselves. But you, President Khrushchev, have stressed, in revealing Stalin's crimes, the power of the cult of an individual. How can a worker obtain justice in such a period if he cannot strike or make any public protest?'

Khrushchev: 'He has his trade union.'

Reuther: 'The trade union is only an organ of the government; it is the Soviet government. Can a trade union ever be at odds with the government? Can you quote me a single case where one of your trade unions has ever been in disagreement with government policy?'

Khrushchev: 'Why do you stick your nose into our affairs?'

Reuther: 'Freedom is an affair that concerns everyone. You are always stressing your interest in the workers of Asia. There is such a thing as the international solidarity of the workers. When I was in Russia I was a member of a trade union . . .'

Khrushchev interrupted excitedly.

Reuther: 'Every time we try to get to the bottom of any question, the President gets angry.'

Khrushchev turned red and said loudly: 'In our country we should call you a lackey of the imperialists.'

Reuther's comment was: 'There can be no disagreement between men of good faith about the essentially immoral character of communism, or on the brutal opposition to and denial by the Soviet dictatorship of human liberty and those democratic rights and values which we, as a free people, love. Since Soviet dogma and propaganda is centred on the myth that communism is the liberator of the working class, it is essential that the leaders of the American trade unions, which represent millions of American workers, should be able to say directly to Mr Khrushchev that the American workers, through their trade union movement, are irrevocably bound to the cause of human freedom and that no dose of communist propaganda will ever succeed in deluding them or shaking their total devotion to our system of human liberty and determined opposition to communism.'

As regards the right to strike Reuther commented: 'We are distressed to see that the new Soviet penal code, published in *Pravda* on December 26, 1958, provides for penalties of up to fifteen years imprisonment for organizing strikes. We reject the explanation that from the time when the people becomes the owner of the factories there is no more exploitation. History has shown us beyond any shadow of doubt that the government may become the most pitiless of exploiters.'

CHAPTER XVIII

Policy towards the Non-Russian
Peoples of the Soviet Union

1

THERE are in the Soviet Union more than a hundred nationalities, from the preponderant Russian or Great Russian, which according to the census of January 15, 1959 accounted for 114,588,000 persons out of a total population of 208,826,650, to ethnic groups numbering a few tens of thousands, the remnants of primitive tribes which before the Soviet rule did not even have alphabets for their languages.

Lenin replaced the imperialist policy of the tsars, linked with the traditions of old style European colonialism, by a bold policy of emancipation of all the peoples which no longer wished to form part of the empire. It recognized their right of cession and of organizing themselves as national states. By giving so unequivocal a proof that the new Russia was diametrically opposed to the old and had renounced its spirit, the Bolshevik régime was able to claim to be the natural protector of all oppressed nationalities and communism to be the standard-bearer of a crusade for the liberation of all peoples groaning under the yoke of colonialism.

Lenin wanted to show by facts the truth of the thesis set out in his book *Imperialism, Last Stage in the Development of Capitalism*, which said that imperialism, because of the financial resources that it required and those that it obtained from its undertakings, was a purely capitalist phenomenon. Imperialism had disappeared in Russia with the triumph of communism; it would only disappear from the world with the destruction of capitalism.

The hopes of all peoples yearning for freedom and who needed help to achieve it began to centre on the new régime. The new possibilities of action allowed Lenin to do what the tsars had never succeeded in doing, namely to destroy the strongholds of British power in the countries bordering on Russia—Afghanistan, Persia and Turkey—and to establish with them relations of special trust, thanks to the reversal of tsarist policy and the repercussions in international affairs of the universally acclaimed policy of the right of self-determination for all peoples.

But that he actually resolved to go so far as the actual emancipation of the non-Russian nationalities of the empire was belied by the unequivocable actions carried out by him, especially after he had emerged victorious from the civil war.

It is, however, fair to admit that his policy was far more delicate and elastic than that of his successors, who lacked the lightness of touch indispensable to his able designs.

2

A clear exposition of the policy that the Bolsheviks proposed to put into force concerning the non-Russian nationalities in Russia was laid down in the book written by Stalin, on Lenin's inspiration and suggestion, in 1913 entitled *The Question of Nationalities and Social Democracy*. Stalin went so far as to renounce the federal link in order to maintain unreservedly the principle of self-determination.

It was therefore to Stalin that, after the Bolsheviks had seized power, Lenin entrusted the task of putting a policy of this sort into operation, by appointing him Commissar for Nationalities. It was as such that, scarcely three weeks after the October days, Stalin proclaimed the recognition of Finnish independence by Russia at the Congress of the Social-Democratic Party at Helsinki. It was the first renunciation, the renunciation of a country that had formed part of the empire for more than a century.

It seemed that the Bolshevik government really wanted to dismantle the imperial edifice of the tsars. It paraded a policy antithetical to that of Kerensky and all the counter-revolutionary forces, which had rejected every idea of renouncing territory in homage to the principle of the inviolate sovereignty of Russia over all the tsarist conquests.

The Bolshevik course, even though imposed by circumstances, none the less wounded the deepest feelings of the Russian people, which proved exceptionally jealous of national power and greatness. It was therefore obvious that in the long run no government could continue to insist on such a policy if it did not want to run counter to public opinion.

At Helsinki, however, Stalin proclaimed full liberty for all the peoples of Russia to decide their own future. He limited himself to proposing an honourable and voluntary alliance between the Russian and Finnish peoples.

3

On November 2, 1917 the new policy towards the non-Russian

peoples was defined in the 'Declaration of rights of the peoples of Russia', based on recognition of the right of self-determination, which left the nationalities concerned free to break away or to live together in association with Russia on a basis of equality and sovereignty, with the abolition of any sort of privilege for one or the other nationality.

The reactions in the heart of the Bolshevik party itself at such declarations were very violent. Bukharin and Dzerzhinski stressed that the new policy favoured the resistance of the bourgeois classes, to whom it gave the chance of weaning the masses from solidarity with the Russian people in order, once isolated, to crush revolutionary movements more easily.

4

What were the real aims of a policy apparently so generous? One can understand them better if one recalls that, simultaneously with the policy of renunciation, a vast programme was put into operation to entice the non-Russian peoples by encouraging revolutionary movements amongst them and renewing, by means of these movements, the bonds which had been loosed in the name of self-determination. Thus the old imperial edifice was demolished in order to erect in its place a new one, vaster and more solid than the old. It was, as subsequent events have proved, a new kind of imperialism, cleverer and more efficient than the earlier one, aimed at undermining the positions of the rival imperialism and reinforcing its own.

Naturally a policy so revolutionary and carried out in the precarious and tragic conditions of Russia at that time could not but run very serious risks and incur very painful losses. Where circumstances were favourable to the bourgeoisie and allowed them to consolidate their position and block the Bolshevik propaganda, the Leninist policy of the liberation of nationalities facilitated the rise of anti-communist states, which were immediately supported by the West, like Finland, Poland and the Baltic states. But where, because of isolation from the West, the influence of Moscow was able to prevail it was evident that the new policy merely replaced the old form of subjection by another, less heavy but no less binding. In the end events justified Lenin's foresight. Little by little as the Soviet state became consolidated its powers of pressure and attraction grew greater, so that almost all the old positions which after the collapse of tsarism seemed to be irretrievably lost were recovered and many new ones acquired. The Soviet Empire, including its vassal states, stretched to frontiers that far surpassed the maximum limits of tsarist domination.

It is true that most of these developments took place in Stalin's time, but the beginnings of the policy of *reconquista* went back to Lenin's time. It was Lenin who outlined the tactics to be followed faithfully in later times, which lent themselves easily to the new expansionist drive by creating forms of spontaneous adhesion to the Soviet state. These tactics, of pure Leninist type, consisted in organizing *coups d'état* with the aid of local communists, supporters of the Soviet system. In this way the Rada in the Ukraine and the Menshevik government in Georgia were overthrown.

If at first these tactics had only partial success, this was due not to the will but to the weakness of the Bolshevik government. But not even after the treaty of Brest-Litovsk, when it was compelled to make the most painful cessions, did it ever undertake to renounce the right of one day reclaiming the ceded territories. Trotsky's words at the session of the Conference on February 10, 1918 made this clear. He announced that he refused to sign the peace treaty. 'The peoples of Poland, the Ukraine, Lithuania, Courland and Esthonia,' he said, 'consider such conditions as a violation of their desire to remain associated with Russia; these conditions are a perpetual threat.'

More than words, deeds testified to the constant intention of the Soviets, despite the solemn proclamation of the rights of peoples to decide their own destiny, to reconstitute the unity of the old empire. Their tactics were to foment communist movements in order to bind the new régimes to the Soviet Union. Thus on December 23, 1918 Moscow recognized the 'Soviet Republics' of Lithuania, Latvia and Esthonia and offered them 'all the aid and support necessary'. The manoeuvre did not succeed because the Western powers intervened and the Soviet forces were driven out of the Baltic states, even as they were driven out of Poland when they tried, under the command of Tukhachevsky, to take Warsaw and set up a Soviet régime there.

These were the precedents for what happened in 1940 and the years following. Finland alone was able to save herself by her dogged resistance to the Soviet forces, on which she inflicted very severe losses.

5

Stalin continued and accentuated Lenin's policy. Since he was acting on the master's instructions, the liberal façade of the new policy had to be maintained; but when Lenin, owing to illness, had to give up taking an interest in current affairs for long periods at a time Stalin gave rein to his despotic temperament and departed from this policy of compromise and formal accommodation which retained the fiction of respecting the freedom of the other party. The most striking conflict was between him and the political currents of his native country of Georgia, which had been satisfied with a small degree of autonomy. Stalin demanded that Georgia form part of a Caucasian federation of soviet republics, whereas Georgia wanted to remain a federated soviet republic all on its own, which in fact it is today.

Lenin, who had at first supported Stalin, was preparing to criticize him and to oppose him openly when he was prevented by death.

The accusations that Lenin prepared against Stalin were never made public.

Once freed from Lenin's directives, the new dictator became the standard-bearer of the old imperialist tradition and the fiercest opponent of any form of regional nationalism. What his ideas really were was shown during the civil war when he tried to seize a strip of Persian territory. This was when the Red armies of Raskolnikov which had routed Denikin's forces pursued them from Baku across the Persian frontiers. On Stalin's instigation Raskolnikov organized the soviet republic of Ghilan, despite the fact that at the same time Chicherin was negotiating an agreement with the Teheran government, which was concluded in 1921, by which Russia renounced all the properties, concessions and privileges that she had enjoyed in Persia from tsarist times.

From some casual remarks by Stalin it may be deduced that his policy was intended to correspond closely to the objectives followed by Lenin, even if the latter acted in more hidden and less brutal ways. For example, when speaking to the XVI Party Congress, he referred to the Leninist policy towards the non-Russian nationalities of the Soviet Union as follows: 'Consider Lenin's attitude on the question of the rights of national self-determination even to the extent of secession from the Union. Lenin sometimes expressed the thesis of national self-determination in the simple formula: Disunion to achieve union. The aim, therefore, must be union.'

That this was really Lenin's idea is confirmed by the strongly unified structure that he gave to the Soviet state, a rigid centralization of power the better to be able to resist separatist tendencies. It was with this aim in view that, when the constitution was remodelled, he even rejected the federative idea.

These precedents made clear how ambiguous, even in Lenin's time, was the much-vaunted policy of the self-determination of peoples. The real aims of such a policy became clearer little by little as Russia began to recover her former power. To get an idea of this change it is enough to consider the thesis supported by Russia when treating with the German delegates at Brest-Litovsk and compare it with that which it supports today when dealing with Federal Germany. Trotsky supported the idea of self-determination and the Germans, though stating their acceptance of it, eluded its logical consequences by an infinity of quibbles. Today it is Adenauer who speaks the language of Trotsky and tries to make the idea of self-determination prevail, while the Russians, by every sort of quibble, reject it. In forty-five years the positions have become entirely reversed. At that time it was the Kaiser's delegates at Brest-Litovsk who refused the Soviet proposal for free and impartial plebiscites in the occupied territories on the excuse that Courland, Lithuania and Poland had already voted; today it is Russia who opposes free elections for the reunification of Germany on the pretext that the Pankow Germans have already voted in plebiscite for the continuance of the present régime.

The Western world and the communist world have changed places and imperialism is now in the Soviet camp. Trotsky's words at Brest-Litovsk have acquired a prophetic flavour. 'We are revolutionaries,' he said, 'but we are also realists and we prefer to speak of annexation than to use euphemisms for the real thing.' Today the use of euphemisms has become a habit in Soviet diplomacy.

6

Khrushchev, in his speech in Paris on April 2, 1960, described the multi-national structure of the Soviet state.

'More than a hundred different nationalities and national groups,' he said, 'live in our country. Before the revolution many of these nationalities led a miserable existence, dying of hunger, poverty and disease. The Soviet motherland has found the right solution for the multi-national problem. The unification of the peoples which lived under the tsarist régime in Russia has been carried out in the Soviet Union with strict observance of the principle of free choice.'

It has already been described how the Soviet Union worked for the reconstruction of the country's unity. In the difficult years of the revolution the non-Russian peoples, rather than make common cause with the central power, broke away to form autonomous governments, in the Ukraine, in Georgia, in Armenia, in Azerbaidzhan, in Central Asia and in Mongol Siberia where the Japanese had the support of the local populations.

It is a fact that on January 11, 1919 the Allies recognized the governments of Georgia and Azerbaidzhan. Hoover, who was appointed by President Wilson as chief of the aid mission to Russia, was able to state in April 1919 that 'the new-born democracies of Siberia, Kuban, Finland, Esthonia, Latvia, Lithuania, Armenia and the other nationalities that surround Bolshevik Russia must have a breathing space to set their affairs in order'. It must not be forgotten that during the civil war most of these peoples found themselves between the hammer and the anvil. Of the two contestants the Whites, who represented the tsarist tradition, were the more dangerous because their programme of 'an undivided Russia' implied the return to their former condition of vassalage. In actual fact, however, the non-Russian peoples did not, generally speaking, collaborate with either side.

It must also not be under-estimated that everything possible was done by the West to facilitate the disintegration of the empire. At the beginning of 1919, at the moment when the Russian state seemed about to collapse from internal disintegration, there was a feeling that it would be willing, as L. Fischer has testified, to renounce its sovereignty over the greater part of Siberia, over northern Russia, over part of the Ukraine and part of the Don basin and the whole of the Caucasus, the Transcaspian lands and the Crimea.

It is also a fact that the peripheral regions, which had been conquered by the tsars, had to be re-conquered by the Red armies, even though the resistance that they found there was slight, not only because of the help they received from the many fifth columns that made their advance easy but also because of the impossibility for these peoples to get help from the West, which rendered useless every effort on their part to continue the struggle. One can therefore say that the inclusion of the non-Russian peoples in the Soviet Union was not an act of free will on their part. It is also true that even as they did not rebel against the tsars once they had been subjected so too they have not rebelled against the Soviet Union. But that is no proof of their desire to remain tied to Russia. Also signs of a contrary desire are by no means lacking.

It would not, however, be just to conceal that the Soviet government is now carrying out a wise and moderate policy towards these peoples, respectful of their national traits and especially aimed at developing, at great expense, the economic resources of their countries. It is therefore possible to agree with Khrushchev when he said that 'under the Soviet régime all the nationalities and national groups have had great possibilities of developing their economy and their national culture and to display their abilities to the full. And they have achieved noteworthy results.'

However, every aspiration for resistance and every latent hope of a future autonomy has been killed by three factors: the large-scale purges they have undergone, the Russification now going on and the centralizing of power in the government of the Soviet Union.

The indictment for the crime of genocide committed against the non-Russian peoples of the Soviet Union was presented by Khrushchev himself at the famous trial of Stalinism at the XX Party Congress. He unreservedly denounced 'the mass deportations from their native lands of whole nations, including all the communists and Komsomol members without exception. Such deportations were not justified by any military considerations'.

'It was thus,' stated Khrushchev, 'at the end of 1943 when on all fronts of the great patriotic war the tide was turning in favour of the Soviet Union, that the deportation of the Karachai from their native lands, on which they had lived till then, was ordered and carried out. About the same time, at the end of December 1943, a similar fate overtook the entire population of the autonomous Kalmuck republic. In March 1944 the entire Chechen and Ingush peoples were deported and the autonomous republics that they had formed were eliminated. In April 1944 all the Balkari people were deported to places very far from the territory of the Kabardin-Balkari autonomous republic which was thenceforth named the Kabardin autonomous republic. The Ukrainians were only able to avoid a similar fate because there were too many of them and it was therefore impossible to find anywhere to deport them. If it had been possible, Stalin would have deported them too.'

In this personal testimony by the head of the Soviet government there is irrefutable proof of the hostility of whole populations against the dominant state; and to cast off its yoke they had made common cause with the German forces at the time of the invasion. In reprisal for their defection, the cruel expedient was devised of uprooting them from the lands where they had been living for generations past.

But Khrushchev's revelations were not complete. They raised only a corner of the veil over a situation which has aroused the deepest feelings and sympathies for the fate of peoples which, after having been cruelly decimated, still groan under the yoke of a master whom they abhor. In a single night in 1941, at the time of the invasion of Latvia by the Red armies, fifteen thousand persons out of a population of two million were deported to Siberia. During the guerilla fighting which devastated Lithuania after the Soviet occupation of June 1940 a fifth of the population was either killed or deported. In Esthonia the NKVD set up a reign of terror. The terrible police in the single night of June 13-14th deported thousands of Esthonians, while thousands more were massacred. The flood of arrests and deportations continued and culminated in the mass deportation of March 1949.

Khrushchev did not even mention the deportation of four hundred thousand Volga Germans, all of whose leaders were shot, nor the Jews, nor the Katyn mass-graves, nor the Tatars wiped out to the last man in the Crimea where their khans had built the splendid palace of Bakcheserai which Pushkin lauded in his famous poem as 'the fountain of tears'.

After such crimes of genocide, the ephemeral value of the guarantee sanctified by Article 117 of the Soviet constitution, which recognizes the right of every nationality to secede from the Union, is evident. The cases quoted by Khrushchev are plainly cases of peoples intolerant of Soviet rule, but there has not been a single case of the application of Article 117. It is one of the many façade articles which have no guarantee that they will ever be carried out and no procedure by which to do so.

8

In order to strengthen the cohesion of an organism made up of so many heterogeneous elements, various measures have been taken to favour their amalgamation. The ultimate aim is to drown the national minorities in a sea of Russians and Ukrainians. The Soviet leaders make no mystery of this. Khrushchev's report to the XXII Party Congress on October 18, 1961 reads: 'There is a merging of nationalities taking place in our country. Naturally we come across persons who deplore the gradual disappearance of national distinctions. To these we reply that the communists do not want to preserve and perpetuate national distinctions. We rely upon the natural process of an even closer amalgamation of nations and nationalities which is now taking place within the communist structure on a voluntary and democratic basis. It is essential to insist on the education of the masses in a spirit of proletarian internationalism and Soviet patriotism. Even the slightest trace of nationalism must be eliminated with unrelenting Bolshevik determination.'

It is clear that this unification must be obtained at the cost of distinctive national characteristics and must end by accentuating the predominance of the most numerous people—the Russian.

This process of unification began in tsarist times according to the standard colonial tradition. It was accentuated by the intermingling caused by the revolution, the war and the intense industrialization of the country.

The census of January 15, 1959 gives an idea of the results achieved:

Region	Total population	Original population	Percentage	Russians	Percentage	Ukrainians	Percentage
Ukraine	41,869,000	Ukrainians	76.1	7,400,000	17.7	—	—
Belorussia (White Russia)	8,055,000	Belorussians	80.0	729,000	9.1	—	—
Moldavia	2,885,000	Moldavians	65.4	293,000	10.2	421,000	14.6
Lithuania	2,711,000	Lithuanians	79.3	231,000	8.5	—	—
Latvia	2,093,000	Letts	62.0	556,000	26.6	—	—
Esthonia	1,197,000	Esthonians	72.9	260,000	21.7	—	—
Uzbekistan	8,106,000	Uzbeks	62.0	1,101,000	13.6	—	—
Kazakstan	9,310,000	Kazaks	29.6	4,014,000	43.1	762,000	8.2
Georgia	4,044,000	Georgians	63.3	438,000	10.8	—	—
Azerbaidzhan	3,698,000	Azerbaidzhanese	67.1	515,000	13.9	—	—
Kirgizia	2,066,000	Kirgiz	40.5	624,000	30.2	—	—
Tadzhikistan	1,980,000	Tadzhiks	53.1	263,000	13.3	—	—
Armenia	1,763,000	Armenians	88.0	56,000	3.1	—	—
Turkmenistan	1,516,000	Turcomans	60.9	263,000	17.3	—	—

From the time of this census the percentage of Russians has increased enormously, especially in Kazakstan because of the cultivation of the virgin lands, so that today Kazakstan has a shattering Russian majority.

The Russification of the country was given a tremendous impetus during the war when whole industrial areas were removed from the European to the Asian provinces to ensure their continued operation at a safe distance from the fronts.

The development of the entire country promoted by the five-year plans based on the principle of exploitation of natural resources of power and minerals 'on the site' also demanded vast movements of manpower, mainly Russian and Ukrainian, and the formation of nuclei of directors, technicians and specialists, also for the most part Russians and Ukrainians.

The rapidity of this population flow from the European to the Asian areas is shown by the following figures. Whereas the Soviet population as a whole increased by 9.5 per cent in twenty years from 1939 to 1959, the increases were as follows:

Area	Percentage
Urals	32
Western Siberia	24
Eastern Siberia	34
Central Asia and Kazakstan	38
Soviet Far East	70

Perhaps the most striking proof is in the zone of the Urals, at one time almost exclusively inhabited by Bashkirs, who are now reduced to less than half a million out of a population of more than fifteen million.

The Russians tend to concentrate in the cities, which have expanded from small rural centres to huge industrial complexes or have been created entirely from scratch. Russian colonization, with the exception of Kazakstan and Western Siberia, is, like the Greek colonization at the time of the Hellenization of the Middle East, for the most part urban.

The impression one gets from a trip in Eastern Siberia, the area east of the Yenisei, is that the Soviet government is systematically strewing these immense areas with urban centres by the creation of more and more new factories, electric power plants and mining installations.

Where conditions are suitable this does not prevent an easy intermingling of races. Thus in Uzbekistan both the cities and the agricultural enterprises welcome people of either race. This is the favourite procedure where the non-Russian ethnic groups are not over-numerous. In Yakutya, for example, of a population of about half a million a third is Russian, a half Yakut and the remainder made up of various minor ethnic groups, Eveni, Chiuki, Yukagiri and the like. In the capital Yakutsk the majority is Russian, even as the manpower in the gold and diamond mines is Russian; but the city officials and teachers are mainly Yakuts.

I did not get the impression that the Russians make any great effort to encourage mixed marriages. But none the less there is no lack of unions between Russians and Yakuts and the children of these mixed marriages are splendid types. But as far as I could judge these unions are not looked on with favour by either race.

I came across similar opposition among the Uzbeks, though even amongst them mixed marriages are far from rare. In the cities with a mixed population, such as Tashkent, Samarkand and Bukhara, the best residential areas are reserved for Russians.

Finally, in the districts where there is a compact Mongol population, the two races seem to live alongside one another without mixing. Irkutsk, Bratsk, Chita, Khabarovsk, seemed to me, even after wandering the length and breadth of them, to be purely Russian cities. They are wedges thrust into a compact Mongol mass. If the aim desired is to split up the non-Russian populations, it must be conceded that such a policy is being carried out with consummate tact, delicately and unostentatiously, trying to offend the susceptibilities of the local people as little as possible, with all that sense of discretion and secrecy which is inborn in the Russians from the most minor official to the man in the street.

9

The main guarantee against any dreams of separation or of slackening the bonds of the federated republics is the strongly centralized organization of the Soviet state and especially the exclusive competence of the centre in the administration of the finances.

The centralization of the essential powers of the Union is in accord with a directive from Lenin himself. In one of his last articles he again returned, it is true, to an insistence on the principle of the autonomy of the nationalities in the Soviet Union and on their freedom to secede from the Union, explaining that any imperialist concept with regard to the oppressed nationalities would cast a doubt on the sincerity of Soviet principles and make the struggle against imperialism impossible. But he none the less recommended the 'maintenance and strengthening of the Union of Socialist Republics' and added: 'There can be no doubt whatever about this.'

This confirms how ambivalent was his directive which, while insisting on the principle of autonomy even if it involved the right of secession, recommended that the idea of the unity of the state be upheld.

During the Stalinist period there was a continual reinforcement of the central powers of the Union. The keystone of this unitary structure was the system of unified budgeting for the whole Soviet state, laid down, in conformity to Article 14 of the constitution, by the laws of 1924, 1927 and subsequent years. The fiscal reform of 1930 in particular, by regulating the turnover tax on Soviet industries, laid down that the income from this tax should go directly to the Union budget, of which it now forms the most important asset. Another step towards centralization was made in 1938 when all the budgets of the fifteen federated republics, of the autonomous regions, of the *krais* and the *oblasts*, were incorporated in the Union budget. It follows that the Soviet budget has nothing in common, in form, with the budget of a federal state but resembles the ordinary budget of a unitary state, since all the local budgets are included in it. In this way the Leninist principle of a unified financial policy has been applied.

This policy was not changed after the administrative decentralization put into force by Khrushchev in 1954 when he upheld the idea of transferring to the federated republics the functions hitherto carried out by a pleiad of central technical ministries. Even more important was the decentralization of industrial organization made in 1957. The State Control Ministry was suppressed and a State Control Committee formed in its place. It has already been noted that in so vast a country as the Soviet Union efficient direction and control of industry becomes impossible. These functions passed to the regional organs, able to take account on the spot of the needs to be satisfied and the most suitable means of satisfying them. These regional organs were the sovnarkhozes, or economic councils, which are the motive force of all economic activities in their area. They acted with a certain amount of autonomy which, as will be seen, was later restricted. The sovnarkhozes are dependent on the governments of the federated republics which, after the reform, found their spheres of competence considerably enlarged.

This decentralization was not limited to the economic sphere but was extended to the judiciary also, since the Union Ministry of Justice was abolished and its functions transferred to the Ministries of Justice of the federated republics. Even the Supreme Court of the Soviet Union had its functions diminished, while those of the Supreme Courts of the individual republics were correspondingly enlarged. Each of these republics has its own Code of Laws which must conform completely to the 'basic laws' of the Union.

Only in the financial field has the unitary structure remained unaltered. It is true that on October 30, 1959, at the session of the Supreme Soviet, a new law on the state budget was approved, the third after those of 1924 and 1927, but that too was based on the rigid principle of the financial predominance of the Union and on the system of a unified state budget. Following these principles the Supreme Soviet, which is the highest organ of the Union, reserved to itself the exclusive right of allotting the budget assets between the Union and the federated republics, as well as that of expanding or restricting the quotas assigned to one or the other. The 'objective' competence of establishing the form and measure of taxation also belongs exclusively to the Supreme Soviet, together with its allocation and methods of collection. 'A unified policy for the collection of the budget income is in force throughout the country' according to the law of October 30, 1959.

In consequence the federated republics have strictly limited powers concerning the total of their budgets and their sources of income. The smaller federated republics especially have not got much revenue at their disposal and would not therefore be able to do without the large sums from the state budget for putting economic programmes into operation. Therefore the whole economic and financial life of these minor republics is dependent on the Union.

Khrushchev's decentralization has not in practice achieved all the results expected of it. The increase in autonomy has encouraged the growth of regional particularism. It has therefore been necessary to reverse the process. In July 1961 the State Control Committee was transformed into a State Control Commission known as the Goskontrol with powers to appoint its representatives to the federated governments and individual enterprises and to act without reference to the federated governments. It is hoped that this stiffening of the central control will be able to cure slackness in production, falsification of statistics, fraud, bad organization and, above all, failure to apply the economic plans which the Gosplan draws up and supervises. *Pravda*, listing these shortcomings, has accused the sovnarkhozes and the technical ministries for the poor yield of the enterprises.

To avoid such shortcomings a decision was reached in February 1962, after long investigations and many meetings from March 1961 onward, to divide the Soviet Union into seventeen economic regions. Each of these would embrace a certain number of 'economic councils' in order to create large economic entities able, thanks to the means and natural resources at their disposal, to develop specified industrial sectors without recourse to continual and complicated requisitions of manpower and material from other centres.

The division of the Soviet Union into economic regions is nothing new; it was adopted for the first time in 1920, revived in 1929 (twenty-four economic regions) and once more in 1958 (thirteen economic regions) but, up to the present, the regions have not had, or at least did not manage to acquire, a specified and co-ordinated function.

This new sub-division is intended to give the economic regions directive powers and each of them has a 'Council of Co-ordination and Planning' with the task of co-ordinating the activities of the economic councils, of developing new techniques and applying the most recent scientific discoveries, as well as maintaining links with the other economic regions.

To conclude; the Soviet Union has a strongly centralized structure. The right of secession is a fiction. The Party with its iron organization does its best to stifle every manifestation of autonomy and every national claim which might imperil the unity of the Soviet state.

CHAPTER XIX

The Anti-Religious Struggle

1

COMMUNISM declares itself to be materialist and atheist. Communists and believers are in total opposition. For communism religion is superstition, an anachronistic survival of a past when myth took the place of scientific truth. In the new world created by communism such irrational influences cannot be tolerated. They obscure and fetter human knowledge and help to keep alive a social order based on class distinctions and therefore destined to disappear. Starting from such premises, the Soviet régime with the considered intention of uprooting all faith has gone to great lengths in the anti-religious struggle. It has thus fallen into the error of all sectarian governments of fighting an idea with violence, which only gives fresh life to the idea.

The Soviet constitution formally guarantees freedom of of conscience to all. In Article 124 it states that 'with the aim of guaranteeing freedom of conscience the Church in the Soviet Union is disestablished and education is divorced from the Church. Freedom of worship and freedom of anti-religious propaganda are recognized for all citizens'. The constitution, therefore, while it does not permit religious propaganda, grants to all the right to make anti-religious propaganda. In this way freedom of conscience, that is the right of the citizen to express his religious convictions, is denied and even violated since the citizen is placed in a position where it is impossible for him to defend himself against anyone who offends his religious sentiments, especially since this offence to his conscience is not only unpunished but even encouraged by the law.

Freedom of worship, that is the exercise of a religious ministry, is all that is allowed the Church, but within very restricted limits, that is only within buildings intended for public worship.

According to Soviet writers the conception expressed in Article 124 is considerably broader than the principles that regulate similar matters in Western legislation which, in their view, lack the essential factor which guarantees true freedom of conscience, that is the right of the citizen not to profess any religion. Such a criticism, on which communist propaganda insists with great frequency, is without foundation, because freedom of conscience in the West is understood in the widest sense, including the right not to believe.

The principles affirmed by the constitution were laid down by Lenin who held the view that the state must consider religion to be a private affair.

2

In commenting on this criterion, Soviet writers start with a subtle distinction; if religion is a private matter as far as the state is concerned it cannot be so for the Party. With that uncertainty of legal criteria so often shown in the decisions of the Soviet government, this bases anti-religious policy on the distinction between state and Party, almost as if the Party were not an organ, even the most important organ, of the state. This makes it possible to uphold the fiction that the state allows freedom of conscience while permitting the Party to carry on a violent offensive against religious convictions which, according to the Leninist principle, should remain for all public organs the private concern of the individual citizen. In this way the shrine of conscience is not sheltered from insult. How many times have Soviet citizens been forced in self-criticism to lay bare their souls and to profane the sanctuary whose threshold no man should be permitted to cross !

A Soviet newspaper has formulated the sophism in this way : 'The Party is the union of combatants, alert and responsible, which promotes the emancipation of the working class and therefore cannot, and must not, remain indifferent to the lack of awareness, the ignorance and the obscurantism reflected in religious beliefs and rites.' The orator does not hesitate to add that 'never has the question of freedom of conscience and guarantees for it been so consistently and wisely resolved as in the Soviet laws'.

3

The Church, as has been pointed out, does not depend on the state. It is a private organization in which the state does not interfere but limits itself to guaranteeing the exercise of religious worship. Every direct action to hinder this is punishable by law, as shown for example by Article 127 of the Penal Code of the Russian federated republic.

All religious buildings and the ground on which they stand belongs to the state. Questions concerning the use of such property are decided by a council for the affairs of the cults and a council for the affairs of the Orthodox Church, under the control of the Council of Ministers.

The administrative organs of the government allot buildings to the religious organizations, concern themselves with repairs and provide paper and presses for the publication of religious books and periodicals.

The Church is exempt from taxation.

When at least twenty adult citizens make a demand to form a religious group, such a group is registered.

Religious instruction outside the Church is punished. Youth is thus safeguarded against religious propaganda.

If the Church, at least formally and within narrow limits, is independent of the state, it is not, nor are the private organizations assimilated with it, independent of the Party, which controls it closely. Since every church is administered by a parochial council in which laymen take part, it is through these laymen, as well as through pressure exercised on the priests permitted to officiate, that the Party makes its will felt and exercises its supervision.

4

It cannot honestly be said that one breathes the air of religious freedom in a country where not even the most elementary forms are safeguarded and where the régime sets out 'gradually to free the whole population from religious superstition'.

If it is not to renounce communism, the Soviet state cannot waver from this line of conduct. It wants to forge the new man, that is to change human nature, by eliminating everything spiritual. For the communist the world is matter and only matter. Therefore Lenin's admonition is apt. 'Our struggle,' he said, 'will not succeed until the myth of God has been extirpated from the spirit of man.'

Consistent with these principles, persecution in the early days of the revolution was very violent and very bloody. The Russian Church as a whole withstood it with great courage and firmness.

After the collapse of tsarism the government supported the principle of full religious liberty and suppressed the office of Procurator-General of the Holy Synod. The Church took advantage of this to summon a Great Council on August 15, 1917. It was the first such meeting since 1696. The Great Council drew up a new statute for the Church which provided for the restoration of the Patriarchate suppressed by Peter the Great. Tikhon, Metropolitan of Moscow, was elected Patriarch by the Council on November 5, 1917.

The exalted responsibility of defending the interests of the Church when it was suffering the maximum violence and hostility of a revolutionary movement which made no secret of wanting to root out Christianity throughout the whole country, moved the Patriarch to hurl an anathema against the enemies of the faith. This action and the Church's refusal in 1922 to hand over the consecrated objects of worship to the authorities embittered the struggle. The tombs of the saints were profaned, churches and convents were sacked, priests and laymen brought to trial. Many were condemned to death. Among these victims sanctified by martyrdom was the meek figure of the Metropolitan of Petersberg, Benjamin, shot with other dignitaries of his diocese.

Patriarch Tikhon also was arrested on May 9, 1922 and kept in prison for a year. After his release he lived only two years. By his last testament the functions of the Patriarch were temporarily entrusted to the Metropolitan of Nizhni-Novgorod, Sergei. With him the storm died down.

5

On January 23, 1918 Lenin had the decree on the separation of Church and State, which was to remain the canon of policy towards the Churches, approved by the Council of People's Commissars. The exhaustion caused by the civil war and more especially the unfavourable reaction of the people's conscience to such rigorous measures weakened the offensive. In 1927 Metropolitan Sergei was authorized to form a Patriarchal Holy Synod to assist him in the administration of the Church. A phase of tolerance began.

At the outbreak of war the Church ranged itself alongside the combatants. Metropolitan Sergei in a very noble message evoked the guardian saints of Russia and blessed the nation. The clergy was allowed to exercise its ministry with the fighting armies, so that the comforts of the faith should not be lacking for those who sacrificed themselves for their country.

A council of bishops was able to meet on September 8, 1943 and elected Metropolitan Sergei as Patriarch. When he died a few months later the Metropolitan of Leningrad, Alexei, mounted the patriarchal throne. He is still reigning.

6

The Russian Orthodox Church, according to the statute that reorganized it, is governed by the Patriarch with the assistance of the Holy Synod made up of six bishops with the Patriarch himself as chairman. A number of 'services' similar to the Vatican Congregations are dependent on the Holy Synod.

Relations with the state are maintained through the Council for the affairs of the Orthodox Church attached to the Council of Ministers. The Secretary of the Council has duties similar to those of the Procurator of the Holy Synod in tsarist times.

The bishops are elected by the Synod; the parish priests are supported by the Church Council and the Control Council, both elected by the General Assembly of parishioners.

Before the revolution there were forty-six thousand churches in Russia, served by fifty thousand priests. In 1935 the churches still open were reduced to little more than five hundred, with five thousand priests. In 1956 the churches where services were being held rose to twenty thousand and the priests to thirty-five thousand. Convents, which in 1917 numbered one thousand and twenty-six, were reduced in the times of trouble to less than forty. Now there are sixty-nine monasteries and nunneries; they have the right to own land, beasts and workshops if these are manned by those in the convent, and must pay a tax on them. There are eight seminaries, each attended by about two hundred students, and two theological academies, one which also organizes correspondence courses. The most famous is that of Zagorsk, a real citadel of religion within the circuit of its ancient turreted walls.

Abroad, the Russian Orthodox Church has exarchs, dioceses, missions and *metochias*.

7

Despite the harmony thus restored and despite the agreement, reached by mutual consent, on the functions proper to the Church and its relations with the state, the vigilance of the Party is detailed and suspicious, always ready to resort to rigorous measures.

Above all, the spiteful anti-religious propaganda never lets up for a moment, prompted by the constant fear of a resurgence of religious fervour and a new ascendancy of the Church over the masses. The press and propaganda therefore aim at undermining the work of restoration that the ecclesiastical hierarchy and the clergy are silently carrying on with great perseverance, tact and discretion. They make use of the most abusive and slanderous campaigns to discredit the new apostles. Its constant themes are the ignorance and depravity of the bishops, priests and monks. Thus in the spring of

1959 they published the names of some bishops of the Patriarchate accused of the vilest crimes by some priests who had deserted the priesthood. Their particular target was Archbishop Sergei of Astra-Khan and Stalingrad. In September 1959 the attack moved on to Archbishop Antonije of Stavropolsk and Baku. The convents, beginning with the most venerated such as the Pecherski Lavras at Kiev and Pskov, are favourite targets for these scurrilous insults. They are accused of deceiving the public by the cult of saints and the sale of fake relics in order to extort money from the faithful. The convents are described as boltholes for lazy and ignorant people who have found a way of living comfortably at the expense of the workers. They broadcast the usual calumnies about the licentiousness of the priests, their perversion of the students and the backwardness of their curricula. The Party incites families to protest against the 'incarceration' of their children in monasteries and nunneries.

But since it has become evident that the scurrilous tone of this sort of campaign based on insults and vulgar calumnies ends by creating disgust and achieves an effect opposite to that intended, an attempt is being made to raise it to a scientific and philosophical plane, above all by stressing that religion is incompatible with science and degrades it, since it admits the existence of forces and phenomena that are beyond the human intellect. Furthermore, religion is the ally of the upper classes to whose advantage it preaches submission and patience, distracting the masses from their struggle against exploiters and slackening their interest in the conquest of the good things of this world.

In order to give the propaganda a new form and wider possibilities of penetration, a new review entitled *Science and Religion* was published at the end of 1959, with some very highly educated contributors. The tone of the review was set by Khrushchev in its first number. He wrote: 'Public instruction, the diffusion of scientific ideas and the study of the laws of nature leave no place for faith in God.'

An idea of the new review may be deduced from an article in it by Academician Ambarzumyan, in collaboration with the mathematical-physicist Kukarkin. The article is entitled: *Man is the Master of Nature*. It says: 'From the time when Copernicus launched his defence of the Catholic Church in the interpretation of the phenomena of nature, and astronomy began to conquer one position after another, expelling God and his angels from the material world, the religious hypothesis of the creation of the world suffered an irreparable defeat.'

But was not Copernicus himself a believer?

It is clear from all this that the struggle against the Church is now based on propaganda and on education, of which the state has a monopoly, rather than on pressure, threats and administrative measures. In fact, contemporaneously with the publication of the review, courses in scientific atheism were introduced in the secondary schools. In the factories the activity of the atheist clubs has been stepped up. In fact there has evidently been an order to intensify the anti-religious campaign.

We are, therefore, in a culminating phase of the struggle. All higher Soviet education is being mobilized against the peril of a resurgence of religious fervour. The editor of the review *Science and Religion*, Pavel Polonitski, summed up in the March 1961 number the main heads of the anti-Christian crusade: 'Whatever stand the Church may take on every historic occasion, whatever policy it may adopt, it remains the standard-bearer and propagandist of a false, anti-scientific and reactionary ideology. Therefore, willy nilly, it is opposed to the building of a new life and is an obstacle to our progress on the road to communism.'

8

The incompatibility between Christianity and communism could not have been more clearly stated and, at the same time, the inexorable nature of the struggle going on between them. The conciliatory attitude of the Church, even if it has won a breathing space in which to reorganize its hierarchy and consolidate the community of the faithful, in fact to restore its framework, does not exempt it from the struggle which is becoming more and more severe and which may compromise, at any given moment, perhaps sooner than one thinks, the work so well begun.

In fact the Orthodox Church does not yet seem to have mastered the crisis that threatens to submerge it. Its upper hierarchy does not seem to understand the nature of this crisis that has lasted for centuries and has made the Church the passive instrument of despotism both in the past and in the present, gradually consuming its vital substance. The Orthodox Church lacks the tradition of struggle, the pride, the militancy, the absolute dedication to the fullness of faith in Christ. How in fact has the Church reacted to the virulent attacks made on it by the Party, the press and the propaganda. It does not react at all. It is intent on one thing only—survival. The ecclesiastical hierarchy is obsequious and submissive to the authorities. To resist is regarded as an absurdity, a folly. There is not the consciousness, so lively in the Catholic Church, that the blood of the martyrs is the seed of new Christians, that only struggle purifies and selects, that the future is for those who struggle, since only struggle stirs the conscience, poses the problems, stiffens the malcontents, affirms the existence of spiritual values and tempers the faithful. As long as communism maintains its pressure on men's consciences, the Church will always be a slave, even if apparently free, because there is no compromise possible between communism and Christianity. The Church must draw the inevitable conclusion. If its faith in Christ is not mere talk but a conviction, it must stake everything on the victory of the faith. It must abstain from renunciations and servility that degrade its dignity and damage its prestige in the eyes of the public.

9

What is the attitude of the Russian masses towards the Church? The rebirth of a religious sentiment is undeniable. We have spoken of the reopening of the churches, mainly by the initiative of the believers who have demanded it. The religious vocation too is flourishing. There are more than five thousand monks. The churches are crowded. After the death of Stalin the number of baptisms doubled. Huge sums flow in to the Patriarchate from all parts of the Soviet Union, to the churches and to the monasteries. Perhaps never as now has the Russian Church had such an abundance of funds at its disposal. 'We could rebuild all the churches in Russia whenever we like,' a high ecclesiastical dignitary told an acquaintance of mine. In only six mouths the Pecherski monastery at Pskov received a thousand donations and, by post alone, two hundred thousand rubles. The abundance of these donations shows the intensity of the feelings of those who send them. Perhaps these offerings are intended to make up for the lack of participation in religious life, to provide a concrete testimony of solidarity. All the churches of any historical importance have been restored regardless of expense, and the golden cupolas surmounted by the cross that triumphs over the crescent once more sparkle in the skies of Holy Russia.

Inside, these Russian churches are parcelled out in the traditional manner into a multitude of tiny areas separated from one another by ikonostases. Almost always the immensity of our cathedrals is lacking, the impetus of our transepts and cupolas that raise the spirit towards the infinite. The Russian worshipper loves his tiny chapel, prostrates himself, kisses the ikon that is the object of his special veneration, searches for the all-enveloping twilight. It is a form of mysticism, made up of humility, of self-pity, of abandonment to the goodness of God. The Russian churches respond wonderfully to this chaste revelation of the soul. No brutal violence can stifle the unrestrained longing of these souls to rise to a world that transcends material reality.

A religion only disappears with the diffusion of another, higher and more spiritual. The rebirth of the Christian faith bears witness to the feeble response that Marxist materialism has aroused in the consciousness of the masses and its incapacity to replace a religion wholly spiritual in the mystical consciousness of the Russian people.

Khrushchev seemed to be aware of this, as may be deduced from the following anecdote told by him at a press conference on June 3, 1960. 'In the first years after the revolution,' he said, 'there were many stupid questionnaires to fill up. They were especially addressed to intellectuals. One of them included the question: "Do you believe in God?" One employee replied: "At home I believe in God but not in the office."'

10

Because of this struggle pushed to the uttermost by every possible means, the ground lost is immense and difficult to recover. The de-Christianization of the masses has been made easier by land-collectivization, by urbanism, by the foundation of new centres and above all by that cataract of humanity which has driven millions of people from one end of the country to the other, uprooting them from their traditional homes. In all the new agricultural enterprises, whether sovkhozes or kolkhozes, there are no churches and no priests, nor are religious rites celebrated. *Kommunist* (No. 8, 1960) quotes the example of one such village, Karavaevo in the Kostroma region, where 'there are no ikons in the workers' homes, no one baptizes the children and no one observes religious festivals'. In the countless new cities that are rising between the Urals and the Pacific, churches are not built, religious life is dead and a completely atheist race is growing up.

In 1959 the Soviet Academy of Sciences held an enquiry in certain districts of historic Russia, specifically in the provinces of Kalinin, Kostroma, Gorki and Yaroslav, to find out the state of religion among the kolkhoz workers.

The investigation showed that the old faith had lost its former intensity because of greater ignorance of religious doctrine, and that the practice of religion was less diffused. In the new agricultural centres there were no religious buildings; therefore services were not held.

Naturally, the investigators point out, the older generation, those

439

aged sixty or over, had kept their beliefs. They are regarded as spreaders of contagion, like microbe carriers. They are the virus for the spread of the faith to new generations.

The Academy of Sciences reports that those between forty and fifty-five who were educated in Soviet schools and alienated from the faith by intense anti-religious propaganda have renounced religious marriage, do not baptize their children and do not keep ikons in their homes. None the less, there are some among them, especially women, who declare themselves believers, though their ideas both about the doctrines and the precepts of the faith are very vague; often they do not even know the prayers, but remain faithful to a tradition which has been constantly observed.

Finally, there is the younger generation. The results of the enquiry might have been expected to show that the young remain indifferent to the anti-religious propaganda either because it has lost its bite or because the whole question no longer interests them. The Academy concludes that this indifference of youth to the religious problem safeguards them from the reactionary influence of religion. None the less the investigators stress that the custom of keeping ikons in the house is once more in fashion, as is also the custom of having new-born babies baptized, customs which almost completely disappeared in the countryside after the revolution. Both those who have themselves been baptized and those who have not have their children baptized. The practice of church weddings and religious services at funerals is also widespread. In fact religious ceremonies are recovering their former ascendancy and even representatives of public organizations attend them.

The most intransigent are still the activists, the propagandists and the 'vanguard', that is to say members of the Party and of the organizations dependent on it.

It must be noted that the enquiry was held in an area traditionally one of the most religious in the country. Taken as a whole, the crisis is still acute and the signs of recovery pretty vague. There was, especially at first, a virtual collapse, despite indomitable courage on the part of some members of the hierarchy and the clergy.

11

When one enquires into the causes of this serious setback to the faith in Russia, one is compelled to admit that the responsibility rests mainly on the Russian Church, which has failed in its task of creating a firm religious faith among the people. Those who wrote about the Russian people in the course of last century stressed the poverty of religious culture. The Church has not carried out the exalted ministry that might have been expected of it, nor has it been, as it should have been, a moulder of character. Therefore the faithful lacked that unwavering conviction of their own rights which is for the Church the surest guarantee of its own rights. It has therefore deserved its fate, since in life and in history every fault inevitably brings its own expiation.

The ignorance of the Russian clergy was proverbial. How far did this formalism, this bigotry, this lack of any urge for reform, in fact the tainted atmosphere of the Russian Church, repulse some of Russia's finest spirits like Pushkin and Tolstoy, who none the less sometimes felt the nostalgic appeal of the ancient religious centres? Monks like Rasputin were far from rare and even more frequent were the visionaries, men like the high-priest Avakum who was hostile to the revision of the Scriptures carried out by Nikon and who boasted of not being a scholar, of knowing neither dialectic nor rhetoric but of only possessing the 'reason of Christ'.

Belinski's famous letter, read by Dostoyevsky at a meeting of revolutionaries and which earned Dostoyevsky a sentence of forced labour in Siberia, said: 'In most cases our clergy is mainly distinguished for its empty and resounding phrases, its scholastic pedantry and its barbarous lack of education.' The same Belinski wrote to Gogol that Russia saw her salvation 'not in mysticism, not in pietism . . . but in the affirmation of that human dignity that has been degraded in mud and filth for centuries'.

Not to have felt the need to raise this human dignity has been, and still is, the great fault of the Orthodox Church. Therefore its clergy have never exercised a true moral ascendancy over the people. De Custine, who had searing words for this passivity of the Russian Church, reproached it for its sterility. 'This Church is dead,' he wrote. The wealth of the monasteries and of the high dignitaries extinguished the spirit of the apostolate. There was a time when the Zagorsk monastery was the greatest landowner in Russia. How different was the spectacle of the ancient *lavras* excavated like catacombs from the hillside overlooking the Dnieper by the very first monks who buried themselves alive there. It is true, however, that this fervour of asceticism lasted scarcely fifty years, after which the monks emerged from their living tombs into the sunlight and built the great monasteries that the Intourist guides take one to see, not forgetting to show the luxurious dwelling of the Metropolitan of the *lavra* amid the picturesque woodlands on the river bank.

The epic of the Russian Church coincides with the period of struggle for independence against Tatar dominion. The Church alone did not betray, did not bargain, and identified the cause of the faith with the cause of the country. It has lived ever since on the memory of this glory. It may well be said that the unity of the nation was re-created on the unity of the Church because wherever the Church preserved the Orthodox faith it at the same time preserved the sovereign rights of Russia. And since the greatest threat was from Catholicism which spread as far as Kiev, the cradle of Russian Christianity, the Russian Church has seemed to identify its reason for existence with its struggle against Rome. Moscow inherited from Byzantium the ancient anti-Catholic hatred, which soon degenerated into systematic opposition to every Western influence.

Thus the ecclesiastical hierarchy and the monks became the most frenzied opponents of every reform, in which they saw a threat to the integrity and the consecrated ritual of Orthodoxy, convinced that relations with the West contaminated the Russian people by diffusing the vices of a corrupt world. Nor were they aware that in their efforts to isolate Russia they would end by isolating themselves and alienating themselves from the living currents of the world.

The beginnings of the crisis can be found in the failure of the attempt by Metropolitan Isidore, a Greek of very high culture and great spirituality, to put an end to the schism between East and West by adhering to the union of the churches proclaimed by the Council of Florence. Having returned to Moscow from the Council in 1441, the Metropolitan was forced to flee and seek asylum in Italy. After his time the Russian Church refused to accept the appointment of the Metropolitan by the Byzantine Patriarch, who was accused of selling out Orthodoxy to the Roman pontiff.

Thenceforward Moscow became the anti-Rome and the anti-Byzantium. The legend arose of a mystical mission conferred by God on Holy Russia to preserve the purity of the faith. It was the legend of the Third Rome, spread by a visionary monk who induced the tsar to extend the confines of the faith. Thus there began, with the support of the clergy, a movement of national expansion which led to the recovery of the former territories and which created the bases of the future empire. This victorious expansion assumed the character of a crusade. Ivan III, when he seized Novgorod, declared that he had come to punish the apostates who had renounced the faith in favour of Catholicism. The Novgorod nobles, who had signed an agreement with Lithuania, were exterminated and the archbishop, Teofil, was deposed. Ivan IV, at the conquest of Kazan, raised the cross above the crescent in memory of the victory and this emblem still crowns the pinnacles of all Orthodox churches in Russia.

In all these events, which were the origins of Russian power, the Moscow Patriarchate had a decisive influence. Its political role became greater and greater, up to the time when the Patriarch Nikon tried to affirm the superiority of the spiritual over the temporal power. Then the uncontrollable decline began. The Patriarch was arrested and exiled. An ecclesiastical council in 1667 proclaimed the supremacy of the secular power over the ecclesiastical and the right of the sovereign to intervene in religious matters. A few years later Peter the Great suppressed the Patriarchate and placed the Holy Synod in control of the Church under the supervision of a Procurator-General.

The mission which the Patriarchate had assumed, the guardianship of Orthodoxy, passed to the tsar who became the protector of eastern Christianity. This ushered in a most dangerous period of united political and religious power. The Church became an *instrumentum regni*, passively subject to the sovereign, and the tool of autocracy.

When it has lost its liberty a Church is in its death-throes. To live, to breathe, it must be free, that is it must feel free and be able to act freely. It is not a matter of material freedom, which does not always depend on it, but of moral freedom, how it behaves before the mighty of the earth and the peoples of the earth, of its unconditional dedication to the cure of the souls and the miseries of men, beginning with the humblest and those most in need. 'The peoples,' observed De Custine, 'who have a sense of freedom will never obey in their hearts a clergy that is enslaved.'

12

The Russian Church has returned to the beginnings of its crisis, when Peter the Great subjected it to the control of the Procurator-General of the Holy Synod. It begins its experience anew. Two roads are open to it: the traditional one, of an historic mission incumbent on the Orthodox Church, which it has inherited from Byzantium and which it cannot accomplish without the support of the power of the state, seconding its plans and justifying its authority; or the apostolic one, of obeying solely the mandate of God to bring the gospel to the people and to rekindle the Christian spirit among the masses which materialism is trying to win over to its principles. The first is the way of conciliation, of living in peace, the way of prudence; the other is the way of struggle, perhaps of martyrdom, but of freedom and of faith in the unfettered rights of the spirit.

The Russian Orthodox Church, in fact, lacks the tradition of a rigid, austere, jealous independence. The tradition handed down to it by Byzantium justifies, from the writings of the Fathers of the Eastern Church, the power of the autocrat and affirms his rights.

Perhaps the Orthodox Church will pay dearly for this period of relative calm, marked by a formal cordiality of relations between Church and state. The submissiveness of the Church accords ill with the intransigence of an atheist propaganda which makes no secret of its determination to wipe out every trace of the Christian faith.

13

For its part the state is satisfied with this submissiveness of the Church and abstains from violent measures. They have attained a sort of compromise that is in the interest of the political authorities to maintain, for more than one reason.

On many occasions Lenin warned his followers not to exasperate a religious reaction by outraging consciences by rigorous measures, though at the height of the crisis he was more than once forced to forego his own principles. Khrushchev reverted to a policy of moderation, without thereby deviating from doctrinal intransigence. On receiving the Lenin Peace Prize in May 1959 he said: 'Although we are atheists we do not preach hostility to believers. We regard those who believe not only with tolerance but even with respect.' These are the words of a great statesman and a man of great intelligence.

Khrushchev also showed that he was not averse to a relaxation of the struggle against the Catholic Church. He could not but be aware of the invincible firmness of this adversary which does not admit to bargaining. The Catholics hold very strong positions in at least two of the communist countries—Poland and Hungary. Here national sentiment is identified with Catholic sentiment; it stands up to oppression and has an insatiable yearning for liberty. It is a force that is always active and which it would be dangerous to exasperate, since religious persecution always strengthens the persecuted whatever his wounds but never the persecutors whatever their violence.

There is, furthermore, the policy of the communist parties in the Western lands to coax political moderates into the popular fronts. To that end they appeal to certain Christian Democrat groups whose religious susceptibilities it is inopportune to offend.

Finally the Soviet government, through the Moscow Patriarchate, has resumed the traditional Russian policy of aid to, and benevolent support of, the hierarchies of the Christian churches of the Levant. It is a form of penetration by means of a subsidized clientele.

Above all, in the Soviet Union itself, the Russian Orthodox Church has proved itself a valuable ally in time of war to sustain the fighters' resistance and in time of peace to support and give validity to the peace propaganda.

Therefore there is now a relatively peaceful pause, for purely contingent reasons. But the origins of the conflict remain and it is not to be expected that they will grow less, since they stem from the inevitable clash of two doctrines, two conceptions of life.

14

Can the Orthodox Church, cut off from Christendom, change its line of conduct and maintain the unequal struggle? Today, in the light of the tragic events of the last forty years, we can see the immense harm to all Christianity of a schism that wounds the brotherhood of those who follow a common faith and stops the circulation of feelings and ideas in the mystic body of the Church. It is hoped that the thinking of the greatest philosophers of Russia, Solovev and Berdyaev, will be deeply studied in the gravity of this hour.

Today the two great branches of the Christian faith are separated in their struggle against a common adversary and are not only divided but, at least on the part of the Orthodox Church, maintain their old feelings of hostility. The Uniate Church, which represented a happy attempt to overcome the old rivalries, like a bridge towards the future, was suppressed, immediately after the last war, both in Belorussia and in the Ukraine. The bishops of Leopoli, of Stanislaviev and of Przemysl, as well as the Apostolic Vicar in Volhynia, were arrested in 1945, together with five hundred priests. A decree of the Synod of Leopoli in 1946 imposed separation from Rome and a return to Orthodoxy. There was a return to the tsarist policy of tolerating Catholics of the Latin rite but of hostility towards all the Uniate communities, regarding with suspicion every attempt to revive them.

15

The Catholic Church in the Baltic lands is regarded with no less suspicion. Priests are forbidden to carry on their ministry on the most futile pretexts; some have been imprisoned on accusations of foreign exchange dealings. Seminarists have frequently been forced to interrupt their studies. Many churches are closed; from time to time the authorities even demand that some in which services are still being held are to be handed over, nor will they allow priests to exercise their ministry outside their own areas, nor even to take part in the solemn ceremonies at one or another shrine. Church-going is regarded with suspicion. The *Sovetskaya Kultura* of September 5, 1959 censured the custom of pilgrimages to Latgaliya in Latvia to venerate the picture of the Aglonskaya Madonna. The participation of young pilgrims is especially censured.

Every practice of the faith is hindered; the vexations are countless. The authorities refuse to recognize the Catholic administrators appointed by the Holy See, nor do they permit bishops of whom they do not approve to celebrate ordinations. Some bishops are forbidden to reside in their own dioceses, like the Bishop of Riga, Monsignor Casimir Dulbinskis, and even worse they are forbidden to perform their episcopal functions. Finally, the Catholic churches are heavily taxed, either on their cubic content or on their artistic value. The churches of Vilno pay at the moment up to three thousand new rubles annually.

In Lithuania religious publications, which before the war had a circulation of seven million copies, have been forbidden. Of the twelve hundred and two churches existing only six hundred are open. The Lithuanian Catholic clergy, which before the war numbered one thousand six hundred and forty-six priests, has now only five hundred priests, mostly of advanced age. At least eleven hundred and forty-six priests have been killed, imprisoned or exiled. There is a single seminary where the number of pupils is limited to sixty.

Thus the Church lives in silence.

But the resistance is unbroken. It is enough to visit the Baltic lands to be aware of the determination of the people, especially the faithful, not to yield. Here there is no compromise, no complaisance. They look towards the example of Poland and Hungary and to the great figures of their Primates, who personify the resistance. What dignity, what pride is in their words! 'It is true that the Church rebels against every oppression,' declared the Primate of Poland, Cardinal Stefan Wyszynski, in reply to Gomulka's attacks on the Roman Church. And since Gomulka affirmed that the Polish laws do not discriminate in religious matters, the Primate retorted that in Poland the laws guarantee freedom of conscience only on paper and that 'the faithful are ready to go down into the catacombs and to conspire for the defence of their religion and their freedom to express it'. These are his words: 'There are times when darkness covers the earth. But when the clouds break once more we shall see Christ who from his cross guides humanity towards the future, lest men be transformed into a pack of wolves which devour one another.'

It is not surprising that faced with such firmness of language, with so serene and confident a resolution, so sure of the support of Him who rules the destiny of peoples, the struggle should be concentrated on the Catholic Church and primarily on the Vatican, despite the blandishments which from time to time try to awake the hope of some conciliatory gesture. Yet the tragedy of this struggle is the impossibility of conciliation, for every compromise is an illusion or a betrayal, at least as long as communism maintains the rigour of its idealogical premises. Therefore the Soviet press at intervals showers the Catholics with calumnies and launches the most vulgar abuse at the Vatican which is described as a den of obscurantism and the inspirer of world reaction against communism.

In so hostile an atmosphere the position of the Catholics in the Soviet Union is most precarious, since they are exposed to every sudden and arbitrary act of the authorities. They number approximately three and a half, or at the most four, million. They are most numerous in the Baltic states, in the Ukraine and in Belorussia. Before the revolution they had fifty-four thousand churches and twenty-four thousand chapels. Now they have one thousand two hundred and forty-one.

There are three thousand Catholics in Moscow. Their only church is St Louis of the French built in 1827 by the Italian architect Gilardi. The priest is Father Withold Broniski, a Pole from the area bordering on Lithuania. The congregation is mostly made up of old people, mainly women. They are sixty to seventy per cent Polish, fifteen per cent Lithuanian and the rest Russian or naturalized Russians of German origin. But what a fervour of faith in this congregation of old derelicts to whom nothing in life remains save the consolations of their religion.

There are only two Catholic seminaries in the Soviet Union, at Riga and at Kaunas (Kovno). Requests for admission are scrutinized by the State Committee for Religious Cults.

16

The Jews share the honours of persecution with the Catholics despite their decisive contribution to the triumph of the revolution. It is estimated that there are about two and a half million Jews, of whom about half a million are in Moscow. All these people live in terror. They are forbidden to emigrate to Israel. There was an attempt to concentrate them in a district in the Soviet Far East close to the Chinese frontier at Birobidzhan, but the experiment failed. Their rights are restricted by every sort of vexation. The use of the Yiddish language is not permitted either for teaching or for the publication of books. They are forbidden to have Yiddish theatres or newspapers.

The threat of fresh restrictions, fresh accusations, fresh trials, fresh sentences, remains suspended over their heads. In the last years of his life Stalin suddenly promoted his 'anticosmopolitan campaign' against them and, if he had not died, the trial of the Jewish doctors would have ended with the condemnation of those healers unjustly accused of criminal activities. In 1961 three leaders of the Israelite community of Leningrad were tried and sentenced for espionage. Other arrests and sentences to forced labour followed. The Vaad Yeshivo, the Presidency of the only Hebrew seminary in the Soviet Union, was dissolved. The seminary was attended by twenty or thirty pupils. In the same year the synagogues in twelve cities were closed by the authorities.

The reason for this persecution of the Jews is the same as that for the persecution of the Catholics. The authorities suspect them of connections with the international Jewish community, even as they fear Catholic solidarity with believers throughout the world. The tactics used against one and the other are the same; an attempt to isolate them from their co-religionists outside the Soviet Union, to decapitate the religious communities by removing their leaders, either by arrest or trial, thus making it impossible for them to carry on their ministry and continually threatening them and subjecting them to the most harassing and vexatious control. At the beginning of 1962 the Israeli Embassy in Moscow was accused of being an espionage centre in contact with the leaders of the Russian Hebrew community. For that reason the leaders of the community were brought to trial.

17

The solidarity of the Moslems in the Soviet Union and the Islamic world is also regarded with suspicion. The authorities try to weaken these ties by hindering pilgrimages to the Holy Places of Islam. Many mosques have been turned into museums, with exhibitions of pictures, drawings and old photographs to draw attention to examples of fanaticism, superstition, slavery and exploitation of the people by the begs. The press too recalls this feudal past to serve as a pretext for attacks on Islam for keeping so large a part of humanity in squalid misery and backwardness. To tell the truth these are now becoming less frequent. By way of contrast it exalts the advances of the Moslem peoples of the Union. These number about fifteen million and include persons of great culture, many of whom hold chairs, or take active part, in the Institutes of Oriental Languages and Culture, of which there are many in Russia in Asia. These institutes encourage the translation of Russian and foreign authors into Arabic or of Arab writers into Russian. They also reproduce and annotate old manuscripts and study problems that concern the Moslem world.

Thus there is a constant exchange of ideas and influences with centres of Islamic culture outside Russia. To facilitate such penetration the anti-Islamic propaganda has been toned down. The Soviet Moslems are for the most part 'Sini', that is to say Sunnites, and their community is presided over by four Mufti: at Ufâ, Baku, Tashkent and Buinsk. The monumental ruins of the palaces, mosques and the splendid tombs of the Timurides and the Tatar khans have been restored with loving care. And, to tell the truth, the influence of the Islamic centres outside the Soviet Union on the Soviet Moslem world, strong in its re-acquired culture, seems to be very slight; this helps to calm the suspicions of the authorities.

18

On the other hand there is great vigilance shown against the expansion of the Protestant religious sects which are trying to profit from the ground lost by the Orthodox Church to increase the number of their proselytes. Many of these sects, which seem to have about three million adherents or sympathizers, display, like the Baptists, an energy, a courage, a novelty of form and a wealth of initiative that create the most favourable response among a people sensitive to any manifestation of faith. This competition by the sects is not new; it goes back to the times before the revolution, but it was especially evident during World War II and showed that the vacuum left by a Church too inactive and hesitant is being filled by others, so general and natural is the need to believe.

The review *Science and Religion* on the one hand and the review *Kommunist*, the official organ of the Party, on the other have broadcast a warning against the activities of the sects. The editor of *Science and Religion*, Pavel Polonitski, launches the accusation that 'they do not obey the Soviet laws and even carry on activities hostile to the régime. . . . Furthermore many leaders of these sects,' he says, 'forbid their followers to go to school, to visit theatres or clubs, or to take part in social work.' These accusations seem to echo the ancient pagan accusations against the Christians guilty of refusing to take part in public life.

Kommunist goes even further. According to it, the Baptists, the Jehovah's Witnesses, the reformed Adventists, the Evangelists, are guilty of 'ideological hostility to communism which in some cases may amount to a lack of political loyalty. . . . Their leaders,' *Kom-*

munist continues, 'tell their followers not to take part in productive work, not to vote in elections to the local soviets, not to enrol in the armed forces and not to send their children to school.'

The most dynamic and expansive of these sects is the Baptists, largely because of the activity of its leader, Jakob Zhidkov. Three-quarters of his followers are Ukrainians. The sect has 5,400 'meeting houses' in the Soviet Union, bare and austere. The congregation includes peasants, workers, students, clerks and, or so I am told, officials and technicians, but the great majority of the faithful are women. The hierarchy has sixty superintendents, 4,500 ministers and 15,000 lay-preachers.

The most serious accusations against the Baptists are that they collaborated with the Germans during the war and that they now have ties with their co-religionists in the United States, in Canada and Great Britain, where they send their most promising young men to perfect their knowledge. The area of diffusion of all these sects, amongst whom must be included the Shakers, who fall into trances, the Pentecostalians, the Molokani and others, stretches from Moldavia into White Russia, from Latvia to Esthonia and as far as the Caucasus, Central Asia and the heart of Siberia.

19

This picture of religious life in Russia shows, despite the hostile propaganda and the administrative measures that do their best to stifle it, that religious sentiment is inextinguishable. It is not, as the Marxists affirm, an artificial phenomenon, the fruit of ignorance and superstition, but a natural need.

Frequently one hears the question asked: what will be the fate of Christianity in Russia? Will the new generations return to the gospels? The facts we have stated allow one to make some suppositions.

Firstly, as happens in all revolutions, after the first outburst of violence, passions die down and bloody persecution ceases. It is above all to the credit of Khrushchev that the anti-religious struggle tends to shift to the plane of propaganda, with a respect for law. There is still a long way to go, but that is the direction. The believer is free to practise his cult, but anyone who holds an official position or is a member of the Party or is enrolled in the Komsomol cannot practise a faith that marxism considers to be opposed to its principles.

Even if restricted to propaganda and education the struggle is still a very hard one for the Churches, which are in a position of absolute inferiority when they try to refute official teaching. To what extent has this teaching brought results? Undoubtedly it has been most effective. But forty-five years of struggle to the death and bloodthirsty persecutions have given more martyrs to the faith of Christ than all the past millennia and have not succeeded in eradicating Christianity. On the other hand it has seen the hierarchy of the Church re-established and its sanctuaries rebuilt.

Perhaps the question should be put in more general terms; is it possible to uproot Christianity? In twenty centuries many have tried but no one has succeeded and the great tree of the Christian faith has continued to grow and to spread its branches over the earth.

Perhaps a more specific question should be : is it possible to uproot Christianity in Russia? To reply one should first investigate the state of mind of the younger generation. The first thing to remember, in such an investigation, is the lack of anti-clerical feeling among the masses. Not only is there no hatred or contempt, despite the violence .of the polemics, but there is very often a sense of respect for the religious authorities and for the sacred rites and ceremonies. One notices in the cities the nostalgic allure of the ancient forms, of the old customs, of the traditions linked with family records. The ikons are returning to the houses. There is a return to the practice of the sacraments. There is a return to participation in the solemn ceremonies, especially at Easter. There are huge crowds on Holy Saturday before all the churches for the blessing of the *kulich*, or Easter cake. The number of communicants increases. The arch-priest of the *Vsekh Skorbyashchikh Radost* (Joy of the Suffering), one of the loveliest churches in Moscow, said that for Easter 1961 there were twenty-five thousand communicants, compared with twenty thousand in 1960 and sixteen thousand in 1959. At the midnight service on the night of April 11-12th at the Yavorski Cathedral the throng was so great as to require a number of ministrants. The crowd of worshippers was made up mainly of young people under forty. The same was true of the other churches in Moscow. The worshippers were from the upper classes, as could be seen from their clothes. They received the consecrated bread and prayed devoutly, taking part in the singing of the liturgical hymns. When the venerable Patriarch Alexei, a hieratical figure in glittering gem-studded vestments with long white hair and beard, appeared in the Easter procession all those present knelt. There was a whistle or two from some scattered groups of Komsomol members, but the choir of the faithful sang louder and drowned the hostile noises. Some of the militiamen saluted.

Wherever I went, from one end of Russia to the other, I always found the churches crammed.

It might be said that all this rather proves the force of tradition, the nostalgia for old times, but does not attest the vigorous outburst of a new and enlightened conscience. But there is also the very significant fact of the numerous religious vocations. I have found among the younger clergy an ardour, a pride and a militant spirit only too often lacking among their superiors. In the course of its history the Russian people has produced figures distinguished by a saintliness, an austerity of manners, an indomitable attachment to the faith. These are the figures which inspired Dostoyevsky, especially those of the blessed Tikhon Zadonski and of Father Ambrosije of Optina Pustin, in delineating the ascetic figure of the *staretz* Zosimus in *The Brothers Karamazov*. The day will come when from the ranks of the younger clergy there will arise, as there has always arisen, some noble spirit, some new phophet, and his voice shall not remain without an echo since the ferment in the conscience of the people still exists.

If Dostoyevsky was inspired by real persons in drawing the *staretz* Zosimus and the exquisite figure of Alyosha, he has also painted from life the choral personality in all his novels, the Russian people 'sensitive, charitable, capable of loving and of being grateful'. That choral personality is not dead. There is no better testimony than that given by the Russian people of the gospel precept of 'the faith that moves mountains'. Whoever has taken part in the services in the Moscow churches, attended the pilgrimage to the holy city of Zagorsk and has seen the crowds, absorbed, ecstatic, rapt as if in visions of a supernatural world, cannot but smile at the attempt to eradicate from the soul of this people a faith which is a part of its very being. Perhaps the old prophecies of the eighteen hundreds which predicted with a baffling exactitude the unleashing of a revolution against Christ will prove true also in their second part which foretells the return of a whole people to the purity of the faith.

It is certain that when the tempest has passed the situation will not be the same as it was before. If a rebirth is to be expected, it will take place in the depths of individual consciences, in the re-thinking of those great problems to which no philosophy, no science and least of all the depressing desolation of materialism has been able to provide the solutions which everyone must, by his own effort and in the light of his own experience, find out for himself. Since man is man the mystery of death will weigh upon him and these problems will not cease to torment him even as they have tormented and at the same time enlightened and enriched him from the earliest times. Russian youth, more than any other, is sensitive to these mysteries. Many ask: what do these young people think about? One might reply what Dostoyevsky made Ivan Karamazov reply to the question: how do the young people in our cities behave? 'They discuss the most important things, naturally: the existence of God and the immortality of the soul. Those who do not believe in God talk about socialism, about anarchy, of how to reform the whole world and the social order.'

But who can pierce the clouds of the future? 'It is not for us,' says the *staretz* Zosimus, 'to know "the times and the seasons" as is said in the Acts of the Apostles: this mystery is in the wisdom of God, in His love and in His providence. That which may still be far off, according to the calculations of men, in the plans of God is perhaps already at the door, is already prepared for His coming.' And before dying he leaves the supreme message: 'Remember. The people will fight against the godless and will overcome them and then shall Russia be united and Orthodox. . . . The Russian people is the messenger of God.'

Index

DATE DUE